ASTROLOGY

A Science or Myth

Sanat Kumar Jain

ATLANTIC®
PUBLISHERS & DISTRIBUTORS

Published by

ATLANTIC®

PUBLISHERS & DISTRIBUTORS

B-2, Vishal Enclave, Opp. Rajouri Garden,
New Delhi-110027
Phones : 25413460, 25429987, 25466842

Sales Office
7/22, Ansari Road, Darya Ganj,
New Delhi-110002
Phones : 23273880, 23275880, 23280451
Fax : 91-11-23285873
web : www.atlanticbooks.com
e-mail : info@atlanticbooks.com

Printed in India
at Nice Printing Press, Delhi

Dedicated

to all those who

enriched the knowledge

of human civilisation

about the vast

UNIVERSE

and

I

could realise my

insignificance

INTERACTION

Fascinated by the twinkling stars since childhood, my curosity about them grew with time and induced me to study Astrology. The exposure to different subjects like Science, Mathematics, Law, Audit, Computer, etc., during my education as well as service has greatly influenced my thinking, causing me to understand all concepts logically and scientifically before reaching to any conclusion. Accordingly, I have always tried to logically understand the basic principles of astrology and the reasons behind their formulation.

I have developed a software on astrology in which all relevant data of a horoscope have been presented in three charts in order to make a comprehensive analysis of various results and also of the interconnected impact of all relevant principles which in turn enable correct prediction. In this novel exercise, I have also designed some Eskain charts which have been incorporated in Appendix 1. Since these charts find no mention in the text matter, they can be studied even before going into the details of the book. When my thirst to discover the unknown was not quenched even by these comprehensive charts, I developed another software on planetarium so as to analyse the celestial sky, beginning from 10,000 BC to the present day, and assess the position of constellations and planets, which prompted our sages to lay down the basic principles of astrology. With these unusual exercises I could able to understand the shifting of celestial position of the planets due to *ayanansh* and the deviation in these astrological principles in the modern concepts of the universe and solar system. Whatever I discovered in this context have already been published in Hindi version, *Jyotish: Kitna Sahi Kitna Galat*. Dignified readers of the book have not only appreciated the contents but also insisted to publish its English version. Consequently, this extended version is being presented to the readers so that they may get acquainted with the factual position of planets and also the reasons behind the framing of principles of astrology in primitive age. Such acquaintances enable one to protect oneself from hangover predictions based on these outdated principles on the one hand, and to have immense benefit from the modern fundamental concept of this wonderful, spiritual and powerful knowledge of planetary impact on the other.

It has never been my intention to hurt the feelings or faith of anybody by the arguments put forth in the book. Instead, I have tried to convey the fundamental concept of planetary impact by blending the primitive knowledge with the modern concepts related to the universe and solar system, so that the uninterrupted flow and transition of know-how of the principles of astrology may be more scientifically logical and useful to the mankind. Still, if sentiments of any person get jolted in any way, I apologize for it.

The present book has been divided into three parts. First part deals with the reasoning behind the formation of fundamental principles of astrology; although they are now considered outdated, irrelevant and illogical in the light of modern knowledge of the universe. Second part contains explanation about some astrological misconception regarding planetary situation, while in the Third part the concept of planetary impact as perceived and laid down by the ancient sages has been blended with the corresponding modern concept, with a view to pursue knowledge that may enable us to mould our destiny according to our wishes.

The contents of the book are entirely logical and have been presented in an easily comprehensible style. In addition to these, relevant diagrams have also been provided for easy grasp of the concepts. For proper understanding, it is essential that the chapters are read serially and sincerely. It is advised that if a reader finds any concept difficult or confusing, just continue with the reading because such concepts are likely to get elucidated in the subsequent chapters. Proper reading and open-mindedness are the main requisites for understanding this book, or better say, astrology. Astrology is a complex subject and I am quite optimistic that the present book will prove a great help in understanding it.

I am thankful to all such persons who have directly or indirectly assisted me in accomplishing this great task. Timely suggestions given by my son Dr. Manish Jain greatly contributed to the quality of the book. I also acknowledge the great cooperation rendered by my wife without whom this book would not have been possible.

I am also thankful to Mr. K.R. Gupta, Chairman, Atlantic Publishers & Distributors, for bringing out this book in record time.

At the end, I would like to mention that all penetrating suggestions from readers are always welcome; do share the reactions as they would be useful in further digging into the subject. Although I have tried my best to sufficiently explain every concept in a simple language and lucid style, anybody who needs more clarification is free to write to me all his queries, I will be happy to answer them.

Sanat Kumar Jain

2, Wagle's Bada, Near Bombay Bakery
Dal Bazar, Gwalior, 474 009
Ph. 0751-2626868
email - sanatkumar_jain@rediffmail.com

CONTENTS

PART 2

PART 3

PART 1

1

INTRODUCTORY

During process of civilisation of mankind, human race was always attracted by the power of Sun, Moon and he curiously observed formation of various faces of Moon. He was frightened by the immense power of these planets and thereby started to worship them in the form of God. By regular observation of the sky, he also identified some more planets among twinkling star and it was also verified by constant observation that these planets are moving in the sky in a fixed track i.e. zodiac. The zodiac was then divided in 12 signs and subdivided in 27 constellations for calculating and identifying the position of the planets. With the improvement of calculations and regular observation, our sages were able to point out the time of eclipse, weather etc. and they also tried to understand the Universe, which is still going on with the help of modern science. It appears that probably scientist will always be on the job of disclosing the mystery of this endless Universe. In the process of gathering the information about the planets, our ancestral also realised that these planets not only have impact on the Earth in the form of change in weather but they also have impact on human race. If we ponder on this finding then it will be clear that this research was first very important scientific conclusion and only thereafter, on this foundation our sages started to peep into the destiny.

To calculate the impact of the planets on mankind, our sages not only continuously observed the movement of the planets in the sky but they deeply analysed the Universe also and only thereafter, they formulated some principles of astrology. The influence of these principles were so deeprooted in our culture that even after more than 2500 years, we are still following those age-old principles and trying to understand the unknown destiny. With the passage of time, as we were able to improve mathematical system and could open new branches of the mathematics, this knowledge was also used in astrological calculations, besides formulations of some new principles for prediction. But any principle, once accepted in any circumstances or on the basis of any information were never rechecked or modified despite availability of new and improved scientific information. *Prima facie* reasons for this mega lapse appears that when the fundamental principles of astrology were being formulated, at that time only and only our sages have the best and up-to-date knowledge, beside this they have unquestioned reputation and thinking, that's why the principles of astrology once formulated by them get recognition and nobody raised any doubt on their knowledge and deep thinking. At present no detailed record is available in support of the basis of formulation of various fundamental principles of astrology and various calculations devised by our sages after observing the planetary position in the sky. Due to lack of this important and vital basic information, later on it was never possible for the learned astrologers to recheck the foundation and soundness of the principles, because till now it was not possible to see the planetary position in age-old sky and secondly, the astrological information and knowledge were only confined to sages or Brahman section of the society, since Primitive age. Hence in absence of such information no further research could be done and the knowledge of astrology has only survived, till date on the shoulders of faith and recognition. Since last 900 years no mathematical development has taken place in this field though only in last 100 years many unknown facts about the planets, solar system, sky and Universe have been disclosed with the help of modern science.

In fact the mathematical calculation and documentation of principles of astrology was only initiated in Primitive age at about 500 BC, when our many learned sages including sage Parashar started to publicise and use the knowledge of the Universe in prediction. At that time, modern mathematics including algebra, geometry or trigonometry was not developed, hence the arithmetical calculations were complicated, vague and were not minute. Beside this correct position of the Earth and planets in the Universe was also not known to sages. Because in Primitive age our sages were neither aware of modern mathematics nor they have modern tools and instruments. Thus after regular observation of the sky followed by vibrant discussion and pondering over various situation from various angles, any theory which seems to be more logical and acceptable was accepted as correct and astrological principles were formulated around this theory. During the period from AD 500 to AD 1100, devising new and minute mathematical calculations supported these astrological principles. From AD 1100 afterwards, only varied principles of prediction was developed. In this way development of formulation of astrological principles after observing the movement of planets in the sky is stagnating since last 2500 years, whereas, no mathematical development has taken place in this field since last 900 years.

In the Primitive age those sages who could develop some new principles were awarded and recognised with the status of Acharya, whereas, now-a-days we can see that anyone who is only practising astrology on the basis of those age-old astrological principles for his day-to-day bread and butter is designating himself as *Jyotishacharya*. What we see now-a-days that either many literate individuals are being misguided and forced to believe the predictions concluded by these astrologers on the basis of out-of-date principles of astrology and calculation, without having any logic behind such prediction and which is against the core idea of this knowledge or remaining individuals have no faith on this marvellous knowledge and best scientific discovery since incarnation of mankind on this Earth. It is a matter of pride that our sages has incessantly tried to unearth the knowledge regarding impact of planets for the benefit of the mankind, at that period of time when there were no modern resources for their help. Contrary to this, now-a-days forget to have a deep thinking and devising some new astrological principles, despite having all sort of modern instruments and information; we are not willing even to peep in to deep to recheck these age-old astrological principles in the light of new scientific information. If astrologers compare their attitude and mental status with that of our sages then it will be crystal clear that definitely they have more logical, mythical approach and thinking within the purview of limited sources and information, that's why they could be able to introduce and establish these astrological principles, after prolonged study of Universe and movement of planets, against all odds.

In this modern scientific age, instead of understanding the circumstances behind the formulation of these age-old astrological principles with a view to support the fundamental concept of planetary impact on the scientific basis, we are not only blindly following the principles formulated on the wrong concept of solar system and Universe but we are also forced to believe that astrological principles are scientifically correct, because the astrological calculations and prediction are now being done with the help of computer on the basis of *Mahadasha*, Friendship-enmity and Exalted-debilitated position of the planets. Now, despite having multiplex modern information of our solar system and the Universe, it has no place in astrology, that's why, there is no progress in this field and we are forced to follow the outcome of age-old principles based on hazy and wrong concept of the Universe, which were being followed by our ancestors since Primitive age. Astrologers are trying hard to establish by hook and crook that any event which is taking place anywhere on this Earth is always supported by astrological principles. For this they have taken help of all sort of astrological principles like *Yog*, *Mahadasha*, *Antardasha*, Friendship-enmity among planets, Aspect, Exalted-debilitated, *Shadbal*, *Saptvargi* horoscopes, Transition of planets etc. and finally get the event supported by any one or other principle. If it is pointed out that a debilitated planet is providing some positive result than they take route of *neech-bhang yog* etc. or if any exalted planet is providing some negative result than they take help of *Mahadasha, Antardasha*, placement of planet in enemy's House, Aspect, *Navmansh*, Transition etc., means to say that if any prediction based on astrological principles is not happening, even then all out efforts are being made to cover the incident by one or another principles. Nobody has ever tried to logically ponder that when a combination or transition etc. of planets in a horoscope is responsible for a particular result in one case then why it is not being repeated again in the same planetary combination or transition etc. in another horoscope. Generally astrologer take shelter by stating that the time of birth may be wrong and due to this mistake other minute calculation of *antardasha* and *navmansh* etc. get changed, hence there may be a variation in the prediction. But nobody has ever asked to any astrologer that in Primitive age, when sage Parashar was formulating the principles of astrology, at that point of time, there were neither watches to monitor the time, nor there was any foolproof system to calculate correct time nor they have any concept of latitude or altitude. At that time our sages used to calculate ascendant with the help of shadow of a stick. Then presently, when we have modern system of calculation of time, even then why we are not able to get correct prediction on the basis of the principles as laid down by our sages.

It is, therefore, our prime requirement of today to analyse and recheck, the foundation of principles of astrology; which were mainly formulated on the basis of following some mythical faith and wrong understanding of planetary position and some vague calculation; in the light of modern astronomical information of solar system and the Universe to enable us to infuse some new principles and create some new calculations, so that stagnated and outdated knowledge of the astrology may be improved and this primitive marvellous knowledge may be carved into more logical, scientific and practical use of mankind and knowledge of India may once again be glittered. As we are making use of four out of five elements of the Universe i.e. Fire, Earth, Water and Air, likewise we may also be able to make use of fifth element Sky i.e. cosmic impact of planets during their movement in the sky while emitting different type of rays, which have been classified as Alpha, Beta, Gamma etc. rays and Magnetic storm, Gravitation etc., because prediction is only an essence of astrological calculations. Thus, if we will not proceed in the right direction in accordance with the understanding of fundamental concept of planetary impact than like our yoga, maths, music, culture, religion etc., it will also be routed through western countries, then only we will be able to realise the correct impact of planets, calculate it scientifically and till then our behaviour in this field will totally be foolish like using the age-old primitive structure of wheel of bullock-cart in aeroplane, instead of technically improving the wheel of bullock-cart with the help of modern knowledge so that it may properly be used in aeroplane. The contention here is not that invention of the wheel of bullock-cart has no significant at all but contention is that this invention by a progenitor who designed a wheel by crystallising his imagination for using it in transportation, during the development of human civilisation was definitely equal to any topmost and technically best invention of today. Because behind every invention there is a basic thinking of doing the best from the available resources and it required same labour, concentration, enthusiasm and deep thinking in the primitive age which is required now-a-days for any scientific invention. In this way any invention is not the best and ultimate but it is only a seed for opening new dimension for improvement of human civilisation, based on which new invention will take place in the future. For classifying astrology as a science it is utmost essential that principles formulated on the basis of the information available in the Primitive age may continuously be modified with an open mind and without any prejudice than only this knowledge may be used in future on the footings of logical science, otherwise it will be in the category like a primitive wheel and may only be used for exploitation of faith, weak mentality, ignorance and blind-faith. Thus the contention that the knowledge of the man belonging to the Primitive age was complete and best is only an indication of our simplicity.

Public at large has a mentality that astrology is a tough subject because it is proclaimed since Primitive age that astrology is a mysterious subject. But in view of the development of scientific consciousness and logical approach of new generation it can be established that the status of the astrology is not more than the standard of science and maths required at the level of Inter.

Preliminary information relating to the subject is being given so that amateur readers may also be able to understand the subject. Certain specific information is being given separately in the concerning chapters.

Planet – There are nine planets in the astrology and they are Sun, Moon, Mercury, Venus, Mars, Jupiter, Saturn, Rahu and Ketu. Because Rahu and Ketu are not visible hence they are considered as shadow planets. But their existence and importance was due to their involvement in effecting an eclipse.

Sign – Circle of 360° around the Earth was bifurcated in twelve segments and every segment of 30° named after a sign. Twelve signs are known as Aries, Taurus, Gemini, Cancer, Leo, Virgo, Libra, Scorpio, Sagittarius, Capricorn, Aquarius and Pisces respectively.

Constellation – Circle of 360° around the Earth was bifurcated in 27 segments and every segment named after a constellation. In this way every sign comprises of two and quarter constellation i.e. two full constellation and one-fourth of third constellation (one *charan*).

Birth horoscope – Planetary position in various sign and celestial position of various sign at the time of birth is depicted in the birth horoscope.

House – Horoscope is divided in twelve parts and every part is termed as a house. That sign which is rising in the east at the time of birth is indicated with relevant number of that sign in the first house of the horoscope and it is called as sign of ascendant. The planets are kept in the relevant house occupied by the sign according to the celestial position of planets in that sign. The sign occupied by the Moon is termed as birth sign. Different aspects of life are studied through the relevant house.

Direct and Retrograde planet – When a planet is visually moving in forward direction i.e. from Aries to Taurus then it is called Direct. Contrary to this, when a planet is visually moving in reverse direction i.e. towards previous sign then it is called Retrograde planet.

Principle – Help of certain fundamental principles like Lord of sign, Friendship-enmity, Aspect of planets, Exalted-debilitated, *Mool-trikon*, Set and retrograde planet, Potential of planets on the basis of different *saptvargi* horoscope, *Vinshottary* periodicity are taken for arriving at some prediction. These principles are being analysed in detail in subsequent chapters. Beside this, planets and signs are also bifurcated in five elements viz. Fire, Earth, Water, Air and Sky; Man-woman, Auspicious-inauspicious, Movable-fix-duel nature. They are also classified as *Vipra, Kshatriya, Vyeshya,* and *Shudra* on the basis of social structure of the society. Prediction is concluded on the basis of intermixing of various principles.

Measurement of distance and time

8 *Jau*	= 1 *Angul*		
6 *Angul*	= 1 *Paad*		
2 *Paad*	= 1 *Vilast*		
2 *Vilast*	= 1 *Hast*	= 1.5 Feet	= 45 cm
2 *Hast*	= 1 *Rickku*	= 90 cm	
2 *Rickku*	= 1 *Dand*		
4 *Hast*	= 1 *Dhanush*	= 180 cm	
2000 *Dhanush*	= 1 *Kosh*		
4 *Kosh*	= 1 *Yojan*	= 14.4 km	
3 *Lau*	= 1 *Nimesh*		
3 *Nimesh*	= 1 *Kshan*	= 1.28 sec.	
5 *Kshan*	= 1 *Kastha*		
15 *Kastha*	= 1 *Laghu*	= 96 sec.	
15 *Laghu*	= 1 *Ghati*		
2 *Ghati*	= 1 *Muhurt*	= 48 min.	
30 *Muhurt*	= 1 Day-night		
2 *Ayan*	= 1 Year		
5 Year	= 1 *Yug*		
1 day	= 60 *Ghati*		
1 *Ghati*	= 60 *Pal*		
1 *Pal*	= 60 *Vipal*		
1 *Ghati*	= 24 Minute		
1 *Pal*	= 24 Second		
1 Hour	= 2.5 *Ghati*		
1 Minute	= 2.5 *Pal*		
1 Second	= 2.5 *Vipal*		

Name of constellation and sign

English and traditional name of sign

Aries	(*Mesh*)	Taurus	(*Vrash*)
Gemini	(*Mithun*)	Cancer	(*Kark*)
Leo	(*Singh*)	Virgo	(*Kanya*)
Libra	(*Tula*)	Scorpio	(*Vraschik*)
Sagittarius	(*Dhanu*)	Capricorn	(*Makar*)
Acquarius	(*Kumbha*)	Pisces	(*Meen*)

Traditional and scientific name of constellation

Ashwini	(Arieties)	*Bharni*	(Musca)
Kratika	(Pledades)	*Rohini*	(Aldebaran)
Mragshira	(Orionis I)	*Aadra*	(Orionis II)
Punarvasu	(Pollux)	*Pushya*	(Cancri)
Ashlesha	(Hydrae)	*Magha*	(Regulas)
Purvafalguni	(Conis)	*Uttara-falguni*	(Denebola)
Hast	(Corvi)	*Chitra*	(Spica)
Swati	(Arcturus)	*Vishakha*	(Libra)
Anuradha	(Scorpii)	*Jyestha*	(Antares)
Mool	(Scorpii-H)	*Purvashada*	(Sagitarii-D)
Uttarashada	(Sagitari-I)	*Shravan*	(Aquailae)
Ghanistha	(Delphini)	*Shatbhisha*	(Aquarii)
Purva-B.pad	(Pegasi)	*Uttara-B.pad*	(Andromeda)
Revati	(Piscium)		

2

DEVELOPMENT OF ASTROLOGY

Before we proceed to analyse the astrological principles, we must have a little idea of history of development of astrology. Therefore, after having a bird's eye view of development of astrology, we will analyse the formation of Universe, Lord of sign, Friendship-enmity between planets, Aspect of planets, Exalted-debilitated planets, Periodicity (*Dasha*) etc. Our learned sages regularly observed the sky and after detecting the movement of planets they ponder about these heavenly bodies for thousand of years. Thereafter, they could be able to formulate the principles of celestial position and transit of planets and linked it with astrology. It is, therefore, essential to know the precise timing of formulation of the principles of astrology, level of intelligence and information which were available with sages about the formation of the Earth, status and position of the Sun, Moon and other planets in the Universe and solar system, at that point of time. To understand the development of astrology, we may divide the period in the following manner :–

Dark age	Before 10000 BC
Rising age	10000 BC to 500 BC
Primitive age	500 BC to AD 500
Pre Middle age	AD 500 to AD 1000
Post Middle age	AD 1000 to AD 1600
Pre Modern age	AD 1600 to AD 1900
Modern age	AD 1900 till date

With the help of such historical information we may ascertain the basis of deriving the astrological principles and modification carried out at different time.

Dark age

Till 10000 BC our ancestral mainly observed the movement of Sun and Moon and by this observation they could understand that weather was controlled by these planets and all seasons including summer, winter and rain etc. were formed only due to these planets. Thus due to having this supernatural power, Sun and Moon was classified as deity and worshipped.

Rising age

This period existed up to 500 BC. By the end of this age, sages and Brahmin who have sufficient knowledge of movement of planets enjoyed special regards in the society, because only they knows before hand about the formation of eclipse etc. In this age, our sages started to divide the period in months and year on the basis of the movement of Moon and Sun respectively. To synchronise these two different periodicity based on twelve circulation of moon and one circulation of sun; they devised an ingenuous method of adding *adhimaas* (extra month). *Veda* was also inscribed in this age and period of five years was termed as *Yug*. *Veda* also has description about the impact of the planets on the mankind. As per *Yazurved*, at the time of inscription of *Veda*, year commenced from the fall of spring season. Whereas, by the end of this Rising age, commencement of year had been shifted to initial period of winter solstice. *Rigveda* have description about the formation of solar and lunar eclipses. According to *Samvayang* composed in this age, Rahu and Ketu were responsible for eclipses. Jain literature, *Surya Pragyapti, Garg Sanhita, Jyotishkarandak* etc. also have description of constellation.

In this age everybody was well aware with the fact that Sun is most essential for living being and life is only possible due to existence of Sun. That's why *Surya Namaskar* got precedence over all form of exercises in *Yoga*. Sun and Moon were regarded as illuminative planets, because they were able to illuminate Earth. Thus formation of eclipse was always treated as fearful and troublesome incident. Various ritual traditions were originated, developed and practised including donations etc. to set free these illuminative planets from the clutches of Rahu and Ketu, during eclipse.

Sky was divided in sign and constellation on the basis of movement of Sun and Moon respectively. Our sages developed the skill to calculate the timing of winter solstice and summer solstice. Winter solstice was never treated as auspicious, because generation of life supporting energy and duration of day reduces during this period. Whereas, contrary to this, summer solstice was always treated as auspicious and celebrated because duration of day increases in comparison to night i.e. darkness, which in turn also increases the energy level. Summer solstice had established its proper auspicious importance before the period of *Mahabharat*. That's why Bhishma Pitamah who was able to choose voluntary death, avoided it till summer solstice and remained on arrow-bed in an uncomfortable situation.

In this age Earth was treated as stationary and it was believed that Sun and Moon rotate around the Earth in an orbit. Jain literature of that time also supported it, with further details regarding rotational orbit of Sun and established that Sun actually takes rotation of *Sumeru-parvat* in full cycle of winter-summer solstice and during this rotation Sun moves about 510 *Yojan*, out of which journey of 180 *Yojan* remains in *Jambu-dweep* (present India) and remaining 330 *Yojan* remains in *Lavan Samudra* (present Indian ocean).

In *Vedic* age, duration of year was calculated on the basis of sayan system and this system prevailed by the end of Rising age. There was no description in the Vedic literature, about the planetary orbit, but *Tettariya Brahmin*, Jain and Bodh literature inscribed during Vedic age had sufficient description about the planets, which emphasised that Earth, Space, Sun, Moon, Constellation were respectively placed over and above the sea. In step 3-11-1 of *Tettariya Brahmin* it was narrated that "... अप:स्थ समुद्रे श्रिता:। पृथिव्या: प्रतिष्ठा युष्मासु।..द्यौरसि वायौ श्रिता। आदित्यस्य प्रतिष्ठा। आदित्योसि दिवि श्रित:। चन्द्रमस: प्रतिष्ठा। चन्द्रमा अस्यादित्ये श्रित:।

नक्षत्राणां प्रतिष्ठा।...". In light of the descriptions available in other literature of the Rising age like *Samvayang* and *Prashnavyakarnang*, it is very clear that situation of orbit of Sun, Moon, Constellation, Mercury, Venus, Mars, Jupiter and Saturn was unanimously considered to be respectively above the stationary Earth. In that age, according to Jain, Bodh and Vedic doctrine, mainland was named as *Jambu-dweep*, with a slight variation in detail of landscape of the Earth, whereas placement of initial order of planets was univocal in all these doctrines and faith. Ending period of the Rising age was fully saturated with philosophical thinking. Philosophy of Mahavir and Budh impressed upon the knowledge and thinking of mankind in general in the last phase of this age and starting phase of Primitive age. Existence of Upper, Middle and Lower world in the Universe had unquestioned approval by all doctrines and cult.

In 572 BC, Revati constellation was considered as *Sampaat* constellation. Whereas, at the time of composition of Vedang Jyotish, summer solstice of Sun was considered in the initial phase of *Ghanistha* constellation.

In this way our sages gathered sufficient information of movement and orbit of planets, impact of planets, equinoxil point, signs of the zodiac, constellations, calculation of time, duration of day, eclipse etc. in respect of all planets including Sun and Moon. Though the details of Universe, which was available with our sages was substantially different from the knowledge and details available in 21st century. In those days basis of prediction was only the merit of a planet. Principles of *Mahadasha*, Friendship-enmity between planets, Exalted-debilitated etc. were not developed and any supportive mathematical calculation for deciding the merit of a planet was also not formulated in this age.

In short, we may say that foundation stone of astrology was laid down in this Rising age. By the end of this age, order of planetary orbit had a univocal support from all faith and philosophy and sages adopted a definite and firm opinion that Earth is stationary and orbit of all other planets was it in the order of Sun, Moon, Constellation, Mercury, Venus, Mars,

Jupiter and Saturn. This concept of the Universe and order of planets was very very important because all the principles of astrology were not only developed on this hub, but they also passed on from generation to generation since then only and only over this hub without any deviation.

Primitive age

This age commenced since 500 BC and on the basis of various information accumulated by our sages by the end of Rising age was used for ascertaining the position and impact of planets in the modified system of *nirayan* year. It will not be out of place to mention that development of all astrological principles were mainly based on the information regarding Universe and planetary orbit with reference to *Jambu-dweep*, which contained in *Samvayang, Prashnavyakarnang* and in other literature of Rising age. After going through the first part of this book, you will also agree with the opinion that knowledge gathered by our sages by the end of Rising age had core impact on the astrology.

During conjunction period of Rising age and Primitive age some important literature was written on the basis of information gathered about the planets. Initial literature in this direction was *Rik-Jyotish*. This literature contained the description about the duration of day, equinoxil point etc. *Surya Pragyapti* and *Chandra Pragyapti* were written in the initial period of this age, which contained the description about the movement of Sun and Moon. Moon was considered as self-illuminative planet in *Chandra Pragyapti* and position of all other planets and constellations were considered in between the distance of 790 *Yojan* to 900 *Yojan*. *Jyotishkarandak* contained the description of constellation and movement of Sun on equator i.e. when duration of day and night is equal.

By the starting of this age it was possible to ascertain the timings of solar and lunar eclipses. Because Sun and Moon were regarded as deities and with the idea that when the correct timing of capturing (eclipse) of these deity planets by demon Rahu and Ketu can be predicted by our learned sages then why they could not predict about course of events stored in future for mankind. Mainly on the basis of this thought, our learned sages started to understand and to work out the impact of deity and demon planets on the mankind and started to formulate different astrological principles on altogether different basis.

Many sages including Surya, Pitamah, Vyas, Vashistha, Atri, Parashar, Kashyap, Narad, Garg, Marichi, Manu, Angira, Lomash, Pulish, Chyavan, Yavan, Bhragu, Shaunak and Pulastya etc. had not only formulated the various principles of astrology, but later on these sages were also regarded as founder and originator of astrology. Sage Parashar wrote *Vrahatparashar-hora* some time in fifth century BC and somewhere in Northern India. We know that political and social set-up always have a definite impact in every sphere of life. Similarly, the then set-up also had its impact over the formulation of principles of astrology and sages developed various mathematical calculation and astrological principles for prediction on the basis of their own findings after regular observation of the sky for watching the movement of planets in zodiac and these principles were improved upon by the system of exalted-debilitated on the basis of social caste system which was described in *Manusmriti* written around 2000 BC, principle of Lordship of sign, Friendship-enmity were introduced on the political pattern, principle of Aspect between planets was motivated on the basis of frequent war fought among kings and some mathematical, predictive principles like *Mool-trikon*, Periodicity of planets, *Shodash Varg, Yog* etc. were based on geometry which was taking shape in those days and on the basis of formula of triangle invented by Bodhayan in 500 BC along with some other calculation.

Sages of this period were aware with the fact after matching the cycle of weather with the position of the Sun that actual position of Sun never coincides with the calculated position of the Sun based on fixed system of calculation i.e. *sayan* system. Thus both system i.e. *sayan* as well as visual system, which was later on known as *nirayan* system were followed in formulation of astrological calculation and principles.

Arastu, who was teacher of Greece born Alexander was able to conclude around 336 BC, on the basis of various calculation relating to lunar eclipse that it was shadow of the Earth which falls on the Moon and on the basis of this shadow he also concluded that shape of the Earth was not flat but it was like a ball. But due to lack of knowledge of gravitation of Earth, he was not able to logically satisfy the queries raised by general public that if Earth is like a ball and we are standing on the top of it than why person standing in the lower part of the Earth may not fall. However, in those days it was believed that no one could live in the southern part of the Earth. But the doubt was not convincingly removed. In the third century BC, another scholar Aeratosthenus of Alexandria was able to ascertain from the businessman, who travels to distant places that sun-light was reaching at the bottom of the deep well of Sienna city on the biggest day (presently 23rd June), whereas on the same day sun-light was inclined in Alexandria. By this fact he was able to prove that the shape of the Earth was like a ball. Subsequently, in AD second century, another astronomer of Greece, Ptolemi was able to draw lines of longitude and latitude on his circular map of the Earth. By this time civilisation of Greece was badly disintegrating and Christian religion introduced by Isa Mashih was picking up momentum. Thus in Europe, the concept of flat Earth was established and it was accepted and recognised for next 1500 years.

As our culture come across the culture of Greece and Egypt nearly in the year AD 100, this subsequently resulted in introduction of Latitude, Altitude, *Char-sanskar*, Sunrise, Sunset in astrological calculation.

In short, astrological principles were formulated in this age after sufficient pondering over a situation and deep thinking on the movement of planets and these principles are still prevalent and recognised.

Pre Middle age

Span of this age was up to AD 1000. Aryabhatt who born in AD 476 wrote *Aryabhatiya* in the year AD 500, in which circumference of Earth was calculated as 4967 *Yojan*, based on presumption of stationary Sun and movable Earth.

Varahmihir, who born in AD 505 wrote *Vrahtjatak* in which principles of Exalted-debilitated, Friendship-enmity between planets, *Mool-trikon* etc. were taken from *Vrahatparashar-hora*. New system of astrological calculation was devised in this age, which also includes calculation of *Chesta-bal* on the basis of calculation of *ahargan*. Brahmgupt who born in AD 598 wrote *Brahmsphut-sidhant* in AD 628 on the basis of stationary Earth. He also discovered the principles of algebra and originated it.

Prashna-shastra was developed in this age on the basis of *Arahachudamanisar* written in the Primitive age by a Jain saint Bhadrabahu. *Kuvlayamala* written by Udyotan Suri had description of the principles of astrology and palmistry. Prediction based on *Shadbal, Muhurat* and *Shagun* etc. was also started in this age.

In short, those principles, which were laid down in Primitive age, were only supported by mathematical calculations and a new concept for supporting prediction by calculations was developed. But the core practice of keeping the track over the movement of planets by regular observation of the sky, which was followed by our sages till primitive age, was continuously reducing day-by-day in this age.

Post Middle age

Span of this age was up to AD 1600. Bhaskaracharya born in 1114 wrote *Sidhantshiromani* keeping Earth as stationary. He also introduced and originated mathematical calculation regarding *Charantar, Udayantar* and *Bhujantar*.

In AD 1478, Makrand developed various tables for calculating *tithi* etc. on the basis of *Surya-sidhant*. Ganesh born in AD 1517 wrote *Grahlaghav* in the age of 13 years according to hearsay. His age is being supported on the basis of calculations used in his book, in which he calculated *arahgan* (calculation of celestial position of the planets on the basis of their average motion worked out after deducting the initial celestial position of planets) for *samvat* 1442 i.e. year

AD 1520. Now-a-days, we are still using *Surya-sidhant* of Makrand and *Grahlaghav* of Ganesh for calculating *tithi* etc. for preparation of almanac.

First time in AD 1522 Captain Sebastian Del Cano of Spain completed his journey around the Earth in three years after travelling towards west on his sailing ship and proved that Earth is like a ball. Thereafter in 1543 Nicholas Copernicus of Poland discovered that all planets including Earth rotate around the Sun in our solar system. But when this novel discovery did not recognised even in Western countries due to religious opposition, then there was no question of its recognition in India.

Due to continuous exposure with the Muslim culture, a novel system of *Tazik* i.e. *Varsh-kundli* was developed along with prediction, *Muhurat, Ramal* etc. Thus during this age everybody was interested only in prediction and thus it had precedence over all other aspect of astrology.

In this age too, Earth was treated as stationary and practice of sky gazing, which prevailed by the end of Primitive age and which was a foundation stone of astrology was completely vanished and bare knowledge gathered from books was recognised as astrological knowledge and expertise. Thus except mathematical development done by Bhaskaracharya none other important mathematical or astrological development took place in this age.

In short, in this age the practice of keeping track on the planetary movement by sky gazing which prevailed in Primitive age and practice of mathematical development which prevailed in Middle age was completely vanished and skill of prediction was only recognised as astrological knowledge.

Pre Modern age

We may take this age up to AD 1900. By the time of starting of this age skill of sky gazing was completely finished. In AD 1608, after gazing the movement of planets with the help of self designed telescope, when Galileo of Italy clarified that the shape of the Earth is like a ball and supported the concept as laid down by Copernicus about the rotation of all planets including Earth around the Sun then he was lodged in a jail as a punishment, where ultimately he died.

Nearly in AD 1680, Meghvijayagani wrote many important books, which contains the description and prediction based on eclipse, planetary movement in sign, retrograde, invisible planet (*Ast*), omen, transition of a planet from one sign to another (*Sankranti*) etc. Nearly in AD 1700, Labdhichandragani wrote *Janampatri-padhati*, in which he describe the details of casting a horoscope *using Ist-kaal, Bhayat, Bhabhog*, Ascendant, Celestial position of the planets in zodiac and prediction based on horoscope. Nearly in AD 1780, King Jai Singh of Amer constructed observatory in Kashi, Jaipur and Delhi mainly to calculate the precise time and to ascertain planetary position in the zodiac. Although all calculation of these observatories were based on the concept of flat Earth and round shape of the Earth was not recognised. In this age, prediction was considered as an only important part of astrology hence procedures for preparation of Almanac, *Muhurat* etc. were developed.

In short, due to influence of Muslim and British culture, neither any astrological principles were developed after sky gazing nor any important and effective mathematical calculation was developed in this age. Because not only all available scriptures but classified and important knowledge like astrology was also confined with a specified section of the society. Thus influential as well as ordinary class of the society was totally ignorant with this knowledge. This fact may be substantiated by a historical event that even brave king like Shivaji was debarred from pronouncing *vedic* script at the time of his coronation. Thereafter, Goga Bhatt of Varanashi pronounced the *vedic* script and completed coronation ceremony. In this way, by the end of this age, primitive concept of Universe and celestial position of the planets was recognised unanimously. Though, when Issac Newton of Britain was able to discover the theory of Gravitation between celestial bodies including Earth, in AD 1687, then concept of Solar system as envisaged by Copernicus get support from this theory and recognised only in the scientific circle, but this concept was never recognised at the level of faith in India and primitive concept of planetary orbit was only acceptable due to religious set-up of the society and ignorance beside absence of scientific aptitude because such scientific findings were against the faith of all religions.

Modern age

Many invention, discoveries and new concept of the Universe have been achieved only in last 100 years. We have easy access to the achievement and knowledge of western world. Many worth mentioning branches of mathematics have since been developed. Though, in India we are not exercising the practice of sky gazing but the Universe is now being continuously gazed with the help of modern scientific technology and instruments including Hubble telescope, which is not only enriching our knowledge and understanding about many secrets of the Universe but we are also able to know much more about our own solar system and planets. Now we know about the existence of many other solar systems and Galaxies. With the help of modern mathematical calculations and by following the concept of solar system as envisaged by Copernicus, scientist was also able in AD 1969 to make foot prints on the Moon which was considered as an important planet in astrological calculation and prediction. In near future next footprints will be on the Mars.

Krishnamurti of South India developed a system of prediction based on sub-division of sign on the analogy of *Mahadasha* and *Antardasha* after casting a horoscope. This horoscope has a difference of about 15° in the span of a House from traditionally casted horoscope as followed in North India. But, as usual, the foundation of this system of prediction also has its roots in the primitive principles of astrology.

Conclusion

We may clearly visualise and come to the conclusion from this whole history of development of astrology that our sages regularly monitored the movement of planets up to 500 BC. Only, thereafter, they were able to formulate some astrological principles on the basis of their the then knowledge of the Universe based on faith, social structure of the society and religious background. Many mathematical and predictive systems were developed in next 1600 years on the basis of these principles. The opinion regarding planetary situation that Earth is stationary and all other planets have their orbit over it, in the order of Sun, Moon, Constellation, Mercury, Venus, Mars, Jupiter and Saturn, which was once decided after deep thinking by our sages and accepted in Rising age have uninterrupted impact on the mindset and later on, only this concept was converted into the foundation stone of astrology. But in India, instead of changing our mindset to bring astrology in the scientific fold and doing some research in the field of traditional astrology with the help of modern technology and know-how, we are only trying to develop our business in this noble field with the help of computers and not only wasting our time in unfounded predictions on the basis of principles based on primitive concept of the Universe but also infusing fear complex in the mind of people in general and foolishly trying to minimise the impact of these heavenly bodies by classifying and treating them as deity and demon.

If we have a bird's eye view on the history of astrology then it will be clear that mathematical part of astrology was only corrected after the introduction of latitude, longitude, calculation of time with the availability of watches and modified *ayanansh* in the 20th century. Besides this remaining various developments regarding prediction were only based on the principles formulated in the Primitive age but without any checking of the fundamental principles of astrology. Though, now we have modern and correct knowledge about solar system, yet in India, the birth place of astrology, we are neither bothered of doing any new sort of research, review of concept of planetary position and principles as laid down in Primitive age or formulation of any new astrological principles at any level nor giving a second thought on this whole subject, but we are only beating the bush of Primitive age. Thus, actually we are at square one of this vast field of astrology and development of its principles.

At one hand, in the primitive age our sages have the then best information about the planets and ancient civilisation like

Greece and Egypt were also impressed with their knowledge and on the other hand, now-a-days not only astrological knowledge has completely turned into blind-faith for general public due to unfounded publicity, but astrologers in general are also lagging behind in the astronomical knowledge due to having their full and final faith over the knowledge of sages of Primitive age and lack of interest in astronomy and their inability to develop astrology on the basis of latest scientific astronomical information, which was actually foundation stone of astrology. Because one section of the society who is well known of astrology is neither willing to modify it nor mentally prepared for completely overhauling it on the basis of scientific information, only due to religious compulsion nor interested in putting labour to discover the scientific reasoning on the basis of latest knowledge nor prepared for reduction in their respect from general public, which is being enjoyed, with a fear that public will taking them to task for wrong statements and misguidance since long after thorough modification in the concept and principles of astrology. Instead of this they are more interested in exploiting the ignorance, fear and faith of the society and want to take commercial benefit by justifying the astrology after systematic propaganda of new sort of blind-faith and fear like a clever businessman. Contrary to this, another section of the society is only being exploited due to their ignorance about the fundamental basis of the astrology. But such exploitation of the new generation will be reduced as-and-when they will be aware with the factual status of the astrology on the basis of scientific information of the astronomy, as contained in this book.

From the next chapter, we will analyse the principles of astrology as laid down in Primitive age, in view of the modern information of Solar system. Universe is the mother of all astrological principles, on which mathematical calculation are based and predictions are being concluded. Hence, first of all we will discuss and analyse the formation of the Universe and only, thereafter, other astrological principles will be analysed, one by one.

Sign and measurement

In the Primitive age period was measured with the help of the position of Moon. It took about 29.5 days or 30 *tithi* in recurrence of the same face of the Moon i.e. period taken from full Moon to next full Moon. Whereas, Moon took about 27 days in passing through the same constellation. Thus sky was divided in 12 signs according to the position of the Sun during 12 months and nearby stars was grouped to form 27 constellations on the basis of daily changing position of the Moon during 27 days. Thus constellation was formed on the basis of single star or group of stars. Name of 12 signs, in which Sun remained during a month, was derived from the shape drawn on the basis of group of constellations and some nearby other stars. Moon takes about 60 *ghati* for crossing a constellation. Transit of Moon during quarter of this time i.e. 3° 20' was called a step (*charan*) of the constellation.

Sky	=	360° / 12 signs / 27 constellations
1 sign	=	30° or 1800' (' = minute) or 30 *ansh*
1 Degree	=	60' or 60 *kala*
1 Minute	=	60" (" = second) or 60 *vikala*
1 sign	=	2.25 constellation
		or 2 const. + 1 step
1 constellation	=	13° 20' or 800'
1 step	=	3° 20' or 200'

3

UNIVERSE

With an idea to understand the concept of astrology and for concluding a pointed prediction, I consolidated all relevant data of a horoscope in three different charts shown in appendix-1, to enable me to simultaneously analyse all parameters of a horoscope at a time. By now you may have gone through these charts detailed in appendix-1 as suggested during interaction. But even after this much exercise, I could not achieve my target of concluding a correct and pointed prediction. Thereafter, I decided to unearth the background of astrological principles and after strolling in the background behind formulation of the principles of astrology, for years together, I could get success only when I prepared a software for detailed observation of the planetary position since 1000 BC to AD 100. It was not possible for the astrologers of the Middle age to recast and observe the sky of Primitive age; otherwise the set of principles of astrology would have been totally different. I surprised with many astonishing facts which came to my knowledge after observing the sky of Primitive age and I also impressed with the deep thinking and labour put in by our sages in formulation of the astrological principles after regular gazing of the sky in Primitive age and that too even when no basic facilities were available to them. It was also clear that how much impact *veda*, religion and faith had on the understanding regarding structure of the Universe, which was accepted in the Rising age. Regular observation of the movement of planets, imagination, deep thinking and the then social and political set-up had so immense impact in formulation of the astrological principles and mindset of the society that in modern scientific age even intelligent section of our society is being pulled up at one hand with the help of these outdated principles and on the other hand they have full faith without any second thought that the principles of astrology are correct.

Now, on the basis of knowledge acquired with the help of modern science, it is beyond doubt and an accepted fact that all planets of our solar system including our Earth rotate around the Sun whereas Moon, which is nearest to our Earth rotate around the Earth. Though our scientists have not only located other planets like Uranus, Neptune, Pluto and Chiron, but they also located Moons of other planets of our solar system. Because our sages not mentioned anything about these new planets and Moons of other planets in any astrological principle, hence we will also not discuss about these planets and Moons.

Before we may start to analyse the principles of astrology, we must keep in mind the level of information regarding the planets and Universe which was available with our sages and celestial position of planets, which were observed by them in Primitive age, when the principles related to Lord of sign, Exalted-debilitated planet etc. were being formulated. We must also keep in mind the level of study related to the Universe and position of planets conducted by our sages. Because it is quite natural that whenever a principle is formulated, it is always based on the best of the then available information, skill, knowledge and interpretation. I repeat that whenever a principle is formulated, it is always based on the best of the then available information, skill, knowledge and interpretation.

What conveyed

We are aware from the description regarding development of astrology that the Earth was considered as a stationary body during Rising and Primitive age. It is very strange that in many countries of the world, it is still believed only due to faith and some religious compulsion that the Earth is stationary. From the very beginning of the Primitive age our sages were well aware with the then information regarding the Universe and they know that there are five more planets besides two illuminative planets i.e. Sun and Moon and they are situated in the order of Mercury, Venus, Mars, Jupiter and Saturn. Thus astrological principles are based on the primitive concept that the Sun is a nearest planet from the Earth and then other planets and constellations were situated in the order of Moon, Constellations, Mercury, Venus, Mars, Jupiter and Saturn respectively at a height over each other. All planets were considered to have their own light and they were treated as a living palace of deities. Sun was considered as nearest planet and all other planets including Moon were considered comparatively at more height in comparison to the Sun. This planetary situation is almost supported by the doctrines of *Vedic, Bodh* and *Jain* religions since Rising age. According to *Vishnu-puran*, Sun is situated at a height of one lakh *Yojan* from the Earth thereafter, Moon is situated at a height of one lakh *Yojan* and all constellations are situated at a height of one lakh *Yojan* from Moon. Thereafter, other planets are situated at a height of two lakh Yojan from each other in the order of Mercury, Venus, Mars, Jupiter and Saturn. According to *Moksha-shastra*, these planets were believed as deities and Sun was believed to be situated at a height of 800 *Yojan* from *Jambu-dweep* i.e. the middle world and Moon was placed at a height of 80 *Yojan* from the Sun, all 27 constellations were placed at a height of merely four *Yojan* from the Moon. Thereafter, Mercury was placed at a height of four *Yojan* and then Venus etc. planets were believed to be situated at a height of three *Yojan* from each other. At that time one *Yojan* was equal to about 14.4 km. Innumerable blinking stars visible in the sky were believed to be situated with constellations i.e. in between the Moon and Mercury. So this was the understanding about the set-up of the entire Universe. Sun and Moon were regarded as illuminative planets i.e. the planets which were able to through the light on the Earth. That's why these two planets were considered as special planets. In this way, in that age it was believed that shape of the Universe was like picture-1. The belief over this shape of the Universe is a very

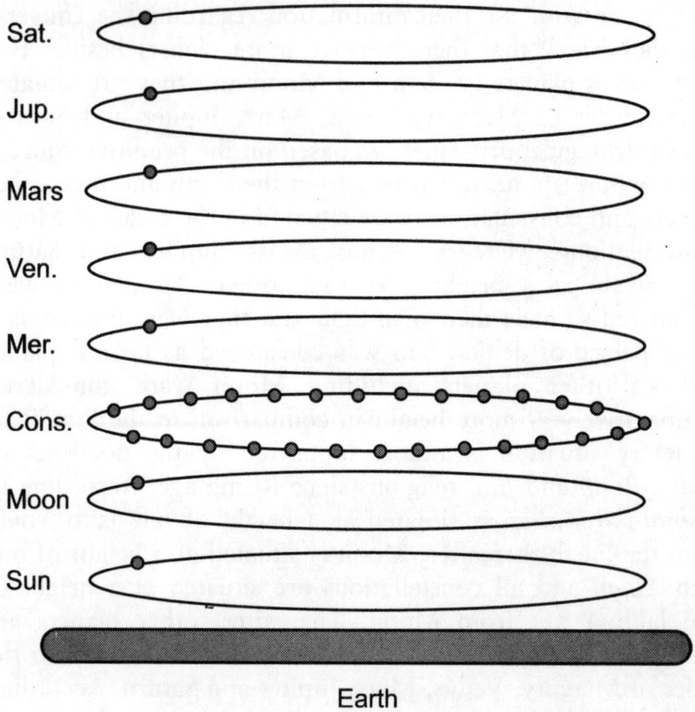

Picture – 1
Universe of Primitive age

very important fact, as we will see that it has a pivotal role on all sort of astrological knowledge and principles which we have acquired or developed till today.

In the Rising age and thereafter too, event of high and ebb tide of sea were never considered to occur due to the Moon. Because, as per faith prevailed at that time, Moon was believed to be situated over and above the Sun and also believed to be far away in comparison to the Sun as shown in picture-1. According to *Tiloypadatti*, high and ebb tide of sea occurs only due to breathe of the deities living in the lower world (*Paataal*). Likewise reason for an eclipse was neither attributed to shadow of the Earth or position of the Moon in between the Sun and Earth nor Rahu Ketu was believed at intersection point of orbit of the Sun and Moon. Because in those days it was believed that Rahu Ketu are some shadow planets and eclipse occurs when they capture Moon and Sun respectively.

You have gone through the description of the development of astrology that this sort of information regarding the Universe believed to be true till last few hundred years. But now everybody knows that only Sun is illuminative and all other planets including Moon which is nearest to the Earth, shines only due to the light of the Sun which falls on them.

At that time our sages had very good knowledge about the equinoxil point and on this basis they were able to know the timing of winter solstice and summer solstice. They were well aware with the duration of daytime and were able to know before hand about the variation in the duration of day and night. Hence, naturally it was auspicious occasion when duration of daytime happens to be more than the duration of night. As per *Sayan* system which prevailed in those days, it was believed that Sun remain at Vernal Equinox, when it transit from the first step (*charan*) of Ashwini constellation i.e. from 0° of Aries sign. From this beginning point on Celestial Equator, situations of other planets were located in the sky. The sky was divided in 27 constellations on the basis of time of 27 days, taken by the Moon in one rotation around the Earth. In the same way time taken by the Sun for reappearing at Vernal Equinox, i.e. when duration of daytime happens to be more than the duration of night, was divided in 12 solar months and accordingly its monthly celestial position was marked by a sign totalling 12 signs for entire sky. By devising the idea of division of sky, not only the knowledge of signs and constellations were improved but the system for locating a planet in the sky was also created.

What observed

There is now substantial change in the information which was available with our sages in the Primitive age, regarding the formation of Universe, Distance of planets from the Earth, Size of planets, Orbit of planets etc., on the basis of which existing astrological principles and predictive astrology were developed. It is quite natural that if there is no change in a situation for over a long period then usually basic concept behind framing of any tradition may get lost. In the same way though so many traditions have now lost their relevancy yet we are following them without giving a second look. For example, whenever Sun enters in a sign, it is known as *sankranti* for that sign. Summer solstice was considered auspicious and celebrated in the Primitive age due to onset of increase in the duration of daytime. Because in those days summer solstice started when Sun transit in the Capricorn sign hence *makar sankranti* had precedence over all other *sankranti*. But now-a-days summer solstice started at about 7° of the Sagittarius (*Dhanu*) sign. Due to gap of substantial time, we forget about the foundation block of celebrating *makar sankranti* i.e. summer solstice, but we only remembered *makar sankranti* and hence instead of changing the celebration of summer solstice to *dhanu sankranti*, we are still celebrating *makar sankranti* as a tradition. Whereas, *makar sankranti* has lost its universal importance which was once linked with summer solstice. Now imagine that in the year AD 7000, when summer solstice will start when Sun will transit in Libra sign then how you will feel in enjoying *mangora* party on 23-3-7000 when *makar sankranti* will fall during onset of summer. This situation will take a very funny turn in the year AD 13300, when *ayanansh* will be 180°. On 23-6-13300, when we would have been celebrating *makar sankranti*, a festival based on summer solstice, but actually at that time Sun would have been taking transit for winter solstice. The main idea behind quoting this situation is only to highlight the fact that while following a tradition we are neither interested to know the basic concept behind that tradition nor concerned to analyse a situation, but we behave like a carrier of custom and continue to follow this without any logic or relevancy. It may now be presumed that society may draw their attention towards above mismatching and may try to correct it. But by the above example you may realise the importance of *ayanansh*, only by which many astrological principles have lost their ground. We will discuss later on about those principles.

Before the discovery done by Copernicus and supported by Galileo in the year AD 1543 and AD 1609 respectively, scholars of the world tried to understand the Universe and planets according to their belief and faith, considering that Earth is stationary and flat. The process of understanding the formation of the world was going on in India since Rising age, whereas the same process was also going on in Greece and Egypt civilisation. Copernicus had discovered for the first time that all planets including Earth rotate around the Sun, whereas only Moon rotate around our Earth. More than 400 years have passed since the establishment of the above fact, yet public at large of many countries of the world including India and Europe, have not recognised the above fact only due to some religious compulsions. You can still come across many persons who still believe that Earth is stationary and will try to classify the event of landing of man on the Moon as a fiction. Only due to existence of such stubborn faith and belief, astrological forecast is being done on the basis of some mathematical principles based on the information and concept of Primitive age, instead of doing some basic research in the field of astrology, on the basis of latest information. That's why we are neither able to improve the astrology nor able to correctly predict an event.

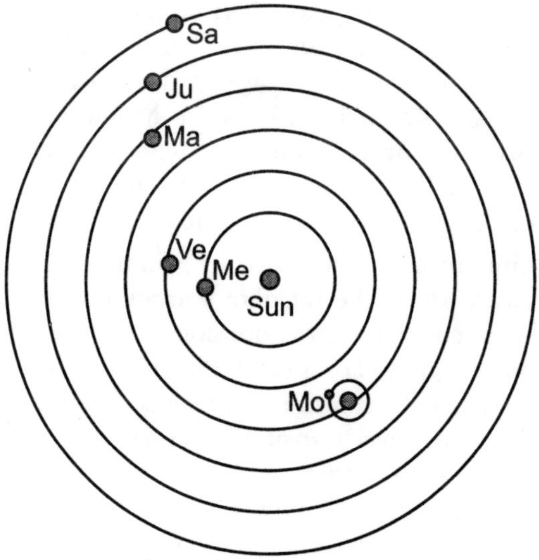

Picture – 2
Actual orbit of planets

Now it is scientifically proved and also uncontroversial that Sun is a Star and Mercury, Venus, Earth, Mars, Jupiter, Saturn, Uranus, Neptune, Pluto, Chiron planet rotate around the Sun, whereas Moon is rotating around our Earth. In view of this fact it is a matter of concern as to how much importance can be provided to the concept of Primitive age regarding the distance and orbit of planets with reference to our Earth as shown in picture-1. Orbit of all planets up to Saturn, discovered on the basis of scientific research is shown in picture-2.

All planets do have their independent Moon, which rotates around their respective planets like our own Moon of Earth. Only Moon rotate around our Earth, whereas all planets including Earth rotate around the Sun. Sun is also rotating in our galaxy around the Black hole. There are lakhs of other galaxies like our own galaxy. In this way no solid body is stationary in the Universe. On one hand every solid body is exerting its impact like gravitation etc. on other solid bodies and on the other hand it is also being effected by the gravitational and other powers of other solid bodies. In this way, we can imagine that every solid body, which is present in our own galaxy or in some other galaxies, is continuously exerting its impact on all other solid bodies like Earth and in turn on all living being. In the Primitive age it was believed that all constellations are situated in between Moon and Mercury. Whereas, now we know from the latest knowledge of the Universe that actually these constellations are not situated even in our own galaxy and they are in different galaxies.

By the time of commencement of Primitive age, our sages were well aware about the retrograde motion of a planet and naturally this phenomenon was not considered as a good sign. Many astrologers of today also think that during retrograde motion, planets actually transit in the reverse direction. Whereas, actually planets can never transit in a reverse direction and it is also not possible for a planet, to change its transit from direct to reverse motion, who is having a size of thousands km and moving around the Sun with an enormous direct speed due to gravitational attraction of the Sun. If we try to rotate a stone tied with a rope then we can see that its direction of movement

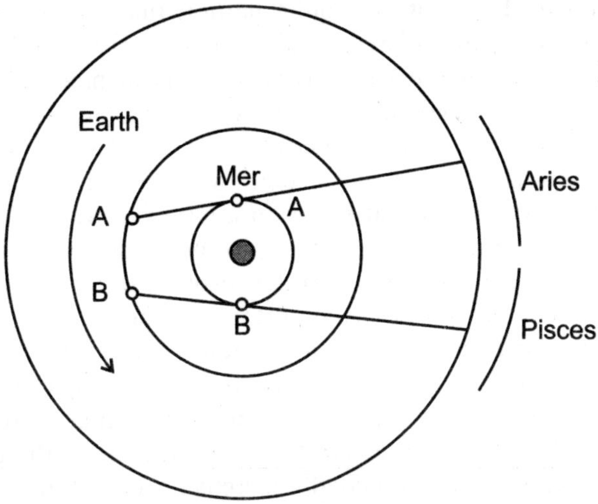

Picture – 3

Retrograde position of a planet with reference to Earth

cannot be reversed intermittently. In the same way any solid body, which is moving in a direction cannot reverse its direction. The actual reason behind visual retrograde motion of a planet in the sky is only due to change in relevant position of the planet with reference to the position of the Earth in the Universe. You can easily understand this fact from the picture-3.

You can see from the picture that the Mercury is visible in Aries sign from the Earth. This position of the Mercury and Earth is marked by 'A'. After completing the half rotation of the Sun by the Mercury in about 44 days, we can see that instead of moving ahead in Taurus sign, Mercury is visible in Pisces sign due to change in relative position of the Mercury and Earth as 'B'. In the same way we visualise the movements of planets as direct or retrograde due to change in the relative position of that planet with reference to the Earth. Whereas all planets always moves in a direct motion with reference to the Sun. Later on we will again discuss this point in detail.

Our sages were neither aware with the actual spherical shape of the Earth nor with the existence of Southern

Hemisphere. Hence it was quite natural that all astrological principles were formulated keeping in mind the flat shape of the Earth. The birth place of astrological principles and where our sages conducted all sort of experiments was in Indian subcontinent situated in Northern Hemisphere. Hence Northern Hemisphere gets importance. Today we know on the basis of scientific information that when duration of daytime increases in Northern Hemisphere then correspondingly duration of daytime get reduces in Southern Hemisphere in the same ratio. Hence if summer solstice is important for the people living in Northern Hemisphere then it is quite natural that winter solstice is must be equally important for the people living in Southern Hemisphere. In view of this explanation there must be some difference in the astrological principles for the people of both hemisphere, but actually there is no such differences in the fundamental principles or predictive astrology for the people of both hemispheres.

Though there were some correct presumption yet there were some natural mistakes due to misconception of the Universe and solar system which emerged from the faith and belief over religious practice followed during Rising age. Beside this with the passage of time, substantial change have also taken place in the celestial position of the planets due to *ayanansh*. But as we have lost our traditions of sky gazing which was the basic foundation stone of formulation of astrological principles, hence we are unable to modify these principles in accordance with the changing situation of the planets in zodiac. We must not forget that sages of the Primitive age were neither equipped with modern mathematics nor they have modern technology. As has been explained earlier that principles of Algebra, Geometry etc. were only developed in the early Middle age after AD 500. Hence it is quite natural and justified that there is mistake in the formulation of astrological principles in the ratio of mistake in the conception of the Universe. Subsequently mathematical calculations, which were developed for predictive astrology was also misalign with the same ratio of mistake.

In the Primitive age it was believed that planet used to transit in retrograde motion and subsequently, order of *mahadasha* was developed on the basis of the phenomena of retrogression and time taken by a planet in one rotation in zodiac, which we will discuss later on.

Conclusion

There is a substantial shift in the celestial position of all planets due to change in ayanansh and there is also a fundamental difference in the concept of formation of the Universe as per modern knowledge based on scientific research in comparison to the concept prevailed in the Primitive age. Hence it is obvious that astrological principles may be wrong in the ratio of mistake in the primitive concept of the Universe.

It has now been finally proved on the basis of scientific research that Moon is the nearest planet from the Earth instead of Sun and Rahu-Ketu are formed due to the movement of the Moon, hence their distance will also be alike the distance of the Moon. Whereas Jupiter and Saturn are moving at a greater distance respectively. Remaining four planets i.e. Venus, Mars, Mercury and Sun are situated after Moon. As per their distance from the Earth their order in the solar system may be arranged like Sun, Mercury, Venus and Mars. This order may also be rearranged with reference to the distance of these planets from the Earth, which keeps on changing due to their rotation around the Sun. The variation in distances of these planets from the Earth during their rotation is as follows :

Distance from the Earth

Planet	Nearest distance	Farthest distance
Moon	3.57	4.07 lakh km
Rahu-Ketu	3.57	4.07 lakh km
Venus	3.73	26.23 crore km
Mars	5.58	39.97 crore km
Mercury	7.90	22.16 crore km
Sun	14.65	15.27 crore km
Jupiter	59.09	96.43 crore km
Saturn	111.54	169.70 crore km

In this way order of Venus, Mars, Mercury and Sun on the basis of distances from the Earth remains under continuous change. Thus order of the planets based on their distance from the Earth will be different for every horoscope according to the time of birth. This revised order of planets will be different in 95% horoscopes in comparison to the order of planets, which were followed in the Primitive age.

Thus it will be clear from the above explanation that there are main mistakes as follows in the primitive concept of formation of the Universe. Thus astrological principles based on this concept are scientifically wrong and incorrect.

1. Moon (satellite) is a nearest planet from the Earth instead of the Sun (star).
2. Earth, Mercury, Venus and Mars rotate around the Sun, whereas Moon rotate around the Earth, hence the distances and order of Sun, Mercury, Venus, Mars and Moon remains under continuous change with reference to the Earth and this scientific concept is totally against the belief prevailed in the Primitive age.

4

LORD OF SIGNS

Any logical description regarding the celestial position of the planets or the basis in support of formulation of the fundamental astrological principles, which are being analysed in the succeeding chapters, are not available now-a-days. Whereas detail of astrological principles can be seen in the literature available in archives. The reasons behind non-availability of any logical description may not be that our sages want to conceal the logic behind the framing of the basics of astrological principles, instead of this concept of celestial position of the planets and formation of Universe was quite common, natural and acceptable to all in those days on the basis of information available in various religious literature, hence there was no reason to record it in the astrological literature. Because in the Primitive age there was scarcity of writing material and transfer of knowledge took place only by hearsay (*shrut-gyan*) system practised in *guru-shishya* tradition. Hence very ordinary reasons behind framing of fundamental principles may not be available in any literature. After analysing the fundamental principles, it also appears and sounds logical that at that time in the Primitive age when astrological principles were taking shape, our sages were trying to formulate various principles as an experiment with the help of which destiny may be ascertained. Hence it was quite natural in the process of experimentation that result of one principle may lead to totally opposite conclusion arrived at with the help of another principle. In this way the principles formulated by our sages were publicised to enable them to analyse the result derived on the basis of these fundamental principles. It was justified that till they were not able to get absolute result, there was no sense in writing down the logic behind framing a principle. Because the results derived from various principles were leading to different directions and secondly predictive astrology was not so important in those days and astrology has not taken a definite shape, hence our sages could not reach to a logical conclusion. In these circumstances there was also no sense in writing down the logic behind every fundamental principles which were being experimented, hence now-a-days we are not in a position to locate any reason behind such fundamental principles. But due to non-availability of the written document behind formulation of the astrological principles it was not possible for the mathematician and thinker who came after thousand of years to reanalyse the core basics of such principles and secondly they have full faith in traditional principles, thus they could only support these principles with the help of new branches of mathematics and tried to develop the infrastructure for correcting predictive astrology. This point is contemplative as to when it was not possible to derive the correct forecast on the basis of astrological principles formulated by our sages in the Primitive age only then it was felt necessary to develop mathematical calculation for deriving correct forecast. Otherwise there was no need to introduce latitude, longitude, correct time of birth, *Shadbal, Charantar, Bhujantar, Mudda* (annual) horoscope etc. and introduction of new theory of prediction by Krishnamurti of south India in 20th century. But how it is possible that astrological principles may correctly be modified and developed when there was fundamental mistake about the information of Universe, Earth and planets. If we consider the present scenario in the scientific background then we can visualise that we are just repeating the same mistake by trying to channelise this whole process with the help of computers instead of understanding the fundamental concept of our sages behind formulating these fundamental principles and without understanding or rectifying the basic mistake committed by our sages in understanding the Universe.

What conveyed

With the help of the different celestial positions occupied by the Sun during twelve months, it was possible to divide the zodiac in twelve signs. Thereafter, the element of the planets and signs were decided, whose description is given below. In view of our sages it was essential to anyhow link these signs with the planets to work out any prediction and hence all signs were linked with the planets in the following manner. Any logical reason behind linking these planets with specified signs is not known.

Element	Nature	Sign	Lord	Element
Fire	Movable	Aries	Mars	Fire
Earth	Fixed	Taurus	Venus	Water
Air	Dual	Gemini	Mercury	Earth
Water	Movable	Cancer	Moon	Water
Fire	Fixed	Leo	Sun	Fire
Earth	Dual	Virgo	Mercury	Earth
Air	Movable	Libra	Venus	Water
Water	Fixed	Scorpio	Mars	Fire
Fire	Dual	Sagittarius	Jupiter	Space
Earth	Movable	Capricorn	Saturn	Air
Air	Fixed	Aquarius	Saturn	Air
Water	Dual	Pisces	Jupiter	Space

What observed

If we compare the element of a sign with the element of their respective lord, then we can see following discrepancies :–

1. Element of the Mercury is Earth, whereas it is lord of Gemini sign whose element is Air and who consider Earth as its enemy.
2. Element of the Venus is Water, whereas it is lord of Libra sign whose Air element is its enemy.
3. Element of the Mars is Fire, whereas it is lord of Scorpio sign whose Water element is its enemy.
4. Element of the Saturn is Air, whereas it is lord of Capricorn sign whose Earth element is its enemy.

What discovered

After deep analysis from all angles on the order of distribution of signs among planets, it transpires that as per belief prevailed in the Primitive age; Mercury, Venus, Mars etc. planets were considered to be situated above constellations. Hence order of distribution of signs was started from Aries of Fire element, which was allotted to the first planet of Fire element i.e. Mars and thereafter other signs were distributed among the planets. The position may be seen from the picture-4 and it may be compared with their planetary position with reference to the Earth in the Universe as shown in picture-1. As per belief in the Primitive age Venus is the next planet which is nearer to the Earth in comparison to Mars, who has already occupied Aries sign, hence next Taurus sign was allotted to Venus and next Gemini sign was allotted to next nearest planet i.e. Mercury. Thereafter next Cancer sign was allotted to next nearest planet i.e. Moon and next Leo sign was allotted to next nearest planet i.e. Sun. Now in the absence of next nearest planet, next planet above the illuminator planets i.e. Sun and Moon and above the constellation was Mercury who was then awarded with Virgo sign and next Libra sign was allotted to next planet Venus, next Scorpio sign was allotted next planet Mars, next Sagittarius sign was allotted to next planet Jupiter, next Capricorn sign was allotted to next planet Saturn. Now in the absence of next

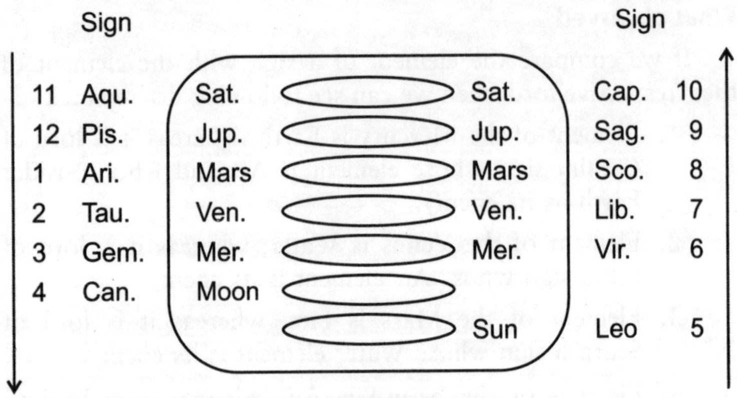

Picture – 4
Distribution of signs among planets

planet and to equate the situation of owning two signs by each planet situated above constellation and excepting illuminator planets, Saturn was awarded with the next Aquarius sign and last Pisces sign was again allotted to the next nearest planet i.e. Jupiter. In this way our sages were able to distribute twelve signs among planets.

In this way all signs were linked with the planets on the basis of the then knowledge and information about the Universe. The basis of this distribution matches the colour of starting four signs and planets. In this way at least eight signs were able to get the lordship of the planets having matching element. Beside this colour of initial four signs i.e. Aries, Taurus, Gemini and Cancer which are red, white, green and bright were matched with the colour of their respective lords i.e. Mars, Venus, Mercury and Moon. It was not possible to distribute the signs among known planets more efficiently then this distribution of signs. Because only by this distribution the colour of starting four signs properly matched. This fact also emerges from this distribution of signs among planets that how much important and exclusive role was played by the primitive concept about the Universe and planetary situation in the Universe with reference to the then stationary Earth.

In this way full matching of the element of all signs with the element of their lords could not be executed, because there was no other best alternative. Details of distribution of Sign and planet among the elements and their predictive quality may be seen from the next table.

Element	Sign	Planet	Quality
Fire	Aries, Leo,	{Sun,	Supremacy,
	Sagittarius	{Mars	Power
Earth	Taurus, Virgo, Capricorn	Mercury	Intelligence
Air	Gemini, Libra, Aquarius	Saturn	Work
Water	Cancer, Scorpio,	{Moon,	Imagination,
	Pisces	{Venus	Comfort
Space		Jupiter	{ Knowledge,
			{ Wealth, Luck

It is evident from the distribution of the signs among seven planets that there are similarities in the qualities of some signs and their lord. Nevertheless, it is not so that quality of some other planet may not have matched with the quality of a sign. It is presumed that sign of ascendant may have impact only on the affair of body and sign of Moon may have impact only on the matter related to mental status. In this way if a sign has some qualities of the House then it may have its impact over the result. But result of a planet situated in a sign may be according to its element and quality. Beside this activator of a House plays an important role in providing the result of that House. Because the activator planet possess more prominently the qualities of that house and it also has leading effect on the result.

During analysis of the formation of the Universe it was mentioned that there is substantial difference in the distances of Sun, Moon, Mercury, Venus and Mars from the Earth as anticipated in the Primitive age as shown in picture-1 in comparison to the modern information about the Universe and solar system. Now we know that Moon is the nearest planet (satellite) and order of another four planets based on their distances from the Earth remain under continuous change due to relative distance of these planets from the Earth during their rotation around the Sun. Because allotment of a sign to a planet as its lord was mainly based on the distance of that planet from the Earth. Hence it is pertinent that lord of all signs may be decided afresh at the time of birth in accordance with the procedure adopted by our sages in Primitive age for every horoscope on the basis of the distance of every planet from the Earth on the basis of modern technology.

Conclusion

Additional four planets discovered so far i.e. Uranus, Neptune, Pluto and Chiron have no place in the distribution of signs. It may also be possible that there may be one more planet, thus by adopting some scientific method, all twelve signs may properly bedistributed among twelve planets for lordship in future. But if we are bent upon to allot every sign to some planet then we will have to revise the principle of lordship of signs due to change in the order of the planets from the Earth on the basis of their distance. It is also possible that if two planets i.e. Uranus and Neptune would have been located by sages before the Primitive age, then these nine planets may have been allotted lordship of twelve signs by our sages in the manner as shown in picture-5.

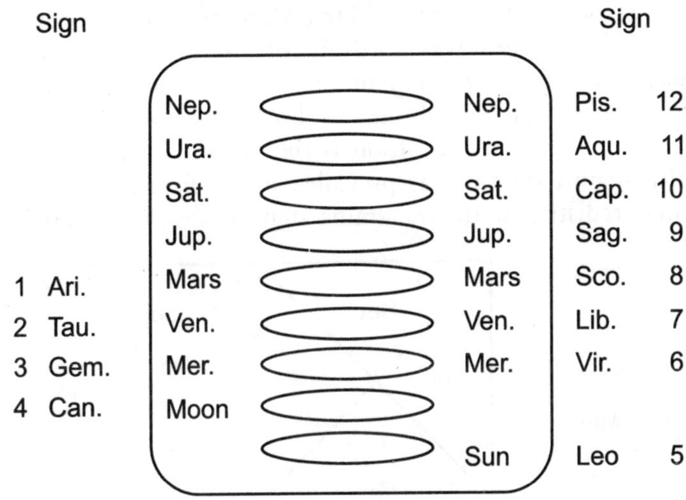

Picture – 5

Probable distribution of signs among nine planets

It was also possible that those planets who possess a sign having opposite element would have been allotted only one sign and in this way Pluto and Chiron may also got an opportunity of lordship.

If we follow the same system which was adopted by our sages for allotting a sign to the planets based on their distance from the Earth then we have to decide the lordship of all signs independently for every horoscope on the basis of the order of distance of the planets at the time of birth, in view of the modern concept of the Universe. If there is no way out and we want to allot the signs among planets and on the other hand do not want to allot any signs to new planets i.e. Uranus, Neptune etc. then as per details shown in the table of

'Distance from the Earth' in previous chapter, it is clear that order of distance of Sun, Mars, Mercury, Venus and Moon may not be according to picture-1. Because Moon will always be nearest, whereas order of Jupiter and Saturn may remain as it is, because there is no change in the order of distance of these two planets as envisaged in the Primitive age and as per modern concept. Order of other four planets on the basis of their distance may be Venus, Mars, Mercury and Sun or in any other order. In this way lordship of Sagittarius, Capricorn, Aquarius and Pisces will remain unchanged. If we also want to allot Cancer sign to Moon, as both have water element, despite the fact that the Moon is the nearest planet, which is totally against the faith as prevailed in the Primitive age then we may redistribute the remaining signs as shown in picture-6.

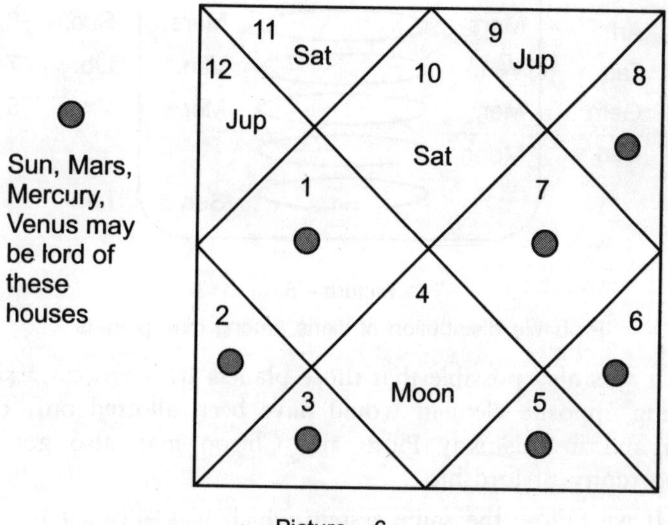

Picture – 6
Distribution of signs among planets

Signs may be allotted among four planets in accordance with the distance of the planets from the Earth and in this way lord of Aries, Taurus, Gemini, Leo, Virgo, Libra and Scorpio signs may be decided. As a second option if we want to allot Aries sign either to Mars or some other planet then entire order of lordship will be changed according to the distance of the planets from the Earth. In both situations, the order of lordship will entirely be different after arranging them according to the distance of these planets from the Earth.

In this way it is clear that instead of deciding a lord for every sign; it is more logical to follow the system of treating a planet as an activator of a house as decided by our sages and shown below. Because in this way planet will respond more suitably for providing a result of the House and only by this method other planets like Uranus, Neptune etc., may also be properly provided with some activator qualities, as and when discovered.

Planet	House	Planet	House
Sun	1, 9, 10	Jupiter	2, 5, 9, 10,11
Mars	3, 6	Venus	7
Mercury	4, 10	Saturn	6, 8, 10, 12
Moon	4		

In this way it will be clear that knowledge of the Universe and planetary position in the Universe gathered till Rising age had a definite impact over deciding the lordship of various sign. It can also be seen that modern information of planets in solar system and primitive concept of the planetary system has only about fifty per cent similarities.

From the above analysis it can easily be concluded that there are following mistakes in deciding the lordship and due to which astrological principles are faulty and not in accordance with the scientific concept.

1. Distances of Sun, Mercury, Venus, Mars and Moon from the Earth continuously changes hence principle of deciding the lordship on the basis of fixed distances of these planets is faulty.
2. Element of the planets and signs are not properly matched.
3. Non-allotment of lordship of any sign to the Uranus, Neptune, Pluto and Chiron planets, which were discovered later on, is faulty.

Planet, motion and element

Sun and Moon were only regarded as planets moving over fixed Earth prior to Rising age. Due to their visual nature and impact they were considered as the representative of Fire and Water element respectively. These two illuminative planets always transit in a direct motion with reference to the Earth i.e. they always move towards next constellation and sign.

Sages discovered by their regular gazing of the sky and after deep thinking that Universe is made up of five elements i.e. Fire, Earth, Air, Water and Sky. Representatives of these five elements were also discovered in the shape of other five planets i.e. Mars, Mercury, Saturn, Venus and Jupiter respectively. These five planets were considered to be situated above constellations and their transit continuously varies between direct and retrograde motion with reference to the Earth. In this way these planets appear to move in forward and backward direction in constellations and sign.

Sages devised imaginary shadow planets in the form of Rahu and Ketu due to solar eclipse and changing face of Moon. It was considered that these shadow planets move in retrograde motion at a speed of 3' 11" i.e. movement towards backward constellation. Sun, Moon, Mercury, Venus, Mars, Jupiter, Saturn, Rahu and Ketu are considered as planets in astrology.

All matter and human being were considered to be effected by an element and their nature was then classified according to the element of the planet. Thus signs and planets were also classified according to the nature of these element. If a person is effected with surplus of any element from Air, Fire or Water then it is presumed that he is suffering from *vaat, pitt* or *cough* respectively in *Ayurved* and then these elements are balanced by proper treatment.

According to latest information Sun is a Star and five planets along with Earth and other four planets i.e. Uranus, Neptune, Pluto, Chiron discovered during last 300 years are rotating around the Sun in direct motion with reference to the Sun. Moon is only a satellite which rotates around the Earth. All other planets have their own Moons, which rotates around their respective planets. Rahu and Ketu is actually the intersection point of the orbit of Sun and Moon.

5

FRIENDSHIP-ENMITY BETWEEN PLANETS

What conveyed

Friendship-enmity between planets was laid down in the following manner :–

Planet	Friendship	Even	Enmity
Sun	Mars, Moon, Jup.	Mercury	Venus, Saturn
Mars	Sun, Moon, Jup.	Venus, Sat.	Mercury
Jupiter	Sun, Moon, Mars	Saturn	Mercury, Venus
Moon	Sun, Mercury	Jup., Mars, Sat., Venus	—
Mercury	Sun, Venus	Jup., Mars, Saturn	Moon
Venus	Mercury, Saturn	Jup., Mars	Sun, Moon
Saturn	Mercury, Venus	Jupiter	Sun, Mars, Moon

As usual, any logical explanation in support of the above principle for deciding the friendship, enmity between the planets is not available.

What observed

After analysing the mutual relations between the planets, based on the principles of friendship and enmity we can observe many discrepancies in this principle, which indicates that mutual relations between the planets are not based on equal footings. The details of these disparities are as follows :–

1. Mercury is even for Sun, whereas Sun is friend for Mercury.
2. Mercury is enemy for Mars, whereas Mars is even for Mercury.
3. Mercury is enemy for Jupiter, whereas Jupiter is even for Mercury.
4. Saturn is even for Mars, whereas Mars is enemy for Saturn.
5. Venus is enemy for Jupiter, whereas Jupiter is even for Venus.
6. Saturn is even for Mercury, whereas Mercury is friend for Saturn.
7. Mercury is friend for Moon, whereas Moon is enemy for Mercury.
8. Mars and Jupiter are even for Moon, whereas Moon is friend for Mars and Jupiter.
9. Venus and Saturn are even for Moon, whereas Moon is enemy for Venus and Saturn.
10. There must be natural friendship in between the planets of Fire and Air elements, and in between the planets of Earth and Water elements. But it is not so. Sun of Fire element has enmity with the Saturn of Air element; similarly, Mercury of Earth element has enmity with the Moon of Water element.
11. There must be natural enmity in between the planets of Fire and Water elements, in between the planets of Water and Air elements, in between the planets of Air and Earth elements, and in between the planets of Earth and Fire elements. But it is not so. Sun and Mars of Fire elements have friendship with the Moon of Water element. Venus of Water element has friendship with the Saturn of Air element. Saturn of Air element has friendship with the Mercury of Earth

element and Mercury of Earth element has friendship with the Sun of Fire element.

12. There must be natural friendship between the planets of same elements. But it is not so. Venus is even for Moon, whereas Moon is enemy for Venus, though both planets belongs to Water element.
13. There is instant enmity between any two planets, if they are situated in same house, fifth, sixth, seventh, eighth or ninth house from each other. Whereas these planets may have friendship between them according to the standard principle of friendship-enmity.
14. There is instant friendship between any two planets, if they are situated in second, third, fourth, tenth, eleventh or twelfth house from each other. Whereas these planets may have enmity between them according to the standard principle of friendship-enmity.

Thus it is clear that there is no uniformity in the principle of friendship-enmity.

What discovered

It is evident from the description of friendship-enmity given above that there is no uniformity and equality in the mutual relations between the planets. Thus if one planet is showing friendship for another planet and another planet is showing enmity towards the first planet. Then it will be clear that neither element of a planet nor principle of equality was given any importance during formulation of the principle of friendship-enmity.

After deep study it was discovered that after dividing the zodiac in twelve signs, lordship of every sign was allotted to some planet according to their distance from the Earth as detailed in earlier chapter. Because element of triangular signs is related to any one element among Fire or Earth or Water or Air. Hence sages given importance to triangular signs and lords of triangular sign were believed as friend, with a concept that they have enmity with the lords of another triangular sign. This position may be explained with the help of picture-7 prepared on the basis of lordship.

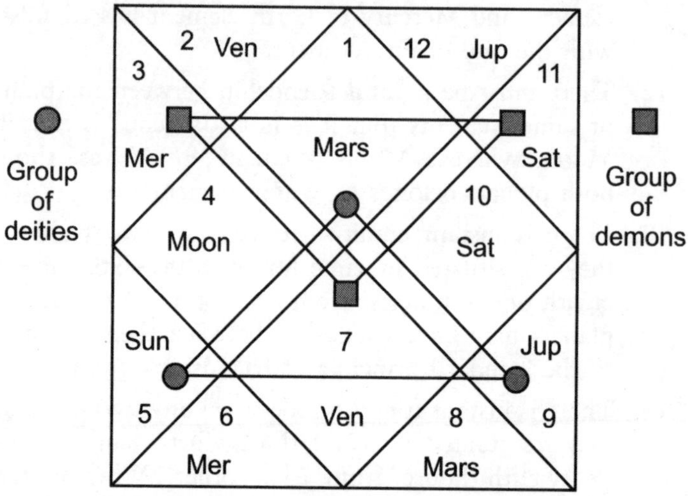

Picture – 7

Triangular position of planet for friendship-enmity

In this way following fact emerges from picture-7 prepared on the basis of sign and their lord, that lords of triangular signs related to Ascendant, 5th, 9th house and lord of another triangular signs related to 3rd, 7th, 11th house are friend themselves but they are enemy for each other. We can also see that the element of the signs of these two triangles are Fire and Air respectively and they are natural friends. Thus it is clear that while formulating the principles relating to mutual relation between the lords of two triangles, sages neither considered the element of signs nor the element of planets. Actually our sages formed two groups of planets on the basis of triangular signs and their mutual relation were decided on the basis of the relation between deities and demons as described in a mythical story. We all know about the story, which highlight the bitter relations between deities and demons and their fight for nectar, which was extracted from the sea, to become immortal. One demon was killed while he was trying to take a sip of nectar and only thereafter the body of demon was divided in two parts, which converted into Rahu and Ketu. Because demons do have full faith on Jupiter who was the instructor of deities hence no planet consider him as his enemy similarly for Moon no planet is enemy.

Ordinarily two planets do not have identical relations with each other; hence there is always a sufficient scope in deriving any prediction according to good wishes of an astrologer. This situation worsen after including the principle of instant friendship-enmity, according to which a planet has instant enmity with a planet placed in the same house, 5th, 6th, 7th, 8th and 9th house and instant friendship with the planets placed in other house. Though net effect is worked out on the basis of net friendship (*panchadha maitry*) yet effect of element of sign of a house in the horoscope remains unattended.

Conclusion

There is a glaring mistake in the principle of friendship-enmity due to absence of any attention on the element (Fire, Earth, Air and Water) of planets and signs. Because friendship-enmity between the lords of triangular signs cannot be termed as scientifically and logically in accordance with the modern concept of solar system in the Universe and allotment of lordship was also not in accordance with the distances of the planets from the Earth at the time of birth. Even if it is essential to form friendship-enmity between planets in accordance with the procedure adopted by our sages then it should be decided afresh in every horoscope after reallotment of lordship of signs based on the distance of a planet from the Earth at the time of birth. Moreover, it is not scientifically fit to create friendship-enmity between the planets on the basis of mythical story based on a fight between deities and demons. We will further discuss this issue in the chapter of aspect of planets.

From the above analysis it can be concluded that there are following mistakes in deciding the relation of friendship and enmity between the planets and due to which astrological principles are imperfect and not in accordance with the scientific knowledge about these planets.

1. It is not correct at all to create false relationship between the planets on the basis of lordship of two

triangular signs, which is further based on the concept of the Universe and lordship of signs which is further based on false and fixed distances of the planets from the Earth..

2. Elements of the planets have not been considered at all while formulating the principles of friendship-enmity between the planets; beside this principle of enmity between planets having natural friendly elements was incorrectly formulated on the basis of a mythical story.
3. Mutual relations between the planets are not identical and principle of instant friendship-enmity leads to much more confused situation, from where correct conclusion cannot be derived. Hence the principle of friendship-enmity cannot be treated as correct.

Degree, minute of sign and constellation

Sky of 360° was divided in 12 signs and 27 constellations as follows :–

Sign	Degree	Constellation	Degree
Aries		Ashwini	0° to 13° 20'
	0 to 30°	Bharni	13° 20' to 26°40'
		Kratika 1 step	26° 40' to 30°
Taurus		Kratika 3 step	30° to 40°
	30° to 60°	Rohini	40° to 53° 20'
		Mragshira 2 step	53° 20' to 60°
Gemini		Mragshira 2 step	60° to 66° 40'
	60° to 90°	Aadra	66° 40' to 80°
		Punarvasu 3 step	80° to 90°
Cancer		Punarvasu 1 step	90° to 93° 20'
	90° to 120°	Pushya	93° 20' to 106° 40'
		Ashlesha	106° 40' to 120°
Leo		Magha	120° to 133° 20'
	120° to 150°	P-falguni	133° 20' to 146°40'
		U-falguni 1 step	146° 40' to 150°
Virgo		U-falguni 3 step	150° to 160°
	150° to 180°	Hast	160° to 173° 20'
		Chitra 2 step	173° 20' to 180°
Libra		Chitra 2 step	180° to 186° 40'
	180° to 210°	Swati	186° 40' to 200°
		Vishakha 3 step	200° to 210°

Sign	Degree	Constellation	Degree
Scorpio		Vishakha 1 step	210° to 213° 20'
	210° to 240°	Anuradha	213° 20' to 226°40'
		Jyestha	226°40' to 240°
Sagittarius		Mul	240° to 253° 20'
	240° to 270°	Purvashada	253° 20' to 266°40'
		U-shada 1 step	266° 40' to 270°
Capricorn		U-shada 3 step	270° to 280°
	270° to 300°	Shravan	280° to 293° 20'
		Ghanista 2 step	293°20' to 300°
Acquarius		Ghanista 2 step	300° to 306° 40'
	300° to 330°	Shatbhisha	306° 40' to 320°
		Purva-B.pad 3 st.	320° to 330°
Pisces		Purva-B.pad 1 st.	330° to 333° 20'
	330° to 360°	Uttara-B.pad	333° 20' to 346° 40'
		Revati	346° 40' to 360°

6

ASPECT OF PLANETS

What conveyed

All seven planets have full aspect on 7th sign, whereas Mars, Jupiter and Saturn have additional full aspect on 4th, 8th, 5th, 9th and 3rd, 10th sign respectively. Though 7th sign falls in front of a planet hence its aspect on this sign may be natural, but there is no logical explanation as to why only these three planets were armed with two additional full aspects. Full description of the aspect of planets is as follows :–

Planet	Full aspect	3/4 aspect	Half aspect	Quarter aspect
Sun	7	4, 8	5, 9	3, 10
Jupiter	7, 5, 9	4, 8	—	3, 10
Mars	7, 4, 8	—	5, 9	3, 10
Saturn	7, 3 ,10	4, 8	5, 9	—
Venus	7	4, 8	5, 9	3, 10
Mercury	7	4, 8	5, 9	3, 10
Moon	7	4, 8	5, 9	3, 10

What observed

The basic reasons behind framing the aspect of the planets may be clear if we go ahead on the basis of relations of friendship-enmity between the planets. If we recollect the history of development of astrology then we can remember that in the Primitive age when our sages were promoting astrology with the help of some principles. At that point of time it was a tradition to understand the nature and qualities of a sign and planet with the help of some symbolic system as prevailed in those days. Thus any prediction was concluded on the basis of symbolic classification of the planet and sign in Male-female, Benefic-malefic, Friend-enemy etc. In this process when every sign was attached with a planet in the shape of their lord and group of Sun, Mars, Jupiter i.e. lord of the trine was classified as deities and another group of Saturn, Mercury, Venus i.e. lord of another trine was classified as demon. After forming these two groups it was quite natural that as per mythological story these groups must have enmity with each other on the analogy of tense relations between them over the issue of ownership of nectar to become immortal. To clear the position of every planet of a group our sages devised a classification by which, Sun and Saturn were termed as king; Mars and Mercury were termed as chief of army and Jupiter, Venus were termed as instructor of deities and demons respectively. This type of nomination of the planets is generally mentioned during identification and effect of a planet. We may also clearly observe the impact of the then political system on the nature of fight between deities and demons.

What discovered

Picture-8 is prepared for understanding the principle of aspect. This picture is prepared after placing the lord of sign in their respective house; and by placing the Sun, Saturn; king of deities and demons respectively in front of each other. If we study this picture keeping in view the nomination of these planets as king, chief of army and instructor then the position of these planets will appear like an army standing in the war-field and mystery of aspect of planets is solved.

After contemplating horoscope as a war-field of planets, our sages allotted strong aspect to the planets who were classified as deities, whereas, weak aspects were allotted to the planets who were classified as demons. In this way our sages also taken the side of deities and tried to pave the way of victory of deities alike their victory in the war fought between deities and demons for nectar. We can also perceive that how our sages differentiate both of them while distributing the aspect to the planets. It is quite natural in the war-field that a soldier may have a direct visual attack on opponent who is standing just in front of him. In conformity of this phenomenon every planet was awarded with this full aspect on seventh sign.

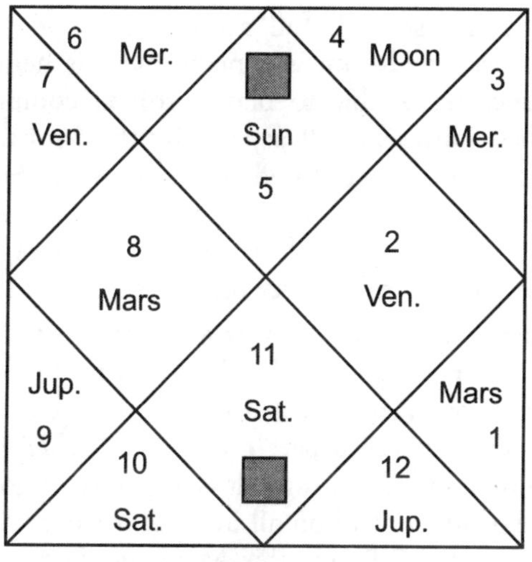

Picture – 8

Aspect of planets

You will agree that winning king or the king who hold strong position in the war-field will always keep a close watch only over the opponent king, because his all other fronts in the war-field are strong. Whereas, a weak king has to take care of every front thus he has to keep a constant watch over his all fronts. Because the planets who have been classified as deities have to win the war, like the victory of deities in the war of deities and demons. Hence the Sun who was classified as the king of deities has seventh full aspect from Leo sign on the Saturn who was the king of demons and standing in Aquarius sign as shown in picture-8. Whereas Saturn who was classified as king of demons has not only seventh full aspect on the Sun, from Aquarius sign but he also has 3rd and 10th full aspect on Mars, who is chief of army of the Sun and available in Aries and Scorpio signs. If we analyse the position of Saturn standing in Capricorn sign then the weak position of Saturn and policies adopted by a weak king emerges, who is willing to do a compromise. Saturn standing in Capricorn sign has a 3rd full aspect on the Jupiter who is the instructor of deities and no body treat him as an enemy and Saturn has 10th full aspect on his instructor Venus who is standing in Libra sign. Beside this he has seventh full aspect on Moon standing in Cancer sign. Because Moon is a planet who is neutral in this fight and hence he is able to play a roll in compromise. By exercising these different full aspects by the Saturn it will be clear that he is totally confused in front of the Sun and his behaviour is alike a weak king and despite providing so much aspect his status was weak, because except an aspect on his chief of army, he has full aspect on all other fronts.

In the same way Mars, chief of army of deities has 4th full aspect from Scorpio sign, on the Saturn, king of demons and 7th full aspect on Venus, instructor of demons, standing in Taurus sign and 8th full aspect on Mercury, chief of army of demons, standing in Gemini sign. It is a quality of good chief of army to have a full control on all important fronts of opponent army in the war-field. Beside this Mars standing in Aries sign has 7th full aspects on Venus in Libra sign and 8th full aspect on himself i.e. on his army standing in Scorpio sign and 4th full aspect on Moon standing in Cancer sign and who is neutral in this fight and capable to play a roll in compromise. In this way Mars was armed with appropriate aspects required for an able chief of army. In the same way Mercury, chief of army of demons, who was also classified as impotent, has no full aspect either on Sun or on Mars, i.e. king or chief of army of deities; instead of this from Gemini and Virgo sign, his 7th full aspect is only on the Jupiter, instructor of deities in confirmation of his impotent behaviour because nobody treat Jupiter as his enemy.

In the same way Jupiter, instructor of deities has 7th full aspect on the Mercury, chief of army of demons from Sagittarius and Pisces signs. Jupiter has 5th full aspect from Sagittarius sign and 9th full aspect from Pisces sign on Mars, chief of army of his side. Whereas Jupiter has 9th full aspect on Sun, his king, from Sagittarius sign, who is standing in Leo sign and from Pisces sign, Jupiter has 5th full aspect on Moon, who is neutral and can lead towards compromise. It is a remarkable quality of an instructor that on one hand he must be able to assess the balance of army power and on the other hand able to safeguard the interest of his king and may also be able to have a slit for entering into a compromise. You can see that the Jupiter enjoyed this quality. Contrary to this Venus, instructor of demons has 7th full aspect only on the Mars, chief of army of deities from Taurus and Libra signs. This quality is in conformity with the nature of instructor of demons, to enable him to cook his line of action by assessing the movement of opponent. By this description of aspect of planets you can very well realise the disparity observed by our sages in allotment of aspects to the planets of both group.

Above description is being extended in short regarding the detail of three fourth, half and quarter aspects of the planets. Sun has 4th, 8th three fourth aspect and 5th, 9th half aspect on Mars, chief of army and Jupiter, instructor of deities, after keeping a full aspect on the Saturn, king of demon. Sun has his least attention as 3rd, 10th quarter aspect on the chief of army and instructor of demons i.e. Mercury and Venus respectively. Which only indicates strong position of the Sun. Correspondingly, Saturn in Aquarius sign also has three fourth and half aspect on his chief of army and his instructor i.e. Mercury and Venus respectively. Jupiter of Pisces sign has three fourth and quarter aspect on Mercury and Venus, chief of army and instructor of demons respectively. Whereas centrally placed and troubled Venus has 4th and 8th three fourth aspect on the Sun and Jupiter; beside this he is also paying an equal attention to his king Saturn from Libra sign. He has 5th and 9th half aspect on his king Saturn and Mercury, chief of army. Due to his crookedness Venus has least attention as 3rd and 10th quarter aspect on the Jupiter and neutral Moon. Like an obedient chief of army, Mars has 5th and 9th half aspect on his king and instructor beside neutral Moon and remaining quarter aspect is again on opponent king and chief of army i.e. Saturn and Mercury, like his full aspect. Contrary to this chief of army of demons, Mercury has three fourth aspect on Jupiter like his full aspect and on Saturn, king and opponent chief of army, Mars. In conformity of his impotent nature he has no attacking aspect instead of this he has half aspect on Saturn and Venus, king and instructor of demons respectively. Remaining quarter aspect of Mercury is on king and chief of army of deities i.e. Sun and Mars respectively, which only indicates his impotent quality.

In this way our sages were able by their sagacity and ensured the victory of deities alike in the war of deities and demons for nectar by allotting weak aspect to the planets belonging to the group of demons and by making his chief of army as an impotent planet. We can also see that all sort of aspect of planets falls only on 3rd, 4th, 5th, 7th, 8th, 9th and 10th sign and house with reference to the position of the planet and there is no aspect on 2nd, 6th, 11th and 12th sign and house. We can see these situations in picture-8 and easily realise that these positions are important in the war-field with reference to the position of every planet. Because it is prime requirement in the war-field that one must go ahead by keeping a watch over the activities which are taking place in both direction as well as in front and one must neither be detracted with his sides (2nd, 11th and 12th house) nor afraid from the support to the opponent from his sides (6th house).

If we review full aspect of every planet then we can see that only Mars has 8th full aspect on himself from Aries sign. In this way his effect was believed to be multiplied. Only due to this reason, effect of Mars was more prominently considered for matrimonial life despite presence of much more powerful and evil planets in the horoscope. Marriage proposal of many well placed individuals is unnecessarily being delayed due to so-called ill-effect of this phenomenon, which is neither scientific nor logical. Nobody is paying any attention towards many marriages performed in the world without considering this phenomenon and still they are leading normal life.

Our sages distributed the aspects on the analogy of the war fought between deities and demons after placing the planets in their respective sign, which were allotted according to their position in the Universe. In this way we can also draw an inference that our sages given the importance only to the fixed aspects on planets, which were categorised as king, chief of army and instructor and not to the signs or houses. By following this system their idea may also be that because every planet have aspect from their respective positions in the Universe on all signs of constellations situated either below from the planets or above the illuminative planets as shown in picture-1, hence every planet of the Universe belonging to any group may always have predecided full, three fourth, half, quarter and zero aspect (as in the case of aspect of the Sun on Moon and *vice versa*) on other planets irrespective of their actual location in the sign or house. For example, Sun may always have full aspect on the Saturn irrespective of his position in any sign, otherwise our sages would have been provided some sort of reshuffling of aspect of the planets during their retrograde motion. Because our sages had sufficient knowledge of retrograde motion of the planets since the Rising age. By analysing the system which is in practice, if Mars situated in Scorpio sign has 4th full aspect on Saturn then this 4th full aspect will turn to 10th full aspect during retrograde motion of the Mars. In this way Mars will have full aspect on the Sun. Because this system was not adopted hence it is evident that intention of our sages was only on fixed aspect on the planets which is also essential in the war field and is also confirmed from the procedure for deciding the aspect of planets. In this way Sun and Saturn may be placed anywhere in the horoscope but they will have mutual aspect on each other and in turn on sign. Contrary to this the system being followed now-a-days appears to be wrong because in this way all aspect of the planets remain only on house or sign and they have no connection with the aspect, which were decided only, on the basis of situation of the planets.

In the Krishnamurti system being followed in southern India, benefic and malefic impact of a planet is decided on the basis of the difference in angle between one planet and the cusp of a house or with another planet. Though in this way it is against the principle of aspect which were decided by our sages yet in this system the impact of the planet changes dramatically due to change in difference in angle between two planets as a result of change in motion of the planet from direct to retrograde or *vice versa*. For example, if a planet is placed at 15° of Aries sign and another planet is at 15° of Cancer sign. If motion of both planets are direct and the transitory speed of first planet is more than second planet then initially the angular difference between these two planets will be 90° and first planet will have benefic aspect on second planet. Whereas in the event of change in motion of first planet from direct to retrograde the direction of transit in zodiac will be reversed and accordingly the angular difference between these two planets may be counted clockwise and it will be 270°. According to Krishnamurti system the aspect of a planet is limited to 180° and because the angular difference in the instant example is more then 180° hence there will be no aspect and first planet will have no impact on second planet. Though in this system, the direction of aspect is reversed in the event of retrograde motion yet there is no explanation that when scientifically a planet is exerting its impact in all direction in the Universe then according to Doppler's effect it may be possible that impact of first planet which is following and moving towards another planet may have some more impact over it as in the case of direct motion but it is not possible at all that the impact may completely be vanished on another planet when it is trailing behind and moving away from the first planet due to retrograde motion of first planet. Beside this we must consider this fact also that in astrology we have to estimate the quantum of impact of both planets on the humanbeing living on the Earth, instead of estimating the impact of a planet on another planet. In this way in the above example, human being living on the Earth will feel the combined effect of both planets when the angular difference between two planets is 90° and human being will also feel combined effect when the motion of a planet changes to visual retrograde motion. Though it may be possible that planet having visual retrograde motion with reference to the Earth may exert some more impact and this will also be possible only when the distance of the planet from the Earth may reduce. If the distance of the retrograde planet from the Earth is increasing then the impact will also be reversed irrespective of the fact that mutual distance of this planet with other planet is reducing.

According to this system fast moving planet will only have impact on the slow moving planet. Here motion of the planet is calculated on the basis of angular difference in their daily position. For example, fast moving Moon is at 15° of Aries sign and slow moving Saturn is at 15° of Cancer sign and both are in direct motion. Thus Moon will have benefic impact over the Saturn due to angular difference of 90° between these two planets. Now if we consider the planetary position of these planets in the solar system than we know that Moon is the nearest planet from the Earth and Saturn is far away from the Earth. In this situation it is not possible at all that impact of Saturn may be changed to benefic impact due to impact of fast moving Moon. Because any sort of impact which would have been exerted by the Moon on the Saturn will move towards the outer periphery of the solar system and will not be returned to the Earth. In second situation, any sort of impact which is emerging from the Saturn and moving towards the Earth and which is either being reflected by the Moon or reaching to the Earth after passing nearby of the Moon will only be modified with the impact of the Moon in the ratio of reflected or modified impact. Because only in this situation, impact emerging from the Saturn will meet the Moon and Earth respectively. Now in this situation it is again a fact that it makes no difference as to whether first planet i.e. Saturn is either fast moving or slow moving, because in both cases the impact of the second planet i.e. Moon, which is moving in-between the first planet and the Earth in solar system will have its mixing effect. For example if we replace the Moon by Mercury in above example than when the direct motion of the Mercury will be less then the direct motion of the Saturn, at that time also Mercury will have its mixing effect on the impact of the Saturn, because it is situated in between the Saturn and the Earth. Beside this, most of the time, the motion of the Saturn will always be less then the motion of every other planet. Thus every planet will exert its effect on the Saturn. Hence this situation as well as all such situations based on the angular difference between other planets too, is faulty.

It may be correct to presume a fixed impact of aspect with reference to the change in angular difference between the planets as per imagination that prevailed in the Primitive age, because at that time the order of the planets with reference to the Earth was presumed as fixed as shown in picture-1. But now on the basis of modern information we know that the distance of the moving planets from the Earth continuously varies in the solar system and accordingly the order of the planets based on the distance from the Earth also varies hence fixed aspect of the planets is faulty. Hence instead of working out the impact on the basis of predecided change in angular position of the planets, actually the impact based on planetary movement must be worked out on the basis of change in distance of the planets from the Earth, which will be discussed later on.

If we consider the impact of a planet in the shape of rays of colour and waves then we can perceive that emerging impact of a planet comprised of different type of rays in the form of wave. It is a scientific fact that two waves which are opposite by 180° and having same wavelength may neutralise each other. But if it is not so then the impact of the different type of waves will not be effected. Scientists have not observed so far any sort of rays, which can neutralise the impact of another planet. Hence two or more different rays may have a mixed effect but they cannot change the nature of each other. Though different type of rays continuously propagates and simultaneously travelled in the Universe yet their nature is never effected. For example, different type of communication waves relating to Radio, TV, Telephone etc. travelled in the atmosphere and get mixed with each other but there is no change in the nature or impact of a wave due to there different wavelength. In Krishnamurti system, the impact due to aspect of all planets is calculated as if they have same wavelength and all planets are at the same fixed distance from the Earth. Thus the system adopted for calculating the impact of the planets on the basis of their motion can only be logical and correct only when all planets may have emerging same waves and moving at a same distance from the Earth. But the actual situation of the planets in the solar system is not so, hence this system is faulty.

Conclusion

There is no scientific basis in support of the principle of aspect, which was once decided for the planets on the basis of the then prevailed faith and belief.

According to the Krishnamurti system it was laid down that planets have their benefic or malefic directional impact up to 180° depending on their angular difference. But this fact is ignored that every planet is moving at a different distance with reference to the Earth and thus they have not calculated the impact of the planet on the Earth keeping in view the motion of that planet with reference to the Earth. In the same way impact of a planet was not calculated with reference to the motion based on their distance from the Earth.

In view of the above situation it will be clear that there are following main mistakes in the principle of aspect between the planets due to which astrological principle is faulty and not supported by scientific concept.

1. It is faulty to discriminatory decide aspect of various planets after dividing them in two groups on the basis of wrong allotment of lordship of signs on the basis of imperfect conception of the Universe and believing them as enemy of each other on the basis of a imaginary story of fight for nectar.
2. In Krishnamurti system, effect of angular difference between two planets is worked out as if they are at the same distance from the Earth and impact of the planet on each other have been worked out instead of their impact on the Earth.

Horoscope

A sign, which is rising in the east is shown in the first house and increasing number shows sign of subsequent houses. Celestial position of the planets in a sign at the time of birth is shown in respective sign under a house. This is called horoscope.

Actual degree out of 30° of a sign, which is rising in the east is shown as degree, minute, second of the ascendant and sign of ascendant is called ascendant's sign. Actual position of ascendant is considered as mid-point of first house of *Chalit* horoscope and span of all other houses is worked out accordingly.

Sign of the Moon at the time of birth is ordinarily called sign of a person and first letter of the name is decided on the basis of the position of the Moon in a particular constellation and a step out of four steps (*charan*) thereof. Constellation of the bride and bridegroom is matched and matching number is worked out for taking a decision of marriage.

Krishnamurti system

Krishnamurti system was initiated in southern India. In this system ascendant is considered as starting point of first house and all other houses are extended accordingly. Prediction is concluded on the basis of lord, sublord, subsublord of a planet which is decided on the basis of its position in a constellation and by matching its degree with the table of *vinshottary dasha*, like *antar* and *pratyantar-dasha*.

7

SET PLANET

What conveyed

Sages presumed that a planet is set when it is within the orb of 12° from the Sun. The main idea behind this concept was that the impact of a planet is completely vanished if it is very near to the Sun. Because the Sun was considered to be the nearest planet from the Earth in the Universe as per belief prevailed in the Primitive age as shown in picture-1. While developing the predictive astrology on the basis of this belief and faith the impact of a planet was considered to be ineffective due to its situation in the orb of the Sun.

What observed

We know that the Mercury and Venus are nearest planets from the Sun. Hence these planets were frequently treated as set. If two planets may be considered as set in most of the horoscope and their impact may not be accounted for then it was observed that some time predictive conclusion may be wrong and some time it may be right. In this way there was natural mistake in the predictive conclusion. Hence subsequently, it was also occasionally presumed by the astrologers according to their choice that Mercury and Venus might not be treated as set, whereas other planets were considered to be set if they were moving in the orb of the Sun.

What discovered

It is logical in view of the faith and belief as prevailed in the Primitive age that a planet may lost its impact as and when it transit from the orb of the illuminator Sun. Because in that age orbit of the Sun was considered to be nearest from the Earth whereas orbit of other planets were considered to be situated beyond the orbit of the Sun. Hence it was quite natural that when all planets were situated beyond the orbit of the Sun then all planets may also be considered as set as and when they transit from the orb of the Sun. But if we compare the situation of setting of the planets with reference to the modern explanation of the solar and lunar eclipses in view of the latest scientific concept of the solar system then position will be clearer. At the time of solar eclipse, Moon actually reduces the impact of the illuminated Sun due to its movement from the front of the Sun and at that time Sun is actually set. In the same way we may have to understand the position of the Mercury in the event of its setting, because Mercury may set in two different ways. In one situation, Mercury may transit from in between the Earth and Sun whereas in another situation Sun may be in between the Earth and Mercury. In the first situation the impact of the Sun will be reduced due to in-between presence of Mercury. Though it may be a different issue that how much impact of the Sun will actually be reduced by small Mercury. Whereas in the second situation the impact of the Mercury will actually be liquidated due to its motion behind the Sun. If Mercury actually transits behind the Sun then the impact of the Mercury may completely be lost on that particular sign. Such situations are continuously repeated in the solar system because the orbits of the Mercury and Venus are nearer to the Sun. Other planets may also be set due to in-between presence of Sun and Moon. For example, if a planet transit behind the Moon then it must be treated at set. Such type of event took place on 24-1-2002 when Saturn actually took transit behind the Moon and it was actually set with reference to the Earth. In the same way Mars, Jupiter and Saturn may only be treated as set as and when they actually took transit behind the Sun or Moon.

Solar eclipse occurred only due to transit of Moon in between the Sun and Earth and impact of Sun, which is being experienced on the Earth may be obstructed by the Moon. Hence it is quite natural that living world may be effected due to obstruction in the direct impact of the Sun. Whereas, during the lunar eclipse there is no such obstruction in the position and impact emerging from the matter of the Moon with reference to the Earth and only reason behind the reduction in the illuminated part of the Moon was due to obstruction in the sunlight due to the shadow of the Earth on Moon. Hence there is no question of reduction in the impact of the Moon, which is being generally experienced on the Earth. Yes, if we are on the Moon at the time of lunar eclipse then we will see solar eclipse due to in-between position of the Earth and impact of the Sun, which falls on the Moon, will be reduced due to the Earth. We will again discuss later on about the set planets.

If we analyse the zodiac then it may be seen that all planets do not transit on the same track, but their position, even in the same sign continuously changing year after year. Though this change in their position is taking place in front of everybody but we failed to notice it. Because we have left the practice of sky gazing since two thousand years. The main reason behind transit of the planets in different track is due to the inclination in their respective orbit in different degrees with reference to the orbit of the Sun or ecliptic of the Sun. Thus even if the angular difference between two planets is less than one degree then at the most we may classify this situation as union of two planets but there is no justification in presuming that a planet is set. In this way though the angular difference between two planets may be less than one degree as per details given in the horoscope and almanac yet the actual celestial difference between the position of two planets may be more than one degree due to inclination in the orbit of the planets. More detail in this regard will be given later on. Likewise astrological principle about the retrograde motion of the planets is also faulty. Reason behind retrograde motion of the planets and its actual position will be discussed in detail in next part.

Conclusion

It was not possible to see a planet, if it is within the orb of 12° of the Sun, even at the time of sunrise and sunset due to glare of the Sun. Hence it was quite natural in view of the knowledge and belief prevailed in the Primitive age that a planet may be considered as set and treated as if it has lost its impact. Whereas if we reanalyse this situation in view of the modern scientific concept then it will be clear that any distant planet may only be considered as set with reference to the nearest planet. As we know that Sun is alike set during solar eclipse which occur only when Moon take transit in-between the Earth and Sun. In the same way if Mercury and Venus take transit in between the Earth and Sun then we must consider the Sun alike set keeping intact the impact of Mercury and Venus. Though it is a different issue that impact of the Sun will only be reduced marginally because the size of these planets are very small in comparison to the size of the Sun and these planets are far away from the Earth in comparison to the distance of Moon. It is also clear in view of the scientific information that there is no justification in accepting a planet as set till it is completely overshadowed by another planet.

In view of the above description it will be clear that there are following main mistakes while accepting a planet as set due to which astrological principle is faulty and not supported by scientific concept.

1. It is faulty to accept a planet as set when it is within the orb of 12° from the Sun, which was founded on the ground of imperfect conception of the Universe in which all planets were kept after the Sun.
2. It is natural that impact of Sun may be reduced during solar eclipse, whereas there may not be any reduction in the impact of the Moon during lunar eclipse.

8

EXALTED-DEBILITATED PLANETS

What conveyed

It was a general practice in the Primitive age to conclude a forecast on the basis of natural presumptive qualities of a planet. Hence sage Parashar and other contemporary sages devised the concept of exalted and debilitated planet after regular gazing of the sky and blending the result of observation with the information of the Universe and natural qualities of a planet. They decided exalted and debilitated position of the planets as follows :–

Exalted planet							
Planet	Sun	Moon	Mer.	Ven.	Mars	Jup.	Saturn
Sign	0	1	5	11	9	3	6
Degree	10	3	15	27	28	5	20
Debilitated planet							
Planet	Sun	Moon	Mer.	Ven.	Mars	Jup.	Saturn
Sign	6	7	11	5	3	9	0
Degree	10	3	15	27	28	5	20

Any description regarding peculiar position of the planets or any event, which leads our sages to formulate this principle of exalted and debilitated position of the planet at some degree, is as usual not available.

What observed

Mythical literature, the then concept of the Universe, conclusion drawn after regular gazing of the planets with the help of ordinary instruments like cone, tube etc., simple mathematical calculations and deep thinking were main ingredient behind the formulation of the astrological principles by sages in the Primitive age. In this way celestial position of the planets was an important key factor behind formulating this astrological principle.

There is neither any *prima facie* reasoning in support of deciding exalted and debilitated situation of every planet at some degree of a sign nor it was ever logically explained hence it is difficult to digest the random explanation put forward in support of this principle. Whereas if we critically examine the exalted and debilitated position of a planet then following discrepancies will immediately emerge out :–

1. How Sun may be exalted in Aries sign, which is owned by an evil planet like Mars?
2. How Sun of fiery element may be debilitated in Libra sign having friendly airy element?
3. How Mars of fiery element may be exalted in Capricorn sign having opposite earthen element and which is also owned by evil Saturn who also treats Mars as his enemy?
4. How Mars may be debilitated in Cancer sign that is owned by auspicious planet Moon and who is also friend of Mars?
5. How Mercury who is an activator of knowledge, may be debilitated in Pisces sign of watery element who is owned by Jupiter which is related with the wisdom and who is treated as even by the Mercury made up of friendly earthen element?
6. How Jupiter may be debilitated in Capricorn sign owned by even Saturn?
7. How Venus may be exalted in Pisces sign owned by Jupiter who treats him as enemy?

8. How Venus may be debilitated in Virgo sign owned by his friend Mercury?
9. How Moon may be exalted in Taurus sign owned by his enemy Venus?
10. How Moon of watery element may be debilitated in Scorpio sign of watery element and owned by his friend Mars?
11. How Saturn of airy element may be debilitated in Aries sign of friendly fiery element and owned by even Mars?
12. When Jupiter is able to give auspicious result in his own Sagittarius sign then how he may be debilitated in Capricorn sign which is merely one second away from Sagittarius sign and how he may be extremely debilitated merely after moving only 5°?
13. Feeble or Moon of dark night is considered as evil. Whereas the angular difference between 10° of Aries sign and 3° of Taurus sign is only 23° i.e. Moon may be in second day after moving 23°. In this way how Moon may be extremely exalted after moving just two days from the dark night?
14. In this way there may be dark night when Moon may be at 3° of Taurus sign. Then how it may be treated as exalted?

If you come forward with some explanation against above mentioned points then you, yourself will find that your so-called explanation is not supported in some other point.

Beside this there is no basis of treating a planet as extreme exalted (*param ucch*) at some particular degree of a sign. What was the reason that no planet was considered as exalted or debilitated in Gemini, Leo, Sagittarius and Aquarius sign? Although it was the wisdom and devotion of sages that could lead them with the help of even primitive instruments to finalise the degree of a sign for exalted and debilitated planet which was 180° apart from each other.

Faulty positions of exalted and debilitated planets at some degree of a sign is examined on the basis of element, friendly-enmity relation between the planets and planetary transit in the sky as explained above. From this it will be clear that there are sufficient contradictions in this principle and no cognisance were given to sign, element of planets, relations between the planets while deciding the exalted and debilitated degree in a sign for planets. Thus it will also be clear that either the principle is faulty or some other situations were considered while deciding the exalted and debilitated degree in a sign for planets.

Explanations in support of exalted-debilitated degrees of a planet in a particular sign are contained in some astrological books and also supported by astrologers. As there is complete lack of logical approach in the explanation, hence short description of these explanation and comments thereon are being given as follows. Table of periodicity incorporated in the chapter of 'Vinshottary dasha' may be referred for understanding linking of periodicity with a constellation.

> **TIP :** If you are amateur reader or find any difficulty at any time in understanding succeeding paragraphs then you may jump to Conclusion and try to understand this left out portion in next reading.

1. Sun is exalted at 10° of Aries sign because this is the position of Ashwini constellation, periodicity (*vinshottary mahadasha*) of which is owned by Ketu and who is competent to deliver salvation.

The point as to whether periodicity of Ashwini constellation is controlled by Ketu or not will be discussed in detail in the chapter of periodicity. But if we consider the explanation itself then another constellation, Magha which is not only owned by Ketu but it is also in Leo sign, owned by the Sun or third constellation, Mula which is also owned by Ketu (as per table of periodicity) and which is in Sagittarius sign owned by virtuous Jupiter and who is also a friend of Sun, would have been more appropriate for exalted position of the Sun, instead of Ketu, because Ketu is responsible for solar eclipse hence it is like an enemy for the Sun.

2. Moon is exalted at 3° of Taurus sign because he is able to get Sun in his Kratica constellation despite impact of amorous Venus on this constellation and who is also lord of Taurus sign.

If Moon is exalted on this basis then Uttarafalguni and Uttarashada who are another constellations of Sun (as per table of periodicity) may also be favourable. Because Sun, Mercury, Jupiter and Saturn own first and remaining three steps of these constellations respectively (see sign and their constellation). It is a funny explanation that on one hand Moon is exalted in Kratica constellation situated in Taurus sign owned by Venus and on the other hand Moon is debilitated because the mood and desire of the Moon is completely destroyed after transiting in first three steps of Vishakha constellation situated in Libra sign and again owned by Venus and thereafter when it transit from the fourth step of Vishakha constellation it is debilitated. It is a matter of consideration as to how Moon may be debilitated while transiting from the fourth step (*charan*) of Vishakha constellation, which is owned by Jupiter, who is not an enemy for any planet and that too when union of Moon and Jupiter in the horoscope claimed to form a so-called powerful *Gaj-kesri yog*.

3. Mars is exalted at 28° of Capricorn sign owned by his enemy Saturn, because it is in his own Ghanistha constellation as per table of periodicity and a brave, strong planet like Mars can only show his power in the vicinity of enemy.

On this analogy Mars must be exalted in entire span of Ghanistha constellation because entire constellation is in the ambit of Capricorn and Aquarius signs which are owned by his enemy Saturn. Similarly, Mragshira and Chitra constellations owned by Mars as per table of periodicity are also situated in the signs of enemy planets

(Mercury and Venus) and Mars may also be exalted in those signs too.

4. Mercury is said to be exalted because during transit in Hast constellation, periodicity of which is owned by Moon, he tries to acquire the ability to understand the problems faced by other like Moon.

On this analogy Mercury must be exalted during entire span of 13° 20' Hast constellation. Beside this other constellation like Rohini and Shravan constellations under periodicity of Moon, which are situated in Taurus and Capricorn signs and whose lords are Venus and Saturn respectively and who are friends of Mercury are also not too bad for exaltation of Mercury. Whereas Mercury treat Moon as his enemy.

5. Jupiter is stated to be exalted in Pushya constellation because only planet like Jupiter is able to witness supreme eternal spirit even when he is in-between emotional Moon who is lord of Cancer and cunning Saturn who owned periodicity of Pushya Constellation.

On this analogy Jupiter must be exalted during entire span of 13° 20' of Pushya constellation. But Jupiter is debilitated when comparatively he is in best situation and transit from Uttarashada constellation, periodicity of which is owned by the Sun, who is more powerful than Moon and concerning constellation situated in Capricorn sign owned by as usual Saturn.

6. Venus is stated to be exalted in Pisces sign owned by his enemy Jupiter because here amorous Venus is able to get the company of Jupiter who has base of wisdom.

But see that this Venus is debilitated in Virgo sign, which is owned by his friend Mercury who also has base of knowledge.

7. Saturn is stated to be exalted in Libra sign owned by Venus because he himself is evil and even after transiting in Swati constellation whose periodicity is owned by curious Rahu and lord is amorous Venus, he is able to touch Vishakha constellation of Jupiter.

So what, if Saturn treat Jupiter as his enemy.

Thus we are not able to get any logical explanation in support of exalted and debilitated situation of the planets. While framing such type of bogus explanation, this fact has not been kept in mind that when a planet is exalted at a point during transit then at 180° away from this point the same planet will be debilitated. This phenomenon itself proves that sages had somewhere considered the transitory pattern of the planets while framing the principle of exalted and debilitated situation. Sages were well aware with the fact that if any moving object is highest at a particular point than it would be at lowest point after moving 180° i.e. when it is just in opposite situation. If we spin a stone tied with a rope, in any pattern then we can see that when the position of the stone is highest from the ground than after moving 180° when it is in opposite situation, the position of the stone will be lowest from the ground.

Secondly, constellations which were decided for assessing the starting Vinshottary periodicity of a planet has no connection for deciding exalted and debilitated position of a planet at a degree in some sign. As this principle has contradiction with the principle of friend-enemy, element, evil etc., in the same way there is no linking with the constellations nominated for deciding the periodicity of a planet. Thus it will be clear that there was no connection of any other fact for deciding the exalted and debilitated position of the planets and main independent consideration was transitory position of the planets. But now-a-days, due to business consideration it becomes a tradition to pick a point from anywhere and go ahead without any deep thinking and logical support.

What discovered

After creating and studying the celestial position of the planets, which would have been observed at the time of ending period of Rising age and early period of Primitive age, with the help of computer, mystery behind deciding degree in a sign for exalted and debilitated planet came to surface. It was not possible for the mathematician up to the Middle age to create and study the celestial position of the planets as prevailed in the Primitive age; otherwise, they would have corrected these linked principles long back. Some particular celestial position of the planets which were observed and considered as an important position for the planets by the sages of Primitive age, were actually the foundation stone of this principle. Formation of the Universe, rising of planet, summer solstice, constellations and intensity of glare of the planet were main factors relating to the planets during their gazing in the Primitive age. Hence it was quite natural that result of gazing form a building block while deciding the degree in a sign for exalted and debilitated planets. As has already been explained during description of picture-1 that planets were considered to be situated on each other in the shape of cylinder. Thus qualities of the Universe were also believed alike cylinder. We know there is a resemblance in both ends of the cylinder. Similarly there is a continuity and resemblance in the orbit of the planets, which were considered to be situated on the surface of the cylinder. Because all planets were presumed to be situated on the surface of the imaginary cylinder, hence on the basis of summer solstice and increase in the glare of a planet it was quite natural to draw an inference that they continuously came closer and move away from the Earth during their transit in the orbit. In this way it was quite logical and natural to come to a conclusion that Sun is moving nearer to the Earth during summer solstice and other planets may considered to be nearer to the Earth if their glare is increased. We must remember that in the Primitive age it was considered that every planet has his own glare like illuminative planets Sun and Moon. Sun and Moon were considered as illuminator planets because they were situated below the constellations and able to throw their light on the Earth. It is only a modern and scientific concept that all planets including Moon gets their illumination from the Sun. But like other scientific discoveries this fact also has no place in the formulations of the astrological principles.

Orbit of all planets is shown in picture-9 from where you can see that how orbit of planets were considered as slanted on one side. Thus during one rotation by a planet it was considered to be exalted at one situation and more effective when it was nearer to the Earth. Contrary to this in opposite situation i.e. 180° away, it was considered to be far away from the Earth and debilitated hence less effective. Now we will discuss the celestial position of the planets in the Primitive age, which inspired our sages to formulate the principle of exalted and debilitated planet at some degree in a sign.

Sun – Since very beginning of the Primitive age, Sun happens to be in summer solstice when it reaches at 10° *nirayan* of Capricorn sign. But despite fall of summer solstice Sun was not able to cross the equator line hence duration of

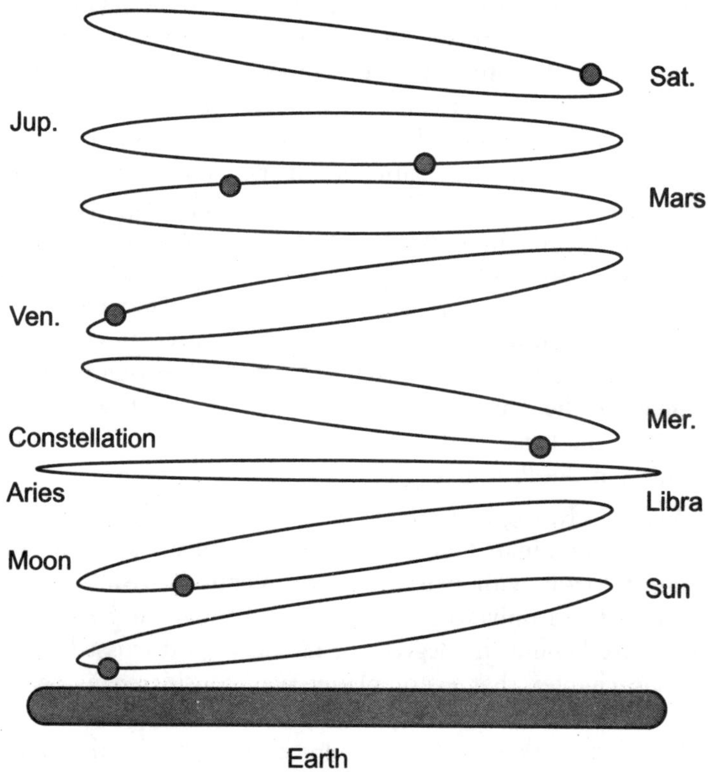

Picture – 9

Exalted and debilitated planetary position

day was less than night. Thus it was quite natural that position of the Sun may not be considered powerful and comfortable so long duration of daytime was less than 12 hours (30 *Ghati*). But as soon as Sun was able to cross the equator line from vernal equinox from 10° of Aries sign, duration of daytime also exceeds in comparison to night. Hence it was quite natural that Sun was considered as exalted at 10° of Aries sign.

Saturn – It was believed in the Primitive age that Universe was extended from Sun to Saturn. All constellations and stars were considered to be situated in between Moon and Mercury (see picture-1 or 9). In this way Sun and Saturn were considered to be situated at both extreme ends of the Universe, which was considered in the shape of a cylinder. Thus Saturn was considered to be situated at the other end of the Universe. Hence when Sun was treated as exalted after moving 10° in Aries sign while crossing the equator line then it was pertinent that Saturn which was situated at the other side of the cylindrical Universe may also be exalted in Libra sign just after moving 10° from the opposite situation of the exalted Sun in 10° of Aries sign. On this logic, after moving 10° from the opposite situation of the exalted Sun i.e. after moving 10° + 180° = 190°, Saturn must be exalted. Thus after moving 190° from 10° of Aries sign we reach at 20° of Libra sign. Thus in considering the Saturn as exalted at this point was quite logical on the basis of the then concept about the Universe as prevailed in the Primitive age.

Venus – Rising of a planet is naturally auspicious. Hence Venus was nominated as morning star when it rises from the eastern horizon with extreme glare. Venus is visible in the eastern horizon only when it is lagging behind the Sun i.e. its degrees are behind the degrees of the Sun. As discussed in the previous chapter that every planet was considered as set so long it is in the orb of 12° (plus minus 12° around the Sun) of the Sun, because naturally it was not possible to see the planet in this situation. However, when it is not believed as set i.e. when it has a distance of more than 12° from the Sun or 13° from the Sun then Venus was not only clearly visible in the

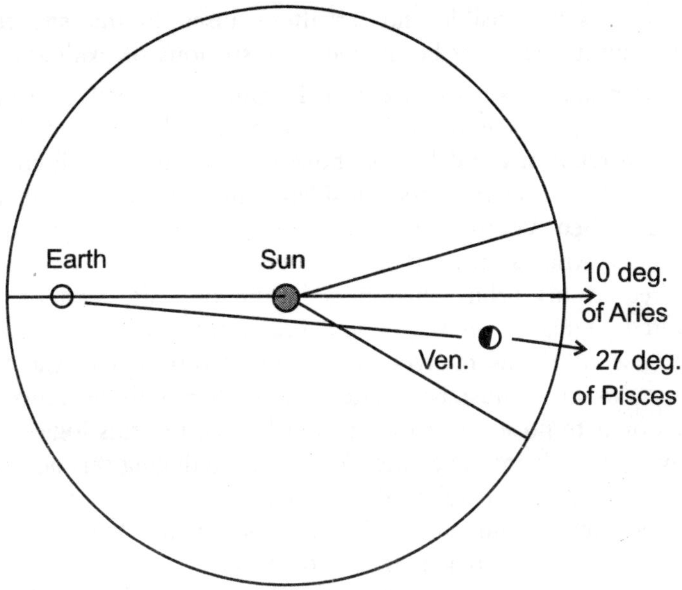

Picture – 10

Exalted position of the Venus with extreme glare

eastern horizon but it also had extreme glare. Now such situation when Venus may be 13° behind the Sun may occur in various signs during the transit of the Sun. But when Sun was considered to be exalted at 10° of Aries sign hence it was quite logical and pertinent that Venus may also be treated as exalted only when it was 13° behind 10° of Aries sign i.e. at 27° of Pisces sign. Thus considering the Venus as exalted at this point was quite correct on the basis of the information available in the Primitive age. This position can also be understood from picture-10 and it may be understood that Venus will be visible from the Earth with its full glare due to light of the Sun only when it is in this particular position with reference to the Sun. This position is like a view of full Moon in the night of full-moon due to the light of the Sun. Venus may also be at a forward distance of 13° from the exalted Sun, with full glare, when it transit from 23° of Aries sign. But in this situation it will rise from eastern horizon after sunrise, hence it is not visible and set after sunset. In this situation naturally it could not be treated as auspicious or exalted.

Mercury – As per concept of the Universe, which prevailed in the Primitive age, Mercury was believed to be situated above the constellations and Venus above the Mercury. As discussed earlier, the Universe was considered in a cylindrical shape. Hence when Venus was exalted at 27° of Pisces sign then Mercury who is situated just below the Venus may also be exalted in his orbit when it is in the opposite sign of the exalted Venus i.e. in Virgo sign. Because 12° was adjusted in the case of Venus to avoid its setting position with the Sun hence Mercury must be exalted 12° earlier with reference to the opposite position of the exalted Venus. On this logic after moving 180° from the exalted Venus and reducing this position by 12°, which were adjusted in the case of Venus, we get 168°. Hence after moving this 168° from the exalted Venus of 27° of Pisces sign we reach at 15° of Virgo sign. Hence it was logical in view of the concept prevailed in the Primitive age to treat Mercury as exalted at this point.

Jupiter – Auspicious Jupiter remains at the best and most impressive celestial position in the northern India, when it transits from Pushya constellation. It is mentioned in *Tettariya Brahmin*, a book of *Vedic* age that Jupiter was born from Tishya i.e. Pushya constellation because in those days Jupiter transit so closely with the Pushya constellation that it was difficult to distinguish them. In this position Jupiter was visible at zenith i.e. at a perpendicular position from India. We can realise that impact of the Sun is more prominent in summer, when it is near to zenith i.e. at a perpendicular position from India. In the same way glare of the Jupiter was best when it was near to Pushya constellation. Thus it was logical to treat the Jupiter as exalted in the initial degree of Pushya constellation i.e. 5° of Cancer sign, in view of the best glare and best position.

Moon – As per primitive concept of the Universe, Sun was believed to be a nearest planet from the Earth and next planet was Moon, as may be seen from picture-1. Sun and Moon were only regarded as illuminator planets. These two planets were never retrograde like other planets during their rotation around the *sumeru-parvat* situated on the Earth. Sages were aware from the study of the orbit of the Sun that during summer solstice after crossing the equator line (though it was not known as equator line but this important position was assessed when duration of day and night was equal), it move toward northern direction till fall of winter solstice. Now we know this situation of 23° as Tropic of Cancer. Hence it was natural to draw an inference that Moon must also be exalted after moving 23°. In this way after moving 23° from 10° of Aries sign i.e. exalted position of the Sun, we came at 3° of Taurus sign. Another reason for going ahead 23° in this direction was that illuminator Moon must also be visible in the night sky after setting of exalted Sun. But if we move backward in the direction of Pisces sign, as in the case of Venus, then Moon will rise in the east before sunrise and it will have no glare throughout the day and also set before the sunset. Hence it was logical to treat the Moon as exalted at 3° of Taurus sign in view of the primitive information.

Mars – As per primitive concept Earth and Saturn were considered as two extreme ends of the Universe. There were two illuminator planets Sun and Moon above the Earth. In the same way there were two planets Jupiter and Mars below the Saturn. There was difference of 23° between the exalted position of the Sun and Moon. Because these two planets were illuminators hence in this case rule of moving to the opposite sign i.e. 180° was not enforced. But Jupiter and Mars were ordinary planets hence Mars may only be exalted in the opposite situation of the exalted Jupiter plus 23°, which was also given to the Moon. It was decided in view of the fact that both ends of the cylindrical Universe were similar. On this logic third planet from the other side of the cylinder must be exalted after moving 180° from the exalted Jupiter and after adding 23°, as given to the Moon, which was at third place (including Earth) from one side of the cylinder. In this way after moving 203° from 5° of Cancer sign, which was the exalted position of the Jupiter we came to 28° of Capricorn sign. Secondly, the difference of 6 sign 23° i.e. 203° between the exalted position of Venus and Saturn would be equal to the difference between the exalted position of Jupiter and Mars, which is in conformity of cylindrical shape of the Universe. Hence Mars was considered as exalted at this point, which was quite natural in view of the primitive knowledge about the Universe.

Because all planets were considered as exalted i.e. nearer to the Earth in one position then it was quite natural that they would be debilitated i.e. treated as far away from the Earth in just opposite position as explained in the example of spinning a stone. Hence after adding 180° in the extreme exalted position we may get extreme debilitated position of all planets. Sages thus decided extreme exalted and debilitated degree in a sign for planets by assessing above important position of the planets and subsequently in the Middle age, mathematical and predictive astrology were developed around this structure.

While deciding the exalted and debilitated position of a planet, sages have not given any importance to the element of the planet and mutual relation based on friendship enmity between them, hence there is a mistake in the proportion of the enmity between two planets. It would be clear from the explanation given above that crossing of Equator line by the Sun, full glare of the Jupiter in Pushya constellation due to its high angle of elevation from the horizon, best glare of Venus and transit of the planets on the surface of the cylindrical Universe were main basis for deciding the exalted and debilitated position of the planets. As per knowledge prevailed in the Primitive age it was believed that every planet has its own glare hence it was quite natural to think and conclude that whenever a planet is nearer to the Earth, its glare may increase. Whereas if we analyse this situation in view of the modern scientific discoveries then we can see that it is not essential that a planet would actually be nearer to the Earth and more effective whenever it transit from exalted degree in a sign.

Sayan system was prevalent in the Rising age. But it was experienced that seasons were not commencing on the due date, due to continuous change in the celestial position of the Sun, and this change in the celestial position of the Sun was going on since Rising age. Due to regular monitoring of the sky, our sages were aware by the commencement of the Primitive age that on every next event of increase in the duration of day time, Sun is not visible at zero degree position i.e. on 0° of Aries sign and Sun is visible at some different position. This visible position of the planets in some degree in a sign were then defined as *nirayan* position and sages given recognition to logically correct *nirayan* position over *sayan* position. As celestial position of the planets continuously changes and any planet, which is visible at a point in the zodiac, will not be again visible at that particular point. Hence *nirayan* system was adopted in place of *sayan* system which prevailed in the Rising age. Position of the planets in the zodiac is still continuously changing since Primitive age. Hence, now we will re-examine the exalted and debilitated position of the planets in view of the changed position of the planets in the zodiac.

If we look at the explanation given for exalted and debilitated planets then we can see that crossing of the equator line by the Sun has a pivotal roll in deciding the exalted degree in a sign for every planet. Sun used to cross this equator line at 10° of Aries sign in the Primitive age. But in AD 2003, Sun as usual crosses this equator line after moving 90° in summer solstice. Now-a-days summer solstice commenced at 7° of Sagittarius sign. Hence naturally Sun crosses this equator line when it is at 7° of Pisces sign i.e. 33° earlier in comparison to the primitive position. Now, if we recalculate the exalted degree in a sign for all planets in accordance with the procedure followed by the sages in the Primitive age by presuming the cylindrical shape of the Universe as shown in picture-1 instead of modern concept of solar system as shown in picture-2, then there would be a difference of 33° due to *ayanansh* and position of exalted and debilitated degree in a sign of all planets would be as follows :–

Exalted planet							
Planet	Sun	Moon	Mer.	Ven.	Mars	Jup.	Saturn
Sign	11	0	4	10	8	2	5
Degree	7	0	12	24	25	2	17

Debilitated planet							
Planet	Sun	Moon	Mer.	Ven.	Mars	Jup.	Saturn
Sign	5	6	10	4	2	8	11
Degree	7	0	12	24	25	2	17

In this way there is considerable fundamental change in the extreme exalted and debilitated degree in a sign for every planets only due to *ayanansh*. What is *ayanansh*, how it changes and how the planetary position in the zodiac changes, due to which exalted and debilitated degree in a sign and periodicity (*Mahadasha*) have fundamentally changed and its importance will be discussed later on in detail.

Conclusion

Primitive concept of the shape of the Universe and summer solstice etc. has pivotal role in formulation of the exalted and debilitated principle. Hence this principle of exalted and debilitated planet is faulty in the proportion of the ratio between the primitive wrong concept of the Universe and modern scientific concept of the solar system. Thus the basis of this principle has altogether been completely changed and now primitive concept of the Universe has no value at all.

No importance was given to the element of the planets and mutual friendship-enmity between them. Hence any prediction worked out on the basis of two diagonally opposite principles is also proportionately wrong. If we consider the prediction based on exalted and debilitated principle then impact of the planet may be correct only when the planetary position matches with the modern concept of solar system and celestial position of the planet. In case we get favourable result despite debilitated position of a planet then it is tried to correct it by quoting the reference of *neech-bhang yog* etc., contrary to this if we face some unfavourable result despite exalted planet even then it is tried to convince that exalted planet in ineffective due to unfavourable present transit (*gochar*) etc. and ultimately astrological principles are forcefully pulled and presumed as correct.

It is a scientific fact that whether we are in Southern Hemisphere or in Northern Hemisphere of the Earth; impact of the planet will be effective only in proportion to the angle of elevation from the horizon. Thus if angle of elevation of a planet is 90° from the horizon then it would be extremely effective. In view of this phenomenon it can be seen that there is similarity in the impact of the exalted Jupiter, because in the Primitive age it was almost at a perpendicular position from India, when it transit from Pushya constellation, whereas in case of other planets, even then the angle of elevation was not 90° but there was also some impact in the ratio of angle of elevation. Hence impact of the planets seems to be somewhat correct. Impact of such planetary position will be discussed later on in detail.

It will be clear from the above explanation that there are following main mistakes in the principle of exalted and debilitated planet. As such this principle is faulty on scientific basis :–

1. It is faulty to decide exalted position of the planets on the basis of their glare, their relative position, crossing of equator line by presuming Sun as a nearest planet in the cylindrical shape of the Universe.
2. There is continuous change in the primitive celestial position of the planets due to change in *ayanansh*. Hence exalted and debilitated degree in a sign have also been completely changed by 33° due to change in *ayanansh* since Primitive age.

Measurement of period and *sayan*

Celestial position of the Moon was an important factor for calculation of period. Duration of *tithi, paksh*, month and year was calculated on the basis of the celestial position of the Moon with reference to the Sun. Angular difference between the position of the Sun and Moon was the basis of Tithi and Tithi was changed on every angular difference of 12° between Sun and Moon. This practice is still being followed. Till mid of Rising age it was believed that rainy season start, whenever Sun and Moon reappear in same original sign i.e. after 12 lunar month of 360 *tithi*. But after passing of time it was observed that rainy season does not repeat despite the same original position of Sun and Moon. Hence a novel method of adding an extra month after every three years was devised to synchronise the position of Sun and Moon, which is still being followed. In this way further calculation were being made on the fixed position of Sun and Moon. The method of calculation regarding celestial position of the planets, which was based on fixed position, was called *Sayan*. In this way, when it was observed that there was a difference between the calculated position based on the principal of adding an extra lunar month and actual celestial position of the Sun and Moon with reference to sign and constellation then both systems i.e. visual (Drag) and calculated position of planets were being followed. Visual (*drag*) position, of the planets in sign and constellation was accepted over calculated position of the planets in the Primitive age after observing the vast difference between them. Calculated position based on fixed system was called *Sayan* whereas visual position of the planet was classified as *nirayan* position.

After passing of time 0° 0' 0" of Aries sign was known as *sayan* position and visual position was as usual known as *nirayan*. Difference of these two positions was known as *ayanansh*. In this way after deducting *ayanansh* from *sayan* we may get *nirayan* position of the planet.

9

MOOL TRIKON

What conveyed

This principle was formulated for ascertaining the position of a planet in *mool-trikon*. Like other principles, the basis of formulation of this principle is also not known. According to this principle Sun treated as auspicious for concluding any prediction if it is placed between one degree and 20° of Leo sign. *Mool-trikon* position of other planets is as follows :–

Planets in *mool-trikon*

Planet	Sun	Moon	Merc.	Venu.	Mars	Jupi.	Sat.
Sign	4 Leo	1 Tau.	5 Vir.	6 Lib.	0 Ari.	8 Sco.	10 Acq.
Degree	1-20	3-30	15-20	1-5	1-12	1-10	1-20

What observed

It has already been highlighted in previous chapters that astrological principles were formulated in Primitive age on the basis of the then available information about the Universe and meditation. Thus there is no justification in supporting the concept of these principles on the basis of modern scientific information. But if we analyse this principle only on the basis of the information available in the Primitive age even then following discrepancies emerges :–

1. When all planets except Moon were considered in *mool-trikon* only in their own sign then why different

attitude was adopted for Moon and it was considered in *mool-trikon* in Taurus sign instead of its own sign Cancer? Whereas lord of Taurus sign is Venus who consider Moon as his enemy.

2. Why Venus of Watery element was considered in *mool-trikon* in Libra sign of Airy element, which is its enemy element?
3. When Venus is considered as extreme debilitated at 27° of Virgo sign then how it is possible that only after moving just 4° it may be considered as auspicious and in *mool-trikon* in Libra sign?

It is evident from the above discrepancies that no importance was given to the principles of mutual friendship-enmity, debilitated position, element and their celestial position; and this principle was formulated on some other grounds, which in turn is leading to such discrepancies.

What discovered

In the Primitive age the concept of formation of the Universe was like picture-1. Till that time geometry in the modern shape was not established. But at the time when different principles of astrology were being formulated; our sages were able to create different type of altars for offering to God. With an idea of giving different shape to an altar, they draw different designs with the help of circle and triangle to enable them to create different type of altars based on these geometrical designs for offering to God. In this way foundation of modern geometry was being initiated. Thus as is evident from its name, principle of *mool-trikon* was formulated after giving due importance to the triangular shape and on the basis of some formulated astrological principles like lord of sign, exalted degree in a sign. Thus this principle is leading to various discrepancies with other astrological principles and prediction is also being defiled in the same ratio. Following procedure was adopted for formulating the principle of *mool-trikon.*

TIP : If you are amateur reader or find any difficulty at any time in understanding succeeding paragraphs then you may jump to Conclusion and try to understand this left out portion in next reading.

Sun - The formation of the Universe as shown in picture-1 was recognised in the Primitive age and it was believed that Sun was the nearest planet and Saturn was at the end of the Universe. In other words it was believed in those days that entire Universe was situated within these two planets. Sun was considered as exalted at 10° of Aries sign and lord of Leo sign. Above position of the Sun, which was believed as nearest planet from the Earth in the Universe may be observed in picture-11, which is drawn after dividing the sky in twelve signs. Location of 10° of Aries sign and Leo sign owned by Sun are appropriately shown in the picture. If we draw a line from the exalted location of 10° of Aries sign to 10° of own

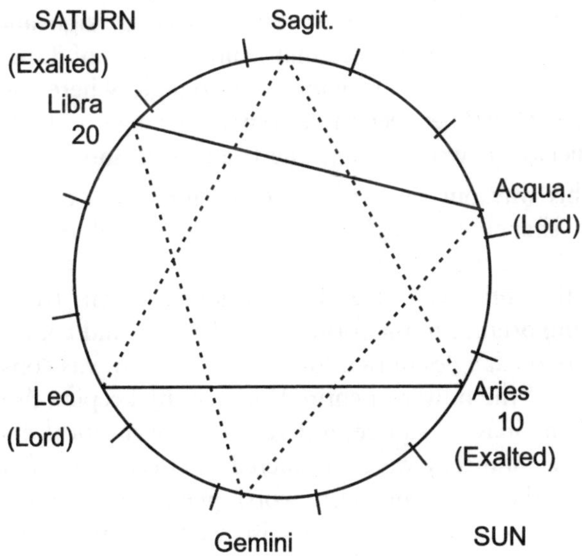

Picture – 11
Position of Sun and Saturn in *mool-trikon*

sign Leo as shown in the circle and calculate the angular difference between these two points. Then this difference will be 120° (20° of Aries + 30° of Taurus + 30° of Gemini + 30° of Cancer + 10° of Leo). If we draw another line from this point of Leo sign, keeping the same difference of 120° then it will touch the point of 10° of Sagittarius sign. After connecting this point of Sagittarius sign to the point of 10° of Aries sign, we can see a shape of triangle. Dotted and dark lines (between lord and exalted point) show this triangle in the picture. We can see that there is angular difference of 120° between these three points with reference to the centre of the circle i.e. triangle drawn in the Universe and there is an angle of 60° between two lines on these points. This is a very ordinary shape in the modern geometry.

Saturn - In the same manner if we draw another line for Saturn, which was situated at the tail end of the Universe, from its exalted position of 20° of Libra sign to 20° of own sign Aquarius then it will also have a same difference of 120° like Sun. Keeping the same difference, if we draw another dotted line from this point to 20° of Gemini sign and then join this point with the original point of 20° of Libra sign, then we can see another shape of a triangle where there are difference of 120° between three points of triangle and difference of 60° between two lines like the triangle of Sun.

In this way our sages observed the formation of same and opposite shape of triangle between exalted and own sign in respect of Sun and Saturn, who were situated at the opposite ends of the entire Universe. The formation of this triangle get specific importance in the form of *mool-trikon* and combination of these two triangles drawn for Sun and Saturn was considered as symbol of the power of entire Universe. By keeping these two triangles in circle or square, different type of mystical diagrams were drawn and they were considered as effective as offering to God. Thus these diagrams were worshipped as symbol of power of Universe. Now-a-days we may also see such various diagrams like '*Shree-yantra*' etc., which are only symbol of the power of entire Universe from Sun to Saturn as per belief prevailed in the Primitive age and based on the principle of *mool-trikon*.

Due to similarities in the triangles formed by the Sun and Saturn, a part of 10° and 20° respectively towards the exalted sign (after counting from exalted Aries sign of Sun we get Leo sign, similarly from exalted Libra sign of Saturn we get Aquarius sign related to own house of these planets) in Leo and Aquarius sign were classified as *mool-trikon* for these planets, as these parts also have the same element of Fire and Air like their planets. In this situation, it was quite natural to conclude that when there was a formation of similar triangle between exalted and own sign of Sun and Saturn who are situated at two ends of the Universe then there must also be some triangular relation between exalted and own sign for other planets too. On this basis our sages worked out the degrees of *mool-trikon* for other planets.

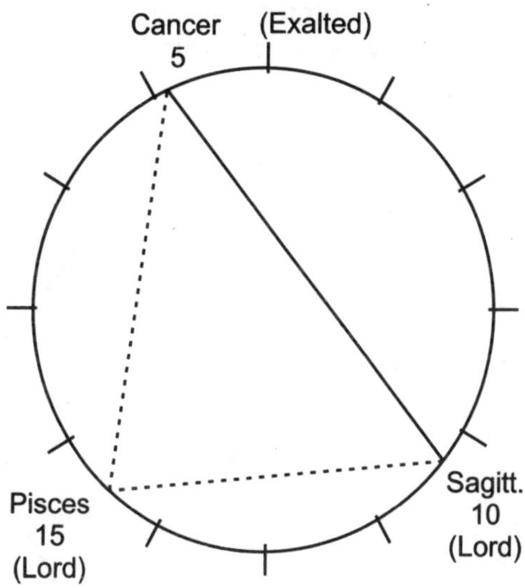

Picture – 12
Mool-trikon position of Jupiter

Jupiter - Jupiter was considered as exalted at 5° of Cancer sign and it is lord of Sagittarius, Pisces signs. There is an angular difference of 95° between zero degree of Aries sign and 5° of Cancer sign (90° of Aries, Taurus and Gemini sign + 5° of Cancer sign). In the same way reversing back 95° from mid-point of Pisces sign i.e. 95° behind 15° of Pisces sign, we get 10° of Sagittarius sign. Thus after joining these three points situated at 5° of Cancer sign, 10° of Sagittarius sign and 15° of Pisces sign, we get a triangular diagram as shown in picture-12. Point in Cancer and Sagittarius sign is linked with a line and another point in Pisces sign is linked with two dotted lines. After going ahead from the exalted sign Cancer of Jupiter, we get Sagittarius sign. Thus part of 10° (one degree to 10°) of Sagittarius sign was quite naturally classified as *mool-trikon.*

Venus - Venus was considered as exalted at 27° of Pisces sign and it is lord of Taurus, Libra signs. If we observe the position of these three signs then it can easily be ascertained that there is a difference of 183° between 27° of Pisces sign and zero degree of Libra sign. Hence with a view to connect these three signs it was natural to locate such a point in Taurus sign so that there may be a triangular relation between the

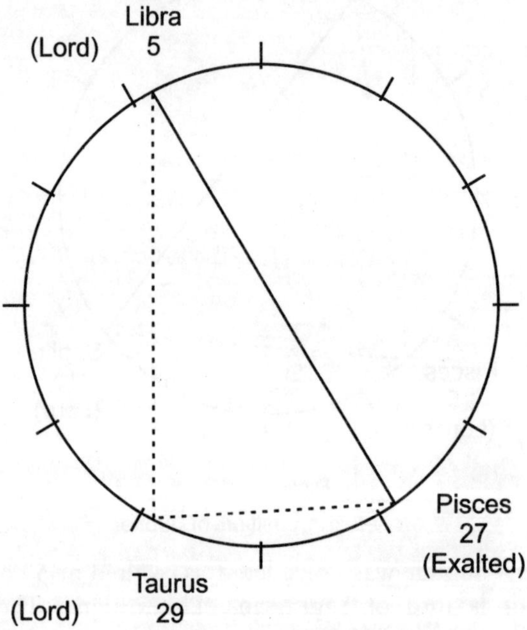

Picture – 13

Mool-trikon position of Venus

point of 27° of Pisces sign and any point of Libra sign. Such triangular relation can be established by keeping the double difference between Taurus-Libra sign with reference to the difference between Pisces-Taurus sign. There is a difference of 63° up to the end of Taurus sign from 27° of Pisces sign. As this difference is up to the end of Taurus sign hence if we go ahead double of 63° i.e. 126° from 1° behind i.e. from 29° of Taurus sign, then we will reach at the point of 5° of Libra sign. Thus by joining these three points a triangular relation between these three signs is formed. Point in Libra and Pisces sign is linked with a line and another point in Taurus sign is linked with two dotted lines as shown in picture-13. As Pisces sign is the last sign of the zodiac thus we have to move backward and reach to the Libra sign where there is a point of 5°. Thus 5° of Libra sign was classified as *mool-trikon* for Venus.

Mars - Mars was considered as exalted at 28° of Capricorn sign and it is lord of Aries, Scorpio signs. It may be observed from picture-14 that there is a difference of 74° between 14° (which is half of 28° related to Capricorn sign) of Scorpio sign and 28° of Capricorn sign. If we move ahead 74° from 28° of Capricorn sign then we will be at 12° of Aries sign. For deciding *mool-trikon*, if we go ahead from Capricorn sign then there is end of zodiac at the end of Pisces sign. Thus we have to move backward from Capricorn sign and reach to Scorpio sign. The Fiery element of Mars has natural enmity with the Watery element of Scorpio sign; hence next Aries sign having Fiery element and at third point of triangle got importance. Thus part of 12° under Aries sign was classified as *mool-trikon* for Mars.

Moon - Moon was considered as exalted at 3° of Taurus sign and lord of Cancer sign. As there was difference of only 87° from 3° of Taurus sign to the end of Cancer sign. Hence it was not possible to create a triangle with the difference of 120°, as was the case of Sun and Saturn. Thus our sages divided 87° in three parts of 29° each. It may be observed from picture-14 that if we move ahead 29° from the point of 3° of Taurus sign then we will be at 2° in Gemini sign as a first point and after moving ahead with next 29°, we will be at one degree in Cancer sign as a second point and third point will be

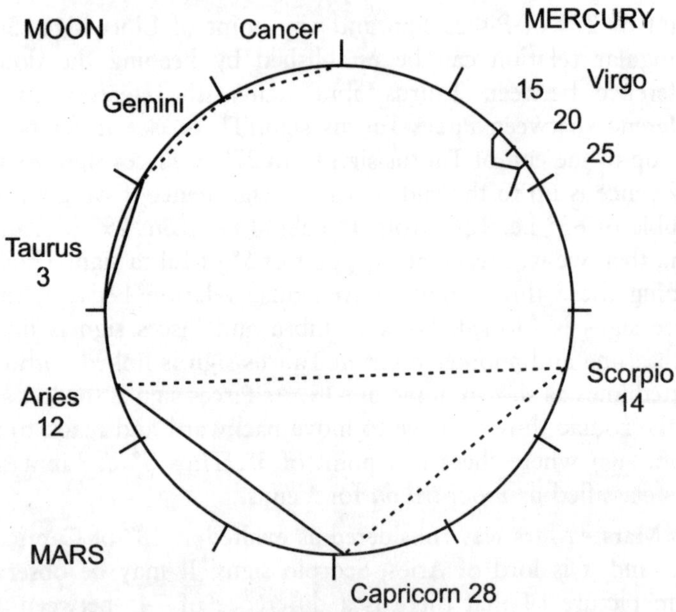

Picture – 14
Mool-trikon position of Mars, Moon and Mercury

at the end of Cancer sign, which is 29° away. The position of these three points may be seen in picture-14. Now, first point is located at 2° in Gemini sign and this is joined by a line but Moon has no relation with this sign. In this situation, it was decided that instead of classifying only 2° of Gemini sign as *mool-trikon* for Moon it would be more prudent to classify the remaining part from 3° of Taurus sign to the end of Taurus sign as *mool-trikon* for Moon, as this point is also towards Cancer sign, whose lord is Moon. In this way segment of 3° to 30° in Taurus sign was classified as *mool-trikon* for Moon.

Mercury - Mercury was considered as exalted at 15° of Virgo sign and it is lord of Gemini, Virgo sign. Mercury has exalted as well as relation of lordship with the Virgo sign and Earthen element of Mercury also matches with the Earthen element of Virgo. Hence remaining part of 15° from the exalted position of Mercury to the end of Virgo sign was divided in three segments of 5° each. Thus first segment was from 15° to 20°, second segment was from 20° to 25° and third segment was from 25° to 30° of Virgo sign as shown in picture-14. Thus as per procedure followed for other planets, it was quite natural to classify the first part from 15° to 20° as *mool-trikon* for Mercury.

It would be clear from the above explanation that while deciding the segment in a sign as *mool-trikon* for a planet, our sages paid importance to the exalted, own sign and lastly to the element of the planet and not to the relation of friendship-enmity. You are quite aware with the procedure adopted in deciding the lordship of sign and degree in a sign for exalted-debilitated position of a planet from the description given in the earlier chapters. You may also be aware as to how these principles were decided on the basis of primitive knowledge regarding formation of Universe and celestial position of the planets. From those chapters you may come across the major differences between primitive concept of formation of the Universe and modern concept of solar system and how the position of exalted-debilitated planets have since been deviated by 33° due to increase in *ayanansh* since the formulation of astrological principles in the Primitive age. As the principle of *mool-trikon* is based on other principles of astrology, and when there is a substantial change and error in the basic principles which leads to the formulation of the principle of *mool-trikon* then it is quite natural that there may also be an error in the same proportion in the principle of *mool-trikon*. Thus it is pertinent to modify this principle on the basis of latest knowledge of the Universe.

Conclusion

Not only this principle got importance due to triangular formation between sign of lordship and exalted position of a planet on the basis of the then available information in the Primitive age regarding situation of the Sun and Saturn in the Universe but triangular design as a symbol, representing entire power of Universe also got importance while creating different type of altars and mystical diagrams. While formulating the principle of *mool-trikon*, utmost importance was given to the principle of lordship of a sign and exalted position of a planet. Because the sign of *mool-trikon* are either own (*swa-rashi*) or exalted sign of a planet hence whenever a prediction is presumed on the basis of this principle than it appears that prediction would be correct as it automatically matches with the principle of lordship or exalted sign. Whereas, actual truth is quite different.

Now everybody knows on the basis of latest discoveries of science that the Universe is not limited from the nearest planet Sun to farthest planet Saturn from the Earth as envisaged in the Primitive age but all planets including our Earth is a part of solar system of the Sun, which itself is a very small part of the galaxy and in turn, of the Universe. Hence whatever is the ratio of mistake in the astrological concept regarding formation of the Universe, lord of sign, exalted position of the planets; same ratio of mistake also exist in the principle of *mool-trikon*.

From the above description it will be clear that there are following main mistakes in the principle of *mool-trikon*, due to which astrological principle is faulty and not being supported with the modern knowledge of the science :–

1. Creating a triangular relation between the position of exalted and own sign (*swa-rashi*) of a planet by imaginary presumption of limited Universe from Sun to Saturn over the fixed Earth is wrong and is not supported by the modern knowledge of the science.
2. Principle of *mool-trikon* is mainly based on exalted and own sign of a planet. There is a vast and fundamental difference between primitive and modern knowledge about the formation of the Universe. As exalted degree of a planet is continuously changing due change in *ayanansh* beside lordship, which is based on the distance of planets from the Earth. Thus when main principle in support of formulation of the principle of *mool-trikon* has completely changed, hence principle of *mool-trikon* is also faulty.

10

PLANETARY STRENGTH

What conveyed

Formulation of principle of friendship enmity and procedure for casting other type of horoscopes was carried out in the Primitive age. Subsequently, Sages of the Middle age developed the mathematical base for calculating the strength of a planet on the basis of these principles. In this way calculation of *shadbal* and predictive astrology were gradually developed on the basis of the potential of a planet. *Shadbal* comprises of six different powers of a planet. They are *Sthan bal, Digbal, Kaal bal, Chesta bal, Nesargic bal* and *Dragbal* respectively. *Sthan bal* was again divided in five parts and they are *Saptvargi bal, Ucch bal, Kendra bal, Ugmaugm bal* and *Drescon bal* respectively. We can realise the impact of *saptvargi bal* on the modern predictive astrology. Strength (*bal*) of a planet is calculated on the basis of principle of friendship-enmity and lordship after drafting different type of horoscopes by subdividing a sign of 30° arc in small arcs of different degrees. But *saptvargi bal* includes the strength of planets in ascendant (birth horoscope), *hora, drescon, saptmansh, navansh, dwadshansh* and *trishansh* horoscopes.

What observed

Basis of all sort of strength of a planet was based on planetary position in birth horoscope, position of planet from respective exalted position, time of birth, *paksh*, *tithi* and a wrong concept, which prevailed since Rising age to believe these planets as living being and deity. Working out the strength of a planet by these age old methods is neither logical nor scientific in the modern age of science. Because many other horoscopes are also being prepared now-a-days along with *saptvargi* horoscopes and prediction is also concluded on these basis. Hence we will analyse only these horoscopes.

Mostly opposite situations are created, which leads to different directions, while concluding a prediction on the basis of different type of horoscopes. For example, if we analyse the position of only Mars in *navansh* horoscope among the various horoscopes drawn for evaluating planetary strength then we may come across following discrepancies :–

1. In birth horoscope, Mars remain in his own Aries sign between 6° 40' to 10° and 16° 40' to 20°. Mars and Aries sign also belongs to same Fiery element. Beside this Mars of 8° to 10° also remain in his *mool-trikon*. But in *navansh* horoscope, this Mars reaches in Gemini and Virgo sign respectively owned by Mercury, who is enemy of Mars.
2. Between 3° 20' to 6° 40' and 20° to 23° 20' of Gemini sign, Mars remain in the sign of his enemy Mercury in birth horoscope. Whereas, in *navansh* horoscope this Mars reaches in Scorpio and Aries sign respectively, which are owned by Mars.
3. In the same way, Mars of 6° 40' to 10° and 16° 40' to 20° of Gemini sign, is in the sign owned by his enemy Mercury, in birth horoscope. Whereas, in *navansh* horoscope this Mars reaches in Sagittarius and Pisces sign respectively, which are owned by his friend Jupiter.
4. Mars of 6° 40' to 10° of Cancer sign, is in the sign owned by his friend Moon, in birth horoscope. Whereas, in *navansh* horoscope this Mars reaches in Virgo sign, which is owned by his enemy Mercury.
5. In the same way, Mars of 20° to 23° 20' and 23° 20' to 26° 40' of Cancer sign, is in the sign owned by his

friend Moon, in birth horoscope. Whereas, in *navansh* horoscope this Mars reaches in Capricorn and Aquarius sign respectively, which are owned by his enemy Saturn.

6. Mars of 6° 40' to 10° and 16° 40' to 20° of Leo sign, is in the sign owned by his friend Sun, in birth horoscope. Moreover, Mars and Leo sign belongs to same Fiery element. Whereas, in *navansh* horoscope this Mars reaches in Gemini and Virgo sign respectively, which are owned by his enemy Mercury.
7. Mars of 6° 40' to 10°, 10° to 13° 20', 20° to 23° 20' and 23° 20' to 26° 40' of Virgo sign, is in the sign owned by his enemy Mercury, in birth horoscope. Whereas, in *navansh* horoscope this Mars reaches in Pisces sign owned by his friend Jupiter, own Aries sign, Cancer sign owned by his friend Moon and Leo sign owned by his friend Sun respectively.
8. Mars of 6° 40' to 10° of Scorpio sign, is in his own sign, in birth horoscope. Whereas, in *navansh* horoscope this Mars reaches in Virgo sign, which is owned by his enemy Mercury.
9. In the same way, Mars of 20° to 23° 20' and 23° 20' to 26° 40' of Scorpio sign, is in his own sign, in birth horoscope. Whereas, in *navansh* horoscope this Mars reaches in Capricorn and Aquarius sign respectively, which are owned by his enemy Saturn.
10. Mars of 6° 40 to 10° and 16° 40' to 20° of Sagittarius sign, is in the sign owned by his friend Jupiter, in birth horoscope. Whereas, in *navansh* horoscope this Mars reaches in Gemini and Virgo sign respectively, which are owned by his enemy Mercury.
11. Mars of 6° 40' to 10°, 10° to 13° 20', 20° to 23° 20' and 23° 20' to 26° 40' of Capricorn sign, is in the sign owned by his enemy Saturn, in birth horoscope. Whereas, in *navansh* horoscope this Mars reaches in Pisces sign owned by his friend Jupiter, own Aries sign,

Cancer sign owned by his friend Moon and Leo sign owned by his friend Sun respectively.

12. Mars of 3° 20' to 6° 40', 6° 40' to 10°, 16° 40' to 20° and 20° to 23° 20' of Aquarius sign, is in the sign owned by his enemy Saturn, in birth horoscope. Whereas, in *navansh* horoscope this Mars reaches in own Scorpio sign, Sagittarius and Pisces sign owned by his friend Jupiter and own Aries sign respectively.
13. Mars of 6° 40' to 10°, 20° to 23° 20', 23° 20' to 26° 40' of Pisces sign, is in the sign owned by his friend Jupiter, in birth horoscope. Whereas, in *navansh* horoscope this Mars reaches in Virgo sign owned by his enemy Mercury, Capricorn and Aquarius sign owned by his enemy Saturn respectively.

There are so many such situations for other planets in the *navansh* horoscope and in respect of all planets in other various horoscopes where a planet may be in opposite situation. In this way if a planet is in comfortable situation in one horoscope then it may be in opposite situation in other horoscope. Thus out of various horoscopes covering Birth, Moon, Transit, *Navansh*, *Hora*, *Saptmansh*, *Drescon* etc., Planetary position, *Yog*, Periodicity, *Gochar*, Aspect, Exalted, Debilitated, *Shadbal* etc. only and only those situations and particular horoscope, which are in conformity with any event in the life of a person may only find place in the magazine and books covering the predictive part as a business propaganda. But actually there is neither a procedure nor it is possible to correctly conclude any prediction with the help of existing astrological principle nor through various horoscopes and there is always a position of dilemma and in this situation astrologer not only predict any favourable or unfavourable event according to the mental status of an individual but also exploit them financially by proper handling them psychologically.

There are many different ways to calculate the strength of a planet. This is calculated from different type of horoscopes on the basis of lordship and relation of friendship-enmity between the planets after assessing the sign of ascendant and planets by matching their degrees from the tables created for this purpose.

If you are interested in calculating the strength of planets on the basis of different horoscopes then you may draw these following horoscopes without taking help of any table and you may be able to work out the sign of planets and ascendant for any type of horoscope only from their degree and sign. Because degrees of a planet is only sub-divided in small portion in such calculations and after dividing this number by 12 we may easily know the new sign of a planet.

Horoscope 1	Part of sign 2	deg/min/sec of one part 3	deg/min/sec of 12 sign 4
Hora	2	15°	—
Drescon	3	10°	120°
Chaturthansh	4	7° 30'	90°
Saptmansh	7	4° 17' 8.5"	51° 25' 42"
Navansh	9	3° 20'	40°
Dasamansh	10	3°	36°
Dwadshansh	12	2° 30'	30°
Shodshansh	16	1° 52' 30"	22° 30'
Vishansh	20	1° 30'	18°
Saptvishansh	27	1° 6' 40"	13° 20'
Trishansh	30	1°	12°
Khavedansh	40	0° 45'	9°
Akshvedansh	45	0° 40'	8°
Shathyansh	60	0° 30'	6°

If we divide 30° by the number shown under column 2 then we get the degree/minute/second as shown in column 3. If we multiply this number by 12 then we get degree/minute as shown in column 4. Hence according to first method we may divide the degree-minute of planets and ascendant by the number shown in column 3, against the type of horoscope which we want to draw. This number may then be reduced by 12, if it is more than 12 or divided by 12. The next number of remainder will be the sign of that planet or ascendant. According to second method simply go on reducing the number shown in column 4 from the degree-minute of a planet till it is more than this and then remainder may be divided by the number shown in column 3 and the next number would be sign of that planet or ascendant. For example, for preparing *navansh* horoscope :–

First method :–

Planet = 15° of Leo sign

= 4 sign + 15° = 135° = 8100 minute

Divide it by 3° 20' = 200 minute of 3rd column

= 8100 ÷ 200 = 40 remainder 100

= 40 + next sign

= 41

Reduce it by 12 or divide by 12 = 5 remainder

Hence sign of this planet in *navansh* is Leo.

Second method :–

After continuously reducing 40° from 135°

remainder would be 15°

15 ÷ 3° 20' = 4 with some remainder

Hence 4 + 1 = 5

Hence sign of this planet in *navansh* is Leo.

Similarly, sign of any planet or ascendant may be calculated for preparing any type of above mentioned horoscopes.

What discovered

It is a matter of consideration that when once we have finalised that a planet is lord of a particular sign covering 30° of zodiac then how another planets may be lord of a small segment of this sign. For defence one may say that adopting this process assesses different aspect of life. Even then prediction may be moulded according to sweet will in various opposite situation of a planet as is pointed out in case of Mars in *navansh* horoscope. If we also consider aspect and exalted-debilitated position of a planet in the birth horoscope and link it with the planetary position in different type of horoscopes created for working out the planetary strength then multifold opposite situation will arise and there is ample scope for fabricated prediction, which may be derived according to the mental status of an individual. You may have understood from the description given so far that how much mistake exist in the principle of lordship, aspect, friendship-enmity, exalted-debilitated etc., which is based on the wrong concept of the planetary position in the Universe as shown in picture-1. In fact our sages were trying to know the future beforehand with the help of different type of calculations, by casting different type of horoscopes and by formulating and adopting the different astrological principles as is being done in any scientific experiment. Later on after hundreds of year, different types of calculation were created to work out the potential of a planet to formulate the principle of predictive astrology on the basis of unfinished incomplete principles of Primitive age.

The existing mistake in the procedure adopted for finalising the principle of lordship, friendship-enmity, exalted-debilitated due to wrong concept of the Universe, is repeated in the same ratio by adopting the primitive methodology for working out the strength of a planet. During the process of development of astrology, sages tried different ways and means to dive in the subject and after failure of a procedure some different procedures were tried. But correct result could not be worked out, because of wrong concept of the Universe. As the basic hub of formation of the Universe was not correctly known in those days, which resulted in subsequent mistakes in finalising the principles of lordship, friend, exalted etc. Principles of lordship and friendship-enmity were only involved in calculating the *saptvargi* strength of a planet. There is no intervention of the principles of aspect and exalted-debilitated planets. Thus when both situation are just opposite to each other then how both principles may be correct which are leading to opposite results.

You may see from column 3 of the table as to how a lordship has been worked out after sub-dividing a sign in small segments. Thus there may never be any uniformity in the lordship, with the lordship and exalted position of a planet in the birth and transitory (*chalit*) horoscopes. Hence any past event can easily be supported from the framework of different type of calculations and horoscopes but there is always a dilemma so far concluding a future event is concerned. Because if we want to give the importance to the strength of a planet then there is no scope of aspect and exalted-debilitated position of a planet. Whereas in the procedure adopted now-a-days any moulded prediction according to sweet will, may be concluded on the basis of supporting principles chosen from all sort of available principles leading to different directions, only for business purpose.

Conclusion

Lord of sign and their mutual relation with reference to friendship and enmity is taken into consideration for working out the *saptvargi* strength of a planet. Whereas it is being mixed with the opposite principles of exalted and debilitated along with aspect between planets for concluding any prediction according to requirement. Basic foundation of all sort of astrological principles is the formation of Universe. Because understanding and concept of the Universe was wrong in the Primitive age, hence there is no relevancy in the strength of the planet and it is now essential that some fruitful and logical efforts may be made in the field of astrology on the basis of scientific information instead of sticking with the age old tradition.

It is clear from the above explanation that there is following mistake in the astrological principle and it is not supported with the scientific information :–

It is wrong and illogical to work out the strength of a planet on the basis of wrong formulation of the lord of signs on the basis of wrong concept of the Universe and treating the planets as enemy of each other on the basis of an imaginary mythical story of fight for nectar.

Ayan

It was believed in the Primitive age that Sun shift towards *Lavan Samudra*, situated in southern direction while rotating around the *Sumeru Parvat* of *Jambu-dweep*. When Sun transit in extreme north direction with reference to the *Jambu-dweep* i.e. when Sun touches the Tropic of Cancer on 23rd June according to latest information, then Sun regularly start to shift towards south direction and in this process Sun actually rise a little towards south. This situation was known as winter solstice. Contrary to this when Sun transit in extreme south direction with reference to the Jambu-dweep i.e. when Sun touches the Tropic of Capricorn on 23rd December according to latest information, then Sun regularly start to shift towards north direction and in this process Sun actually rise a little towards north. This situation was known as summer solstice. Duration of day and night was equal to 30 *ghati* when Sun touches the *ayan*. Now-a-days these situations are created on 23rd March and 23rd September.

Bhayat-bhabhog

Angular span of every constellation is 13° 30' or 800'. Periodicity (*mahadasha*) of a planet is decided on the basis of the constellational position of the Moon at the time of birth. *Bhayat* is the proportionate period of the *mahadasha* of the relevant planet in the ratio of the portion of the constellation which has already been crossed by the Moon i.e. the minutes which has been crossed by the Moon from 800' and it is considered that this much period has already been passed before the birth. Remaining proportionate period of *mahadasha* is called *Bhabhog*.

Sampaat constellation

It took about 29.5 days or 30 *tithi* in recurrence of the same face of the Moon i.e. period taken from full Moon to next full Moon. In the same way, while rotating around the Earth, Sun took one year or recurrence of the seasons took place after a little more time than 12 lunar months. Since Rising age it was devised to add one extra month of 30 *tithi* after three lunar years to synchronise lunar year of 354 days with solar year. In this way there was still a difference of 1.25 days between the actual duration of a year of 365.25 days and calculated duration of a year of 364 days. Due to this discrepancy it was not possible to correctly ascertain the *sampaat* constellation and season also not reoccur on the same constellational position of Sun and Moon. Year commenced with the fall of spring season in those days as per description given in *Yazurveda*, whereas by the end of Rising age, year commenced in rainy season at the time of first day of winter solstice (It may be possible that word '*Varsh*' may be devised after the *Varsha* season, because in Rising age word *Samvatsar* was used for a year).

It was known and believed by the sages that orbit of the Sun and Moon with reference to the Earth was like picture-1. Hence at mid of summer solstice, when both these illuminative planets transit at same degree in a constellation then that constellation was regarded as *sampaat* constellation. Sun and Moon used to transit at about same degree during the fall of spring season when they were in the mid of summer solstice, hence Revati constellation was regarded as *sampaat* constellation, because Sun used to cross the equator in spring season. Due to correct calculation of 365.25 days of a year, now-a-days, Sun crosses the equator on 23rd March in spring season and it is now possible to correctly ascertain the *sampaat* constellation.

In this way *sampaat* constellation was that constellation in which Sun crosses the equator during summer solstice and Moon also touches the same constellation in dark-night. Now-a-days Sun crosses the equator line when it transit through Uttara-bhadrapad constellation in spring season and Moon also transit through the same constellation in dark-night. Hence now-a-days Uttara-bhadrapad is *sampaat* constellation which will be changed in future due to increase in *ayanansh*.

11

VINSHOTTARY DASHA

What conveyed

Vinshottary periodicity (*dasha*) of nine planets and their distribution among 27 constellations may be seen in the linking table given below. But what was observed in the Universe, which lead sages to decide this order and periodicity of the planets is as usual not available.

Sun	Moon	Mars	Rah.	Jup.	Sat.	Mer.	Ket.	Ven.
6	10	7	18	16	19	17	7	20
Kra.	Roh.	Mra.	Aad.	Pun.	Pus.	Ash.	Mag.	P.F.
U.F.	Has.	Chi.	Swa.	Vis.	Anu.	Jye.	Mul.	P.S.
U.S.	Shr.	Gha.	Sat.	P.B.	U.B.	Rev.	Ash.	Bha.

What observed

Correct prediction could not be concluded with *Vinshottary* periodicity hence this periodicity was also not recognised by the astrologers since Primitive age. Hence sages formulated and tried different type of periodicity like *Ashtottary, Yogini, Kaalchakra, Shodshottary, Dwadshottary, Panchmottary, Shatabdika, Chaturshitisama, Dwisapratisama, Shasthihayini, Shatyishtsama, Char, Sthir, Yogardh, Kendradhi, Kaarak, Brahmgrah, Manduk, Shule, Trikon, Drag, Panchswar, Pind, Nesargik, Ashtvarg, Sandhya, Pachak, Tara, Varnad, Nisarg dasha* etc. to conclude correct forecast. *Mudda* periodicity based on annual horoscope (*Tazik*) was only devised in the Post-middle age but this periodicity was also based on the principles of *vinshottary* periodicity. *Vrahatparashar Hora* itself contains the description of about 42 different type of periodicities. Beside this, details for consulting a particular periodicity was also mentioned therein. According to this, if born in the *navansh* of the Venus then *dwadshottary* periodicity, if Rahu is in *kendra* or *trikon* house except in first house then *ashtottary* periodicity, if Jupiter is in Cancer sign and in the *Dwadshansh* of Cancer then *Panchamottary* periodicity, if ascendant is *vargottam* then *shatabdi* periodicity, if lord of tenth house is placed in tenth house then *chaturshitisama* periodicity, if lord of ascendant is placed in seventh house or lord of seventh house is placed in ascendant then *dwisapratisama* periodicity, if sign of ascendant and Moon is same then *shasthihayini* periodicity may be consulted for concluding any prediction.

Now it is proved that like other planets our Earth is also rotating around the Sun four new planets have also been identified during last 300 years beside seven planets which were known since Rising age. Hence on the basis of following analysis it is obvious that *vinshottary* periodicity as well as other periodicities, based on the similar base of constellations and their related calculations, are also fundamentally wrong. We may observe following discrepancies after deep pondering over the periodicity of the planets :–

1. Periodicity of only seven planets, which were known since Rising age have only been included for concluding the prediction, which is incomplete. Because the periodicity and order of other four planets which have also been identified till now must also be included.
2. If the periodicity of these four planets may also be included than total period will be more than 120 years and this will be much more than the expected life of an individual.
3. If we include these four planets in the major periodicity then it will not be possible to divide 27 constellations among 13 planets.

4. It is presumed that Sun and Moon return back to their original constellation after completing 120 years of *vinshottary* periodicity. But it is not so. In fact Sun takes about 25920 years in returning to its original position after completing a change of 360° at the rate of 50" (*vikala*) per year. Celestial position of the constellations situated in other milkyways will also be changed after such a long time. In this situation it is definite that though the position of the Sun may be repeated with reference to the degree yet its position will never match with reference to the relative position of other constellations.
5. Occasionally, it is also written here and there that sages decided the *vinshottary* periodicity keeping in view the age of an individual as 120 years. This statement is also not logical because about 99 per cent persons died by the age of 75 – 80 years despite best medical facilities which are available now-a-days. Even then suppose we admit the age of 120 years for human race then too after adding the periodicity of four new planets either the age of the human race will be more than 120 years or we may have to reduce the periodicity of all planets to adjust it within 120 years.
6. Position of Rahu and Ketu were differently presumed in the Primitive age in comparison to the latest concept of their formation, because correct formation of the Universe was not known at that time. But in view of the latest concept of the solar system, it is not prudent to place the Rahu above Mars and Ketu above the Mercury as has been done during finalisation of the order of the periodicity of various planets. Whereas it is now a well-known fact that Rahu and Ketu are formed in the orbit of the Moon after crossing the orbit of the Sun by the Moon and hence their distances from the Earth are also alike the distance of the Moon from the Earth.
7. There is no any justification as to why 6 years periodicity was decided for Sun, who was most nearest

(see picture-1) and effective illuminative planet in comparison to Venus, who was awarded with 20 years periodicity.

What discovered

There is no any visible *prima facie* connection between the order of the planets, their periodicity and distribution of constellations among them. But if we try to understand the whole situation in view of the standard of the information which was available with sages at that point of time in the Primitive age then every thing will be clear. At the time of sage Parashar it was a well accepted uncontroversial ordinary fact that Earth is stationary and Sun, Moon, Constellations, Mercury, Venus, Mars, Jupiter and Saturn were respectively situated over each other and they rotate around the *Sumeru-parvat*, which was situated on the stationary Earth as may be seen in picture-1. From the earlier analysis you may now be well aware with the fact that how much importance was assigned to the cylindrical formation of the Universe in formulation of the various astrological principles. In the same way various information, which were gathered till the Primitive age like distance of the planets from the Earth, their retrograde motion, their celestial position with reference to the Sun, constellational position of the Moon, time taken by the planets in reaching their original position beside formation of the Universe and *sampaat* position of the Moon had very important contribution in deciding the order and periodicity of the planets for *vinshottary* periodicity.

> **TIP :** If you are amateur reader or find any difficulty at any time in understanding succeeding paragraphs then you may jump to Conclusion and try to understand this left out portion in next reading.

While formulating the principle of *vinshottary* periodicity it was a natural and pertinent question and it was also considered as to who would be the first planet and first constellation from where this periodicity will be commenced.

Because fall of summer solstice commenced in the first step of Uttarashada constellation in 572 BC and Sun crosses the vernal equinox in Revati constellation situated at an angle of 90°. Thus Revati was nominated as *sampaat* constellation. I have also verified this fact from own developed software that as per *sayan* system summer solstice started at 270.55° i.e. first step (*charan*) of Uttarashada, on 22-12-572 BC. In this way, as per *sayan* system, Sun and Moon coincide at vernal equinox in March - 572 BC, while they were in Revati constellation. Thus it was correct to consider the Revati constellation as *sampaat* constellation in the Rising age. Because as per belief prevailed in the Primitive age, Mercury was the first planet, which was situated above the illuminator Moon and constellations. Hence in this circumstances it was quite natural and logical that Mercury and Revati constellation may be nominated as an initial starting point of the *vinshottary* periodicity. From the table earlier given in this chapter you may see that periodicity of Mercury was linked with the Revati constellation. But with a view to give an unnecessary modern look to the *vinshottary* periodicity, Sun and Kratica constellation are being shown as the starting point in the tables shown in the modern books. But it makes no difference in the order of planets and constellations as laid down in the original principle.

After solving the problem of initial constellation and planet, next question before the sages was, as to whether the order of the planets for periodicity may be kept as per the order of their existence in the Universe as shown in picture-1 or some other order may be derived. Help of the orbit of the planets was taken for solving this question. Because during one complete rotation of the zodiac, Mercury retrograde thrice, whereas Venus retrograde only once. Beside this only these two planets were always remain in the close ambit of the illuminator Sun. Hence during formulation of the periodicity, these two planets were kept on one side of the Sun and Moon. It was believed that change in the face of the Moon and solar eclipse were created only due to the impact of Rahu and Ketu respectively, beside this these two shadow planets were always remain in retrograde motion. Hence during finalising the order of the periodicity these planets were kept on both side after one planet. Rahu, which was regarded as head of the demon, was kept in between Mars and Jupiter i.e. on top side of the Moon and Ketu, which was the lower part of the demon was kept in between Mercury and Venus i.e. on the lower side of the cylindrical Universe. Thus Rahu was kept on one side of the illuminator Sun and Moon whereas Ketu was kept on the other side. Above position of the planets may be seen in picture-15.

In this way order of planets was decided to be arranged so that Ketu may be placed after Mercury, which retrograde thrice and thereafter Venus, which retrograde once was placed just before illuminator Sun and Moon. Because Mars retrograde once during its complete rotation of zodiac hence it was placed just before Rahu as per earlier explanation, thereafter, Jupiter and Saturn were placed, which retrograde twelve times in one rotation of zodiac, completed in 13 and 30 years respectively. The entire position may be understand from table-1. In this way those planets which could not be seen in the mid-night i.e. who always transit in the close ambit of the day-lord Sun, were placed on the side of the Sun; whereas those planets which may be seen in the mid-night were placed on the side of the night-lord Moon.

Table – 1

From Sampaat constellation Revati

Complete one rotation of all signs in one year (Remain with Sun)					Complete one rotation of all signs in more than one year			
Ret. three times	Ketu	Ret. once	Illuminators		1.5 year retro. once	Rahu	13 yrs.	30 yrs.
Mer.	Ketu	Ven.	Sun	Moon	Mars	Rahu	Jup.	Sat.

In this way after deciding the initial constellation, Planet and order of planets for Vinshottary periodicity, the question of periodicity for every planet remain unsolved. As has been described in the chapter of 'Mool-trikon' that in the Primitive age, shape of triangle and circle was given much importance for using them in altar. Hence the shape of simple triangle as symbol of the power of Universe, cone, circle and time taken by Rahu and Moon in one rotation were used as follows for deciding the periodicity of the planets.

MOON – When Revati was *sampaat* constellation in 572 BC, then in those days Moon took about 10 years to meet the Sun in Revati constellation during summer solstice. Hence it was quite natural to fix 10 years as the periodicity of the Moon.

RAHU – In the same way Rahu took about 18 years in returning to its original position with a retrograde motion of

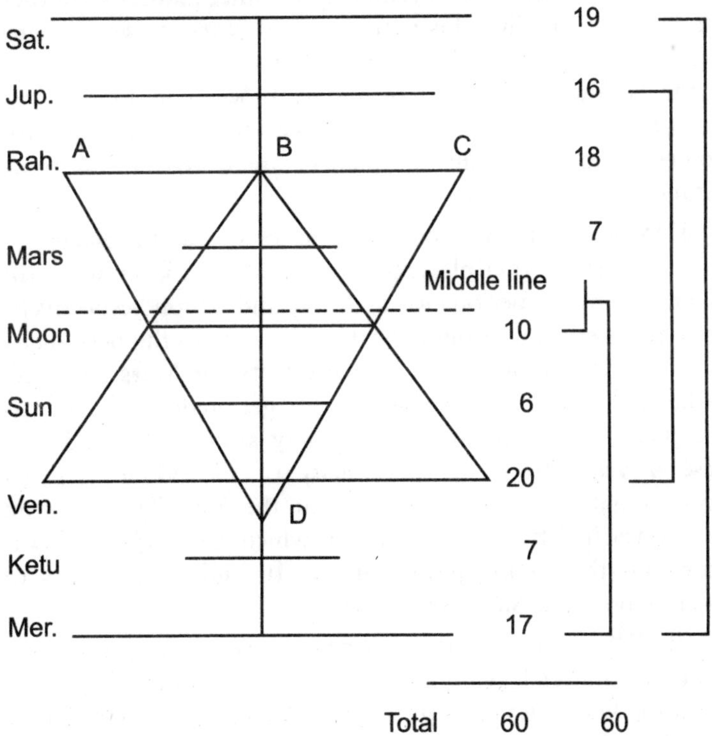

Picture – 15
Procedure for deciding the periodicity of planets

3' 11" per day. Hence 18 years was fixed as periodicity of the Rahu.

These two planets are still taking roughly same time in returning to their original position on the basis of angular motion decided for them. What was the mistake in deciding the retrograde motion of Rahu Ketu will be discussed later on. The cylindrical shape of the Universe, conical shape of two triangles as shown in picture-11 and planetary position played a significant and decisive roll in finalising the periodicity of other planets on the basis of the periodicity of these two planets. We get 120 years by multiplying the periodicity of 10 years decided for the Moon by 12 signs. Hence it was natural to confine the duration of Moon based *vinshottary* periodicity to a period of 120 years. Periodicity of other planets were then decided after dividing this period of 120 years in two triangles of 60 years each. This period of 60 years is also corresponding to the period of 60 *ghati* of a day. Process of deciding the periodicity of other planets may be understood from the picture-15 in which line of planets are drawn at an equal distance.

SUN – It may be seen from the order of the planets as shown in table-1 that placement of the Mars is in between the 18 and 10 years periodicity of Rahu and Moon respectively. Thus after reducing proportionate 4 years from the periodicity of Rahu, we may get 14 years periodicity for Mars and after further reducing these 4 years, we may get predecided 10 years periodicity of Moon. In the same way after further reducing these 4 years from the periodicity of the Moon, we get proportionate 6 years periodicity of the Sun. This position may be verified from picture-15. In which a triangle A C D is drawn on the ending points of 18, 10 and 6 year lines of Rahu, Moon and Sun respectively.

VENUS – Line of 10 years periodicity of the Moon may be obtained after leaving one planet Mars from the mid-point 'B' on the line of Rahu in picture-15. A triangle is formed after drawing a line from this mid-point 'B' by touching the end-points of the line of Moon and extending it in the same proportion. On the basis of simple mathematics relating to triangle, it can be verified graphically that after leaving the line of Sun from Moon, the periodicity of the Venus must be 20 years. As distance between point B to line of Moon and line of Moon to line of Venus are same. Thus when horizontal line of Moon represents 10 years, hence horizontal line of Venus may simply represent 20 years.

JUPITER – That part of the cone, which is below the mid-line of the triangle A C D, contains only 10 and 6 years line of Moon and Sun respectively. In this way combined periodicity of the Sun and Moon is 16 years. Hence according to the quality of a cone constructed from two triangles, this much periodicity i.e. 16 years was allotted to the next planet Jupiter, which is situated after Rahu on the other side of the cone.

MARS – So far the periodicity of the planets situated in the cone made up of two triangles have been decided as follows :

Venus	Sun	Moon	Mars	Rahu	Jupiter
20	6	10	14	18	16

According to the qualities of the cone, its middle part is always smaller in comparison to the outer part of the cone. Whereas if the middle part of the above table is observed in view of this analogy then total of the periodicity of Moon and Mars is 24 years (periodicity of 14 years for Mars was calculated while deciding the periodicity of the Sun) and the total of the periodicity of next planets Sun and Rahu is also 24 years. Thus it is in the shape of a cylinder instead of cone. To convert this shape into cone, it is essential to modify the periodicity of the Moon and Mars, which are situated in the middle part. 10 years periodicity of Moon was fixed in view of the time taken by it in returning to its original position; hence it could not be modified. Thus to obtain a correct shape of a cone, periodicity of Mars can only be reduced in correct multiplicity and this was achieved by halving the 14 years periodicity of the Mars to 7 years. Thus 7 years periodicity was fixed for the Mars. In this way the total of periodicity of Mars and Moon situated in the middle part of the cone become 17 years and the total of periodicity of next planets Sun and

Rahu situated on the both sides become 24 years and the total of periodicity of next planets Venus and Jupiter situated on the both sides become 36 years. These numbers resembled with the cone as well as with a large triangle.

KETU – If Sun is kept in the middle of a smaller cone then it can be seen from picture-15 that periodicity of next planet Mars was 7 years, which was situated after the line of Moon on the one side of the Sun. On the same analogy decision of finalising 7 years periodicity of the next planet Ketu, which was situated after the line of Venus on the other side of the Sun was quite logical and natural in view of the mathematical process of triangle and cone. In this way 7 years periodicity was decided for Ketu.

SATURN – Periodicity of the Sun was 6 years. After adding 4 years each for the planets Moon, Mars, Rahu, Jupiter and Saturn situated after Sun as per picture-15, we get 26 years periodicity for the Saturn. If both triangles of the cone may be kept as upside down then outer points will form a shape of circle. From this shape of circle it can be realised that the size on both ends will be same. As has been mentioned earlier in the description of Mars that total of the periodicity of three pair of the planets situated in the cone was 17, 24 and 36 years. Hence to synchronise the shape of cone with the shape of circle it is essential that the total of next pair will be reduced. Saturn is fourth planet on the above side of the middle line. Whereas Ketu is the fourth planet on the lower side of the middle line for which 7 years periodicity has already been decided. Hence after reducing this 7 years from 26 years calculated periodicity of the Saturn, net 19 years periodicity was left for Saturn. Beside this total of periodicity of four planets i.e. Mars, Rahu, Jupiter and Saturn kept in the above part of the cone is also 60 years.

MERCURY – The total of periodicity of the pairs of planets of both sides from the middle line of the cone is now 17, 24, 36 and 26 respectively. From this it can easily be concluded that to match the shape of circle next total must be 17 years, whereas now only Mercury is left in the lower part of the cone from where the order of planets was initiated. Hence these 17 years periodicity was allotted to the Mercury. In this way not only the shape of the circle is matched but the total periodicity of five planets i.e. Moon, Sun, Venus, Ketu and Mercury, which were kept in the lower part of the cone was also 60 years, alike the total periodicity of the planets of the upper part of the cone.

While calculating the periodicity of the Sun we have reduced 4 years for every planet. In this way if we continue then we may get 36 years for nine planets. Thus *yogini* periodicity was formulated on this 36 years and three frequency of these 36 years form 108 years, which form the basis of formulating *ashtottary* periodicity. It was further concluded that maximum periodicity must be 36 years. This phenomenon also matched with the total of 17 years periodicity of Mercury, from where *vinshottary* periodicity was initiated on the basis of *sampaat* constellation and 19 years periodicity of the ending Saturn planet was 36 years. In this way the mathematical calculation and procedures adopted for formulation of the principles of the *vinshottary* periodicity is exposed.

Sages were not only able to create different form of altar on the basis of triangular design for performing religious offerings to God but they were also able to create different *yantra* like '*Shri-yantra*' by enclosing these triangular shapes (see picture-11) representing cosmic power in a circle or square. There are two triangles in picture-15 drawn by adjoining the ending points of lines of periodicity of Rahu and Venus with Moon. If we draw a triangle by adjoining the ending points of top line of Saturn with Mars situated at two lines below and another triangle by adjoining bottom line of Mercury with Sun situated at two lines above then any resembling shape with these four triangles may be seen in any *yantra*. In this way *vinshottary* periodicity got prominence over other periodicities because it was based on the design of power of Universe.

Now we will examine the suitability of *vinshottary* periodicity for 21st century. Only by following *sayan* system Revati constellation may repeatedly be *sampaat* constellation after every 10 years. Because only *sayan* system was practised during the ending period of the Rising age and early period of the Primitive age. Hence Revati constellation was categorised as *sampaat* constellation and all other constellations were accordingly distributed among all other planets as described earlier in this chapter. As has been mentioned in the earlier chapter that *nirayan* system was started due to detection of shifting of planets in the zodiac and due to non-recurrence of the season on scheduled time. But in the Primitive age mathematical calculations were based on *sayan* system, whereas celestial planets were detected by *nirayan* (*drag* or visual) system and subsequently *nirayan* system was fully adopted for astrological calculations. Now we must follow any one of the following methods for preparing the horoscope.

1. If position of the Moon in the zodiac in deg.-sign may be calculated as per *sayan* system instead of *nirayan* system by following the practice of Primitive age then there is no need to change the linking table of constellation and planets, which is available in all sort of books. Because Revati may be still a *sampaat* constellation as per *sayan* system which prevailed in the Primitive age.
2. Now-a-days horoscopes are being prepared only on the basis of *nirayan* system. Position in deg.-sign of all planets including Moon is calculated only by following the *nirayan* system. Thus if we want to calculate the position of different periodicity after calculating the position of the Moon by *nirayan* system then *sampaat* constellation must also be calculated by *nirayan* system and all constellations must be distributed among the planets afresh only then correct periodicity may be calculated.

A very funny situation has been created in the present scenario. Because degree and sign of the Moon is being calculated by *nirayan* system and *vinshottary* periodicity is being worked out by consulting the table, which was prepared on the *sayan* system.

When it was observed in the Primitive age that planet was not visible at a particular point, which was calculated by *sayan* system, only thereafter sages devised the principle of *nirayan* system and calculated *ayanansh*. In this way initially Revati constellation was also a *sampaat* constellation by *nirayan* system too during the year AD 285 to year AD 1242, because till this year the *ayanansh* was 13° 20'. During this period *nirayan* system was well established and this was the period when the eminent mathematician was developing new sort of mathematical calculations. Because Revati was *sampaat* constellation hence there was no need to change the order of planets and devising new distribution of the constellation. But after the year AD 1242, Uttara-bhadrapad was the new *sampaat* constellation by *nirayan* system. As has been mentioned earlier that there was no mathematical development during last 900 years and political position was also unfavourable. Hence no body cares about this phenomenon. Now today in the year AD 2005, Uttara-bhadrapad is a *sampaat* constellation and this constellation will hold this position till the year AD 2202.

In this way Revati will always be a *sampaat* constellation by *sayan* system. After the year AD 285, Revati was *sampaat* constellation by *nirayan* system too. Because Revati remain as a *sampaat* constellation for such a long time hence there was no need to reallocate the constellations among the planets and subsequently, we lost this concept.

In this way it will be clear that Revati was a *sampaat* constellation in the Primitive age, hence all constellations from Revati and onward were distributed among the planets commencing from Mercury etc. But when Uttara-bhadrapad is a new *sampaat* constellation then even if we keep aside the planetary position as shown in picture-2 depicting modern concept of the Universe even then it is essential that constellations may now be distributed afresh commencing from the Uttara-bhadrapad constellation in the following manner.

Sun	Moon	Mars	Rah.	Jup.	Sat.	Mer.	Ket.	Ven.
Bha.	Kra.	Roh.	Mra.	Aad.	Pun.	Pus.	Ash.	Mag.
P.F.	U.F.	Has.	Chi.	Swa.	Vis.	Anu.	Jye.	Mul.
P.S.	U.S.	Shr.	Gha.	Sat.	P.B.	U.B.	Rev.	Ash.

At present the periodicity of a planet is being reduced in the same proportion in which the period of a constellation has been passed before the birth by treating this period as *bhayat*. In the same way if we consider the minute mathematical calculation then it can easily be realised that *sampaat* position of a constellation is also not changed in a moment. But it continuously changes retrogradely according to *ayanansh* at a speed of 50" per year. Hence Mercury has not to observe the entire periodicity of *sampaat* Uttara-bhadrapad constellation (according to present practice you may treat Revati for understanding) but we have to calculate the balance periodicity of the Mercury on the basis of the degree when Sun actually crosses the equator. For example, if *ayanansh* is 23° 20' then it indicate that Sun will cross the equator at 360° – 23° 20' = 336° 40'. The span of the Uttara-bhadrapad constellation is from 333° 20' to 346° 40'. Hence we have to deduct the starting point 333° 20' of the Uttara-bhadrapad from 336° 40' to get 3° 20' or 200', which has already been covered by the Mercury before crossing the equator line by the Sun and now Mercury has to cover only proportionate periodicity of 600'. Because number of remaining minutes will increase as long as *ayanansh* will increase. Hence remaining minutes will only be considered for remaining periodicity. Planet has to cover entire periodicity in the case of 800' balance of a constellation as in the case of other planets. Thus simple meaning of remaining 600' of a constellation is that out of 17 years of entire periodicity of Mercury, it has already covered 4 years and 3 months, before crossing the equator line by the Sun and now it has to cover only balance periodicity of 12 years and 9 months. Thus it will be clear new tables of periodicity must be drawn for every year on this basis, in which balance periodicity of *sampaat* constellation must be shown.

If we consider the order of the planets for *vinshottary* periodicity in view of the modern information of the solar system then it would be clear that entire planetary position has been changed. The distances and order of the Sun, Moon, Venus, Mercury and Mars planets continuously remains changing with reference to the Earth. Accordingly the order of the planets for *vinshottary* periodicity must also be changed for every horoscope. Order of the Jupiter and Saturn is always fixed in view of their distances from the Earth, as has already been explained in earlier chapter.

Conclusion

If Vinshottary periodicity would have been correct in the critical study made by the sages in the Primitive age then there was no need to device so many other types of periodicities. But none of the periodicity was ever studied with a scientific approach after Middle age. Because we have already forgotten to carry out any deep study of the astrological principles since last 2000 years and period of last 1000 years was only spared in developing simple calculation in support of primitive principles and so-called prediction. Reference of this periodicity in the literary book and use of it by sage Parashar beside simple calculation of *vinshottary* periodicity, were main factors due to which this periodicity is still being recognised and it is also being used in the software developed for astrological calculations without any scientific basis.

Planets were distributed among the constellations on the basis of *sayan* system. But now horoscopes are being prepared on the basis of *nirayan* system hence order of periodicity of planets must also be decided as per *nirayan* system. Because order of periodicity was decided on the basis of retrogression and duration of time taken by the planets for complete rotation in zodiac by keeping them on the both sides of the Moon. Hence order of periodicity of planets may be decided independently for every horoscope on the basis of the distances of the planets from the Moon, at the time of birth by following the same principle. This point must also be considered that there is no scientific justification for distributing the planets on either side of the illuminator Sun and Moon on the basis of retrogression of the planets for deciding the order of the periodicity of the planets. Because now we know that planet can never be transit in retrograde motion but there is only an illusion of the retrograde motion and it is not logical at all to frame a principle on the basis of an illusion. Actual position of a planet during retrograde motion will be discussed later on in detail.

According to the procedure adopted for deriving a prediction in the Krishnamurti system of south India, lord, sublord, subsublord of a planet are decided on the basis of a constellation and they are derived like *antar-dasha* and *pratyantar-dasha* in *vinshottary* periodicity. Hence this system is also mathematically faulty to the extent of change in *sampaat* constellation etc.

From the above explanation it will be clear that there are following mistakes in deriving the periodicity of the planets. That's why the astrological principles are faulty and not supported scientifically.

1. It is wrong to consider that Sun is nearest planet from the Earth in comparison to the Moon by arranging the planets at a fixed distance on the basis of wrong primitive concept of the Universe.
2. Rahu and Ketu are only formed by the Moon while transiting in its orbit; hence these planets must be kept beside the Moon for deriving the periodicity.
3. Table of periodicity in vogue is based on *sayan* system. Hence it is wrong to determine the periodicity of a planet of the horoscope which is being prepared by adopting *nirayan* system.
4. Table of periodicity was prepared on the basis of *sampaat* constellation, which has since been changed due to change in the *ayanansh*. Hence the present position is totally misleading.
5. Non consideration of the balance periodicity of a planet, on the basis of actual position of the *sampaat* constellation, like *Bhayat Bhabhog*, is wrong.

Latitude and longitude

Astronomer Ptolemy of Greece prepared, the map of the Earth in 2nd century on the then knowledge and imagination of the Earth, by adjoining various important places with the parallel and perpendicular line with reference to equator. Though these lines are different from the present lines of latitude and longitude and shape of the Earth was also not believed like a ball. But present form was developed on the concept of Ptolemy. Basic latitude i.e. 0° latitude is equator line. Parallel lines with reference to equator, drawn in Northern Hemisphere and Southern Hemisphere are regarded as + and – latitude respectively. Their measurement is based on the angle formed with equator line at the centre of the Earth. Likewise basic longitude i.e. 0° longitude is perpendicular line on equator adjoining North Pole and South Pole through London. Longitude is measured on the basis of angle formed from any place with this basic longitude at the centre of the Earth and they are classified as eastern and western longitude up to 180° on either side. Any place on the Earth may be located on this basis.

For example, latitude and longitude of Gwalior is 26.14° north and 78.10° east respectively. It means that there is a northern angle of 26.14° between equator and Gwalior at the centre of the Earth. Likewise Gwalior is situated at an eastern angle of 78.10° from the longitude passing from London. This angle is also formed at the centre of the Earth.

Ecliptic

If we presume the sky as a big screen with stars printed on it and mark the daily position of the Sun on this screen with reference to the star for a year. Thereafter at the end of the year we will see a circular shape passing through all signs and constellations. This is orbit of the Sun and known as 'Ecliptic'. In the same way, if we continue to mark the position of the Moon among stars for a month then at the end of the month we will see another circular shape passing through all signs and constellations. This is orbit of the Moon. These two orbits are distinctive and they intersect each other at two different points due to an angle of about 5° among them. These two points are Rahu and Ketu. More details in this regard are also given in the chapter of "Actual Rahu Ketu".

12

RAHU AND KETU

What conveyed

As per belief prevailed in the Primitive age, Rahu and Ketu demons were considered behind lunar and solar eclipses respectively. But now-a-days it is being mentioned in astrological books that Rahu and Ketu also known as Node and Antinode are those two points where ecliptic and orbit of the Moon intersect each other. Daily retrograde motion of Rahu and Ketu is fixed as 3' 11". What were the reasons and calculation behind fixing the retrograde motion of Rahu and Ketu is now not known like all other astrological principles.

What observed

Now-a-days in astrological calculations neither primitive nor scientific theory is being followed. Because now it is not supported that Rahu and Ketu demons are behind these eclipses, instead of this it is mentioned that Rahu and Ketu are those two points where ecliptic of the Sun and Moon intersect each other. But neither a very important factual position that solar and lunar eclipse occurred due to transit of Moon in between the Sun and Earth; and transit of Earth in between the Sun and Moon respectively, nor the fact that these full eclipses created only when ecliptic is crossed by the Moon, has been used and taken into consideration at all. Whereas retrograde motion of Rahu and Ketu as decided in the Primitive age is still maintained at 3' 11" and followed.

What discovered

As has already been explained that due to wrong concept of the Universe it was believed that solar and lunar eclipses occurred due to Ketu and Rahu respectively. The imaginary shape of the Universe, as believed in the Primitive age has already been shown in picture-1. Where Moon was considered to be situated above the Sun. Hence there was no reason to believe that solar eclipse may ever be occurred due to transit of Moon between the stationary Earth and Sun. But sages perhaps observed after regular gazing of the sky and calculation of interval between various eclipses that cycle of eclipses repeated after 223 lunar months. Because presence of Rahu/Ketu demons was considered behind every eclipse hence this belief get recognition that after 223 lunar months these demons may returned to their original position after completing their retrograde rotation. In those days lunar year and transit of Moon was prominently observed and calculation of *tithi* etc. was based on transit of the Moon through various constellations. Hence retrograde motion of the Rahu Ketu was calculated on the basis of recurrence of the various eclipses. If we calculate the retrograde motion of Rahu Ketu on the basis of recurrence of eclipse with reference to the Moon then we can see the basis of calculation adopted by sages. Though today general public may not know it but it is a fact that eclipses recurred in the same order after 18 years 11-12 days i.e. after 6585-6586 days. On the basis of latest system of calculation we know that average duration of one lunar month is 29 days 12 hours 44 min. 2.9 sec. i.e. 29.53055 days. Whereas average duration of lunar month as 1774 *ghati* 44 *pal* 48 *vipal* i.e. 29 days 13 hours 52 min 19.2 sec was calculated by our sages with the help of primitive instruments. In other words Moon took 29.578 days to cover 30 *tithi*. It can be realised after comparing these two results that the calculation of sages was also not too much wrong. In this way Moon took 354.941 days in 12 lunar months on the basis of 29.578 days of a lunar month. Because sufficient importance was given to the Moon in the Primitive age, hence it was believed that Rahu Ketu came to their original position with reference to the Moon after retrograding 354.941° and in turn eclipses recurred. There are 6690 *tithi* in 223 lunar months of 30 *tithi* each. If we divide 354.941° by 6690 *tithi* then we can get retrograde motion of 191" per *tithi*. In this way basis of formulating the retrograde motion of Rahu Ketu as 3' 11" was devised in the Primitive age. On this basis it can be presumed that the calculation of retrograde motion of Rahu Ketu was correct with reference to the instantaneous information, which was available in the Primitive age. This fact is quite important that retrograde motion was decided for a *tithi* in the Primitive age and not for a day of 24 hours as is being followed now-a-days.

> **TIP** : If you are amateur reader or find any difficulty at any time in understanding succeeding paragraphs then you may jump to Conclusion and try to understand this left out portion in next reading.

Occurrence of eclipse is a very important astronomical event. Because various scientific information related to motion, distance, relative mutual motion etc. are collected during an eclipse and these information get analysed to correctly ascertain the position of these planets. But the planetary position during an eclipse is not being used in astrology at all. Now-a-days it is being stated on the basis of scientific information against the primitive belief that those two points where ecliptic and orbit of the Moon intersect each other due to inclination of the orbit by 5° among them, are actually Rahu and Ketu. But actually this statement is unnecessarily being made to show that astrology is supported by science. Whereas this fact in not being followed in the astrology. Hence this statement is not correct and misleading. Why there is an eclipse when Rahu/ Ketu is up to 14° away from the Sun/Moon. This point will be discussed later on. But at present we will confine our discussion only on full eclipse and summarily understand how these two points are formed in ecliptic to unable us to analyse the retrograde motion and position of Rahu Ketu. Ecliptic and other related information may be seen in picture-16. In this

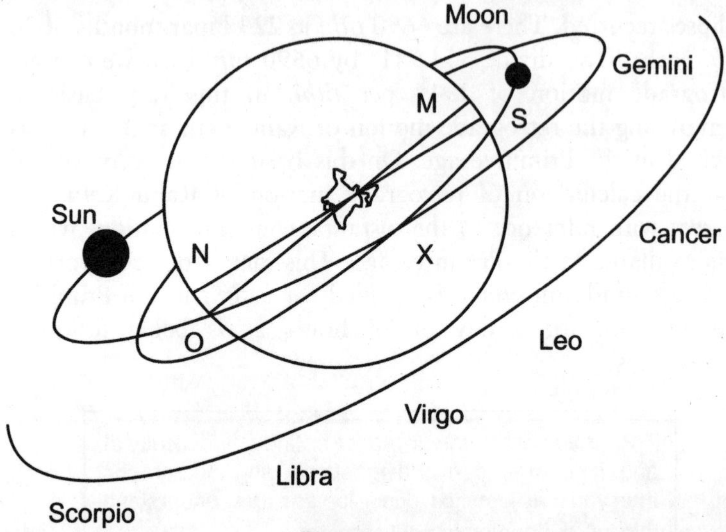

Picture – 16
Formation of Rahu and Ketu

picture smaller monthly (visual) orbit of the Moon and thereafter larger yearly orbit of the Sun is shown around Earth. In the outer most half circle position of six signs of winter solstice is shown. Moving planets are visible in front of these signs. If we draw perpendicular lines of visual orbits i.e. ecliptic and orbit of the Moon on Earth then we can see that there is an angle of about 5° between these two lines. These lines are shown as S N and M O respectively. Moon will appear to intersect the ecliptic at point X. Thus celestial location of this visual intersection point of these two orbits is Rahu / Ketu. As per picture this intersection point is created by the Moon while moving in his orbit and when moving towards southern direction with reference to the ecliptic. Thus this visual point of intersection which is visible at the backdrop of the sign is point of formation of Ketu. In the same way, Moon will again intersect the ecliptic when it will transit behind the Earth, while moving towards northern direction with reference to the ecliptic. Thus that visual point of intersection will be point of formation of Rahu as seen at the backdrop of a sign. In this way it can be seen and understood that there are twelve pairs of crossing of the ecliptic by the Moon during a year. Thus Rahu Ketu are actually formed only twelve times during a year.

On one hand it is being mentioned in the astrological books that intersection points of ecliptic and orbit of the Moon are actually the point of Rahu and Ketu and on the other hand retrograde motion of Rahu and Ketu has been

Table – 1

Full and annular solar eclipse during 1981 to 1999

S. No.	Dark night	Date	Degrees of			
			Sun/Mn	Rahu	Ketu	Diff.
1.	–	31-07-81	104	97	–	– 7
2.	23	11-06-83	56	61	–	5
3.	6	04-12-83	228	–	232	4
4.	6	30-05-84	46	43	–	– 3
5.	6	22-11-84	216	–	213	– 3
6.	12	12-11-85	206	–	194	– 12
7.	11	03-10-86	166	–	177	11
8.	6	29-03-87	345	348	–	3
9.	6	23-09-87	156	–	159	3
10.	6	18-03-88	334	329	–	– 5
11.	6	11-09-88	145	–	140	– 5
12.	17	27-01-90	283	293	–	10
13.	6	22-07-90	95	–	104	9
14.	6	16-01-91	271	274	–	3
15.	6	11-07-91	84	–	85	1
16.	6	05-01-92	260	256	–	– 4
17.	6	30-06-92	74	–	66	– 8
18.	23	10-05-94	26	–	30	4
19.	6	03-11-94	197	201	–	4
20.	6	29-04-95	15	–	12	– 3
21.	6	24-10-95	186	182	–	– 4
22.	17	09-03-97	324	–	335	11
23.	12	26-02-98	313	–	317	4
24.	6	22-08-98	125	127	–	2
25.	6	16-02-99	303	–	298	– 5
26.	6	11-08-99	114	110	–	– 4

retained. To analyse this position, all full eclipses occurred during the year 1981 to 1998 i.e. for 18 years, which is the duration of recurrence of eclipses, have been incorporated in table-1 and table-2 for solar and lunar eclipses respectively. Full eclipse that reoccurred after 6585 days from the full eclipse occurred on the date shown at s.no. 1 of both tables is incorporated as a last entry in both tables. As subsequent eclipses will be repeated in the same order after an interval of 223 full-moon/dark-night, though size of eclipse may slightly change. Because all these full eclipses occurred with reference to the Earth hence it may be possible that some eclipses could be observed from India. Degree of the Sun and Moon is same at the time of full solar eclipse hence degree of both planets is shown as a single entry in table-1. Whereas degree of the Sun is

Table – 2

Full lunar eclipse during 18 years (Sun + 180)

S. No.	Full Moon	Date	Degrees of Moon	Rahu	Ketu	Diff.
1.	–	10-01-82	85	89	–	4
2.	6	06-07-82	260	–	259	– 1
3.	6	30-12-82	74	70	–	– 4
4.	29	05-05-85	200	–	205	5
5.	6	28-10-85	11	15	–	4
6.	6	24-04-86	190	–	186	– 4
7.	6	18-10-86	0	356	–	– 4
8.	29	20-02-89	128	–	131	3
9.	6	17-08-89	300	302	–	2
10.	6	10-02-90	116	–	112	– 4
11.	35	10-12-92	53	–	58	5
12.	6	04-06-93	229	228	–	– 1
13.	6	29-11-93	43	–	39	– 4
14.	29	04-04-96	170	173	–	3
15.	6	27-09-96	340	–	344	4
16.	12	17-09-97	330	–	325	– 5
17.	29	21-01-00	96	100	–	4

always 180° ahead of the degree of the Moon during a full lunar eclipse hence degree of the Sun is not incorporated in table-2. Number of difference of dark-night and full-moon in-between two full solar or lunar eclipses respectively is also incorporated under column 2 of the tables. Grand total of the number of dark-night / full-moon in both tables is 223.

In the Primitive age and thereafter other mathematician developed the predictive principles on the basis of fixed retrograde motion of Rahu and Ketu who were active behind lunar and solar eclipse respectively. This primitive concept is still being followed with a little modification that if the position of Rahu or Ketu is equal or within the range of 14° from Moon and Sun then there will be solar eclipse. Likewise when the Sun and Moon are 180° apart from each other and the position of Rahu and Ketu is equal or within the range of 14° from the Moon then there will be lunar eclipse. This fact may also be seen from the both tables.

The position of Rahu or Ketu at the time of a full eclipse is also shown in table-1 and 2. From the detail shown at s.no. 1 of table-1 it can be observed that solar eclipse was not due to Ketu as believed in the Primitive age but it was due to Rahu who was at 97° and Sun was at 104°. Thus there was full solar eclipse due to difference of –7° in-between them. Likewise other solar eclipse occurred due to Rahu may also be seen in table-1. Similarly from the detail shown at s.no. 4 of table-2 it can be observed that lunar eclipse was not due to Rahu as believed in the Primitive age but it was due to Ketu who was at 205° and Moon was at 200°. Thus there was full lunar eclipse due to difference of 5° in between them. Likewise other lunar eclipse occurred due to Ketu may also be seen. From the above explanation it will be clear that belief of Primitive age about the presence of Rahu and Ketu demons for lunar and solar eclipses respectively was totally wrong. Now we will analyse these data during solar and lunar eclipse with a scientific angle.

Solar eclipse – Scientifically, solar eclipse occurred only when Moon transit in between the Sun and Earth. Thus Sun is not visible due to Moon. Position of partial and other solar eclipse is slightly different but for full solar eclipse it is not only essential that degree of Sun and Moon must be same but it is also essential that ecliptic and orbit of the Moon must also intersect at the same point with reference to the location on the Earth from where this full solar eclipse is visible (detailed description will be given in next section). Rahu or Ketu will not be formed, so long Moon transit in its orbit, which is inclined by 5° and remain at a distant position from the ecliptic. But on dark-night when Moon is in such a position that it is not only in his own orbit but it also came over the Sun and cross the ecliptic then only required condition for full solar eclipse created. Thus Sun and Moon came in a line with reference to a location on the Earth and full solar eclipse may be seen. Undoubtedly and scientifically position of Rahu or Ketu must be the position of Moon and Sun, only then full solar eclipse may occur. If there is a slight difference between the position of Rahu or Ketu i.e. point of visual intersection of orbits and Sun/Moon then there is no question of full solar eclipse, because then location on the Earth will not be on the line of centre of Sun and Moon. In this way on other dark-nights when there is no solar eclipse and inclination of Moon with reference to the ecliptic happens to be zero degree then the position of Moon matches with the ecliptic but degree-sign position of Moon will altogether be different from the degree-sign position of the Sun. On this day when degree-sign of Sun and Moon happens to be the same then there is difference of more than one degree between these two planets with reference to the southern horizon due to inclination of the orbits by 5°. Hence there is no solar eclipse.

Lunar eclipse – Scientifically, lunar eclipse occurred only when the Earth transits in between the Sun and Moon. Thus Moon is not visible due to shadow of the Earth. Position of partial and other lunar eclipse is also slightly different. For full lunar eclipse it is not only essential that degree of Sun and Moon must be 180° apart but it is also essential that orbits of the Sun and Moon must also intersect at the location of Moon. Rahu and Ketu will not be formed, so long Moon transit in its orbit, which is inclined by 5° and remain at a distant position from the ecliptic. But in the night of full-moon when Moon is in such a position that it is not only in his own orbit but it also came on the ecliptic then only required condition for full lunar eclipse created. Thus the Sun and Moon came in a line with reference to Earth but in opposite direction and full lunar eclipse may be seen due to shadow of the Earth on the Moon. Undoubtedly and scientifically position of Rahu or Ketu must be the position of Moon, only then full lunar eclipse may occur. If there is a slight difference between the position of Rahu or Ketu i.e. point of intersection of orbits and Moon then there is no question of full lunar eclipse, because then centre of Earth will not be on the line of centre of Sun and Moon. In this way on the other nights of full-moon when there is no lunar eclipse and inclination of Moon with reference to the ecliptic happens to be zero degree then the position of Moon matches with the ecliptic, but degree-sign position of the Moon will not be exactly 180° apart from the degree-sign position of the Sun.

From the above explanation it would have been quite clear that most important factor for full solar eclipse is that degree of Rahu or Ketu must be equal to the degree of Sun and Moon; likewise for full lunar eclipse, not only degree of Rahu or Ketu must be equal to the degree of Moon but position of Sun must also be exactly 180° away from the Moon. Thus for both types of full eclipses the position of Rahu or Ketu will only match when Moon will cross the ecliptic. If Moon is slightest away from the ecliptic then though there is a possibility of other type of eclipse but there is no possibility of full solar or lunar eclipses. If we review the table-1 and 2 with this angle then it can be clearly observed that Rahu or Ketu who was responsible for a particular full eclipse was away from the Sun or Moon by 11° to –12°, which is shown in the column of difference. When the diameter of these planets are less than one degree then if the position of Rahu or Ketu, which was formed during crossing of the ecliptic by the Moon, was slightly away from the Sun then there is no possibility of full eclipse. Now on the basis of full eclipse, which occurred on the dates given in the table-1 and 2, we can easily draw a conclusion that degree-sign position of Rahu Ketu and their believed retrograde motion is totally wrong.

Full lunar and solar eclipse occurred in the night of full-moon and dark-night falling on 28-10-1985 and 12-11-1985 is shown in table-2 and table-1 respectively. The interval between these two full eclipses was only 15 days. Similarly, another full solar and lunar eclipse occurred on 3-10-1986 and 18-10-1986 respectively, were within 14 days. Necessary details of Sun, Moon, Rahu and Ketu are again being shown. The motion of Rahu and Ketu is only being shown in degree to avoid further complication in the subject matter.

Moon was at 11° at the time of full lunar eclipse in the night of 1985, whereas Rahu was four degree away from this point and shown at 15°. It is essential for full lunar eclipse that Rahu must be at 11°. Likewise Sun was at 206° at the time of full solar eclipse and for full eclipse; Ketu must be at 206° instead of 194°, which was being shown in the almanac. Accordingly Rahu must be at 26° i.e. 180° away from Ketu. In this way Rahu moved from 11° to 26° and hence shifted by direct 15° within 15 days with a direct motion of one degree per day. Whereas, as per present astrological principles, Rahu may be shifted retrogradely only by 47' 45" during this period with a fixed motion of 3' 11" and thus may moved to 14° from 15°. Likewise Ketu may also moved to 194° from 195° and full eclipse is not possible in both these conditions. Similarly, Sun and Moon were at 166° at the time of full solar eclipse, in the example of year 1986 and Ketu was 11° away from this point and shown at 177° in the almanac. It is essential for full solar eclipse that crossing point of orbit of the Sun and Moon must be at 166°. Likewise, at the time of full lunar eclipse in the night of full-moon, when Moon was at zero degree of Aries sign then Rahu must also be at zero degree of Aries sign instead of 356°. Accordingly, Ketu must be at 180°. In this way Ketu has shifted from 166° to 180° and hence shifted by direct 14° within 14 days with a direct motion of one degree per day.

Full lunar and solar eclipse (Year 1985)

Date	Degree of		Wrong deg.		Correct deg.	
	Moon	Sun	Rahu	Ketu	Rahu	Ketu
28-10	11	191	15	–	11	–
12-11	206	206	–	194	–	206

Full solar and lunar eclipse (Year 1986)

Date	Degree of		Wrong deg.		Correct deg.	
	Moon	Sun	Rahu	Ketu	Rahu	Ketu
03-10	166	166	–	177	–	166
18-10	0	180	356	–	0	–

From the above analysis you may think that Rahu Ketu may take complete round of zodiac within one year instead of 18 years with this direct fast speed, whereas eclipse reoccurred roughly after 18 years. From the above examples of continuous eclipse, it appears that direct motion of Rahu and Ketu may be 59' per day. But actually the motion of Rahu and Ketu is not direct. Otherwise on every dark-night, there would be difference of hardly one degree between the position of Rahu/Ketu, which formed at the crossing point of ecliptic and the position of the Sun, which also transit with an average motion of 59'/ day. Thus there would be a solar eclipse on every dark-night. Because it is believed that if there is a difference of less than about 14°, between the position of the Sun and Rahu/Ketu, then there must be a solar eclipse (this point will be discussed later on). But it is not so. Hence it is clear that motion of Rahu and Ketu is not direct. Such confusion is created only because it is believed that alternate formation of Rahu and Ketu are moving with a fixed retrograde motion with a fixed distance of 180° between them. Full solar eclipse occurred on 31-7-1981, when Sun and Moon were at 104° 21' and thereafter, during next cycle of eclipse after 6585 days, full solar eclipse occurred on 11-8-1999 when Sun and Moon were at 114° 34'. Thus during this period Rahu Ketu moved retrogradely by 349° 47' (104-21 + 360 – 114-34). If we divide 349° 47' by 6585 days then we may get 3' 11.225" as apparent average retrograde motion of Rahu Ketu. Which is very near to the retrograde motion being followed at present. But this average retrograde motion cannot be accepted because neither Rahu and Ketu remain at a fixed distance of 180° between them as they are formed alternately and may be formed at a distance of 195°, which is evident from the two continuous eclipses nor their calculated position with this average retrograde motion matches with the position of full eclipses. You may have understand by now that Rahu or Ketu is formed as and when Moon crosses the ecliptic; and thereafter Moon continuously transit to remain forward or in backward situation with reference to the Sun and Earth in the Universe. Thus Moon has to cover different distances for reaching to Ketu from Rahu or *vice versa* and these distances also varied continuously. With this explanation it will now be clear that actual and correct position of Rahu Ketu cannot be ascertained by calculating their position on the basis of average apparent retrograde motion, but their correct and precise position can easily be ascertained at the time of full eclipse.

If we analyse the details of two ordinary solar eclipses and one full lunar eclipse in-between, occurred on 21-6-1982, 6-7-1982 and 20-7-1982 then it can be understood that after an ordinary solar eclipse occurred on the day of dark-night on 21-6-1982 due to Rahu; Moon crossed the ecliptic from a distance of little less than 14° and full lunar eclipse occurred on 6-7-1982 due to Ketu in the night of full-moon eclipses may be seen in table-1 and 2 to understand as to how Rahu and Ketu interchanges their position. Then after the ordinary

Continuous three eclipse

S.	Date	Degree of		Wrong deg.		Correct deg.	
No.		Sun	Moon	Rahu	Ketu	Rahu	Ketu
1.	21-06-1982					Sun eclipse	
		66	66	80	–	–	–
2.	06-07-1982		(After 15 days)			Full eclipse-Moon	
		80	260	79	259	80	260
3.	20-07-1982		(After 15 days)			Sun eclipse	
		94	94	79	–	–	–

solar eclipse on the day of dark-night on 20-7-1982, Moon crossed the ecliptic before 14°. Hence there was ordinary solar eclipse due to the difference of less than one degree altitude between them from the southern horizon, despite the same degree of both Sun and Moon as shown at s.no. 1 of the table. Whereas after 15 days there was full lunar eclipse and again after 15 days another ordinary solar eclipse occurred. Correct position of Rahu is not shown on the dates of ordinary solar eclipses as the position of Rahu, which formed after the crossing of the ecliptic by the Moon, was at a distance of up to 14° from the same celestial position of the Sun and Moon.

There is an angle of 5.14° between the ecliptic and orbit of the Moon. Hence Moon may swing by 5.14° south and north with reference to ecliptic during rotation around the Earth. Thus there may be a net difference of 10.28° in the altitude of the Moon from southern horizon. After any full solar eclipse due to Rahu i.e. when there is no difference in the altitude of the Sun and Moon; there is an increase in the altitude of the Moon by 5.14° till next three dark-nights. Thereafter the altitude of Moon decreases by 5.14° till next three dark-nights. In this way after forming Ketu, the altitude of the Moon is further reduced by 5.14° in next three dark-nights and then altitude again increases by 5.14° till next three dark-nights. Thus Moon may be in original position to form Rahu by crossing the ecliptic. In this way original position i.e. when there is no difference in the altitude of the Sun and Moon, may reappear after forming Rahu and Ketu 12 times in 12 dark-night / full-moon nights of a lunar year and in this situation an eclipse may occur. Consult table-1 and see that full solar eclipse occurred on 12-11-1985 after 12 dark-nights. Some time this whole process may be completed and solar eclipse may occur only after 11 dark-nights due to change in rotational motion of the Earth, as may be seen from table-1 that solar eclipse occurred on 3-10-1986 after 11 dark-nights. If a solar eclipse reappear after 11 or 12 dark-nights then these both eclipse would either be only due to Rahu or only due to Ketu. As has been explained that full rotation of 5.14° inclination is completed in 11 or 12 dark-nights. Likewise if a solar/lunar eclipse occurred due to Rahu / Ketu and it reoccur only after 17-18 / 6 dark-nights / full-moon nights then it would be in reverse order of Ketu / Rahu. Because during this period Moon would have completed either its one and half or half rotation of swing of its inclined orbit. This position may clearly be understood from table-1. Full solar eclipse occurred on 23rd dark-night after the full eclipse of 31-7-1981. This eclipse occurred due to Rahu because of 11+12 dark-nights. After this next solar eclipse occurred after 6 dark-nights. By then Moon has completed its half swing of 5.14°. Hence this eclipse occurred due to Ketu because of interval of 6 dark-nights. Likewise position of other eclipses may be seen in table-1 and table-2 to understand as to how Rahu and Ketu interchanges their position.

From the above description it would have been quite clear that Rahu and Ketu are only created, as and when Moon crosses ecliptic. If this is created on the day of dark-night or night of full-moon then there will be solar or lunar eclipse respectively, because the difference of angle of altitude between the Sun and Moon from the southern horizon will be less than one degree and both are at the same degree-sign or equally inclined in opposite direction due to opposite degree-sign with reference to equator respectively. Likewise there will be no eclipse if Rahu Ketu are created before or after two days from the day of dark-night or full-moon, because then on the day of dark-night or full-moon, despite the same or just opposite position of the Sun and Moon, the difference of angle of altitude from southern horizon or equator will be more than one degree respectively.

Motion – If we analyse the motion of Rahu or Ketu on the basis of full eclipses occurred due to Rahu or Ketu as detailed in table-1 and 2 then position will be quite clear. Full solar and lunar eclipses occurred due to Rahu or Ketu, have been segregated in table-3 and 4 respectively along with interval between two eclipses, difference of degree during this period on the basis of correct position of Rahu or Ketu, average motion thereof. From this table it is evident that average retrograde motion of Rahu between two eclipses varies between

1' 41" and 7'. Average retrograde motion of Rahu was 1' 41" for next 354 days from 11-6-1983. Whereas average retrograde motion of Rahu was more than 4' and 6' till adjoining other eclipses. Thus it is clear that some time during the period of 354 days daily 'direct' motion of Rahu must have been 3', otherwise it is not possible to get average retrograde motion of 1' 41". Likewise average motion of Ketu between two eclipses varies between 'direct' motion of 1' 53" to retrograde motion of 8' 53". Average motion of Ketu during the year 1985 and 1997 was direct. Average retrograde motion of Ketu was about 6' till adjoining other eclipses. Whereas average direct motion of Ketu was about 1' 53" during these years. Thus it is

Table – 3

Full eclipse due to Rahu during year 1981 to 1999

Eclipse	Days	Date	Degree of			Retro mot.	
			Sun	Moon	Rahu	diff.	Mi/Se
S	–	31-07-81	104	104	104	–	–
M	163	10-01-82	265	85	85	19	7'00"
M	354	30-12-82	254	74	74	11	1'51"
S	163	11-06-83	56	56	56	18	6'37"
S	354	30-05-84	46	46	46	10	1'41"
M	516	28-10-85	191	11	11	35	4'04"
M	355	18-10-86	180	0	0	11	1'51"
S	162	29-03-87	345	345	345	15	5'33"
S	355	18-03-88	334	334	334	11	1'51"
M	517	17-08-89	120	300	300	34	3'56"
S	163	27-01-90	283	283	283	17	6'15"
S	354	16-01-91	271	271	271	12	2'02"
S	354	05-01-92	260	260	260	11	1'51"
M	516	04-06-93	49	229	229	31	3'36"
S	517	03-11-94	197	197	197	32	3'42"
S	355	24-10-95	186	186	186	11	1'51"
M	163	04-04-96	350	170	170	16	5'53"
S	870	22-08-98	125	125	125	45	3'06"
S	354	11-08-99	114	114	114	11	1'51"
Total - Days 6585,				Retro. diff./motion 350,			3–11

Table – 4

Full eclipse due to Ketu during year 1982 to 2000

Eclipse	Days	Date	Degree of			Retro	mot.
			Sun	Moon	Rahu	diff.	Mi/Se
M	–	06-07-82	80	260	260	–	–
S	516	04-12-83	228	228	228	32	3'43"
S	354	22-11-84	216	216	216	12	3'02"
M	164	05-05-85	20	200	200	16	5'51"
S	191	12-11-85	206	206	206	+6	+1'53"
M	163	24-04-86	10	190	190	16	5'53"
S	162	03-10-86	166	166	166	24	8'53"
S	355	23-09-87	156	156	156	10	1'41"
S	354	11-09-88	145	145	145	11	1'51"
M	162	20-02-89	308	128	128	17	6'17"
M	355	10-02-90	296	116	116	12	2'02"
S	162	22-07-90	95	95	95	21	7'46"
S	354	11-07-91	84	84	84	11	1'51"
S	355	30-06-92	74	74	74	10	1'41"
M	163	10-12-92	233	53	53	21	7'43"
M	354	29-11-93	223	43	43	10	1'41"
S	162	10-05-94	26	26	26	17	6'17"
S	354	29-04-95	15	15	15	11	1'51"
M	517	27-09-96	160	340	340	35	4'03"
S	163	09-03-97	324	324	324	16	5'53"
M	192	17-09-97	150	330	330	+6	+1'53"
S	162	26-02-98	313	313	313	17	6'17"
S	355	16-02-99	303	303	303	10	1'41"
M	516	16-07-00	90	270	270	33	3'50"
Total - Days 6585,				Retro. diff./motion 350,			3–11

clear that some time during these years 'direct' motion of Ketu must have been up to 7', to get average direct motion of 1' 53" or more. Similarly, during the year 1986 average retrograde motion of Ketu was 8' 53". Thus actual retrograde motion of Ketu may be up to 13' to get the average retrograde motion of 8' 53". Likewise if we analyse data of other eclipses contained in these two tables by expanding other average motion then it will be quite clear that direct or retrograde motion of Rahu and Ketu has no mutual impact on each other and instead their independent daily motion may reach up to 20' direct or retrograde, instead of so called fixed retrograde motion of 3' 11" per day, as they are not physical planets but they are actually created at the time of crossing of ecliptic by the Moon.

Angular difference – Because motion and distance (from Earth) of the Moon remains under continuous change hence obviously there is corresponding change in retrograde motion of Rahu and Ketu. Beside this position of the Sun and Earth with reference to the orbit of the Earth and Moon respectively are not in the centre but their positions are slightly off the centre. Hence angular difference between Rahu and Ketu is not remain fixed as 180° but continuously swinged within 15° and remain changing between 165° to 195°. Above fact can clearly be checked from the details of two full eclipses, which occurred within 15 days as shown earlier and details of all eclipses incorporated in table-5. Correct position of Rahu and Ketu at the time of full eclipse and their average motion from the date onward on the basis of table-3 and 4 is incorporated in table-5. Accordingly calculated position of Ketu or Rahu is also shown in the bracket on that date, on the basis of average motion from the previous date. For example according to table-5, full lunar eclipse occurred on 6-7-1982 due to Ketu and at that time Ketu was actually at 260°, i.e. its position must match with the position of Moon due to full lunar eclipse (see table-4) instead of 259° (19° of Sagittarius sign) as shown in table-2. Similarly at the time of next full solar eclipse, which occurred on 4-12-1983 after 516 days due to Ketu, it must be at 228°. In this way average retrograde motion of Ketu after 6-7-1982 was 3' 43" per day due to change of 32° during this period. Thus detail of retrograde motion as contained in table-5 is based on table-3 and 4. In this way, Ketu moved retrogradely to 249° with an average retrograde motion of 3' 43" till 30-12-1982 when next full lunar eclipse occurred after 177 days. Thus on this date angular difference of Ketu from Rahu was 175°. Daily motion of Rahu is indicated by R in the table-5 and other motion relates to Ketu. Likewise other details incorporated in table-5 may be understood and it can clearly observed on the basis of angular differences given in the last column that how difference of Ketu from Rahu may vary in between 165° to 195° on various dates and how two full eclipses occurred within 15 days in the year 1985 and 1986, when angular difference between Rahu and Ketu was 195° and 165° respectively. Further details in this regard have already been explained.

Some wise astrologers may come forward with the arguments that when situation of crossing of ecliptic by the Moon was not observed from India i.e. full eclipse was not visible from India hence above position of Rahu-Ketu cannot be recognised. In other words the full eclipse must be visible from the perpendicular position of the Sun / Moon from Earth. In this way it leads to a position that not only situation of crossing of ecliptic by the Moon must be visible but position of Sun / Moon must also be perpendicular (from India). In this circumstance this point needs attention as to whether formation of Rahu-Ketu will not be recognised at the time of lunar eclipse as per present practice of retrograde motion of Rahu-Ketu by 3' 11", if Moon is not in the sky of India and eclipse is visible only from USA at the time of crossing of ecliptic by the Moon. For example on 6-7-1982 and 29-11-1993 full lunar eclipse occurred at 1.00 PM and 12.00 noon (Indian standard time) respectively. These eclipses were visible only from USA because at the time of eclipse it was noon in India. At this time Ketu was considered at 259° and 39° respectively as per table-2. In this situation Ketu must not be considered anywhere near to Moon. But an argument may put forward that it makes no difference if crossing of ecliptic was not observed from India, because next eclipses were visible from India. Thus by this point of argument it is clear that not only crossing of eclintic by the Moon must be visible from concerning place but celestial position of these planets must also be perpendicular with reference to the Earth then only Rahu-Ketu may be recognised or in other words

Table – 5

Angular difference of Ketu from Rahu in degree

Eclipse	Days	Date	Degree of Rahu	Degree of Ketu	Retro. motion Mi./Se.		Diff. of Ketu - Rahu
M	–	10-01-82	85	–	R	1' 51"	–
M	177	06-07-82	(80)	260		3' 43"	180°
M	177	30-12-82	74	(249)	R	6' 37"	175°
S	163	11-06-83	56	(239)	R	1' 41"	183°
S	176	04-12-83	(51)	228		2' 02"	177°
S	178	30-05-84	46	(222)	R	4' 04"	176°
S	176	22-11-84	(34)	216		5' 51"	182°
M	164	05-05-85	(23)	200		+ 1' 53"	177°
M	176	28-10-85	11	(206)	R	1' 51"	195°
S	15	12-11-85	(11)	206		5' 53"	195°
M	163	24-04-86	(6)	190		8' 53"	184°
S	162	03-10-86	(1)	166		1' 41"	165°
M	15	18-10-86	0	(165)	R	5' 33"	165°
S	162	29-03-87	345	(161)	R	1' 51"	176°
S	178	23-09-87	(340)	156		1' 51"	176°
S	177	18-03-88	334	(151)	R	3' 56"	177°
S	177	11-09-88	(323)	145		6' 17"	182°
M	162	20-02-89	(312)	128		2' 02"	176°
M	178	17-08-89	300	(122)	R	6' 15"	182°
S	163	27-01-90	283	(117)	R	2' 02"	194°
M	14	10-02-90	(282)	116		7' 46"	194°
S	162	22-07-90	(277)	95		1' 51"	178°
S	178	16-01-91	271	(90)	R	1' 51"	179°
S	176	11-07-91	(265)	84		1' 41"	179°
S	178	05-01-92	260	(79)	R	3' 36"	179°
S	177	30-06-92	(250)	74		7' 43"	184°
M	163	10-12-92	(240)	53		1' 41"	173°
M	176	04-06-93	229	(48)	R	3' 42"	179°
M	178	29-11-93	(218)	43		6' 17"	185°
S	162	10-05-94	(208)	26		1' 51"	178°
S	177	03-11-94	197	(21)	R	1' 51"	184°

Table 5 (Contd.)

Eclipse	Days	Date	Degree of Rahu	Degree of Ketu	Retro. motion Mi./Se.	Diff. of Ketu - Rahu
S	177	29-04-95	(192)	15	4' 03"	183°
S	178	24-10-95	186	(3)	R 5' 53"	177°
M	163	04-04-96	170	(352)	R 3' 06"	182°
M	176	27-09-96	(161)	340	5' 53"	179°
S	163	09-03-97	(152)	324	+1' 53"	172°
M	192	17-09-97	(143)	330	6' 17"	187°
S	162	26-02-98	(134)	313	1' 41"	179°
S	177	22-08-98	125	(308)	R 1' 51"	183°
S	178	16-02-99	(120)	303	3' 50"	183°
S	176	11-08-99	114	(292)	–	178°
M	163	21-01-00	96	(281)	–	185°

position of eclipse must be perpendicular from the cities of India. Such argument may put forward just to oppose the explanation given in this chapter about the position, angular difference and motion of Rahu-Ketu but actually this argument will lead to much more complex situation and then we have to accept that there was no Rahu-Ketu in the horoscope of the persons born in north India. This point will be discussed later on in detail.

Conclusion

Fixed retrograde motion of these shadow planets was decided on the basis of recurrence of eclipse according to the then calculation of time and faith that these eclipses occurred due to Rahu and Ketu demons as believed in the Primitive age due to wrong information and concept about the Universe and solar system. But now on the basis of latest scientific knowledge it is unquestionable that there is an inclination of 5° between ecliptic and orbit of the Moon. Thus these two orbits intersect each other at two different points. Hence eclipse occurred due to transit of a planet in between other two planets. Though average apparent retrograde motion of Rahu Ketu for 6585 days is 3' 11.225". But the position of these shadow planets never agrees with the position of full eclipse during entire 18 years as shown in table-1 and 2, because their motion continuously swing between direct and retrograde. Thus it is quite clear that to ascertain the position of these shadow planets on the basis of fixed average retrograde motion is totally wrong. Because angular difference in their position of creation also continuously varies between 165° to 195° as is shown in table-5. Correct motion and position of these planets may perhaps be available in future in the almanac otherwise for ascertaining the correct position of Rahu Ketu on the basis of their average motion between two eclipses will comparatively be more justifiable. In fact actual location of Rahu or Ketu may only be correctly ascertained at the time of full eclipse. Because their motion may continuously vary and they may be formed within 7 days before or after the day of dark-night or full-moon.

Though there is no direct impact of eclipse in the predictive astrology. But their impact is considered in transit. Beside this impact of Rahu and Ketu is more prominent in predictive astrology and considered to be even more effective than planets. Now it is a matter of grave concern as to when the position of these planets are not correct in the horoscope then how a prediction may be correct. When average motion of any other planet is not being taken for ascertaining their position in any sign while drafting the horoscope then it is a gross mistake to calculate the position of these so-called important shadow planets on the basis of average retrograde motion. Their position in the horoscope may deviate by 15° forward or backward after calculating their actual position. When these planets may take up to 9 months for covering the distance of 15° with the average motion then what is the use of correct time of birth? Actually, positions of these planets are totally wrong in the horoscope of every individual and so-called existence of many fearful and baseless *yog* like *Kaal-sarp yog* based on these shadow planets are also wrong.

When the actual position of Rahu and Ketu varies by +15° to –15° and they are not even fixed at an angular difference of 180° then Krishnamurti system of prediction which is based on a small portion of a constellation known as sub-sub-lord, may also be termed as wrong and baseless.

From the above description it would be clear that the position of Rahu Ketu who have active part in eclipse, is wrong due to following reasons :–

1. Actual position of Rahu / Ketu at the time of full eclipse is not matching with the degree-sign position that is being shown in the almanac.
2. The daily motion of these planets is being continuously changing and at times it may be direct instead of fixed retrograde daily motion of 3' 11".
3. The angular difference between Rahu and Ketu is not fixed at 180°, but it continuously varies between 165° to 195°.
4. Rahu Ketu are actually formed at the time of crossing of ecliptic by the Moon as per present concept. Hence it is also wrong to move them with a fixed retrograde motion for demons as conceived in Primitive age.

Name and location of House

Combination of some houses of a horoscope is known by a specific name. Some of them are as follows :

House	Name
1	Ascendant house (*Lagn bhav*)
1, 4, 7,10	Central house (*Kendriya bhav*)
1, 5, 9	Triangle house (*Trikon bhav*)
6, 8, 12	*Trik* house

Location of house is fixed for every horoscope and they may be identified in any horoscope as follows :–

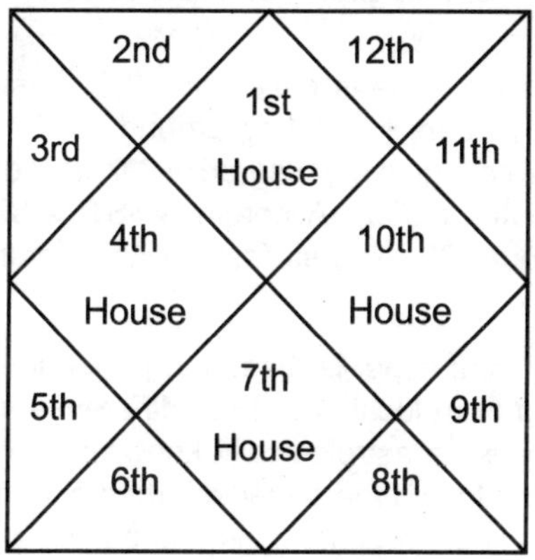

Picture – 17

Location of house

Standard time and local time

Standard time : Longitudinal line of 0° passes through Greenwich (a city of England). Hence standard time of England is known as GMT and this time is used as a standard time throughout the world for all sort of navigation etc. and other standard times are related with this time. Every country has its own standard time. Indian standard time is known as IST and it is 5 hour 30 minutes faster than GMT or in other words it is noon in the England when it would be 5-30 of evening in India.

Imaginary longitudinal lines are drawn between North Pole and South Pole of the Earth and every longitudinal line crosses the equator line. Thus longitudinal position is identified as Eastern and Western longitude with reference to 0° longitudinal line.

Indian Standard Time is based on 82.5° Eastern longitude. As Sun takes 24 hours in rotating around the Earth or rotating 360°. Thus in rotating every degree it takes four minutes (24 hours x 60 minutes / 360). Accordingly IST is 82.5 x 4 = 330 minutes or 5 hours 30 minutes faster with reference to GMT.

Local time : Local time is based on that longitudinal line, which is passing from local city. Time difference at the rate of 4 minutes per degree is astrologically known as 'Deshantar'. It is essential to know local time because when Sun happens to be at 82.5° longitudinal (meridian) line and it is actual noon at 82.5° (Near Benaras), but at the same time Sun will neither be at meridian line of Mumbai nor of Guwahati.

13

ASCENDANT AND VIVID PLANET

What conveyed

Position of ascendant may be calculated on the basis of degree-minute of a sign, which is rising from the East direction at the time of birth and vivid planets may be calculated in deg.-min. on the basis of celestial position of these planets.

What observed

Modern research in medical science regarding birth of test-tube babies is going to pose an intricacy matter for astrology. Since all hereditary factors are determined at the time of conception and cosmic effect of planets also immediately begin to influence the destiny, body and mind etc. of an individual. Hence, it is difficult to pinpoint the time of birth between conception in test-tube and actual delivery. Cosmic effect at the time of conception in test-tube can neither be avoided nor ignored scientifically. If conception in the test-tube may be taken as the birth time, which may be scientifically correct, then it leads to another trap in case of normal birth. Because, then in such cases too, time of birth must also be taken as time of conception in the womb, which is impossible to determine. As hereditary and cosmic effect also begin influencing since conception in the womb through mother. This has already been proved scientifically that embryo get effected with day-to-day activity of mother. In this way a question arises as to what would be the time of birth among conception in test-tube/womb, normal delivery, operated delivery, dissociation of navel string, weeping of child for calculating ascendant of an individual? Because there is no uniformity and astrologer support different timings.

Rough time was measured with the help of celestial position of the Sun, length of shadow, position of a constellation etc. since primitive age till widespread use of watches. Ascendant was calculated on the basis of position of Sun or system of *lankodaya*. Likewise, position and motion of a planet was measured on the basis of change in their celestial position. Position and transitory motion of planets are being calculated as per method contained in '*Grahlaghav*', since last 400-500 years.

What discovered

Vivid position of planets for drafting a horoscope was calculated since primitive age on the basis of their celestial position from respective place of birth. Presently correct time of birth is ascertained with the help of watch and correct time of sunrise, ascendant and position of planets are being calculated after correcting the effect of longitudinal change. But still it is not possible to calculate ascendant for the places like Alaska, Norway, Finland, Arctic circle etc., which are situated at higher latitude, because no planet is visible for several weeks, months in row. Beside this, at North Pole there is no other directions except southern direction and likewise there is no other directions except northern direction at South Pole.

> **TIP :** If you are amateur reader or find any difficulty at any time in understanding succeeding paragraphs then you may jump to Conclusion and try to understand this left out portion in next reading.

There is a difference of data in the table used for calculating Ascendant and position of planets as contained in almanacs and this difference is mainly due to incorporating the position of planets for a particular place and based on local time, due to using different principles, tables and due to rough calculation of celestial position of the planets. There are only two methods for ascertaining the celestial position of the planets for drafting horoscope.

First method is use of almanac, which is prepared after essential correction in the position of the planets, which is being calculated by following the methods contained in '*Surya-sidhant*' and '*Grahlaghav*' etc. Such almanacs have vast difference in the relevant basic data of planets and it is also mandatory to correct these data for different place of birth i.e. other than a particular place for which almanac is prepared. Nevertheless there is no guarantee of correctness of calculation of the almanac at all. In the same way there is vast difference in working out the ascendant for different latitude, longitude, by using an almanac, which was basically prepared for different latitude, longitude.

Now-a-days another method of ascertaining the vivid position of planets is based on the calculation performed by a computer. It is very difficult to ascertain the principles and method that were followed for preparation of a particular software for computer. However, I find that vivid position of planets as calculated by the computers is not based for a particular place of birth but their position is with reference to the centre of the Earth. Only time difference is calculated by the computer on the basis of longitude for a particular place of birth. In this way there is always a difference between the vivid position of planets and ascendant that may be calculated for a particular place and with reference to centre of the Earth. If we cast same horoscope with the help of different software then it can easily be ascertained that there is a difference in vivid position of planets and ascendant due to difference in basic principles followed while preparing various software. The importance of this difference may easily be ascertained, because such difference ultimately leads to substantial difference in other calculation linked with the analysis of a horoscope like calculation of *vinshottary* periodicity, *saptvargi* horoscope and subsequently in calculation of potential of a planet (*shadbal*) etc. and ultimately in prediction.

Now-a-days horoscopes prepared with the help of computer are being treated as correct. Hence it will be appropriate to analyse the discrepancies in the vivid position of planets and ascendant. For this, we have to understand the position of the Earth in the solar system and birth-place as shown in picture-18. Because all planets remain at north or south with reference to the equator while rotating around the Earth, hence Earth is shown in the picture in such a way so that North Pole P may coincide with the centre of the Earth and equator may remain at periphery, which is shown as A, B, C on the surface of the Earth. Moon, Sun, Mars, Jupiter and Saturn are shown as N, S, M, J, T along with degree-sign position of Cancer sign in zodiac. Position of Mercury and Venus is not included in the picture hence their position may be presumed nearby Sun. Celestial position of the planets as may be seen from the centre of the Earth is taken into calculation by the computer instead of position of planet as seen from a particular birth-place. For

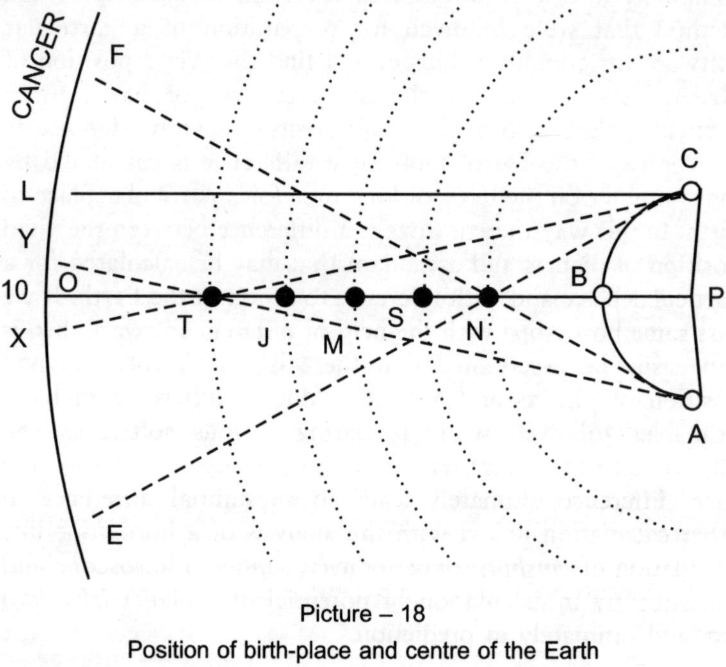

Picture – 18
Position of birth-place and centre of the Earth

example, position of Moon and Saturn is visible at 10° of Cancer sign from the centre of the Earth. Line adjoining the centre of the Earth and planets passes through point B on the surface of the Earth. Hence above planets may be seen at a point O of 10° of Cancer sign from point B like their view from the centre of the Earth. But if we see Moon and Saturn from point A, which is about 6328 km (radius of Earth) away from the centre of the Earth then they will be visible at different points F and Y instead of point O on Cancer sign. Likewise Moon and Saturn will be visible at E and X from point C on the Earth. Different lines show these visual situations in the picture. In the same way Sun and other planets may also be visible at distinctive degree of Cancer sign instead of point O. In the same way position of ascendant from birth place at C may actually be at point L of Cancer sign. Because sky below this point L of ascendant cannot be observed from point C. But if we calculate the position of ascendant with the help of computer or otherwise then it will be shown at 10° of Cancer sign, which is actually at eastern side from the centre of the Earth and ahead from point L. In this way calculated position of ascendant and vivid planets remain faulty.

Since primitive age it was believed that sign and constellations are situated just above the Moon and all astrological principles were based on this theory. If presently we follow the same theory and consider that distance of constellation and Moon is almost same then there will be difference of angle N, C, L or angle formed at point N like an angle C, N, B in ascendant. If we calculate the angle formed for Moon, Sun and Saturn then it will be equal to the angle formed at point N, S and T respectively and these angle may be measured with the help of following equation of trigonometry.

Angle C, N, B at Moon

= Arctangent (radius of Earth / distance of Moon) × 180 / 3.1428

= Arctangent (0.06328 / 3.57) × 57.2727

= 1.015°

Angle C, S, B at Sun in second

= (Arctangent (radius of Earth / distance of Sun) × 180 / 3.1428) × 3600

= (Arctangent (0.06328 / 1465) × 57.2727) × 3600

= 8.9"

Angle C, T, B at Saturn in second

= (Arctangent (radius of Earth / distance of Saturn) × 180 / 3.1428) × 3600

= (Arctangent (0.06328 / 11154) × 57.2727) × 3600

= 1.16"

In this way there is a difference in the celestial position of planets as seen from any birth-place situated on the surface of the Earth or from the centre of Earth. To avoid precise calculation we may left the difference for Saturn etc., which are only in seconds. But if we follow the principle of existence of constellations and signs just above the Moon (see picture-1), for calculating the ascendant as practised in the primitive age then there will be difference of one degree in ascendant like the difference of Moon and it may not only change whole analysis of a horoscope but difference of one degree for Moon may also change *saptvargi* horoscope, *vinshottary* periodicity, potential of planets (*shadbal*) etc. due to precise calculation.

Above difference of one degree for Moon may not be applicable in all horoscopes. If birth place is situated at point B of picture-18 then there will be no difference because in that situation Moon will be in tenth house of the horoscope. In this way there will be no difference in case of those planets who are situated in 4th and 10th house of the horoscope, because they are on the line drawn from the centre of the Earth and place of birth. But as the position of these planets shifted towards ascendant (point C of picture) from 10th house or 7th house (point A of picture) from 4th house then this difference will also increase as shown in earlier calculation and contrary this difference will decrease when these planets find their place towards 4th house from ascendant and 10th house from 7th house.

Conclusion

Now-a-days calculation of the computers for calculating vivid planets and ascendant is based on their relative visual position with reference to the centre of the Earth instead of actual visual position from place of birth. Whereas place of birth may be about 6328 km away from the centre of the Earth. In this way there may be difference of one degree in ascendant and vivid Moon which leads to other errors while calculating *vinshottary* periodicity, *saptvargi* horoscope, potential of planets etc. and ultimately so-called prediction.

House

There are 12 houses in a horoscope. Every house covered 30° of zodiac and the number of the sign shows sign of the house in ordinary birth horoscope.

Different aspect of life is ascertained from the different houses in the following manner :–

House	Aspect of life
1	Body, Mind, Beauty, Fame, Strength, Nature, Age, Knowledge, Wisdom
2	Voice, Wealth, Primary knowledge, Eye, Singing, Transaction
3	Bravery, Servant, Tour, Satisfaction, Brother
4	Comfort, Mother, House, Conveyance, Friends, Sympathy, Cheating
5	Learning, Son, Writing, Policy, Womb, Craft, Intelligence
6	Enemy, Disease, Defame, Grief, Theft, Leg, Injury
7	Spouse, Partner, Marriage, Tour, Business, Transfer, Death
8	Age, Worry, Mysterious knowledge, Poverty
9	Fortune, Intuition, Glory, Pilgrimage, Intuition, Holiness, Conveyance,
10	Father, Work, Business, Respect, Fame, Power
11	Income, Profit, Wealth, Elder brother, Uncle
12	Death, Expenditure, Enemy, Eye, Foreign tour

14

NAME OF WEEK DAYS

What conveyed

Everybody knows that order of the days of a week are from Sunday to Saturday. The English name of these days was decided after the name of their deities by the Greek civilisation on the basis of the concept derived by the sages of India. Subsequently other countries adopted these names.

What observed

What was the logic behind framing the order of the days is not known like other astrological principles. But the reasoning put forward in support of keeping the order of the days as practised today is mentioned as follows.

By quoting the reference of *Surya-Siddhanta* it is argued that in the astrology Saturn, Jupiter, Mars, Sun, Venus, Mercury and Moon were respectively regarded as nearest planets from the Earth. *Hora* whose duration is one hour is another type of measurement for measuring the time after *Ahoratra* and it is a synonymous of Hour. There are 24 hours or 24 *hora* in a day. Hence first *hora* was assigned to the Sun to form Sunday and after counting 25th order towards Venus from the Sun in the above order of the planets; first *hora* of the next day will be of Moon. Hence Monday was decided for the next day. After counting 25th order from the Moon, we may get Mars, hence Tuesday was decided for the next day. In the same way after counting 25th order we will get other days of the week in the existing order. On this argument it is stated that it was quite logical to decide the order of the days in a week.

What discovered

Above statement may appears to be quite correct and probably you may also be convinced with the above argument. But you have not paid your attention towards the fact that above order of the planets was neither accepted in the Primitive age nor it was ever approved by any sage till today nor it is accepted by any scientific theory in which Mercury and Venus may respectively be kept in between the Moon and Sun with reference to the Earth. In other words Mercury may be regarded as nearest planet from the Earth in comparison to Venus.

Correct position is that since Primitive age, accepted order of the orbit of the planets was Sun, Moon, Mercury, Venus, Mars, Jupiter and Saturn respectively with reference to the Earth as may be seen in picture-1, whereas according to the modern scientific knowledge we know that the correct order of the orbit of the planets is Moon, Venus, Mercury, Sun, Mars, Jupiter and Saturn. In this way according to the latest scientific information Venus and Mercury are respectively placed in between the Moon and Sun and not in the reverse order as Mercury and Venus, as is being stated in the order of the planets for deciding the name of days. But someone has skilfully tried to convince that mathematical calculation behind deciding the name and order of the days was correct by cunningly reversing the order of these two planets without in depth study. Only on the basis of above manipulation it is being stated in many astrological books that order of name of the days is correct.

Secondly, Indian sages and mathematicians always used *Ghati, Pal* and *Vipal* for all sort of time based calculation in astrology since Rising age. They have neither used hour for time based calculation nor *hora* is synonymous of hour used in English language. By this argument it appears that initially duration of a day was 24 hours and then its synonymous *hora* was used and then sages decided the order of the seven days of a week, by taking 24 hours (*hora*) in calculation after reversing the order of Venus and Mercury without any logic. Thus this explanation is totally foolish, because hour was used in India during the rule of Britain and there is no question of using 24 *hora* (hour) by our sages and reversing the order of two planets. In this way after digging you may realise that there is lot of adulteration in the astrology by infusing such irrelevant description.

Whereas correct position is that name of days was decided by Indian sages and during interaction of the Greek philosophers with the Indian civilisation they adopted this concept and renamed the days in English after the name of their gods. Subsequently these Greek names were adopted by the entire world during the rule of Britain.

Lunar month based on transitory position of the Moon was always important since Rising age for calculating period and four frequencies of known seven planets was almost equal to the lunar month of 27–28 ($7 \times 4 = 28$) days. Hence week of seven days was devised by allotting a day to every planet. If sages had known about the existence of Uranus and Neptune at that time then definitely we would have been using a week of nine days. By now you may be convinced that concept of Universe and order of the planets as known in the Rising age (see picture-1) had full impact on formulation of various astrological principles. Similarly decision regarding order of days of a week was also influenced with the same concept.

It was believed in the Rising age that there are seven planets above the Earth. Their orbit was in the order of Sun, Moon, Mercury, Venus, Mars, Jupiter and Saturn as shown in picture-1. Sun and Moon were specially regarded as illuminator planets, out of these seven planets. Because these two planets were responsible for light on the Earth. It was also believed that constellations are situated just above the Moon. In that age time was measured in *Ghati, Pal. Ahoratra* or full duration of day and night was comprised of 60 *ghati* and *hora* means 30 *ghati* i.e. half of this time. *Hora* horoscope is also prepared by dividing 30° of a sign in two parts by following the same analogy. Day started just after the rise of the Sun and it remain till setting of the Sun. At that time when Sun happens to be on equator then the duration of the day and night was equal to 30 *ghati*. Hence first of all Sunday was decided on behalf of the

Sun on the basis of 30 *ghati* of daytime and thereafter Monday was decided on behalf of another illuminator Moon who was lord of night and also responsible for the light in the night, on the basis of remaining 30 *ghati* of night. Thus *Var* is the synonymous of *hora*. Now after distributing 30 *ghati* at the rate of one *ghati* for every planet among the known order of the planets in the Primitive age i.e. Sun, Moon, Mercury, Venus, Mars, Jupiter and Saturn. First *ghati* was allotted to Mercury situated after the Moon, next *ghati* was allotted to next planet Venus and similarly next *ghati* was allotted to next planets in the order of Mars, Jupiter, Saturn, Sun etc. In this way all 30 *ghati* may be distributed by the time we get Venus. Hence Tuesday was decided in the name of next planet Mars. (You may be aware that similarly *Ist-ghati* is also being distributed among the planets and next planet is being nominated as *Horapati* while deriving *Kaal-horapati.*) By repeating the same process and after allotting next one *ghati* to next planet Jupiter and so on. All 30 *ghati* may again be distributed till Saturn and next planets are Sun and Moon, to whom days had already been decided, hence Wednesday was decided in the name of next planet Mercury. Now after repeating the same process of distributing 30 *ghati* from next Venus onward, all *ghati* may be distributed by Mars. Hence Thursday was decided in the name of next planet Jupiter. Now following same process of distributing 30 *ghati* from next Saturn onward, all *ghati* will be distributed by Sun. As days have already been decided for Sun as well as next Moon and Mercury, hence Friday was decided in the name of next planet Venus. Thus name of six days were decided for six planets out of seven planets. Hence seventh day as Saturday was allotted on behalf of Saturn. In this way order of seven days was decided for seven planets.

You are aware that it was believed in the Primitive age that Sun is the nearest planet from the Earth and other planets rotate over the stationary Earth in their orbit, which were situated one above the other (see picture-1). Whereas now we know that Moon is the nearest satellite from the Earth and it is not a planet. This fact is totally against the belief prevailed in the Primitive age. Distance of four other planets (Venus, Mercury,

Sun and Mars) from the Earth continuously varies. Hence order of these planets may also alter according to their distance from the Earth. Beside this four new planets have also been discovered so far. Hence if we critically review this whole situation about the decision of finalising the order of name of days on the basis of wrong order of the planets as believed in the Primitive age then it will be a matter of guess to anybody that how much unscientific and unrealistic it was. Hence we must ponder and review this whole issue with an unbiased deep thinking.

Conclusion

Prima facie there is no impact of the name of the days over the prediction. But this is extensively used for deriving auspicious time etc., *shadbal* of planets, calculation of *kaal-bal* and for deciding one effective significator out of many significator planets in almost all sort of prediction based on the Krishnamurti system of southern India. Because the order of the planets based on the distance of the planets at the time of birth is different for every individual horoscope. Hence name of the day calculated on the basis of actual order of the planets will definitely be different from the day followed on the date of birth. Thus prediction will also deviate in the same ratio of the mistake.

In this way as per basic principle and intention of our sages, effective name of the day may be calculated for every individual horoscope, based on the actual order of the planets according to their distance from the Earth at the time of birth for calculating auspicious time, *shadbal* etc. This will definitely be different from the known and practised day. It will be a matter of research as to which unit may be adopted out of hour and *ghati* for calculating *hora* used for deriving the name of the day.

It would be clear from the above explanation that there is following main mistake in deriving the name of the day, due to which prediction based on the principles of name of the day may be faulty and scientifically wrong :

1. Calculation of the day on the basis of fixed order and distance of the planets in misconceived structure of the Universe in which Sun was considered as a nearest planet from the Earth is faulty.

Top ten principles of prediction

There are certain following fundamental principles for deriving the forecast of a horoscope :

1. Planet placed in *trik* house or lord of *trik* house (6, 8, 12) give unfavourable result.
2. Auspicious (Jupiter, Venus, Moon, Mercury) and inauspicious (Sun, Mars, Saturn, Rahu, Ketu) planet give favourable and unfavourable result respectively.
3. Every planet gives favourable result if placed in 11th house.
4. Every planet gives favourable result if placed in centre (1, 4, 7, 10) or *trikon* (5, 9) house.
5. Result of a house depends on the planets placed in the house and aspect on the house.
6. Exalted planet, planet in own house, planet with friend, planet in the house of friend, planet with aspect from friend gives favourable result.
7. Debilitated planet, planet with enemy, planet in the house of enemy, planet with aspect from enemy gives unfavourable result.
8. In *navansh* horoscope any planet in own house, planet with friend, planet in the house of friend gives favourable result and planet with enemy, planet in the house of enemy give unfavourable result.
9. *Vinshottary* major-minor periodicity (*dasha-antardasha*) of auspicious planet give favourable result and periodicity of inauspicious planet give unfavourable result.
10. Auspicious and inauspicious position of a planet in transit (present movement) is assessed from their position in centre-*trikon* house and other house respectively from the Moon horoscope (horoscope drawn by placing the sign of Moon in ascendant and placing other planets according to their sign).

By analysing any horoscope with the help of above rules we get various opposite results. But astrologer predicts any result according to the status of the mind of an individual and psychologically these predictions appears to be correct.

15

FORECAST

Your forecast

Now I will try to forecast something about you. You may be desirous to know as to how I can forecast anything without analysing your horoscope. This is a mystery and later on I will disclose as to how I manage to read your horoscope. So first you go through your forecast, which may also be definitely forecasted by some astrologer and check the percentage of correctness.

You are interested in delicious food, music, impressive clothing and sight-seeing due to relation of auspicious planet with the ascendant. You have a long-life, generous, intelligent, able to understand the intention, sweet spoken but jealous, follower of tradition and religious. You may have an injury on head. You may feel shortage of money despite sufficiency. Your wife is gentle and son is obedient but may have occasional dispute and you may be angrier due to influence of inauspicious planets. After cooling down, with your ingenuity, you may be able to reconcile your dispute. You may feel that your words are not getting that much importance in the house, which in your opinion they must be. Occasionally, you may not be mentally satisfied with your wife and you may be attracted towards another woman. You may have suffered with a serious illness in your childhood. Generally, your health is good but you must be more careful about your health after middle age because you may suffer from a long lasting disease. There is an indication in your horoscope that there may at least be one interruption in your education. You may slowly rise in your life. You may have dispute with your brothers due to bad influence on Mars. You may not get equal affection from mother and father. You may have to move to another city due to your profession. You may occasionally get attracted towards mysterious subjects but left it at an early date. You may have immediate and excessive believe on your friends. But except one friend, who may unexpectedly enter in your life, you may not be able to get any important help. You may not get support up to your expectation from your in-laws due to influence of planets on seventh house. Other person may not be agreeing with your views due to his inability to judge the depth of your views. Your friends will not act upon according to your advice despite understanding your advice. You may desire and continuously try hard to have all modern accessories in your house during *vinshottary* major-minor periodicity of lord of tenth house and whenever it will be in favourable transit position. Due to your farsightedness you may be able to well furnish your house. You may not be able to get post and status according to your ability; hence occasionally you may be disappointed. You may be in trouble whenever there is a union between Sun and Rahu, hence be extra careful and avoid those things, which may catch fire. There is an indication in your horoscope about loss of money and theft hence be careful from any servant living in the house. Due to impact on seventh house, which is also related with stomach it appears that you may suffer from maggot in stomach and it may turn into some disease due to excessive use of wine or spicy food. Try to avoid it. You expose yourself as a warrior in front of others but occasionally due to lack of mental concentration you are internally very timid, hence worship your god regularly. There are fair chances of financial loss in litigation. You may be worried due to lack of support from your superiors in your working field. You may have experience of hurdles in achieving your target. Due to difference of opinion your son may disobey you. There may be financial loss due to deposing extra faith on some familiar person. Due to negative impact on 11th house there is little chance of getting benefit from gambling, contract and share business. After the age of 36 there are good chances of rise. After completing middle age you may like to have pilgrimage. Your eye-sight may be effected and you have to wear spectacles due to mixed position of impact on 2nd and 12th house.

Analysis

Most attractive and important aspect of the astrology lie in the so-called fact that after analysing a horoscope with the help of astrological principles one may be able to know before time about those incidents which are stored as his fate. As mysterious future store all favourable as well as unfavourable incidents, hence an astrologer having capacity to forecast about an incident naturally get importance and faith from general public. Astrologer, after accessing the mental status of an individual also try to do such fabricated forecast with the help of such relevant astrological principles which appears to be somewhat correct in a particular state of mind. In this way an individual may either be able to get instant relief, confirmation of fulfilling a desire or not but bare fact is that the feeling of happiness generated, in getting presumptive relief by diverting any mishappening with the help of so-called timely suggestions provided by the astrologer to get remedy from unwanted incident, worries or satisfaction provided in fulfilling the hope of bright future with all dreams came true, is definitely most useful and beneficial for improving and boosting the mental status of that individual. It is like that, a patient after suffering for a long period may intimately be informed by a good doctor, in his opinion, that he has a minor disease which will be cured very soon. Such heeling dialogue play an important role in improving the mental status as well as self-confidence of the patient due to his faith on the doctor and he internally feels that he is getting cured. On the same analogy an individual may not only get subdued by any forecast made by an astrologer but his mental status also modified accordingly because his inner conscious continuously enforce him to believe the correctness of any forecast due to his consecration. For example, while going through 'Your forecast' given in the starting of this chapter, you may have a feeling that mostly it is describing your past and future. Whereas, above forecast is actually based on your mental status and when any astrologer will tell same forecast along with many other fabricated dialogues mixed with your mental status by staring on your horoscope then you will definitely trapped in his wordiness and mentally convinced that astrology is correct.

Whatsoever scientific or otherwise knowledge we do have now-a-days was actually in the primitive form in Primitive age. For example, knowledge related to astrology, which was a part of religion in the Primitive age has since been developed and bifurcated in predictive astrology, astronomy, geography, geometry, psychology etc. In other words, astrology comprised of all these subjects and astrology treated as correct or scientific only on the basis of correctness of all these subjects. Whereas predictive astrology was actually and completely based on psychology, which was not known in the Primitive age. In the same way feeling of correctness of a forecast based on so-called various position of the planets in a horoscope was actually primitive stage of discovery of psychology and its applied use. But sages were actually not aware with the psychology and its impact hence any prediction, which appears to be psychologically correct was unknowingly categorised as correctness of astrology. Subsequently, logical principle behind psychology was discovered by Sigmund Freud by the end of 19th century. Now-a-days everybody knows about this subject. But they are unable to understand that knowledge of this subject is being continuously, unknowingly and cunningly used in astrology since long and all forecast appears to be correct because they are based on psychology. In other words we can say that psychology was practically used by our sages in astrological prediction before discovering it as a separate subject of modern science. As for half-filled glass with water, one may either say that it is half filled or may also say that it is half-empty. In the same way some achievements of the life can be presumed as success or also as unsuccess. Everything depends on the fact that how we visualise our achievements and present status of life or how astrologers conclude the study of our horoscope. If an astrologer predicts about our unsuccess then we are mentally forced to visualise our little success as unsuccess like half-empty glass or if he predicts about our success then we forget our unsuccess and visualise our little success like half-filled glass and our capability get effected according to mental status, which in turn exaggerate the result accordingly.

In the primitive age, it was really very laborious task to extract any prediction after performing difficult astrological calculation; hence any prediction which was extracted after lot of calculation may naturally be believed. But now-a-days it is a very easy job to extract a prediction with the help of computer. Because, now prediction can be concluded on the basis of various astrological principles and existing planetary combination in a horoscope. If you go through various forecast delivered by computer and take an advise from any astrologer about some contradictory prediction then they will say that prediction made by a computer may never be correct and only calculation part is correct, because correct prediction can only be concluded by an astrologer after comparative study of all planets. Now, a very natural and pertinent question may arise as to when a prediction is extracted by a computer on the basis of some astrological principles then how a different prediction may be concluded by an astrologer on the basis of same principles. Whereas, actually this is the swirling point which is used by an astrologer and accordingly mould a prediction favourably or unfavourably after accessing the mental status of an individual and try to influence his mind by psychologically controlling his mental status. Because an individual is quite ignorant about the astrological principles and after quoting some reference of astrological principle of his choice and by invisible mental pressure exerted by an astrologer, an individual is forced to believe on a particular prediction. In this way an individual is not only financially exploited by an astrologer but also trapped him easily in the zigzag of planetary transit for rest of his life. Whereas, such juggler is not possible by a computer, subject to condition that astrological software would not be prepared with a business consideration otherwise an individual may also be misled by favourable or unfavourable prediction. Although prediction concluded by computer may also appear to be correct due to psychological reasons and it has nothing to do with the hard fact of life.

Even if we believe on the correctness of astrological software or integrity of the astrologer even then there is no possibility about the correctness of a prediction. Because, error in the prediction will still remain because it is based on erroneous unscientific astrological principles which have already been highlighted in previous chapters. Beside this, the whole knowledge of predictive astrology relates to moulding of our mindset hence by referring any astrological principle in support of any past incident, we are forced to believe that whatever is being predicted will also be definitely correct. Now we will discuss in short as to how a desired prediction can be concluded from opposite results emerging on the basis of following fixed astrological principles.

1. If a planet is in a sign, which is owned by him then it will provide a favourable result. But there is another principle that it will provide an unfavourable result if a planet is in a sign having opposite element (For example Mars of Fiery element in Scorpio sign having Watery element).
2. If a planet is placed with his friend then it will provide favourable result. But contrary to this there is another principle that if another planet is placed in the same house then first planet will provide unfavourable result due to instant enmity with the second planet.
3. If a planet is in his own sign and having aspect from auspicious planets (Mercury, Venus, Jupiter and Moon) then it will provide favourable result. But another principle says that if any planet is placed in *trik* house (6, 8 and 12th house) then it will provide unfavourable result due to its aspect or position.
4. If a planet is in his own sign and having aspect from a friendly planet then it will provide favourable result.

But there is another principle, which emphasise that if a planet is placed with an enemy planet or having aspect from enemy planet then it will provide unfavourable result. Whereas generally every house has aspects from auspicious as well as inauspicious planets, because every planet exert its aspect on seven houses out of twelve houses.

5. If a planet is in his own sign then it will provide favourable result, but another principle says that if a planet is in *trik* house then it will provide unfavourable result.
6. If a planet is in his own sign and *vinshottary mahadasha* or *antardasha* (major or minor periodicity) of that planet is running then it will provide good result. But another principle says that if this planet is placed with some enemy planet or in *trik* house then it will provide bad result.
7. If a planet is in his own sign then it will provide good result but as per another principle if a planet is placed in the house of his enemy planet or in *trik* house in *navansh* horoscope then it will provide bad result.

Above all position may be repeated, in case of placement of a planet in central house (1, 4, 7 and 10th house), *trikon* house (5 and 9th house), *Mool-trikon* house, exalted sign, *navansh* and *mudda* (annual) horoscopes, and two just opposite results may be derived.

Beside this if a planet is placed in the house of his enemy planet then it will give bad result, but another principle says that if a planet is aspected by any auspicious planet or by a friendly planet or placed in central house, *trikon* house, exalted sign then it will give good result. In this way two opposite results may be derived (For example Moon is exalted in Taurus sign which is owned by his enemy Venus) and in such situation their is ample scope of exploitation and astrologers are free to conclude either favourable or unfavourable results.

8. *Vinshottary Mahadasha* or *antardasha* of lord of central house or lord of *trikon* house will give favourable result. On the other hand there is another principle that *vinshottary Mahadasha* or *antardasha* of inauspicious planet (Sun, Mars, Saturn, Rahu, Ketu) will give unfavourable result (*antardasha* of all planets remain effective under *mahadasha* of a planet).

Above all position may also be repeated and two just opposite results may be derived in case of placement of a planet in his own house, *mool-trikon* house and exalted sign.

9. Every 12th house is harmful for a particular house (As 12th house is harmful for first house, First house is harmful for second house, Second house for third house and so on). In this way fourth house is harmful for fifth house and ninth house is harmful for tenth house. These central and *trikon* houses are also considered as auspicious house. Thus both type of opposite results may be concluded.
10. Auspicious planet provide favourable result. But as an opposite principle, if this planet is lord of central house than it becomes inauspicious planet and provide unfavourable result.
11. Inauspicious planet provide unfavourable result. But as an opposite principle, if any inauspicious planet is lord of first house i.e. ascendant than it will provide favourable result.
12. Sun or Jupiter destroys the result of the house in which they are placed. But as per another principle every planet provide favourable result if they are placed in central, *trikon* and 11th house.
13. Aspect of Saturn on any house may destroy the result of that house. But as an opposite principle *vinshottary* periodicity of lord of central house, *trikon* house and 11th house is best.
14. If you study the result of placement of a planet in a house in any astrological book then you will find that

result of a planet is just opposite to the result of some another planet.

If we also include *chalit* horoscope, set and retrograde position of planets, various *yog* in above discussion then we come across many more opposite results. In short we can conclude that as we go on in deep in analysing the mutual relation of lord of sign, position of auspicious and inauspicious planets in horoscope, auspicious and inauspicious house (2, 3, 6, 8 and 12th house), aspect of planets, exalted and debilitated planets, set and retrograde planet, position of planets in other horoscopes like *chalit*, annual (*mudda*), *navansh* etc., *vinshottary* periodicity, planetary combination (*yog*), transitory position of planet (*gochar*) etc., we came across much more contradictory results. Because as per principle of prediction any particular result related to any house will materialise only when lord of house, planet accompanying the lord, planet placed in a house, aspect of other planets on lord and concerning house, position of planets in *saptvargi* horoscopes, *vinshottary* periodicity and transit of planet etc. are favourable. Such critical situation that every condition is either favourable or unfavourable in a horoscope will never arise. In this misleading situation, astrologer may predict any result just to impress and subdue an individual by following any principle of his choice.

Result of a planet in a sign and house

Most of the astrological books contain the predictive description that what will be the result of a planet placed in a sign and house in any horoscope. Generally for a reader it is first and initial introduction with the astrology. While keeping a horoscope in front of him and going through the various predictive results by comparing a particular combination he feels deeply emotional fluctuation and due to psychological effect on his sub-conscious mind he convince with the correctness of astrology even after finding a remote match with his present condition. Generally every reader never try to read a book keeping in mind the transitory planetary position and logically applying the result of a planet in twelve sign and house to whole population. Because his knowledge of astronomy is almost zero and his interest is also limited to predictive astrology, hence he may easily fall in a trap as he go on reading the astrology or so-called understanding it. Because all astrological books push him on the same track and he is confined only in predictive astrology, hence he remain totally ignorant about the hollowness of astrology. I myself find that so-called reputed astrologers are not aware with the traces of astronomy, which is mother of astrology. Whereas astrology without the knowledge of astronomy is just like paper flower.

Now we will study only two astrological principles in short and their result with reference to a planetary position in a sign keeping in mind the transit of planets. According to astrological principle, an individual may entrap in a case of murder if Saturn is in Scorpio sign and one may have more than one wife if Saturn is in Taurus sign. If we keep in mind the transit of Saturn then easily understand that Saturn take about 30 years in passing through all twelve signs and it remains in a sign for about two and half years. Now, one must apply his mind and think logically, practically, scientifically, socially etc. that is it possible that all new born during two and half years in whole country and in whole world may be murderer or all new born during two and half years in whole world may have more than one wife (except Muslim countries)? In this way if we include the position of other planets and analyse the time taken by them in passing through a sign on the basis of their transit in twelve signs then after equally distributing the constant birth rate it can easily be concluded that every 12th person may have same impact of the planet. Likewise ascendant of horoscope also passes through twelve signs in 24 hours and all new born during two hours do have same ascendant. If we analyse horoscopes in this light then it can easily be understood that every 12th person will have same ascendant and in this way result of a sign in a house will also be same. If we conduct a comparative study of the composition of the society then this fact proves to be totally incorrect. Because every person have a different future and different activity. One may say that result of a planet of horoscope may get effected by the result of *navansh* horoscope, *vinshottary* periodicity, transitory position of planets or annual (*mudda*) horoscope. But there is no such firm principle in astrology that which particular result will completely be destroyed or reduced in case of existence of which other situation and instead of this both opposite results are taken into account that's why an astrologer may predict any conclusion according to his sweet will. If you draw your attention on any prediction then easily understand that all descriptive prediction are based on sign of planet, position of planet in a house, and lord of a house, which is fixed and decided on the basis of ascendant. Whereas *navansh, vinshottary* etc. are meant for concluding a particular event by the astrologers among as usual opposite results, as stated earlier. If we distribute the result of a principle related to planet among 1/12th population of the city or whole population then we can easily realise the quantum of correctness in the result based on these astrological principles. Which may definitely be far from truth.

Now we will study and analyse in short the truth behind some planetary combination (*yog*), which is used for prediction. Astrological books may contain description of different type of *Raj-yog* but here we will analyse only Powerful *Raj-yog* (*prabal Raj-yog*) and thereafter, you may yourself go ahead to analyse other *Raj-yog* and understand that when result of Powerful *Raj-yog* is wrong then what would be the position of other *Raj-yog* or other miscellaneous *yog*.

Powerful Raj-yog

There are many *yog* for doing a prediction on any horoscope but *Raj-yog* is considered as a most important *yog* among all for having a commanding position. According to the rule of prediction if lord of 9th and 10th house may interchange their position (lord of 9th house may be placed in 10th house and *vice versa*) or both may be in 9th house or in 10th house or any one is in his own house then it is termed as powerful *Raj-yog*.

Sign of ascendant remain changing after every two hours hence all planets have a daily opportunity to be lord of 9th and 10th house. For example Jupiter and Saturn in case of Aries as ascendant, Saturn in case of Taurus as ascendant, Mars and Venus in case of Leo as ascendant, Mercury and Moon in case of Libra as ascendant, Moon and Sun in case of Scorpio as ascendant are lord of 9th and 10th house. Likewise these planets remain as lord of these houses during ascendant of some other sign. Now, if we only examine the position of Taurus as ascendant and left description of other ascendants to avoid unnecessary expansion of the subject then we find that Saturn is the lord of 9th and 10th house. Saturn continuously generates powerful *Raj-yog* for five years by remaining in Capricorn and Aquarius sign. Saturn was in these sign during 1-2-1961 to 8-4-1966 i.e. in his own sign. Beside this, Sun was exalted in Aries sign during fourteen April to fourteen May and remains in his own sign Leo during 17-8 to 17-9 every year. Moon was exalted in Taurus sign and remains in his own sign Cancer in every month for five days. Mars was exalted in Capricorn sign during 25-1-1962 to 3-3-1962, 5-1-1964 to 11-2-1964, 15-12-1965 to 21-1-1966 and remain in his own Scorpio sign during 5-11-1961 to 16-12-1961, 17-10-1963 to 26-11-1963, 25-9-1965 to 5-11-1965, in his own Aries sign during 20-5-1962 to 29-6-1962, 29-4-1964 to 8-6-1964. During this period Mercury and Venus remain many times either in their exalted sign or in their own sign. Jupiter also remains in his own sign Sagittarius upto 9-2-1961 and in Pisces sign from 8-3-1963 to 14-3-1964. Now if we left various situation generated by all other planets due to their exalted or in own house positions for creating miscellaneous *Raj-yog*, boosting the effect of Powerful *Raj-yog* and also left various ascendant in which lordship of 9th and 10th house may match for creating Powerful *Raj-yog* during above period even then whether all 60 lakhs new born, in two hours of Taurus ascendant during the span of five years are getting the benefit of powerful *Raj-yog* in India (forget about the world)? Because during this period children belonging to the poor, illiterate, backward etc. sections of the society including girl baby were also born. Children born during this period have now reached to a level in his life, where effect of powerful *Raj-yog* may be checked. Answer of this checking and analysis will definitely be that except some, all children are not at best of life and thus there is no effect of powerful *Raj-yog*.

If we study the horoscope of members of most prominent royal family like Queen Victoria, Queen Elizabeth (Mercury and Jupiter are debilitated in her horoscope yet she enjoy great respect) or many Indian politician, Prime Minister like Mrs. Indira Gandhi (no planet is exalted or in his own house yet she was powerful Prime Minister), Atal Behari Vajpayee (debilitated Moon yet full of imagination, which is required for a poet), many actors like Amitabh Bachchan (Venus is debilitated yet he has unparalleled image in glamorous film industry), many players like Sachin Tendulkar (Mercury and Jupiter are debilitated yet he has extraordinary judgement during batting in cricket), many industrialist like Dhirubhai Ambani (*Kaal-sarp yog* yet he was one of the topmost successful industrialist) etc. etc. then you will find that neither powerful *Raj-yog* nor even great personage *yog* (*panch mahapurush yog*, which you are going to read) related to fame is available in their horoscopes (see picture-19, where S = Sun, M = Moon, Ma = Mars, Me = Mercury, J = Jupiter, V = Venus, Sa = Saturn, R = Rahu, K = Ketu). Whereas, what is their commanding position and fame in India and world is well-known to everybody.

Five great-personage Yog

Five great-personage *yog* is mainly considered for predicting fame and extensively used like *Raj-yog*. For this *yog*, it is essential that any one planet out of Mars, Mercury, Jupiter, Venus or Saturn must be in central house (1, 4, 7, 10th house) and may either be in his own house i.e. in his own sign or in exalted sign for creating *Ruchak, Bhadra, Hansh, Malvya* or *Shash yog* respectively. According to astrological rule, person having such *yog* may be a great personage.

If we examine this *yog* keeping in mind the transit of the planets then we find that Saturn alone will create *Shash yog* for a period of eight hours per day during seven and half years (when it is in own two signs and one exalted sign) out of 30 years, when it will be placed in central house due to different four ascendant. Likewise new born for three years out of

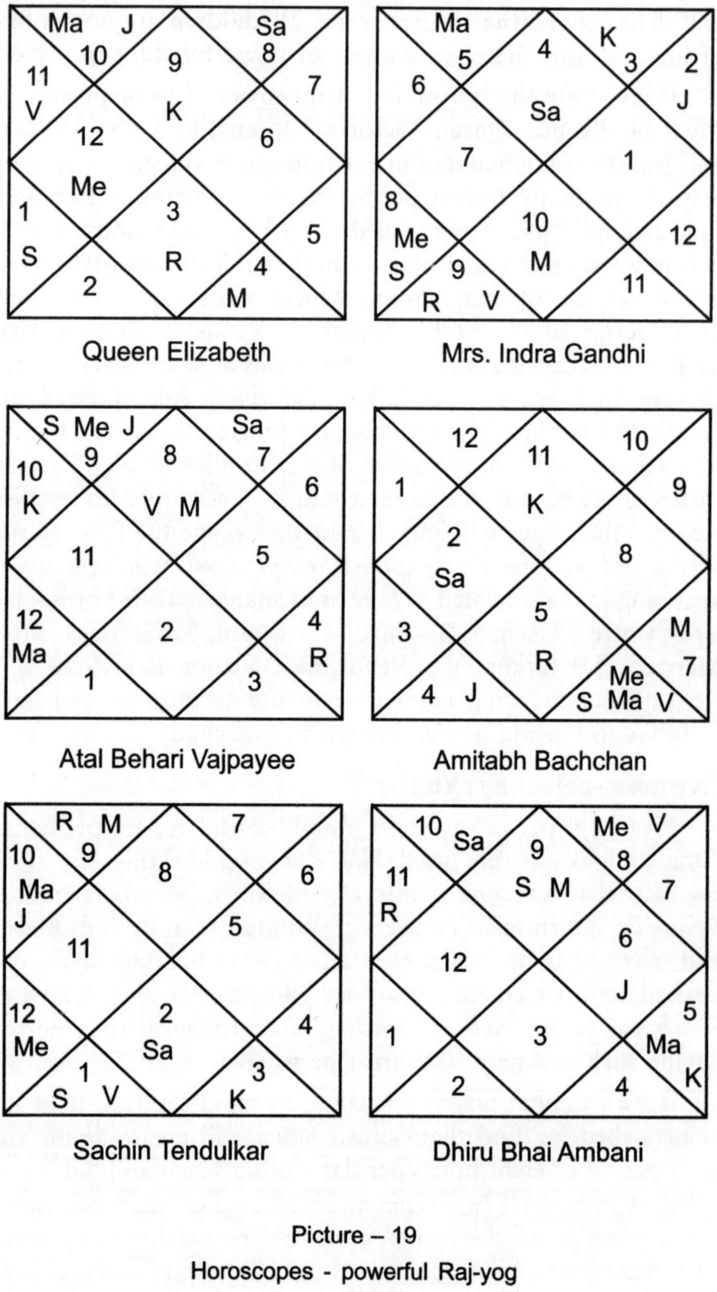

Picture – 19

Horoscopes - powerful Raj-yog

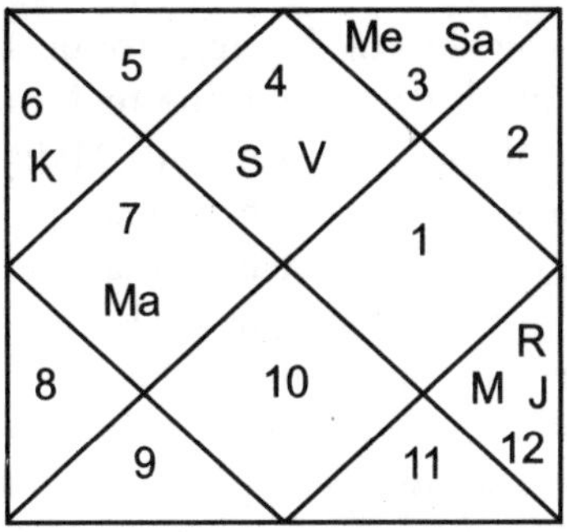

Lokmanya Tilak

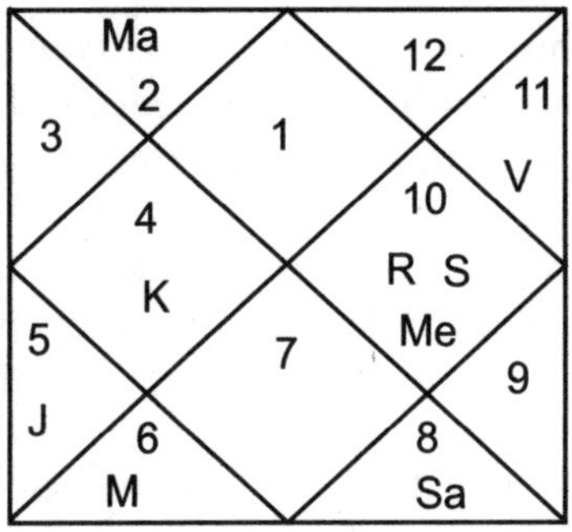

Subhash Chandra Bose

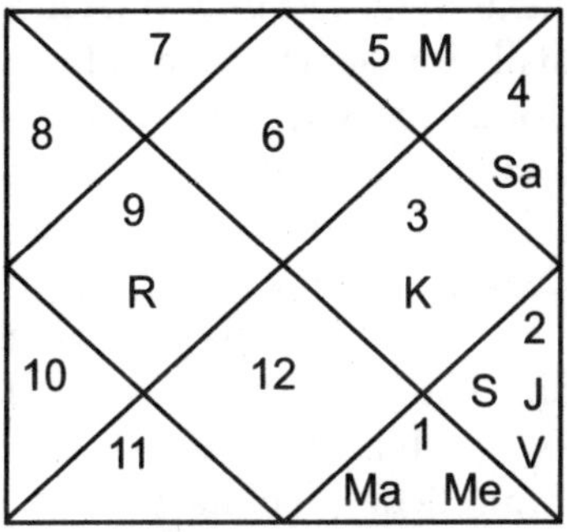

John F. Kenedy

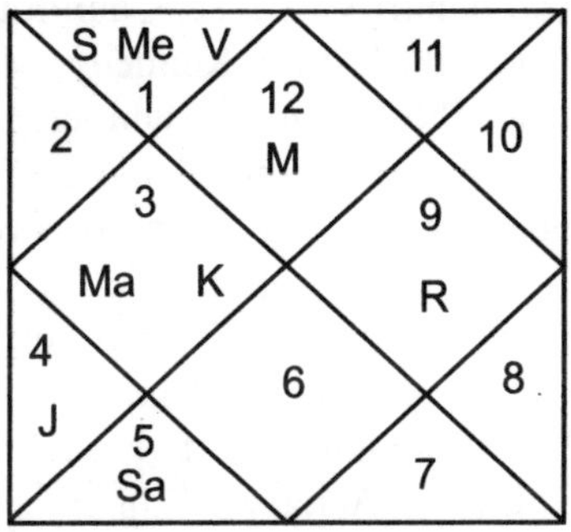

Ravindra Nath Tagore

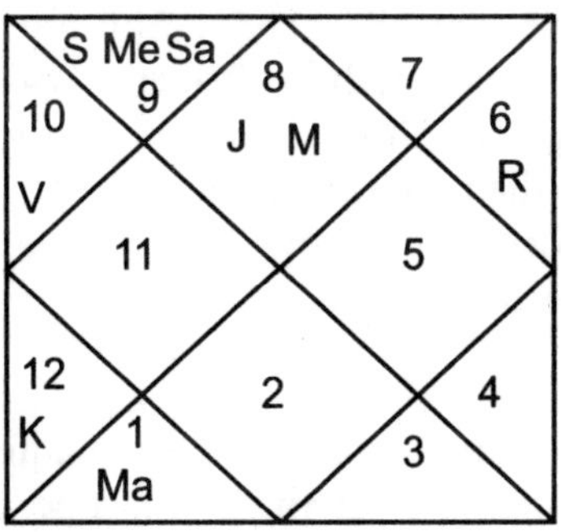

Kapil Dev

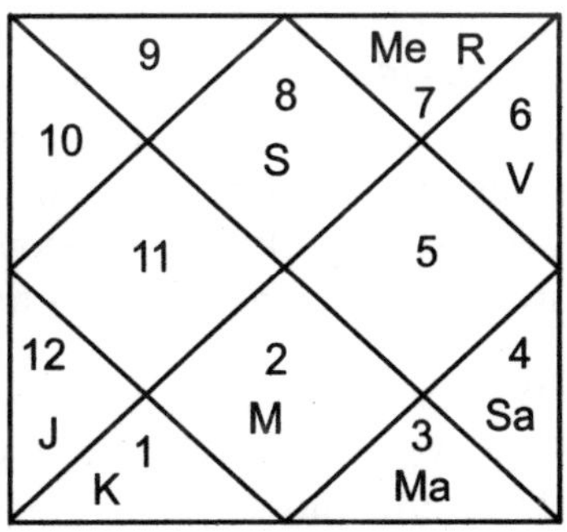

Shushmita Sen

Picture – 20

Horoscopes

thirteen year will have *Hansh yog* due to Jupiter, about six months out of two years will have *Ruchak yog* due to Mars, about three months every year will have *Bhadra* and *Malvya yog* due to Mercury and Venus and great-personage will continue to born for such a long period. Whereas, actually it is not possible that great-personage may continue to born for such a long period and contrary to this actually there is no contribution of this *yog* at all for becoming a great-personage, as may be seen from the horoscope of great personage like Lokmanya Tilak, Subhash Chandra Bose (no planet is exalted or in his own house), Rajgopalacharya, Mrs. Indira Gandhi, Atal Behari Vajpayee, Chandra Shekhar, Queen Victoria, Queen Elizabeth, John F. Kennedy, Mikhail Gorbachev, Martin Luther King (Nobel prize winner), Morarji Desai, S.B. Chavhan, N.T. Ramarao (no planet is exalted or in his own house), Jyoti Basu (debilitated Jupiter), Navin Patnaik (no planet is exalted or in his own house), L.K. Advani, Digvijay Singh, Rajesh Pilot (debilitated Mars, Sun and Venus), Mulayam Singh, Murli Manohar Joshi, Ravindra Nath Tagore, Dhirubhai Ambani, Henri Ford (Industrialist - debilitated Venus), Chiro (Palmist), Acharya Rajneesh, Kiran Bedi (debilitated Jupiter and Moon), T.N. Sheshan, Amartya Sen (Economist), Kapil Deo (debilitated Moon), Sachin Tendulkar, Vishwa Nath Anand (debilitated Saturn), Abhitabh Bachchan, Shushmita Sen (debilitated Venus), Rajesh Khanna, Julia Robert (Oscar winner Actress - debilitated Sun) etc. All of them have earned name, fame and respect due to their judicious decision, good deed, hard work and self-confidence and none of them have any Great-personage *yog* in their horoscope.

Other

If we examine the effect of planet in own house, exalted planet and most fearful *Kaal-sarp yog* in the horoscope of many great personage like Subhash Chandra Bose, Indira Gandhi, Navin Patnaik, Jyoti Basu (Debilitated Jupiter), N.T. Ramarao, Rajesh Pilot (Debilitated Sun, Mars, Venus), Acharya Tulsi (Debilitated Sun, Jupiter), Kiran Bedi (Debilitated Jupiter, Moon), Vishwa Nath Anand (Debilitated Saturn), Martin

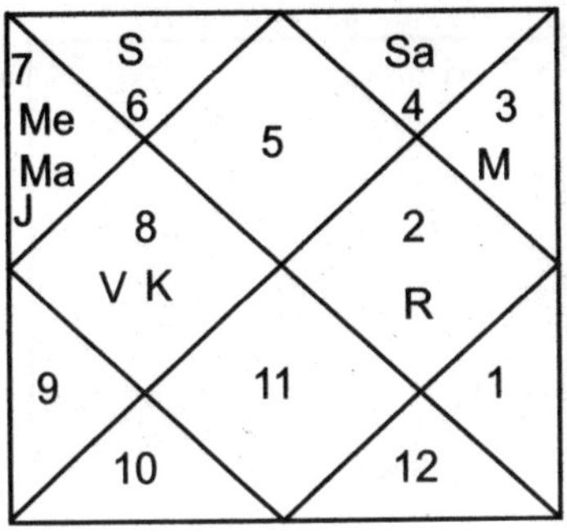

Navin Patnaik

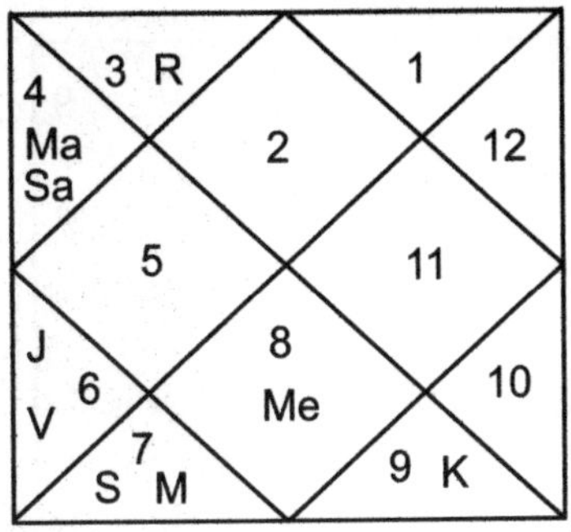

Rajesh Pilot

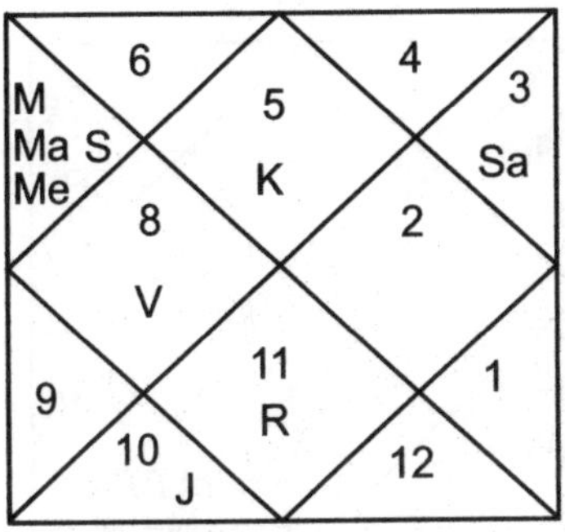

Acharya Tulsi

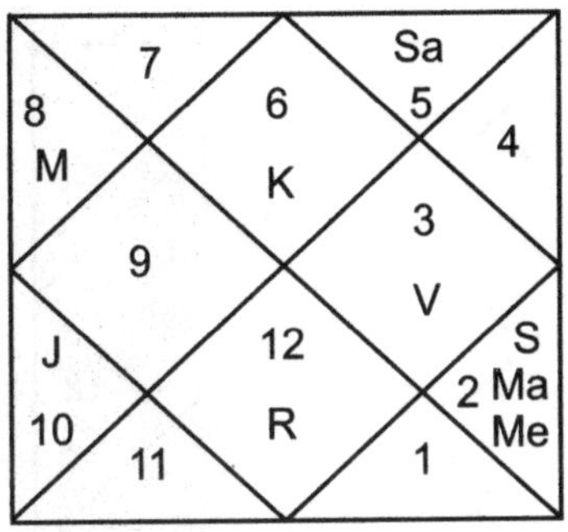

Kiran Bedi

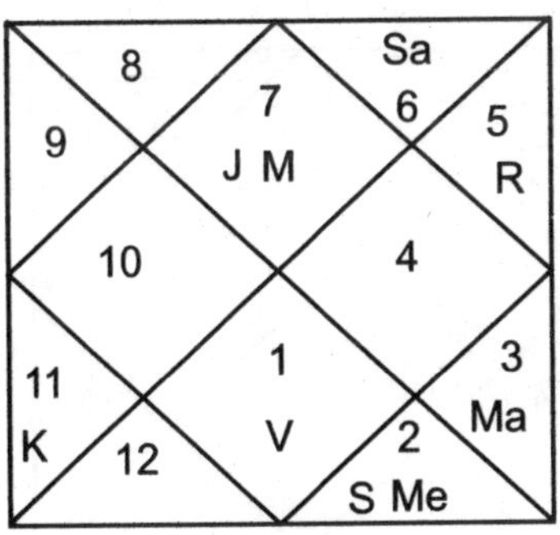

N.T. Ramarao

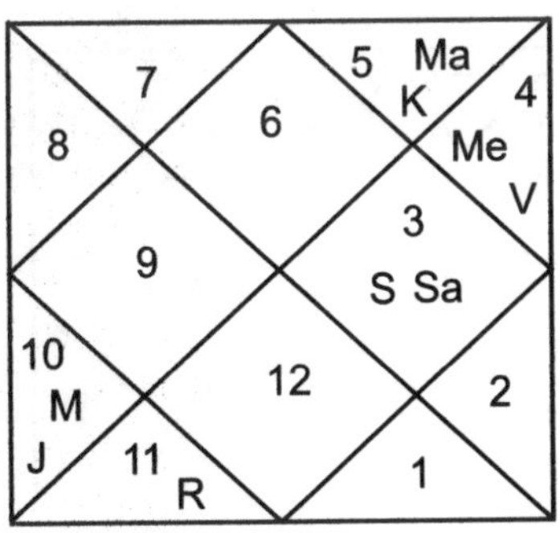

Jyoti Basu

Picture - 21
Horoscopes

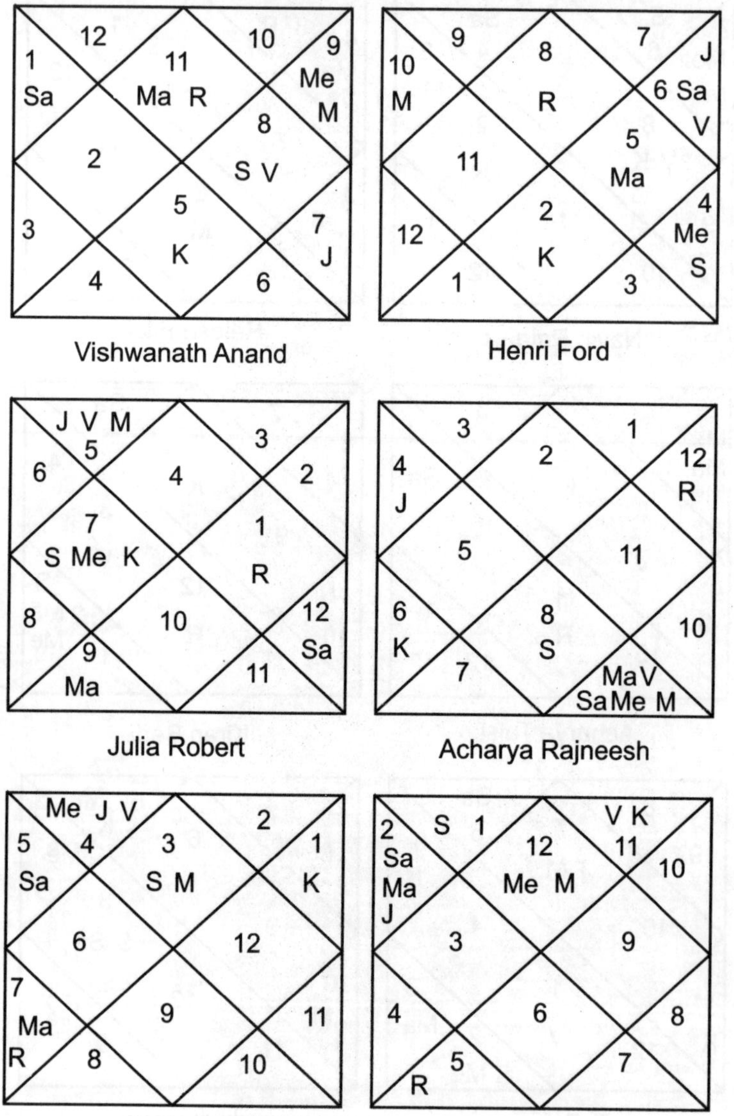

Picture – 22
Horoscopes

Luther King, Henri Ford (Debilitated Venus), Julia Robert (Debilitated Sun) etc. then we can easily verify that neither any planet is Exalted nor placed in his own house but contrary to this in many cases planet is Debilitated as detailed above, even then they are able to earn name, fame, wealth and respectable status in the society. It is also worth mentioning that five planets are placed in 6th and 8th house in the horoscope in the great personage like Amitabh Bachchan, Acharya Rajneesh whereas astrologically planets placed in these houses are not considered as auspicious or good from any angle. Beside this horoscope of Dhirubhai Ambani, S.B. Chavhan, Margaret Alva etc. has *Kaal-sarp yog* (If all planets are placed from Rahu to Ketu) and horoscope of Jawahar Lal Nehru has opposite *Kaal-sarp yog* (If all planets are placed from Ketu to Rahu). Though there is no mention of *Kaal-sarp yog* in old astrological scriptures yet it is propagated for business consideration and for misleading innocent public at large that any task will never be completed if an individual has *Kaal-sarp yog* in his horoscope. In this way a fearful atmosphere is created in the society. Whereas, factual position is quite different and it can be seen in above cases that these individuals have created their status in the society by their honesty, self-confidence, hard labour and judicious decision.

There is one more prominent *yog* known as '*Gaj Kesri yog*'. It is believed that this *yog* is created whenever Jupiter and Moon happens to be in same house; and due to this *yog* one may get name, fame and wealth. If you go through various horoscope given earlier then you will find that this yog was not in the horoscope of many personalities like Queen Elizabeth, Mrs. Indira Gandhi, Atal Behari Vajpayee, Amitabh Bachchan, Sachin Tendulkar, Dhiru Bhai Ambani, John F. Kenedy, Shushmita Sen, Kiran Bedi and so on. But everybody knows about their name, fame and wealth, which have been earned only by hard labour and judicious timely decision. I know many individuals having '*Gaj Kesri yog*' in their horoscope but they are neither famous nor wealthy nor having any powerful status. This *yog* may easily be traced in 10% horoscopes because during transit Moon and Jupiter remains in same house for more than two days in every 27 days required for one rotation of the zodiac by the Moon. Thus it is not essential that only these persons may get name and fame.

If all other *yog*, rule of prediction etc. may be analysed in view of planetary transit then this fact will automatically emerge that any prediction based on any *yog* or astrological rule has no relation with the reality. Because any planetary position considered for a prediction is repeatedly created due to transit of a planet and there may be many individuals having same planetary position in their birth horoscope. You know that any ascendant remains effective for two hours; it means that planetary position in the horoscope will generally be same for the individuals born during two hours. Even than any one out of the individuals born during these two hours may be Prime Minister, President, successful industrialist etc. If there is slightest truth or scientific support behind astrological principles then individual born during this two hours would be at the top or near to top in the society. For example, if one individual is Prime Minister than another individual born during same two hours would definitely be Cabinet Minister, Chief Minister etc. and if first individual happens to be most successful industrialist then another individual must at least be owner of some factories. But neither it is so nor there is any minute astrological principle, which may distinguish these situations. For this, you may analyse the life of those twins, who may brought up in different circumstances. Thus it is clear that if someone is able to achieve some thing then it is only the result of deeds executed according to knowledge and judicious decision taken in that particular time and situation. Is it possible to predict beforehand that a particular horoscope belongs to a Muslim or Hindu lady, who may be one among four wives or single wife respectively; or a Muslim or Hindu man, who may have more than one wife or marry with a single woman respectively? Answer will definitely be, no. Bare fact is that it can neither be predicted nor even concluded from the horoscopes that which one belongs to male or female or eunuch. Whereas social, financial, intellectual, political, household, religious, dresses, physique etc. of male and female are totally different since Rising age even though they may be twins having same horoscopes, because complete lifestyle is totally and drastically changed merely due to the fact as to whether one individual is male or female. Only in previous century it could be discovered that sex is decided by chromosome and not by any planetary situation. One may put forward an argument that despite same planetary position there is vast difference in the *vinshottary* periodicity hence there may be difference in actual happening. But in view of the fact that when every second there is a birth (if you may have seen population watch) and there may also be some birth in adjoining time of birth of great-personage then in this situation there may not be any substantial difference even of one second (*vikala*) in the planetary situation etc., which may be distinguished by any astrological calculation so significantly that it may subsequently lead to diagonal change in prediction in such a way that one may be rich and famous whereas other individual born within one/two seconds may be no where. Secondly from the mathematics involve in deciding *vinshottary* periodicity one may easily understand that same periodicity may not match for a particular time but after some time same *vinshottary* periodicity will be in force, even then there is no matching in actual incidents. Now, for getting escape there may be another argument that present transitory position of the planets may change hence there is no question of same result. But actually there is no astrological principle that any prediction based on planetary position in the horoscope and *vinsottary* periodicity will be true only in some particular very precise transitory position of that planet. Whereas, all type of transitory predictions are mainly based on the planetary position with reference to the birth position of Moon. As fear of *saade-saati* is infused in case of transit of Saturn in the sign of Moon (as per birth horoscope), next and previous sign i.e. transit time of Saturn through three signs. As any women can easily be frightened by any adverse prediction about her husband or son. In the same way any sound minded and balanced person may be shattered by any adverse prediction about his son, business and wealth etc., though he may not have faith on astrology even then he may be depressed psychologically and become easy prey for the astrologers.

Paul Couderc astronomer of Paris observatory analysed the horoscope of 2817 musicians and concluded that position of the Sun has no significance role as they all born throughout the year in different months and no fraction of zodiac or sign has any favour or disfavour to them. Thus it can be understand that any individual may achieve his target and respectable position only by his judicious decision, hard work etc. and not with any so-called supportive *yog* or favourable planetary position in the horoscope. Contrary to this you may came across many perplexed or dreaming persons in many offices or doing small business etc. who are sitting idle due to having full faith on exalted position of planets, *Raj-yog*, *vinshottary* periodicity, transit of planets etc. and they always try to bridle planet by wearing different type of rings etc. on the advise of astrologers, but they never succeed in life and thus always accuse their destiny and wander from one astrologer to another with the hope to control these inanimate planets by hook and crook. Because every astrologer has adopted a different system for prediction. Result of these systems may diametrically opposed to each other but claimed to be correct. For example, *sayan* system is being followed in western countries and *nirayan* system is adopted in India. Whereas there is a difference of 23° (*ayanansh*) in between these two systems. In the same way some astrologer will follow result derived on *vinshottary* periodicity, another will follow *mudda* periodicity (annual *dasha*), third will follow transit of planet (*gochar*), fourth will follow navansh etc. and next will follow Krishnamurti system and so on. Actually non of them is correct and it is also not possible to conclude same result from different opposite systems, but psychologically every prediction appears to be correct because our internal feeling, which was fed and stored in our subconscious mind in early ages always compel us to believe that astrology is a science and it is correct; and it always match with our condition, as you may have observed while going through 'Your forecast'. Moreover every astrologer has independent method for putting bridle on the planet either by gem or *vastu* or offering or worshipping or by some spell narrated in well propagated 'Laal Kitaab'.

Now-a-days astrologers generally do some forecast about the victory of any political leader after accessing present situation with a view to get immediate fame and in case of reverse happening they came with new arguments in support of some other leader. They offer verbal guarantee or through print or visual media regarding 'treatment' of a planet for getting desired result and planets are 'treated' with the help of some spell, *Vastu*, Fengsui, Gem, Mystical diagram (*Yantra*) etc. according to the mental status of an individual. Likewise astrologers do some forecast about weather and predict rainfall or draught on the basis of some particular planetary position. Now one may ask these astrologers as to whether that particular planetary position is only meant for India or it is for entire Earth? Definitely their celestial position is same throughout the world. In this way if Mars is in forward position from Sun in the zodiac then this celestial position of the planets is not limited for a particular city or region of India but this planetary position is actually with reference to the Earth. Then why there is draught at one place and continuous rainfall at another place? Whereas it is very funny to do any weather forecast on the basis of any astrological principle. Actually many weather forecasts are being followed in our country in the shape of regional proverb from generation to generation and they prevailed in a particular region but misused as an astrological forecast to misguide the innocent public for believing that astrology is scientifically correct.

Conclusion

It is presumed that any prediction based on planetary position is correct. Whereas if correctness of any prediction is actually analysed scientifically and logically then this fact can easily be understand that different incidents took place in same planetary position. Because every astrological principle leads to some different and opposite results hence most suitable prediction is concluded by an astrologer for psychologically subduing the mental status of an individual and which is convenient to his business interest. In this way desired forecast relating to victory of politicians, promotion of an officer, transfer, success in examination, profit in business, birth of a male child, marriage etc. are being concluded by the astrologers without any scientific basis. In case of failure of a prediction, defensive attitude may be adopted by astrologers stating that horoscope may be wrong or effect of some other suitable astrological principle according to actual incident may easily be narrated. As astrological principles are quite unscientific hence there is no fixed parameter or effect of any prediction.

In-depth study and analysis was conducted by 186 prominent scientists including 18 noble prize winner personalities for ascertaining scientific basis of astrology, who concluded in 1975 that there is no scientific basis in any form for assuming that planets foretell events. We may realise a very funny situation, if we observe the different type of remedies being followed by an individual to get rid off from any so-called problem being initiated by a planet and it appears that poor planet cannot sustain any harm because as and when it try to catch hold an individual in compliance of so-called destiny based on his horoscope, at the same moment that individual may set free himself then and thereafter doing some suitable remedies as per timely advise of astrologers and that poor confused individual feels that how easily he overturn the whole story of destiny by putting the bridle on the evil effect of planet.

It is evident from the analysis of astrological principles that they are having following deficiencies :–

1. Different astrological principles leads to opposite results due to illogical formulation of principles of prediction and any prediction may appears to be true due to psychological effect.
2. There is not a unified principle with same result for same planetary position.
3. Even not any *yog* or placement of planets is effective for getting success or failure, gain or loss in life.

16

ONE MOMENT

If we have an overview on what we have studied so far about the astrological principles then following fact emerges :–

1. Universe – There is lot of difference between the primitive and modern concept of the Universe. The belief which prevailed in the Primitive age that nearest planet Sun rotates around the stationary Earth; Moon and Constellations were situated over and above the Sun; and confused conception of imaginary Rahu and Ketu in the cylindrical shape of the Universe have been completely overturned by the modern scientific concept according to which Earth and other five planets along with Uranus, Neptune, Pluto, Chiron rotates around a star Sun (which is not a planet); actual position of the constellations are in the other different galaxies; Moon, which is not a planet but a satellite rotate around the Earth and we have modern knowledge about the Rahu and Ketu. Thus basic foundation of formulation of the astrological principles have totally been changed. Not only it has a negative impact on all astrological principles based on the primitive knowledge of the Universe but astrological calculation and prediction are also meaningless in view of the major cracks in the foundation of astrology due to fundamental change in the concept of the Universe.

2. Lord of signs – In the Primitive age, signs were subsequently distributed among the planets according to their distance from the Earth. There was no relation between so-called element of the planet and sign. Now the basis of deciding the lord of sign is completely changed in view of the continuous varying distance of the planets from the Earth. Thus order of the lord of the sign must also change according to the distance of the planets with reference to the Earth in every individual horoscope.

3. Friendship-enmity – The nature of the element of the planets were not taken into account while framing the principles of friendship-enmity among the planets. There will be substantial deviation in this principle, if we reorganise the order of the planets according to their distance from the Earth at the time of birth and thereafter, reallocate the lordship among the planets and then decide the relationship of friendship-enmity among the planets based on the unscientific primitive principle of lordship of two triangles in accordance with the fight between the deities and demons, then there will be substantial fundamental change in this principle.

4. Aspect of planets – Principle of aspect of planets was influenced by the mythical stories, political and social environment. There will be substantial deviation, if we reorganise the aspect of the planets after deciding the revised friendship-enmity based on the lord of the sign according to their distance from the Earth.

5. Set planet – There is lot of confusion about this since Rising age due to wrong concept of the Universe. But according to latest scientific information, Sun may also set due to Mercury, Venus and Moon with reference to the Earth. Now-a-days the position of setting of Sun due to Moon is known as solar eclipse. Whereas in the Primitive age solar eclipse was considered to occur due to Ketu instead of Moon.

6. Exalted-debilitated – Confusion is persisting since Rising age due to wrong understanding of the Universe. Because the reasons due to which it was considered that a planet is nearer to the Earth was itself not correct. Beside this whole situation of exalted and debilitated position of the planets as conceived in the Primitive age has since been deviated by 33° (*ayanansh*) due to change in *nirayan* position of the Sun since then. There will be sufficient deviation in the prediction if we derive it in accordance with the basic idea of the sages, on the basis of the scientifically known minimum distance of the planet from the Earth and the impact of the planets at the time of their highest altitude like Jupiter. The procedure to calculate the potential of a planet according to this basic idea will be discussed later on.

7. **Mool-trikon** – This principle was based on triangular relationship among lord of sign and its exalted position in a sign. When these two basic principles were wrongly based on misconcept of Universe. Then it is quite natural that principle of *mool-trikon* may also be wrong to that extent.

8. **Potential of planet** – Main ingredient to work out the potential of a planet i.e. lordship, friendship etc. are itself worked out on above mentioned wrong concept. Hence it is quite natural that potential of a planet may also be wrong.

9. **Vinshottary Periodicity** – Table of periodicity is wrong because it was based on *sayan* system and there is a difference due to change in *sampaat* constellation on the basis of *nirayan* system. It is totally wrong to calculate the periodicity of a planet of a horoscope, which is prepared by following *nirayan* system and by matching it with a table prepared on *sayan* system. Beside this basis of formulation of periodicity is also misconceived due to wrong concept of the Universe.

10. **Rahu and Ketu** – Position of Rahu and Ketu is not matching with the position of full lunar and solar eclipse. Because retrograde motion and mutual distance among Rahu Ketu is not correct. Hence correct position of Rahu Ketu are not being shown in horoscopes.

11. **Ascendant** – Ascendant and vivid planets are being calculated with reference to the centre of the Earth instead of actual birth place, which may be far away from the centre of the Earth.

12. **Days of the Week** – There is mistake in conclusion of a forecast, which is derived on the name of days, in the ratio of the difference of the order of the planets and formation of the Universe.

13. Forecast – Any prediction derived with the help of primitive astrological principles may not be correct in case of applying same principles in another horoscope. Thus prediction may appears to be correct due to psychological effect.

You may realise from the above description that there is very little correlation between various fundamental principles of the astrology. Lordship of a sign was based on the respective position of the planets from the Earth. Lord of sign of two triangle houses was then classified as enemy of each other. The aspect of the planet was decided on the basis of an imaginary fight between deities and demons. Retrograde, Set, Exalted, Debilitated was decided on various transitory and celestial position of the planets in the Universe. Periodicity of the planets was decided on the basis of rotational transit of planets and their respective situation in the Universe. Existence of Rahu Ketu and their retrograde motion was decided on the basis of deities-demons, lunar year, its linking with recurrence of eclipse. In this way there is no correlation between various principles viz. lordship, friendship-enmity / aspect, exalted-debilitated and periodicity of planets etc. and result drawn from these principles do not supplement each other but they lead to diagonally opposite directions. Just imagine what would happen if a mathematical problem independently solved with the help of arithmetic, geometry, algebra and trigonometry leads to different result. Present status of astrological principles is just like that, because astrology as a whole was only developed on the framework of order of distances of the planets in the Universe with reference to the Earth. Now the order of the planets as believed in the Primitive age proved to be totally wrong on the basis of latest scientific knowledge. Hence there remains no validity or importance of the astrological principles formulated in the Primitive age. Beside this other minor principles formulated for analysing a horoscope also lost their grounds in view of the above explanation. Because the basic idea behind formulating all these principles was based only on the wrong concept of the Universe.

You may have observed that how we get two or more different results on the basis of the astrological principles.

Hence flourishing business is being done with the help of modern equipments like TV, Computer, after matching any past incident of any celebrity with the result of astrological principles, which were formulated on unscientific and wrong primitive concept and public at large is being lured by misleading publicity. Because public are not being informed about those forecasts which were not materialised.

At that point of time when astrological principles were being formulated by our sages, there was complete lack of correct information about the orbit, speed, position etc. of the planets and astrological principles were formulated by treating the planets as deities etc. on the basis of mythical stories, knowledge, belief and as conceived by their deep thought. The level of belief and astronomical knowledge about the Universe was almost same till Pre-modern age. At present astrologers are exploiting the weak mentality of an individual for their material gain by forecasting any so-called favourable or unfavourable event with their eloquent and impressive speech in pleasing or fearful manner in such a way that event of past or future appears to be correct and public at large who is not aware with the basic foundation of this knowledge is being mislead. You may have heard the story of a King who once told his Minister that brinjal (*beingun*) is useless vegetable then Minister confirm the fact by adding that yes it is useless that's why it is black and its name itself suggest that it has no quality. After few days the King praised the brinjal and told to his Minister that this is a very good vegetable then Minister again confirm the fact by supporting the contention of the king and replied that yes it is very good vegetable that's why it is crowned. In the same way astrologer also praised or infuses some fear in the mind of an individual after judging his mentality for getting the handsome fee or publicity. Whereas, with the help of present primitive astrological principles, when it is not even possible to forecast a Himalayan promotional event in one's life, like who will be our next Prime Minister among the present parliamentarian and when? Likewise when an extremely highest jolting event of death will occur in one's life? Then it is merely a joke to predict about a minor promotion in service or business or unfavourable period for an ordinary person. It is like that when one who can't predict about the Himalayan event and then he claim for predicting a minor event like particle of sand.

You may have experienced that astrologers may refer some astrological principles in support of any past or present event. But after going through the previous chapters you may have armed yourself with the contention that every astrological principle leads to different prediction and there was no relation among them. For example, if a person is suffering from the subjects related to those planets (As Jupiter is related to fortune, wealth etc.) which is placed in house number 6, 8, 12 in the horoscope of that person or concerning planet is lord of the sign of these houses then it can easily be concluded and convinced that past event was not favourable only because the concerning planet is placed in unfavourable house or it is lord of unfavourable house. In the same way, for some favourable event related to that planet may be linked to the aspect of good planet, *vinshottary* main periodicity, inter-periodicity, transit of planet, *mudda* periodicity, exalted planet, retrograde, planet is itself auspicious etc. and if it is still not much to the satisfaction than many reasons may be explored from other type of horoscopes including *chalit, navansh* etc. and likewise some favourable or unfavourable prediction may be narrated by keeping in mind the financial benefit or publicity according to the mental, financial etc. status of the individual. If later on, events turn up according to the prediction then astrology is correct. Otherwise, in the event of some other incidents, linking the unforeseen events to some other astrological principles may convince concerning individual. You may have experienced that many times even full prediction may also be turned up to wrong, whereas every prediction is based on the astrological principles, but even then one may not only lost his time, money and mental peace by indulging himself in the articles like Gem, *Vastu*, Fengsui, *Yantra* etc. but may also destroy his life by believing in fixed destiny instead of doing some sincere hard work. Because to get desired success in the life one must not only be faithful to himself but he must be able to take correct and judicious decision with positive thinking and put hard labour to implement it. Thus destiny may be carved out, which may not only provide a success in the present life but if we believe in the next birth then it also support as a so-called destiny in next life. Hence we must understand the astrological principles in correct perspective and in accordance with the original study of impact of the planets, which was conducted by our Indian sages and we must develop these astrological principles by doing further research and develop this like any other scientific development. So that we may take full advantage of this knowledge by following the correct path and there is no need to sit idle in temptation of some so-called misleading forecast of the businessman astrologer on the basis of illogical principles in the modern age of science. We must come out from the mental set up that only the principles and knowledge of the past is best and finally correct and should follow scientific approach. Because faith is only supported by belief, whereas science is supported by logic and accuracy.

During general discussion you may find that those who have faith and believe in astrology will come forward with the argument that astrology is a science, because only by astrology we may know about the solar and lunar eclipse beforehand. Thereafter they will tell any one forecast about age, death, marriage, birth, business or education etc., which was correctly predicted long back by some known astrologer. By these arguments they will try to prove that astrology is science as well as correct.

We know that the scientists process any invention in laboratory with the help of available resources, knowledge and deep thinking. Likewise new knowledge was undoubtedly generated in the hermitage of sages with the help of the then resources, knowledge and meditation during the course of development of civilisation. Now we have many branches of every sort of knowledge and science but in the Rising age there was no such branches and the then whole knowledge was used to pass on through hearsay (*shrut-gyan*) method and it was subsequently made available in *ved, puran*, scripture, religious literature etc. This whole knowledge was fully influenced by religious myth. Hence astrology was developed in the form of 'Jyotish', which was derived from 'Jyoti of Ishwar' i.e. Jyoti+Ish. But actually all that knowledge, which was learned and acquired under astrology has since been bifurcated in various branches of science and other disciplines during last 3000 years. Some important subjects are Astronomy, Physics, Mathematics, Geometry, Trigonometry, Algebra and Psychology etc. Astronomy and Physics has again been bifurcated in many subjects only within last 200 years. The way in which astrology is being propagated as correct, on the basis of solar and lunar eclipse, was actually primitive form of Astronomy when eclipse were anticipated after mathematical calculation regarding imaginary shadow planets Rahu, Ketu instead of correct concept of intersection points of orbit of Moon and ecliptic. How much wrong this primitive imagination was, has partly been studied in previous chapters and will do detailed study in forthcoming chapters. In the same way primitive form of psychology was inadvertently used in predictive astrology due to which so-called prediction appears to be correct. Because it was not known at that time that correctness of prediction was due to psychological effect like half-empty or half-filled glass may be referred in any way. When any classified prediction which is being referred by an individual in support of correctness of astrology, then it is a matter of little review as to why only that type of classified correct prediction may not be narrated as an expert in such prediction by that astrologer in respect of all individuals by using same astrological principles, if so. For example, if even one astrologer who could so-called correctly predict about the age or death then he may have definitely being consulted for predicting about the death at the time of matching of horoscopes before marriage; or horoscope would have been referred for examination to that astrologer by every metropolitan hospital instead of providing any treatment; or horoscope of a client would have been referred by Life Insurance Corporation to that astrologer for examination before executing any life insurance policy and definitely that astrologer would have been at the top level in the Corporation.

Whereas actually it is not so because primitive astrology contains many subject in infancy which were subsequently developed as science hence astrology is being inadvertently classified as science. Whereas the present form of astrology as propagated is actually predictive astrology. The basis of which was limited for concluding a prediction after accessing the impact of planets on the basis of astrological principles and unfortunately it has nothing to do with science. Some gambler, stock broker, hoarder, *satte-baaz* etc. can very well assess future position from their past experience and act accordingly for getting profit. Occasionally they may be correct, but even then they cannot be regarded as astrologer. Likewise some so-called correct predictions concluded on the basis of some unscientific principles or psychologically cannot be accounted for in support of predictive astrology. Because according to principle of permutation combination, 50% conclusion may automatically be correct as you may have experienced from 'Your forecast' in the chapter of 'Forecast'. Extra 25% conclusion may be correct, by chance and remaining 25% conclusion may be correct because the astrologer concluded it after studying the status of an individual, his intuition and psychological experience. Thus there is neither a scientific reason nor any planetary effect, which may lead to perform any act, hence actually astrology is not a science but pseudo science based on experience and psychology.

Generally, starting chapter of almost all astrological books comprises the description of latest scientific information about the solar system, planets and their orbit etc. Thus everybody presumes that astrology is correct and scientifically supported, thus get confused. Whereas till now you may have gathered that how astrology was developed on the wrong concept of the Universe. Any knowledge can only be classified as science when their result may be verifiable, there may not be any fallibility and same result may be repeated in same situation. If we critically examine the predictive astrology in view of this parameter then it is undoubtedly, univocally fact that by applying same astrological principle same result cannot be expected during so-called same celestial planetary position. In this way neither result can be verified nor they are repeated but there remains only fallibility. All these outcomes are totally against science. As has been explained that due to combined effect of psychology, eloquency of astrologer and internal faith about the correctness of astrology, it appears that prediction may be correct. Hence predictive astrology is scientifically not correct from any angle and it is only pseudo-science. Whereas those infant subjects which were once included in astrology have already been developed as science after proper study and research. Thus I emphasize and want to state very loud and clear that future events cannot be predicted on the basis of present astrological principles formulated in Primitive age and based on planetary position in zodiac.

There is a continuous process of accumulation of knowledge during development of human civilisation, which is still going on. As a first stage during this process some 'belief' supported with unfounded explanation, regarding some subject, matter etc. about whom we are totally ignorant is created. For example due to unawareness of factual position regarding Universe during Rising age there was ample scope of generating 'belief' hence scripture, *puran* etc. are mainly based on such belief. After creating some belief, efforts are being made, as a next stage, to know about that thing, nature etc. After accumulating sufficient knowledge about the nature, efforts are being made to control it. So that we may control it according to our wishes. After getting the capacity to control it we try to use that, as a last stage. Knowledge regarding fire, irrigation, animal husbandry, conveyance etc. was acquired by following the same procedure. Astrology has also followed the same procedure and as a first stage, shape of Universe was believed like picture-1 and planets were believed as deities or demons. Thereafter, process to know about these planets was initiated by our sages, who may be regarded as the then scientist, and who studied their motion, celestial position, eclipse, impact, constellation etc. The process of such study is still going on under astronomy, as a result of which we could know about the solar system as shown in picture-2 and it was verified that primitive concept and belief was wrong. Our sages devised the procedure for drafting horoscope, worship, donation, holy dip etc. to minimise the negative planetary impact and for using their positive impact so that future may be ascertained and modified. Because scientifically there is still no system by which planetary impact may be controlled. Hence primitive practice is still being followed. But uncontrolled planetary impact like gravitation, spectrum etc. is being scientifically used for studying the Universe. Scientific procedure for calculating the astrological planetary impact is given in the third section of this book.

I have only discussed the facts behind those astrological principles which have sufficient impact on the astrological predictions and foundation of which were based on some wrong concept and belief about the Universe in the Primitive age. As a result mislead public at large wasting his time, energy and money in the process of conquering the planets in accordance with these outdated and unscientific principles. Anyhow, beside the astrological principles, which were discussed and proved to be baseless in previous chapters, some principles formulated by the sages like activator planet (*kaarak*) of a house, ascendant, house etc., which appears to be somewhat logical. Beside this the basic idea of the sages behind formulating the astrological principles was to know the impact of the planets on the human being and this was most important factor, because they were the first to move in the direction to assert the impact of the planet on the human race in the light of the then knowledge and information. Though it may turned out to be wrong, but anyhow it was and it is the only way to acquire any knowledge by following the procedure of trial and error.

In the forthcoming chapters we will try to understand the impact of the planets on the Earth and on mankind in accordance with the basic concept of the sages with a scientific view. Hence first of all we will understand the formation of the Universe, which was the building block of astrology.

Grahlaghav

Shri Ganesh s/o Shri Keshav, who himself was a mathematician of astronomy, born in AD 1507 (*shak samvat* 1429) was Author of '*Grahlaghav*'. It is proclaimed that Shri Ganesh wrote '*Grahlaghav*' in the age of 13 years and in its support, it is stated that he opted the data of *shak samvat* 1442 in the procedure adopted and written in '*Grahlaghav*' for calculating the celestial position of the planets. Because at that time he was 13 years old hence this rumour spread that in the age of 13 years he wrote '*Grahlaghav*'.

Prior to '*Grahlaghav*', *ahargan* i.e. number of days were worked out in accordance with religious belief from the formation of the Universe by calculating solar year, solar month, lunar month, extra month (*adhimaas*), lost days (*kshya tithi*) till date. Position of a planet in degree, minute, second was worked out by multiplying this *ahargan* by the motion of that planet and after doing various correction known as *sanskar* relating to retrograde motion etc. Lot of mathematical calculation were involved in this procedure.

To cut short this long process, Shri Ganesh developed a method for working out the celestial position of the planets, by taking the celestial position of *Chaitra shukla pratipada* of *shak samvat* 1442 as starting position (*kshepak*). Thereafter, he worked out the change in celestial position of the planets during 11 years cycle (*chakra*) as *dhruvank* and after calculating the remaining days i.e. *ahargan*, left out after *chakra*, was multiplied by average motion of that planet. This position added to starting position (*kshepak*) and *dhruvank*.

In my opinion, celestial position of planets for *shak samvat* 1442 as prepared by his father would be available to him. Thereafter, in the age of 24 (*shak samvat* 1453), the change which took place in celestial position of the planets during last 11 years were considered as *dhruvank* and as usual calculated *ahargan* for remaining period. Thus due to adopting cycle (*chakra*) of 11 years, it is clear that in the age of 24 years i.e. in *shak* 1453, after 11 years from the starting position (*kshepak*) i.e. *shak* 1442 (when he was 13 years old), he wrote '*Grahlaghav*'.

PART 2

17

MODERN CONCEPT OF UNIVERSE

So far scientists have discovered that there are crores of moving galaxies in the Universe, which are moving away from each other. We can see many galaxies from bare eyes. Out of crores of galaxies, our own one galaxy has a diameter of about one lakh light-year. Whereas one light-year is equal to 9,46,080 crore km. Speed of light is 2,97,431 km per second and distance covered by the light in one year with this enormous speed is called one light-year. Our Sun is only a star out of crores of stars in our galaxy. All planets i.e. Mercury, Venus, Earth, Mars, Jupiter, Saturn, Uranus, Neptune, Pluto and Chiron are rotating around our star Sun due to its gravitational force, in their own orbit, which are respectively one after another as shown in picture-2. These planets may have one or more their own satellite i.e. Moon. These satellites rotate around their respective planet. We are also living on a planet i.e. Earth. Our Moon is a satellite, which rotate around our planet Earth. In the same way our star Sun along with solar system comprising of all planets also rotates around the Black-hole situated at the centre of our galaxy, due to its gravitational attraction.

Similarly all galaxies are also individually under control of their respective Black-hole and collectively under control of some unknown centre of attraction. As satellite rotate around the planets, likewise all planets rotate around the star and all stars of a galaxy rotate around the Black-hole. In this way every body in the Universe is moving and every body is in

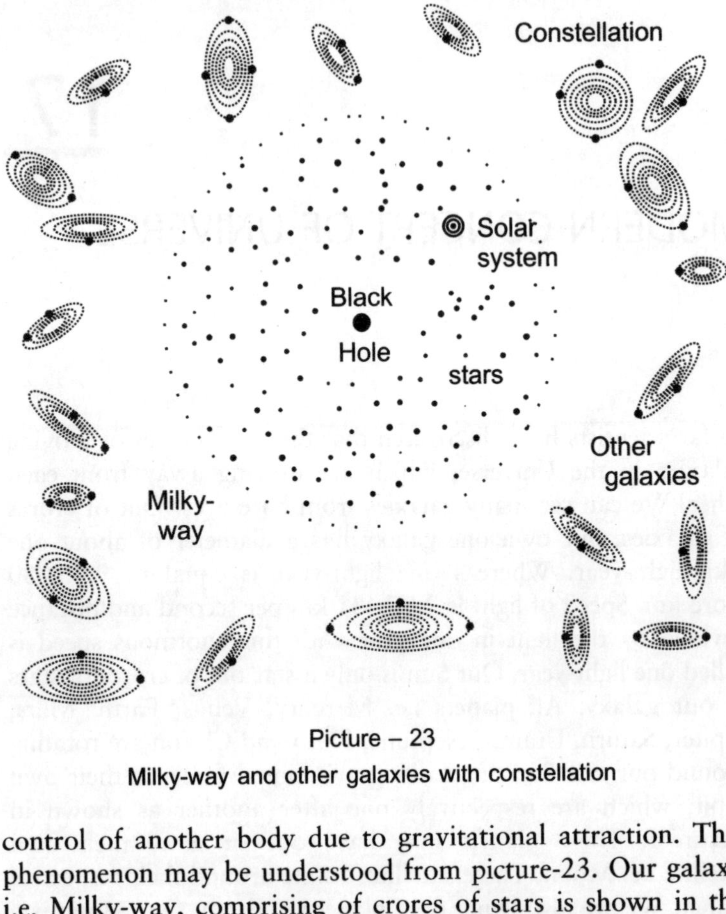

Picture – 23

Milky-way and other galaxies with constellation

control of another body due to gravitational attraction. This phenomenon may be understood from picture-23. Our galaxy i.e. Milky-way, comprising of crores of stars is shown in the centre. You may see our galaxy with these stars only in a clear night, because these stars are dim. Black-hole is shown in the centre of our galaxy. Our star Sun rotating around the Black-hole with solar system is also shown in the picture. Constellations situated in many other galaxies, whose individual distance is still not known, are also shown around our galaxy. We observe these constellations, who are building block of 12 signs, in the background of our planets. Sun along with solar system moves with a speed of 7.69 lakh km per hour and takes 2250 lakh years for completing one rotation of the Black-hole. Our solar system is 23000 light-years away from the Black-hole, which is in the centre of Milky-way galaxy, having diameter of one lakh light-years. Farthest galaxy, which can be observed with naked eye, is Andromeda galaxy, whose distance is 22 lakh light-years.

With the help of astrology we the people living on the Earth, simply study the impact of our satellite Moon, our star Sun, another five planets and 27 constellations situated in other unknown galaxies. Thus you may realise that impact of how much small portion of the Universe is being studied through astrology. Whereas 27 constellations are neither in our galaxy nor different galaxies in which these constellations are situated is still known. Because planets appears to move in front of these constellations, as if any thing moving in front of a curtain, hence our sages allotted name to these constellations to enable them to locate the celestial position of a planet. Subsequently, signs were formed and named after plotting a shape after conjoining the constellations and some other stars.

As all bodies in the Universe have their impact on all other bodies or on their material. Likewise our Earth which is also a body and bodies of the human beings, who are living on the Earth, are also made up of some matter hence we all experiences some sort of impact of the planets. We are continuously exposed to this impact, which is reaching in the form of attraction and waves having different wavelength and propagate in the Universe in the form of light, x-ray etc. Now it is natural and scientifically proved that any body, which is closer to another body, has impact on other bodies in the ratio of their distance. Because Moon is nearest from the Earth hence its impact on the Earth and human beings i.e. on the matter and living world would be more experienciable in comparison to the impact of other bodies of the Universe. In the same way the impact of a body which is respectively away from the Earth would correspondingly be less in comparison to the impact of the Moon. You can understand from the solar system as shown in picture-2 that the distance of all planets from the Earth continuously varies during their rotation. Thus order decided on the basis of the distance from the Earth in respect of four planets Mars, Venus, Mercury and Sun placed after Moon are continuously varying. In this way Moon is always nearest from the Earth and Jupiter, Saturn, Uranus, Neptune, Pluto are always far away in the same order, in every horoscope, whereas order of Mars, Venus, Mercury and Sun may vary in every horoscope. In this way quantum of impact of planet will also naturally vary from person to person depending on the composition of the various matter present in individual human being. Presence of Uranus, Neptune, Pluto was not known in the Primitive age, hence they were neither included in astrological calculations nor in astrological principles. Because it was believed that Saturn was situated at the end of the Universe. But after latest scientific discoveries it is being generally told in defence of astrology that Uranus, Neptune and Pluto have no significant impact on the human being, because they are far away from the Earth. If we analyse the impact of the constellations on the same analogy then the quantum of impact of these constellations would be nil because these constellations are not even in our own galaxy and they are scattered in various unknown galaxies, which are at a distance of millions of light-year. Thus actually there is no increase in the impact of a planet in a particular constellations as believed in the Primitive age but the impact of a planet actually increases only due to increase in its altitude. For example, it was believed that Jupiter might exert favourable impact when it is in Pushya constellation (not now). This favourable impact was not due to Pushya constellation, but it was due to the altitude of Jupiter, which may be 90° with reference to India. We will discuss this point in detail later on. Thus presently constellation may only be used for locating the celestial position of planets and not more than this.

Some astrologers may put forward their argument that Sun was placed nearer to the Earth in comparison to the Moon as shown in picture-1 because Sun is more effective and planets, constellations were arranged according to their influence, because sages know about the entire Universe with the help of meditation. These learned astrologers must realise that astrology was developed on the basis of Universe as described in primitive scriptures and not other way round to incorporate the shape of

Universe in the scriptures on the basis of influence of the planets. Beside this attention may also be drawn on the description of picture-1, where it is clearly mentioned with appropriate reference of primitive scriptures that according to *Vishnu Puran*, Sun is one lakh *yojan* above from the *Jambu-dweep* (stationary Earth) and Moon is again one lakh *yojan* above the Sun. According to belief of other religion, Sun is nearer from the Earth and Moon is far away from the Sun. Hence arguments of astrologers are not factually correct and they only misleads. So far argument of knowing the Universe with the help of meditation is concerned, it is enough to say that when sages were not able to know the shape of the Earth like ball, about its rotation around the Sun and distance of constellations with the help of so-called meditation then it was completely impossible to know about the Universe. These astrologers also try to cover-up the lacuna of non-inclusion of impact of Uranus, Neptune and Pluto in the astrology with the argument that there is no impact of these planets due to their enormous distance from the Earth. But while giving such trifling arguments, astrologers forget that all 27 constellations are not even in our Milky-way having a diameter of 94,60,80,000 *arab* km (billion km) i.e. one lakh light-year, then why they were included in astrological principles despite such enormous distance? In this circumstances the impact of constellations is questionable. Whereas factual position is that since Rising age it was believed that these constellations were present in between the Moon and Mercury as shown in picture-1 and on this logic these constellations were included in astrology.

If we compare the size of other planets with reference to star Sun which is situated in the centre of the solar system then we may realise that the diameter of the Sun is 13.80 lakh km, whereas the diameter of so-called biggest planet Jupiter is 1.42 lakh km, diameter of Saturn is 1.2 lakh km, diameter of our Earth is only 12.75 thousand km, diameter of Venus is 12.2 thousand km, diameter of Mars is 6.78 thousand km, diameter of Mercury is 4.9 thousand km and diameter of Moon is 3.37 thousand km. The average distance of the Pluto from the Sun is 591 crore km, whereas the distance of the next nearest star

Proxima Centauri from the Earth after our Sun is 4.28 light-years i.e. 40,23,608 crore km.

Because the distance of the planets is beyond our imagination hence we have to reduce the size of solar system to bring it in our imagination for proper understanding. I tried to exhibit the reduced distance and size in a table, in which 12,500 km is shown by 1 mm or 10 lakh km is shown by 8 cm. In this way distance of one light-year may be represented by 757 km and diameter of our galaxy may be 757 lakh km. The actual distance of all constellations is still not known as they are in different other galaxies. With the help of this table, if we draw a map then we can see that if our Earth may be shown by a size of one mm then size of the Sun will be about 11 cm and Earth may be kept at a proportionate distance of about 12 meters. Size and distance of other planets may also be understood in the same way. Rotational time of each planet around the Sun, with the number of their Moon is also given in the table. As Jupiter takes 11 years and 314 days for one rotation around the Sun and it has 14 Moons in its sky. Distance of nearest star Proxima Centauri will be 3240 km in this map.

Table

Planet etc.	Diameter	Distance from Sun	Rotational time	Moon
Sun	111 mm	—	—	—
Mercury	1/3 mm	4.62 meter	88 day	—
Venus	1 mm	8.64 meter	225 day	—
Earth	1 mm	11.97 meter	365 day	1
Mars	0.5 mm	18.22 meter	687 day	2
Jupiter	11 mm	62.32 meter	11 yr 314 day	14
Saturn	9.5 mm	114.4 meter	29 yr 167 day	10
Uranus	4 mm	229.44 meter	84 year	5
Neptune	4 mm	360.64 meter	165 year	2
Pluto	0.5 mm	472.64 meter	245 year	—
Moon	1/4 mm	3 cm (From Earth)		—
Proxima Centauri		3,240 km		
Milky-way		757 lakh km		

If we try to understand the gigantic size of the solar system and Universe by drawing a map according to the details given in the table then not only we can very well imagine the impact of the planets but can also realise the vast difference between the belief of Primitive age in comparison to actual scientific discoveries. From the above map, if we also try to understand the impact of the planets and constellations situated outside the galaxy, on the basis of their distance from the Earth and the diameter of our galaxy then it can easily be concluded that when we are not considering the impact of Uranus, Neptune and Pluto, who are situated in the radius of merely half kilometre as per map, due to unawareness of their presence in the Primitive age and presently due to their enormous distance from the Earth; then what is the logic in considering the impact of constellations who are not only situated outside from our galaxy having a diameter of 757 lakh km as per map but even their actual distance from the Earth is also still not known. In fact it is totally illogical to consider the impact of a constellation on the Earth. Because any change in the impact of planets was not due to their movement in a constellation (it was actually just moving in front of constellation), as considered in the Primitive age but change in impact was due to the change in altitude of the planets from the southern horizon or their relative angle from any location on the Earth. This point will be discussed later on.

Further if we compare the impact of all planets in percentage basis even when they are situated just few degrees away from each other, even then impact of the Moon will be prominent because it always remains nearest from the Earth. The impact of other planets will vary according to their distance from the Earth. We will also discuss this point later on.

If we visualise the three dimensional orbit of the planets of solar system with reference to the Black-hole then we can realise that all planets are moving in a direction and simultaneously they are also rotating around the Sun. You can understand this three dimensional orbit of the planets from picture-24.

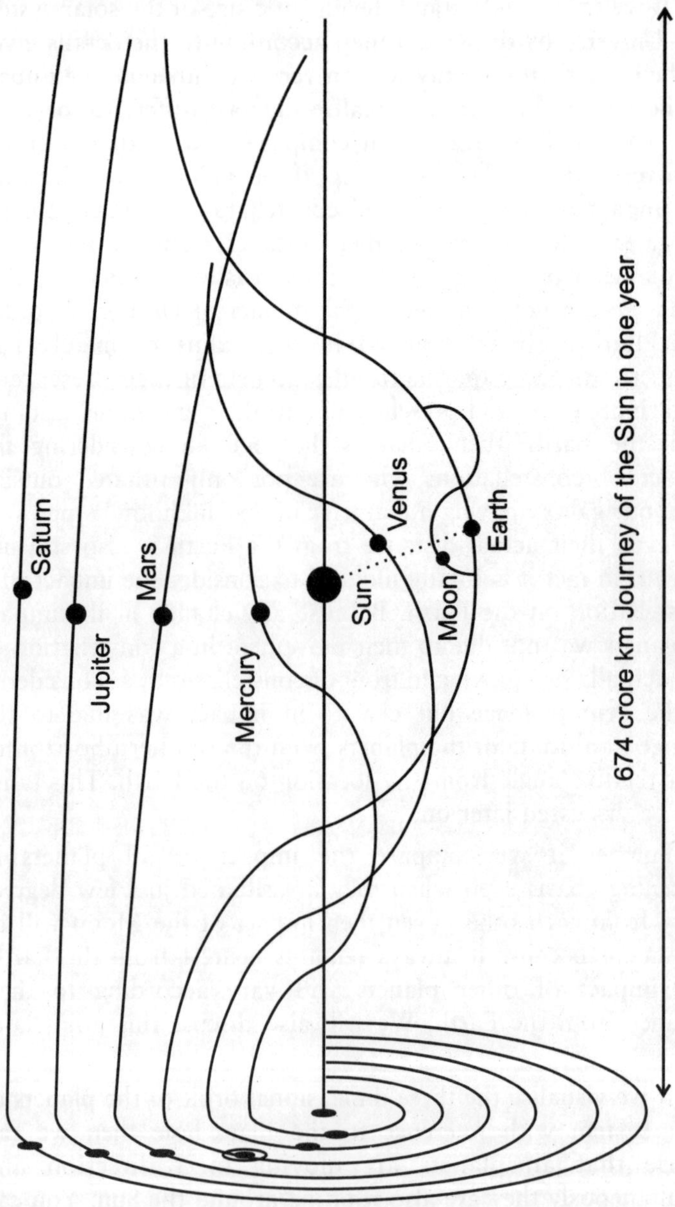

Picture – 24

Three dimensional transit of planets in the Milky-way

You can see from this picture that during a year when Earth complete its one rotation around the Sun; in the same time, Sun also travel a distance of 674 crore km in the galaxy while rotating around the Black-hole. During this whole process all planets not only move ahead with the Sun but they also remain in their individual orbit. During journey you may also have noticed that mosquitoes rotate around the illuminated bulb of a moving train and simultaneously they also move ahead with the speed of the train. Similarly the same process is also continuously going on between the Sun and planets in the Universe. In this process you may see that Earth has three type of speed. Firstly, it is rotating once around its pole in 24 hours by which there are day and night and every point of the Earth at the equator has to move by about 40 thousand km per day. Secondly, it is rotating in a circular manner around the Sun in a year by which there are seasons and the Earth has to move by about 94 crore km per year as shown in picture-2. Thirdly, it is moving 674 crore km in a year in the Milky-way with the Sun as shown in picture-24 by which *ayanansh* is increasing.

Earth rotates around the Sun in a year. Beside this Moon also rotates around the Earth in about 29.5 days. One rotation of the Moon is shown in the picture-24. Moon takes twelve rotation of the Earth in 354 days. Hence sages devised the system of introducing one extra month in three years to synchronise the lunar year with the solar year. When Moon remains at an outer most position with reference to the orbit of the Earth, as shown in the picture, then it is the day of full Moon and if Sun, Earth and Moon happens to be in a line then there is a lunar eclipse. Contrary to this, when Moon remains in the inner most side from the orbit of the Earth then there is dark night, and if Sun, Moon and Earth happens to be in a line then there is a solar eclipse. Hence position of the Rahu Ketu are according to the position of the Moon. But as per practice, which is being followed now-a-days position of the Rahu Ketu at the time of full eclipses is not matching due to mistake in astrological calculations relating to their retrograde motion. You have already studied this.

Now, we will study scientifically in deep about the concept of Retrograde, Set, Rahu / Ketu and Ayanansh.

> **TIP :** If you are amateur reader or find any difficulty at any time in understanding succeeding chapters then you may left these chapters and continue your study from the chapter of 'Deep thought', remembering that present status of these terms as used in astrology is scientifically not correct. Try to understand these left out chapters in next reading.

Tropic of Capricorn and Tropic of Cancer

Sun swing towards Northern Hemisphere and Southern Hemisphere during summer solstice and winter solstice respectively. The latitude from where it reverse the swing is known as Tropic. It was believed in the Primitive age that this reverse swing commences when Sun transit in Capricorn sign and Cancer signs respectively. Later on after implementing the concept of longitude and latitude, these Tropics were known as Tropic of Capricorn and Tropic of Cancer.

As per modern Gregorian calendar, Sun commences its motion in summer solstice and winter solstice on 23rd December and 23rd June respectively and at that time latitude of the Sun remains at 23.5° south and 23.5° north with reference to the equator. In other words, Sun remains at exact vertical position at noon from these latitudes. Hence lines of these latitude are known as Tropic of Capricorn and Tropic of Cancer. But now-a-days due to effect of *ayanansh* Sun happens to be in Sagittarius and Gemini sign at the time of summer solstice and winter solstice instead of Capricorn sign and Cancer sign respectively.

18

RETROGRADE AND SET PLANET

At present there is a complete illusion among many astrologers about the retrograde planet. Hence during retrogression of a planet either the result is unfavourable or favourable then in both situations astrologers will take shelter in the statement that planet is retrograde hence it is giving that particular result. Retrogression of a planet was never considered as a good sign since Rising age. Because in those days it was believed that negative impact of a planet may increase during retrogression. This belief still persists among the astrologers. Whereas there is complete ignorance about the correct astronomical situation of a planet during retrogression. I also find some remarkable fact during retrogression of a planet from self-developed software.

Now it is a well accepted fact that all planets including Earth rotate around the Sun in one direction and Moon is rotating around the Earth. Because Earth is rotating around the Sun in one direction hence Sun always appears to move in a direct motion from the Earth. Similarly, Moon rotates around the Earth in one direction hence Moon also appears to move in a direct motion from the Earth. Whereas, all other planets from Mercury to Chiron rotate around the Sun in one direction but with different individual circular motion. Hence it appears from the Earth that a particular planet is occasionally in retrograde motion. It is shown in picture-3 that how Mercury appears to be retrograde from the Earth whereas Mercury remains always in direct motion with reference to the Sun.

Position of Jupiter

S. No.	Date	Jupiter Deg.	Jupiter Dist.	Sun Deg.	Remark
1.	20-08-2003	124	9546	123	Coming closer/Set
2.	05-09-2003	128	9517	138	
3.	20-09-2003	131	9419	153	
4.	05-10-2003	134	9254	168	
5.	20-10-2003	137	9028	182	
6.	05-11-2003	140	8729	198	
7.	20-11-2003	142	8406	213	
8.	05-12-2003	143	8057	229	
9.	20-12-2003	144	7701	244	
10.	05-01-2004	145	7338	260	Jupiter retrograde
11.	20-01-2004	144	7041	275	
12.	05-02-2004	143	6795	292	
13.	20-02-2004	141	6656	307	
14.	05-03-2004	140	6617	321	Going away
15.	20-03-2004	138	6677	336	
16.	05-04-2004	136	6847	352	
17.	20-04-2004	135	7091	6	
18.	05-05-2004	135	7393	21	Jupiter direct
19.	20-05-2004	135	7732	36	
20.	05-06-2004	136	8108	51	
21.	20-06-2004	138	8454	65	
22.	05-07-2004	140	8777	80	
23.	20-07-2004	142	9062	94	
24.	05-08-2004	145	9314	109	
25.	20-08-2004	148	9490	124	
26.	05-09-2004	152	9607	139	
27.	20-09-2004	155	9645	154	Coming closer/Set

It is also true that there is a change in the impact of a retrograde and set planet. Hence picture-25 may be seen for correct understanding of the impact of retrograde and set planet along with their actual astronomical position. Movement of 30° of the Jupiter has been analysed in this picture. For this analysis, 27 actual data has been taken for the period from 20-8-2003 to 20-9-2003 with an interval of 15 days. Distance of the Jupiter from the Earth is shown in lakh km.

Position of the Earth along with serial number of the data of the table, is shown in picture-25. Likewise all position of the Jupiter has been incorporated in the picture with specific indication of the position of serial number 1, 10, 18 and 27. Sun is shown in the centre of the picture. Because like all other planets, Jupiter also moves in a direct motion with reference to the Sun, hence Jupiter is shown as small circle moving ahead in the picture.

From the data of distance incorporated in the table, we can find that Jupiter was moving towards the Earth from s.no. 1 to 14 and it was moving away from the Earth during 5-3-2004 to 20-9-2004. Whereas if you consider the position of the Jupiter with reference to degree-sign then you can see that it was in direct motion from s.no. 1 to 10 while it directly transit from 124° to 145° i.e. up to the 25° of Leo sign. After which it appears to be in retrograde motion till s.no. 18 and take reverse transit up to 135°. Thereafter from 5-5-2004 it reappears in a direct motion.

If we consider various position of the Jupiter in picture-25 on the basis of data given in the table then we can see that the Earth and Jupiter were situated in just opposite position with reference to the Sun in accordance with the data at s.no. 1. Jupiter was far away from the Earth in this position i.e. 9546 lakh km. The instant position of the Earth, Sun and Jupiter in the solar system may be seen and understand from picture-2. We can also see from the data given in the table that there was minimum difference in the degree-sign position of the Jupiter and Sun as these two planets are situated on one side of the zodiac and solar system with reference to the Earth. It is believed since Primitive age that whenever such position exist between Sun and any other planet then other planet may be considered as set and impact of that planet is also destroyed. Whereas factually the impact of the planet is reduced only because in such situation planet is far away from the Earth. Further, if we analyse the position of the Sun and Jupiter from

8-9-2003 then we can see that degree-sign i.e. longitudinal difference between them would be more than 12°. In this situation Jupiter may no longer be considered as a set planet and it may be presumed that then onward Jupiter will exert its full impact. Whereas if we analyse the position on the basis of the data then it is evident that the distance of the Jupiter was still 94.19 crore km in comparison to maximum distance of 95.46 crore km. In this way if we scientifically analyse the impact of the Jupiter then it is quite clear that there was no substantial change in the impact of the planet. We can feel the substantial change in the impact of the Jupiter as and when it would be in-between the maximum and minimum distance from the Earth. In this way the impact of the Jupiter would be substantial as per details shown against s.no. 8, when Jupiter would be at a distance of less than about 80 crore km from the Earth i.e. since 5-12-2003. Motion of the Jupiter was retrograde from the position shown at s.no. 10. Thus if we match Jupiter came nearest on 5-3-2004 as per details against s.no. 14 when it was 66 crore km from the Earth. Whereas the planet was still in a retrograde motion. The impact of the planet on this date would be maximum due to its minimum distance from the Earth, which was increasing day by day since 20-8-2003. The planet appears to be retrograde till 5-5-2004 as per details given against s.no. 14 to 18. Whereas Jupiter was moving away from the Earth and its distance from the Earth was increasing, which may also be seen in picture-25. Hence the impact of the planet would also be reduced in the same ratio. Retrograde planet was not considered as a good phenomenon since Primitive age because it was believed that impact of the malefic planets increases during this period. In this way this belief has 50% support with reference to the modern concept. But you have seen as to how the impact of a planet starts to reduce even when it is retrograde. Thus it may be clear that during first half period of the retrogression a planet came closer to the Earth while during second half period of the retrogression it actually move away from the Earth. Hence during first half period between retrograde and direct motion, the impact of a planet increases whereas during

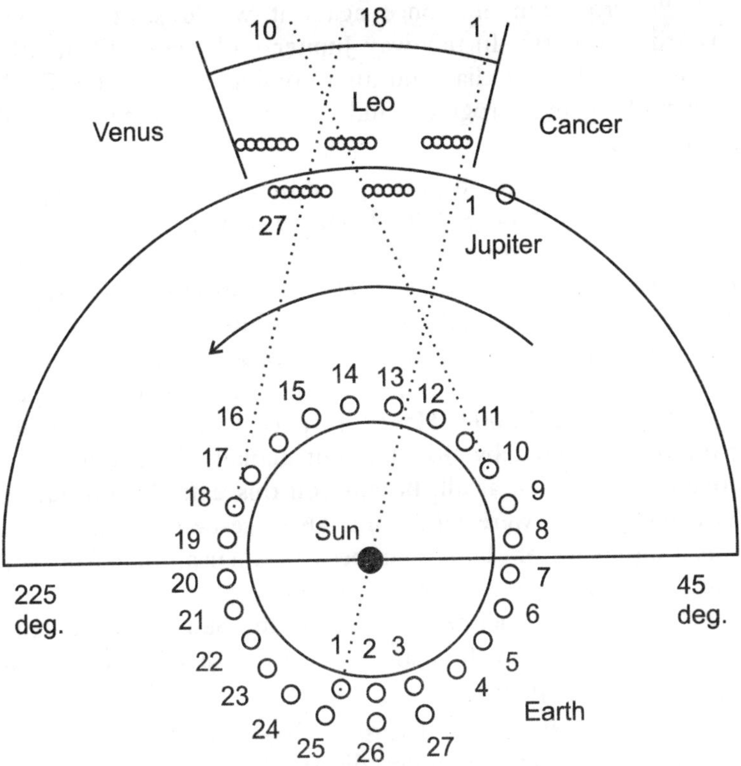

Picture – 25
Actual position of retrograde Jupiter

second half period the impact is actually reduced due to increasing distance. Now if we analyse the position of Jupiter after 5-5-2004 then it can be observed that the planet was in direct motion. Astrologer will consider it as a favourable situation in accordance with the principles as laid down in the Primitive age. Whereas despite direct motion of the planet, actually it was moving away from the Earth till 20-9-2004 as per details up to s.no. 27. Hence its impact would also reduce continuously. Degree-sign or Longitudinal position of the Sun and Jupiter was again very close to each other on 20-9-2004 and Jupiter would again be considered as set with least impact. Distance of the Jupiter from the Earth on that date was 96 crore km and once again it would start to move towards the Earth. In this way Jupiter took about 13 months in moving 31° of zodiac and after coming closer to the Earth it would again retrograde and this cycle will be repeated continuously.

Longitudinal i.e. degree-sign difference between Jupiter and Sun was 12° on 6-9-2004. Hence it was considered as a set planet in accordance with the belief prevailed in the Primitive age. Whereas scientifically the impact of a planet can actually be destroyed only when it is behind the Sun or Moon and it is fully covered by the Sun or Moon. Longitudinal i.e. degree-sign position of the Jupiter and Sun was almost equal i.e. 155° on 22-9-2004. Hence it appears that Jupiter would have been covered by the Sun. But actually Jupiter was not covered by the Sun at all. Because on this date the altitude of Sun and Jupiter were 64.2° and 66.1° respectively i.e. there was a difference of about 2° in between their altitude from the southern horizon and Jupiter was moving 2° above the Sun hence Jupiter was neither covered by the Sun nor is actually set. Later on we will again discuss in detail about such situation of the planets.

Detail of distances as discussed above will not match with the minimum and maximum distances as shown in earlier chapter because during every rotation there is a slight difference between the mutual distances of the Earth and planet from the Sun and accordingly the distance of the planet from the Earth also varies in the same ratio during every rotation.

To have a more clear conception about the relation between distance and longitudinal position of the planet. Just have a look on the picture-26 based on the actual data given earlier. From which you can clearly understood the relation between the distance and retrogression of a planet.

We can see that Jupiter was far away from the Earth when it was at 124° and 155° as shown by 'A' in the picture. It was moving towards the Earth till position 'B' of 145°. From here onward it became retrograde till position 'D' of 135°. During the mid-period of retrogression it came at point 'C' which was nearest to the Earth. The planet moves away from the Earth

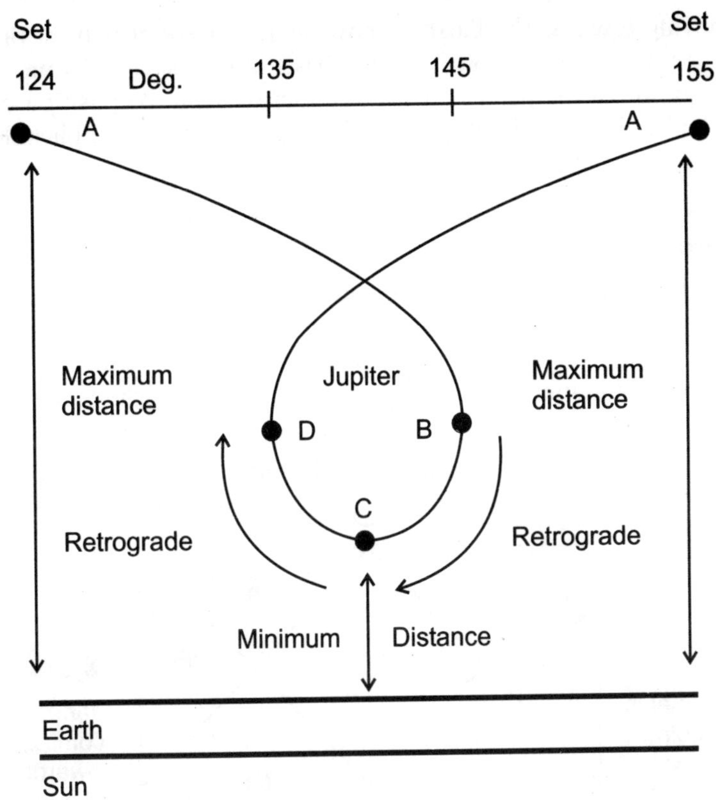

Picture – 26

Relation in distance and retrograde motion of Jupiter

after crossing this point. Whereas after point 'D' it was still moving away from the Earth though it was now in direct motion.

Likewise distance of Mars, Jupiter and Saturn from the Earth varies during direct and retrograde motion due to their outer orbit with reference to the orbit of the Earth and the distance of the planet is maximum during so-called set position. Whereas distance of the planet is minimum during the mid-period of retrogression.

It can also be worked out from the horoscope as to whether a planet was moving away from the Earth or it was moving towards the Earth or how far they were near from the Earth at the time of birth, on the basis of simple calculation of longitude of the planets i.e. degree-sign or from the position of the planets in the house. The following procedure is applicable only for Mars, Jupiter and Saturn.

Procedure for determining the position of planet from horoscope

Picture-27 may be seen for understanding the procedure. If any one out of the above three planets is positioned till sixth sign behind the Sun then that planet was coming towards the Earth. If a planet is positioned till sixth sign after the Sun then

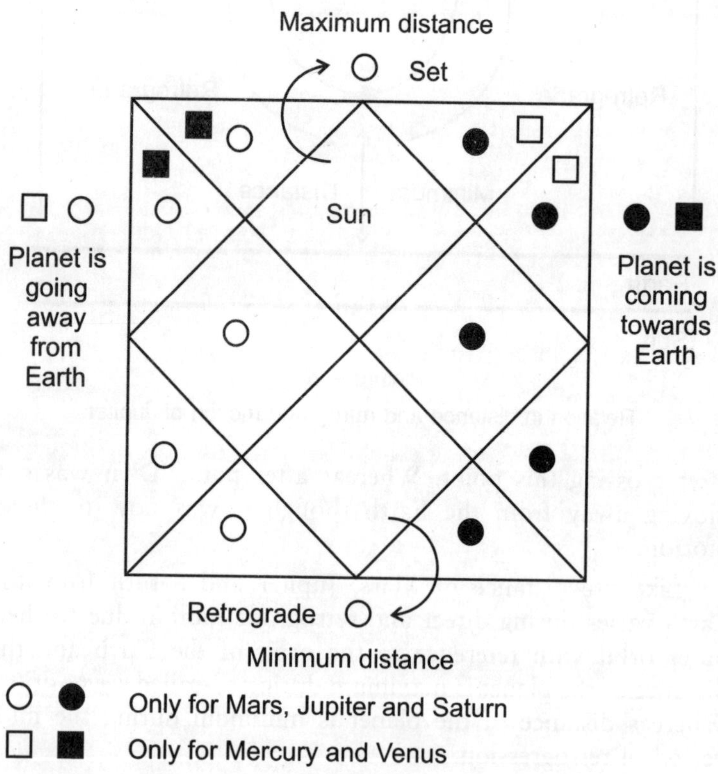

Picture – 27
Distance of the planet on the basis of horoscope

the planet was moving away from the Earth. If the planet is placed in seventh sign from the house of the Sun then planet would be retrograde as well as nearest from the Earth. If it is with the Sun then planet would be far away from the Earth as well as may be treated as set, if they were very close to each other, as believed since Primitive age.

Procedure for calculating the position of planet

If the difference between the planet and Sun is less than 180° then planet was coming towards the Earth. For this purpose, convert the degree-sign of the planet in degrees and add 180° to it. If it is more than 360° then 360° may be deducted. If these degree is more than the degree, obtained after converting degree-sign to degree, of the Sun then planet was coming towards the Earth.

For example :–

A – If Jupiter is at 15° of Taurus sign and Sun is at 20° of Libra sign then

Degree of Jupiter = 35° and

Degree of Sun = 200° then

35° + 180° = 215°

This is more than 200° of the Sun.

B – If Jupiter is at 15° of Scorpion sign and Sun is 20° of Aries sign then

Degree of Jupiter = 235° and

Degree of Sun = 20° then

235° + 180° = 415°

It is more than 360° hence deduct 360°

415° – 360° = 55°

This is more than 20° of the Sun.

Hence Jupiter is coming towards the Earth in both of the above situations.

Contrary to this if after adding 180° in the degree of a planet, it is less than the degree of the Sun i.e. difference between the planet and the Sun is more than 180° then planet is moving away from the Earth.

For example :–

If Jupiter is at 15° of Capricorn sign (285°) and Sun is 15° of Leo sign (135°) then according to the procedure :–

285° + 180° = 465°

It is more than 360° hence deduct 360°

465° – 360° = 105°

It is less than the 135° of the Sun.

Hence planet is moving away from the Earth.

Beside this the correct impact based on the distance of a planet can be worked out in accordance with the original motive of the sages. Which will be discussed later on.

Position of Mercury and Venus is quite different from the other three planets due to their inner orbit with reference to the orbit of the Earth. Actually there are two different situations of these two planets, whenever they are considered as set in accordance with the present practice and primitive belief. This can be understood from picture-28.

It would be clear from the picture that these two planets are considered as set twice during their one rotation when their degree-sign or longitudinal position match with the Sun, because orbits of the Mercury and Venus are inside the bigger orbit of the Earth and they are on the line of Sun and Earth. But actually when these planets are far away from the Earth and in position number 2 as shown in the picture and when they are moving behind the Sun then only these planets may be considered as set and it may be presumed that the impact of a planet is destroyed. Whereas these planets are actually more effective due to their closeness to the Earth on retrogression in position number 1. At this time Sun must be treated as set because in this situation these planets are moving in between the Sun and Earth though there may be negligible reduction in the impact of the Sun. Whereas presently the impact of these planets are being moulded according to the requirement in

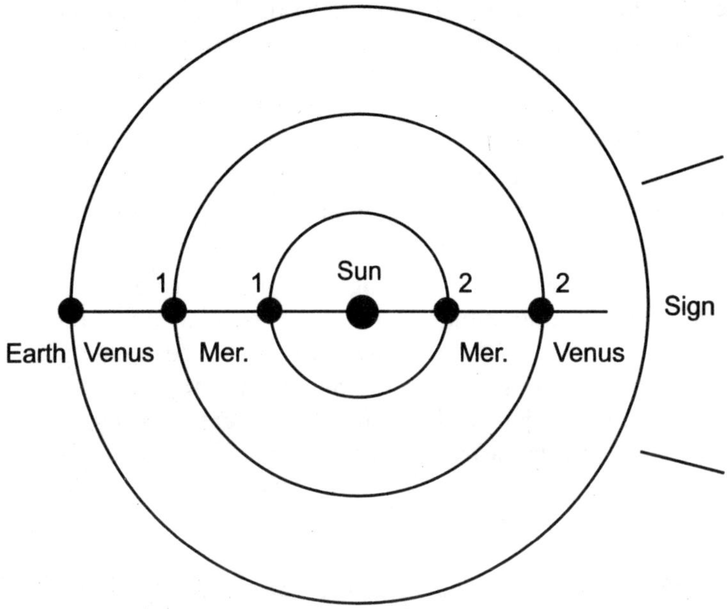

Picture – 28
Set position of the Mercury and Venus

prediction by quoting that these planets are either set or these planets are not considered as set.

For example, Mercury was far away in comparison to the Sun on 4-3-2004 as shown in the table. Hence it may be treated as Set as longitudinal position of both planets were same. But Mercury was nearer from the Earth in comparison to the Sun on 16-4-2004. Hence Sun must be treated as Set because it was behind the Mercury.

Date	Longitude of		Distance in lakh km	
	Sun	Mercury	Sun	Mercury
04-3-2004	320	320	1484	2039
16-4-2004	3	3	1501	868

We can work out from the longitude i.e. degree-sign of the Sun and these two planets as to whether these planets were coming towards the Earth or they were moving away from the Earth. Planet was coming towards the Earth if longitude i.e.

degree-sign of the planet is more than the longitude of the Sun i.e. the planet is either placed in the next house from the Sun or if in the same house and the degree of the planet is more than the degree of the Sun. Contrary to this, planet was moving away from the Earth if the Sun is placed in the next house of the planet or if in the same house and the degree of the planet is less than the degree of the Sun.

The position may also be assessed from the retrograde position of the planet. If the longitude of the retrograde planet is more than the longitude of the Sun then planet was coming towards the Earth and if the longitude of the retrograde planet is less than the longitude of the Sun then planet was moving away from the Earth. But during retrogression these two planets are always nearer from the Earth. The above position of these two planets may also be understood from picture-29.

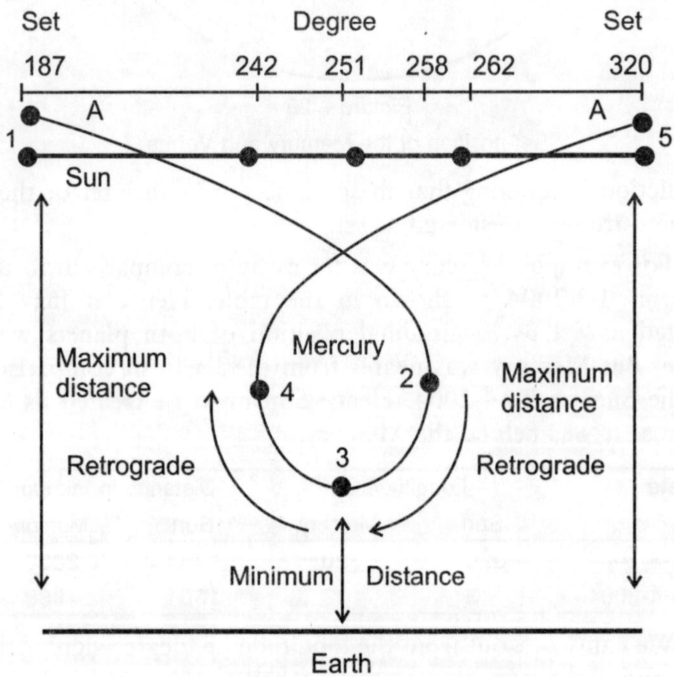

Picture – 29
Set and retrograde position of the Mercury

You can also match the transitory position of the Mercury from 25-10-2003 to 4-3-2004 on the basis of the data given in the table. We can see from the picture that Mercury was far away from the Earth and was behind the Sun as per data at s.no. 1. As both these planets were situated at 7° of Leo sign with reference to the Earth hence Mercury was considered as set. By the passage of time, Mercury would move ahead from the Sun as per their longitude and simultaneously Mercury was coming towards the Earth. In this way by 18-12-2003, longitude of the Mercury would be 16° (258° – 242° = 16°) more with reference to the longitude of the Sun as shown by position number 2 in the picture in accordance with data at s.no. 2. After this Mercury would retrograde. According to present practice, Mercury was considered as set on 27-12-2003, when these two planets were at 11° of Sagittarius sign as shown by position number 3 in the picture according to data at s.no. 3. Whereas actually the Mercury was more effective due to its closeness from the Earth. Because the Mercury was situated in between the Sun and the Earth. Actually Sun would have been considered as set, because it was behind the Mercury with reference to the Earth, in the Universe. After this Mercury would lag behind the Sun in comparison to his longitude though Mercury was still in retrograde motion till 7-1-2004 as shown by position number 4 in the picture according to data at s.no. 4. It would retrograde and lag behind by 20° (262° – 242° = 20°) from the Sun by the time when its longitude was 2° of Sagittarius sign i.e. 242° and it would also continue to move away from the Earth. Because

Table
Data of Mercury

S. No.	Date	Deg. and dist. of Mercury		Degree of Sun	Remark
1.	25-10-2003	187	2134	187	Coming closer/Set
2.	18-12-2003	258	1180	242	Retrograde
3.	27-12-2003	251	1009	251	Nearest to Earth
4.	07-01-2004	242	1218	262	Direct
5.	04-03-2004	320	2040	320	Away from Earth

Mercury actually start to move away from the Earth in the middle of retrogression i.e. from 27-12-2003. After the situation as shown at position no. 4, the planet would be in direct motion and start to increase its longitudinal position. Whereas it was still lagging behind the Sun and its distance from the Earth is also continuously increasing. Thus these two planets would reach to the position number 5 in the picture on 4-3-2004 when the longitude of these planets were 20° of Aquarius sign i.e. 320°. Where Mercury was considered as set due to Sun and position number 1 will reappear, with different longitude.

Thus you may have clearly understand as to why there is a deviation in the impact of these planets during retrogression and set. The above analysis match by 50% with primitive belief. But if the position of planet may be analysed in view of the modern knowledge then only correct impact of these planets may be assessed.

When a planet may be considered as set, quantum of deviation in their impact due to change in distance from the Earth during transit, retrogression, set will scientifically be discussed later on.

19

ACTUAL RAHU-KETU

So far you may have read in many other books that those two points on the ecliptic (orbit of the Sun) at which orbit of Moon intersect it, are Rahu and Ketu. But nothing is clear from this statement. Do you know that every planet has its own Rahu and Ketu? Our own Moon creates those Rahu Ketu, which we are studying in astrology. There was no clear and correct conception about the existence or Rahu / Ketu in the Universe since Rising age. Many astrologers of today may also be not aware with the correct concept of Rahu and Ketu. Rahu was considered to be responsible for changing face of the Moon since Rising age. Whereas now we know that the illuminating portion of the Moon is actually the light of the Sun which is falling on it and actually brighten portion of this light is responsible for changing face of the Moon. Similarly during solar and lunar eclipse, Sun and Moon are neither being destroyed nor eaten away nor captured by the Rahu or Ketu as is being believed since the Rising age, but solar and lunar eclipse occurred only due to movement of the Moon in between the Sun, Earth and movement of the Earth in between the Sun, Moon respectively.

Though Universe is a three-dimensional creation, in which every body is moving due to gravitation of Black-hole, star and planets. But with a view to have a clear understanding about Rahu / Ketu, we may imagine that Sun is stationary and place it on a two-dimensional plane while Earth is moving

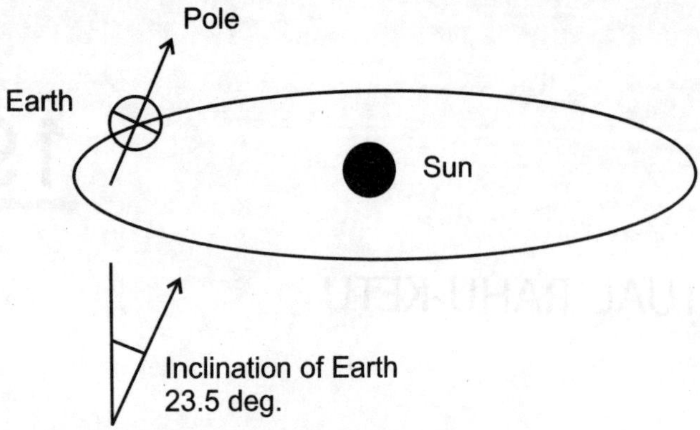

Picture – 30

Orbit of inclined Earth

around the Sun with an inclination of about 23.5°. This position may clearly be understood from picture-30.

Now if we lift this plane and visualise it in three-dimension. Then we may see that space, above and below of the plane is empty. It has now been proved and well-known that Moon is rotating around the Earth. But Moon is not rotating on the above mentioned imaginary plane, which is formed by the situation of the Sun and orbit of the Earth, but the orbit of the Moon is also inclined and during its rotation it moves above and below sides of the first plane. In this way if we keep Earth and Moon on a plane then it will be a second plane. The orbit of the Moon is always on this second plane. You may clearly understand this phenomenon from picture-31. While moving on this second plane, Moon will cross the first plane and will continue to move on the second plane but at the below side of the first plane. Similarly, Moon will again cross the first plane and will come on the above side of the first plane but it will continue to move only on the second plane. In this way Moon crosses the first plane during its rotation around the Earth. Those two points on which Moon actually crosses the first plane are formation points of Rahu and Ketu. That point from where Moon emerges from the first plane during its rotation or that location of the Moon in the zodiac

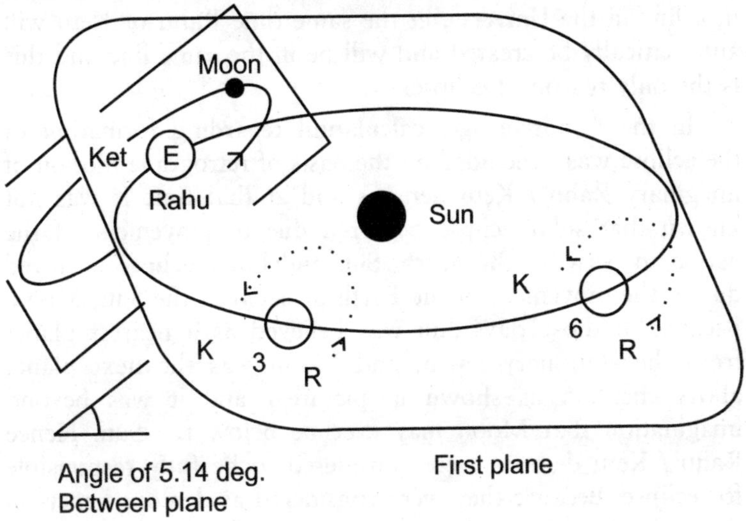

Picture – 31
Creation of Rahu Ketu due to rotation of Moon

is the location of the Rahu whereas that point from where Moon move beneath the first plane during its rotation or that location of the Moon in the zodiac is the location of the Ketu. During next rotation i.e. during one complete rotation through all signs in about 29.5 days, Moon will not cross the first plane from the earlier point or from where the Rahu or Ketu was formed. But Moon will re-emerge after 27 days from a point or cross the first plane which is 1° 26' (27 × 3' 11" = 85' 57") behind the earlier point with a daily retrograde motion of 3' 11". Here retrograde motion of 3' 11" has only taken to clarify the concept of the subject. Actual correct position of Rahu / Ketu may only be ascertained at the time of full eclipse and angular difference of 180° between Rahu and Ketu is also not correct because their mutual difference is dependent on the motion of the Moon and its relative position with reference to the Sun. At present we kept the Earth, Sun on the first plane and Earth, Moon on the second plane. The inclination of the second plane with reference to the first plane is 5.14°. This whole position may clearly be understood from picture-31. In this way whenever Sun, Earth and Moon came in a line in the Universe, at the same time Rahu or Ketu will automatically be created and will be in the same line and this is the only reason of eclipse.

In the Primitive age, calculation regarding formation of the eclipse was concluded on the basis of retrograde motion of imaginary Rahu / Ketu demons and at that time it was not known that solar eclipse occurred due to movement of the Moon in between the Earth, Sun and lunar eclipse occurred due to the movement of the Earth in between the Sun, Moon. Because in those days Sun was believed as a nearest planet from the stationary Earth; and Moon was the next planet above the Sun as shown in picture-1 and it was beyond imagination that Moon may ever be below the Sun. Hence Rahu / Ketu demons were considered to be fully responsible for eclipse. Because they were considered as demons hence on the basis of eclipse their daily retrograde motion as 3' 11" was calculated. Now we know on the basis of latest knowledge of the solar system that eclipse appears only due to shadow of the Moon and Earth. Now it is being mentioned in the books of astrology that intersection points of ecliptic and orbit of the Moon are actually Rahu / Ketu. In this way they are effectively created during an eclipse i.e. only when Moon transit on the line, which may be drawn by joining the Sun and Earth; and while crossing the first plane as described in picture-31. Otherwise in other situation the shadow of the Moon will fall somewhere else in the solar system instead of falling on the Earth during crossing the first plane and in this situation there will be no eclipse, as may be seen from picture-31 against location no. 3 where Moon crosses the first plane by forming Rahu and Ketu but they are not in the line of Sun, Earth; hence shadow of the Moon will not fall on the Earth. Thus there would be no visual impact whatsoever of the imaginary Rahu / Ketu and the physical position of the Sun, Earth and Moon will be on a plane instead of in a line. Thus from the above description it would have been quite clear that Rahu / Ketu are effectively formed with reference to the Earth as and when there is some eclipse i.e. when Sun, Earth and Moon happens to be in a line, otherwise in other situation imaginary Rahu / Ketu will be formed as and when Sun, Earth and Moon may be in a plane and not in a line.

When Moon rotates around the Earth, at the same time Earth also rotates around the Sun. Thus when Rahu or Ketu are formed in between the Earth and Sun or at outer part of the orbit of the Moon at the time of solar or lunar eclipse respectively as is shown in picture-31. Then position of the Earth after three and six months along with Rahu and Ketu is also shown in the picture and indicated by 3 and 6 respectively. From this it would be clear that how solar or lunar eclipse, which occurs after five-six months might be reversed and formed due to Ketu or Rahu instead of Rahu or Ketu. More details in this regard have already been provided in the chapter of "Rahu and Ketu".

The position of Moon at Rahu / Ketu as shown in picture-31 is enlarged and shown in picture-32 to clear the subject matter. From this picture it will be quite clear that what is the position of Rahu / Ketu at the time of full solar and lunar eclipse and scientifically why there is a so-called eclipse when Rahu or Ketu is up to 14° away from the Sun and Moon as explained by calculation contained in '*Grahlaghav*'. Straight line number 5 is ecliptic of the Sun, whereas all other inclined line numbers 1 to 9 indicates various transitory path in the orbit of the Moon. Orbit of the Moon has inclination of 5.14° with the ecliptic. Line nos. 1, 2, 3, 5 and 6 are moving towards downward. The point where these lines cross the straight line no. 5, is the position of formation of Rahu. Because after crossing this line, Moon transit towards the upper part of the first plane i.e. towards the north direction or Moon is in a forward position in the Universe with reference to the Sun and Earth. Line numbers 4, 5, 7, 8 and 9 are moving towards upward. The point where these lines cross the straight line number 5, is the position of Ketu. Because after crossing it, Moon transit towards the lower part of the first plane i.e. towards the lower direction or Moon is in a backward position in the Universe with reference to the Sun and Earth. This phenomenon may also be understood from picture-24, where Moon is behind the plane i.e. line joining Sun Earth, in the Universe.

Solar eclipse

Sun is shown at left-hand side end of the straight line number 5 in picture-32. This line is made up from various points on the first plane, from where the Moon appears to cross it and Sun visually transit on this line i.e. ecliptic. Your eye is the position of the Earth. Moon is shown at right-hand side. There is difference of 14° between the position of the Sun and Moon. Transit of the Moon is visible on any inclined line. Slide a circular cutting of paper of the size of the Moon by keeping its centre on any line. Now you may observe that when you slide this paper moon on line no. 3 then it will move over and above the Sun and it will move upward after moving in between your eyes (Earth) and the Sun; and it will cross the straight line no. 5 from the centre of the Sun. Only in this situation there will be a full solar eclipse and position of the Rahu would also be equal to the degree-sign position of the Sun and Moon. If you slide your paper moon over the line no. 7 then it will again move over and above the Sun and it will move downward after moving in between your eyes and the Sun and it will cross the straight line no. 5 from the centre of the Sun. Again in this situation there will be a full solar eclipse and position of the Ketu would also be equal to the degree-sign position of the Sun and Moon. If you slide your paper moon over the line no. 2 or 8 then it can be observed that it will not move over and above the Sun but it will pass away from very near to the Sun and cross the straight line no. 5 somewhere at an angular distance of about 14°. In both these situations, position of Rahu or Ketu would be about 14° from the degree-sign position of the Sun. If you slide your paper moon over the inclined lines no. 5 then it can be observed that again it will not move over and above the Sun but it will pass away from very near to the Sun. But the Moon has initially crossed the straight line no. 5 at an angular distance of about 14°. In both these situations, position of Rahu or Ketu would be 14° earlier from the degree-sign position of the Sun. Likewise if you slide your paper moon on

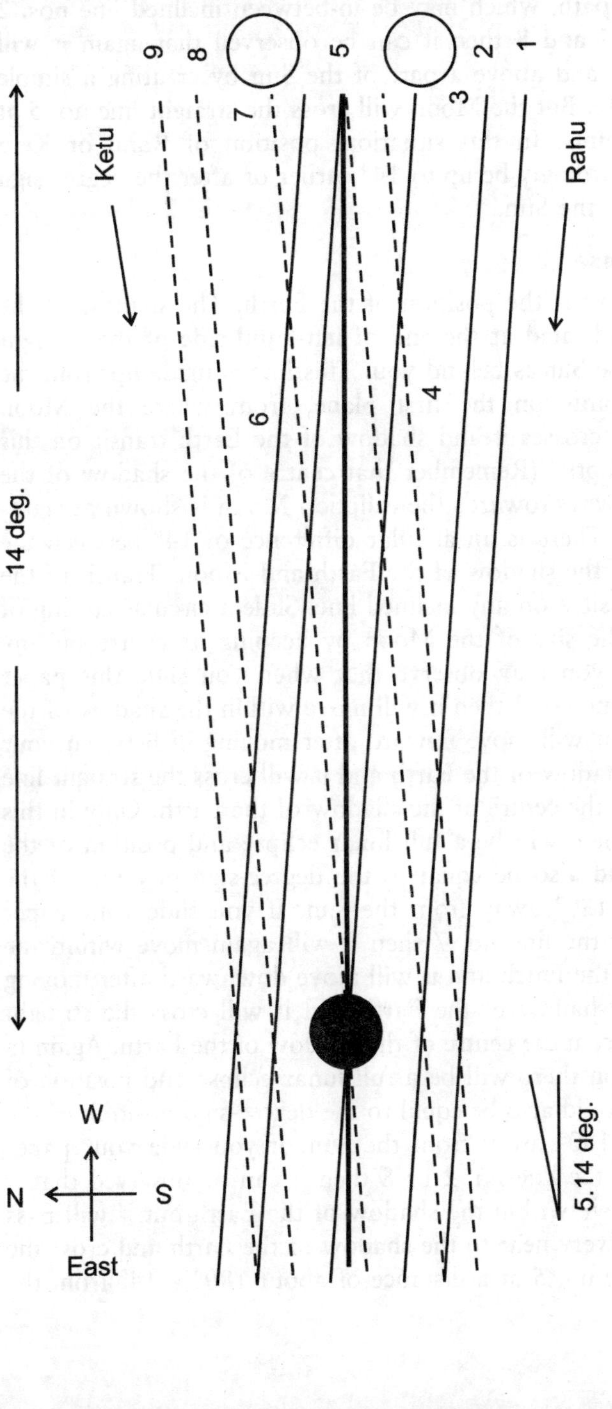

Picture – 32
Full solar and lunar eclipse

any other path, which may be in-between inclined line nos. 2 and 5 or 5 and 8 then it can be observed that again it will move over and above a part of the Sun by creating a simple solar eclipse. But the Moon will cross the straight line no. 5 at various points. In this situation, position of Rahu or Ketu would accordingly be up to 14° earlier or after the degree-sign position of the Sun.

Lunar eclipse

Your eye is the position of the Earth. The shadow of the Earth is indicated at the end of left-hand side of the straight line because Sun is behind you. This line is made up from the various points on the first plane, from where the Moon appears to crosses it and shadow of the Earth transit on this line i.e. ecliptic. (Remember that centre of the shadow of the Earth is always towards the ecliptic.) Moon is shown at right-hand side. There is an angular difference of 14° between the position of the shadow of the Earth and Moon. Transit of the Moon is visible on any inclined line. Slide a circular cutting of paper of the size of the Moon by keeping its centre on any line. Now you may observe that when you slide this paper moon on line no. 3 then it will move within the shadow of the Earth and it will move upward after moving in between your eyes and shadow of the Earth and it will cross the straight line no. 5 from the centre of the shadow of the Earth. Only in this situation there will be a full lunar eclipse and position of the Rahu would also be equal to the degree-sign position of the Moon i.e. 180° away from the Sun. If you slide your paper moon over the line no. 7 then it will again move within the shadow of the Earth and it will move downward after moving within the shadow of the Earth and it will cross the straight line no. 5 from the centre of the shadow of the Earth. Again in this situation there will be a full lunar eclipse and position of the Ketu would also be equal to the degree-sign position of the Moon i.e. 180° away from the Sun. If you slide your paper moon over the line no. 2 or 8 then it can be observed that it will not move within the shadow of the Earth but it will pass away from very near to the shadow of the Earth and cross the straight line no. 5 at a distance of about 180° + 14° from the

Sun. In both these situations, position of Rahu or Ketu would be about 180° + 14° from the degree-sign position of the Sun. If you slide your paper moon over the inclined lines no. 5 then it can be observed that again it will not move within the shadow of the Earth but it will pass away from very near to the shadow of the Earth. But the Moon has initially crossed the straight line no. 5, hence in both these situations, position of Rahu or Ketu would be 180° – 14° from the degree-sign position of the Sun. Likewise if you slide your paper moon on any other path, which may be between inclined line nos. 2 and 5 or 5 and 8 then it can be observed that again it will partly move within the shadow of the Earth by creating a simple lunar eclipse. But the Moon will cross the straight line no. 5 at various points and accordingly the position of Rahu or Ketu would be changed. In any other situation Moon will cross the ecliptic from an angular distance of more than 14° from the shadow of the Earth.

If ecliptic is crossed by the Moon at an angular distance of 90°, earlier or after, from the position of the Sun then as-and-when the degree-sign position of the Sun and Moon was or will be opposite to each other by 180° i.e. on the day of full-moon then in both situations the visual altitude of the Moon will be 5.14° from the ecliptic. Because at that time Moon will be 5.14° away from the ecliptic due to its inclined orbit. From this you can very well understand as to why there is an eclipse when intersection point of both orbits and formation of Rahu or Ketu is within 14° from the Sun or shadow of the Earth.

If you desire then only by observing an eclipse you can understand as to whether a particular eclipse is due to Rahu or due to Ketu. Beside this it can also be ascertained as to whether after this eclipse Moon will move in a forward or backward position in the Universe with reference to the plane of Sun and Earth. For this you may hold and uplift the picture-32 towards sky facing east direction according to the direction shown in the picture and ascertain all above fact by matching the transit of the Moon in its orbit with the shape of the eclipse.

In this way you may have clearly understood the fact explained in the chapter of "Rahu and Ketu" that at the time of full eclipse position of Rahu or Ketu must match the position of the Moon, otherwise there is no question of full eclipse. You may like to see the difference in position of Rahu or Ketu as contained in table nos. 1 and 2 incorporated in the chapter of "Rahu and Ketu" and verify how far position of Rahu / Ketu is matching with the position of Sun and Moon at the time of full eclipse. When this position is not matching then in this situation it is totally wrong to move them with an average retrograde motion of 3' 11" by keeping them at an angular distance of 180° from each other. Because this system was formulated and practised in the Primitive age due to classifying the Rahu and Ketu as demons. From the above explanation it would have been quite clear that actual Rahu / Ketu are created only when Sun, Earth and Moon happens to be on the same plane. Now in this situation it must be reconsidered as to how far it is correct to move them retrogradely with a fixed motion, when they are actually formed alternately after 27 days while crossing the plane of Sun and Earth, by the Moon during rotation around the Earth. For example you may have seen blinking lights in the electric frill, in which light appears to slide. But what happens in this frill is that when light of first bulb is off only then second bulb situated at a distance gets on. Hence there is an illusion that light is sliding. Whereas this illuminated light never travelled physically between these two bulbs, and illumination was only created at two different points at different times alternately. Likewise shadow formation of Rahu / Ketu never travelled between two points, but they are formed alternately at different degree-sign. Thus they must only and logically be shown in the horoscope according to the degree-sign of their just previous formation because it is totally wrong to show their position by adding about maximum 86' with an average retrograde motion of 3' 11" in their previous formation, by the time of next formation after 27 days on the basis of considering them as demons as believed in the Primitive age, because based on latest information, it is now mentioned in the astrological books that visual intersection points of ecliptic and orbit of the Moon are formation point of Rahu / Ketu.

Rahu / Ketu of other planets

All other five planets like Mercury, Venus, Mars, Jupiter and Saturn are also not remained on the first plane formed by Sun and Earth as shown in picture-31, while rotating around the Sun, but they separately rotate around the Sun in their respective individual plane like second plane formed by Moon and Earth. Whenever these five planets crosses the first plane formed by the Earth and Sun like the Moon, during their rotation around the Sun in their individual plane, then these intersection points are actually Rahu / Ketu for that planet. There is no description about these Rahu / Ketu of the planets in any astrological principles since Primitive age. Whereas after intersecting the visual ecliptic, these planets are able to cross the first plane formed by the Sun and Earth. In this way all these planets move ahead in the Universe with reference to the plane formed by the Sun and Earth, after forming their individual Rahu. Similarly these planets trails behind in the Universe with reference to the plane formed by the Sun and Earth, after forming their individual Ketu. The individual plane, formed by every planet with Sun due to their rotation around the Sun, has different angle with the first plane formed by the Sun and Earth. In this way plane of Earth-Moon has an angle of 5.14°, Sun-Mercury has an angle of 7°, Sun-Venus has an angle of 3.39°, Sun-Mars has an angle of 1.85°, Sun-Jupiter has an angle of 1.3°, Sun-Saturn has an angle of 2.49°, with the plane of Sun and Earth. Rahu / Ketu of these planets are also formed with a different retrograde motion like the Rahu / Ketu formed by the Moon. The impact of the Rahu / Ketu of individual planets has not been studied so far in the astrology because when sages were studying the impact of the planets and formulating the astrological principles in the Primitive age, they were not aware with these Rahu / Ketu because at that time the formation of the Universe was believed in the shape as shown in picture-1, hence there was not question of considering Rahu / Ketu of individual planets. But now when we realise that Rahu / Ketu are actually the intersection points of the orbit of the Moon and ecliptic then we must also consider the effect of formation of Rahu / Ketu of individual planets. Whereas beside studying the impact of the Rahu / Ketu of the Moon, it is also equally or rather more essential to study the impact on the living world in northern and southern hemisphere of the Earth at the time and after crossing the first plane from individual Rahu / Ketu by the individual planets. Mind and thought may be perplexed whenever Moon is near about to Rahu / Ketu. Because actually at this time Moon is transiting either in leading or trailing position in the Universe with reference to the first plane formed by the Sun and Earth. Similarly, there may be uncertainty in the related subject matter with the planets, due to the change in the impact of these planets on the Earth, whenever these planets are near to their respective Rahu / Ketu. Because actually they were transiting either in leading or in trailing position in the Universe with reference to the first plane formed by the Sun and Earth. Hence it will be prudent and justified to take care in the matter related with the planet.

Earth also transit either in leading or in trailing position in the Universe with reference to the vertical plane formed by the Sun and Black-hole, at the time when Sun appears to cross the equator i.e. at the time when day and night are equal. This fact may be understood from picture-33, where Sun is shown as rotating around the Black-hole. There may be a plane on which Black-hole and orbit of the Sun around the Black-hole may be placed. This plane may be understood in the form of page of the book. Another perpendicular plane with Sun and Black-hole may also be formed on this plane. This perpendicular plane is shown by a line joining Sun and Black-hole. Earth rotates around the Sun by maintaining an inclination of 23.5° with this second perpendicular plane or in other words there is an angle of 23.5° between orbit of the Earth around the Sun and perpendicular plane with Sun-Blackhole. This angle is known as angle of inclination of the Earth as shown in picture-30. Earth crosses this perpendicular plane of Sun-Blackhole twice in a year, during rotation around the Sun. Duration of day and night is equal at the time of crossing of this plane i.e. on 23rd March and 23rd September. Earth moves ahead in the Universe with reference to the perpendicular

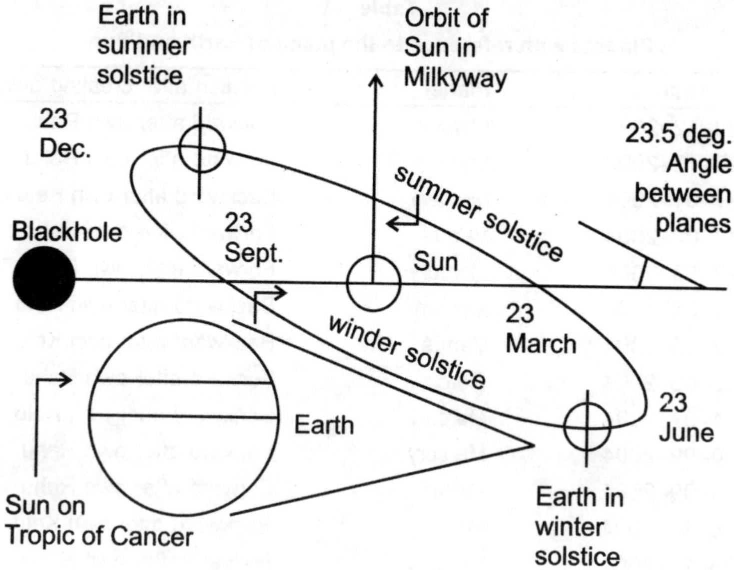

Picture – 33

Inclination of orbit of the Earth

plane of Sun-Blackhole after passing from its Rahu on 23rd September. Likewise Earth trails behind in the Universe with reference to the perpendicular plane of Sun-Blackhole after passing from its Ketu on 23rd March. Sun remains perpendicular on the equator line at the time of crossing of the Earth from its own Rahu / Ketu, that's why duration of the day and night is equal on these dates. At the initial time of winter solstice i.e. on 23rd June, Sun is perpendicular on Tropic of Cancer. This position is also shown in the picture. Such rotation of the Earth is also the cause of *ayanansh*, which we will discuss later on.

At present Jupiter is moving ahead in the Universe with reference to the plane of Sun and Earth (understand it from picture-31 by forming separate individual plane for Jupiter etc. with Sun inclined on first plane) since January-2002 after creating its own Rahu and it will move behind this plane after creating its own Ketu in April-2008. The position of all other planets from December-2003 to January-2005 is shown in table-1.

Table – 1

Planets with reference to the plane of Earth and Sun

Date	Planet	Position after creating own
20–12–2003	Mercury	Forward after own Rahu
29–12–2003	Mars	Forward after own Rahu
27–01–2004	Mercury	Backward after own Ketu
17–02–2004	Venus	Forward after own Rahu
17–03–2004	Mercury	Forward after own Rahu
24–04–2004	Mercury	Backward after own Ketu
06–06–2004	Venus	Backward after own Ketu
13–06–2004	Mercury	Forward after own Rahu
21–07–2004	Mercury	Backward after own Ketu
10–09–2004	Mercury	Forward after own Rahu
29–09–2004	Venus	Forward after own Rahu
15–10–2004	Mercury	Backward after own Ketu
05–12–2004	Mercury	Forward after own Rahu
09–01–2005	Saturn	Forward after own Rahu
11–01–2005	Mercury	Backward after own Ketu
15–01–2005	Mars	Backward after own Ketu
17–01–2005	Venus	Backward after own Rahu

You may have understood from the description given in previous section as to how there may be a mutual angular difference of 165° to 195° between Rahu and Ketu; and how their motion varies from retrograde to direct on the basis of this angular difference. Beside this you may have also studied in the present chapter as to why a solar or lunar eclipse took place when Rahu or Ketu is within 14° either from Sun or shadow of the Earth respectively (refer picture-32). In this way you may have sufficient knowledge about the creation of Rahu / Ketu of Moon and other planets. Hence, now we will scientifically study in little deep about the Rahu / Ketu actually created by the Moon and understand about their actual motion, position, size and part of the Earth, which may be under the direct impact of creation of Rahu / Ketu for the purpose of astrology.

TIP : Succeeding description may appear to be most difficult. Hence it is essential to pay more attention and keep in mind three-dimensional image of solar system to understand it. If you are amateur reader or find any difficulty at any time in understanding succeeding description then you may left this chapter and continue your study from next chapter of 'Ayanansh' accepting that scientifically there is mistake in astrological calculations relating to fixed retrograde motion of Rahu / Ketu, their astrological position based on formulas given in *Grahlaghav* and their region of impact on the Earth etc. Try to understand this left out portion in next reading.

Motion of Rahu / Ketu

Now we knows that Moon is a satellite of the Earth and it rotates around the Earth and we observe it moving in front of twelve signs and 27 constellations. We also knows that Moon took about a little more than 27 days in one rotation around the Earth i.e. time taken for reappearing at same degree-sign or at same constellational position. But during this period of 27 days degree-sign position of the Sun also changes due to rotation of the Earth around the Sun. Thus Moon took about 2.5 days extra to cover this change. That's why night of full-moon or dark-night recur after every 29.5 days. As described in detail of picture-31 that after every rotation Moon crosses the plane a little earlier i.e. about 86' earlier. In this way in general speaking, daily retrograde motion of Rahu / Ketu works out to 3' 11" and calculation relating to eclipse is being performed on the basis of this motion since Primitive age. Same motion of Rahu / Ketu was also incorporated in *Grahlaghav*, which was written in sixteenth century, but it was also mentioned therein that necessary correction may also be carried out in the calculations on the basis of actual celestial position of the planets. But actually no corrections have been carried out in the calculation; and timings of next eclipse is being worked out on the basis of angular difference of 14° of Rahu / Ketu from the Sun on night of full-moon or day of dark night; and it is further corrected on the basis of timing of previous eclipse formed before 223 lunar months or old ready-made tables for showing accordingly in the almanac. But daily retrograde motion of Rahu / Ketu is being kept fixed at 3' 11".

We will again understand about the creation of Rahu / Ketu before going ahead to know about their motion. Now on the basis of scientific information we know that every mass which exist in the Universe is under the influence of gravitation of another mass. In this way gravitational force drag a mass towards inside whereas circulational force tries to throw it away. Any mass actually start to rotate around another mass due to counterbalance of these two forces. Only due to this counterbalance of forces, all planets including Earth rotates around the Sun; and Moon i.e. satellite of Earth and other planets rotates around their respective planets. Due to combined

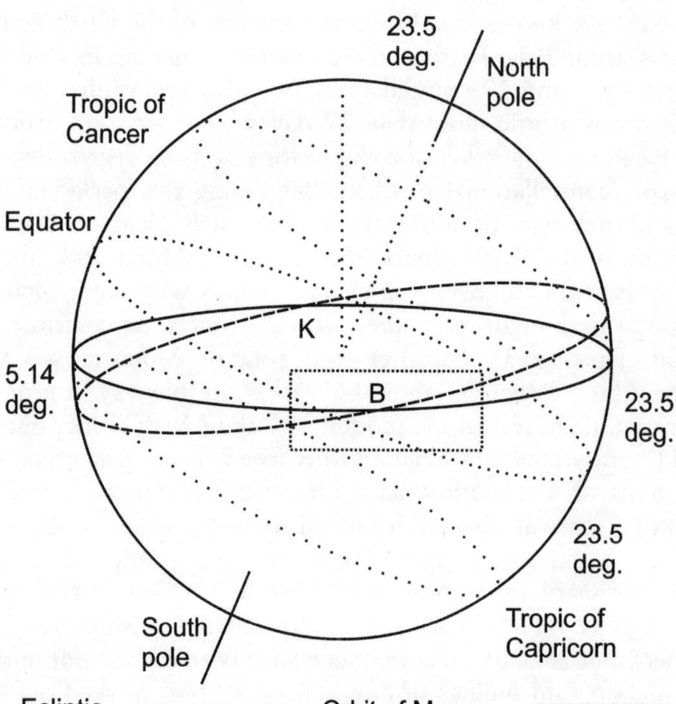

Picture – 34

Orbit of Moon and Sun

effect of the Earth and Sun, Moon actually rotates around the Earth with an inclination of 5.14° from the ecliptic. This phenomenon may clearly be understood from picture-34. Earth is shown as inclined in the picture by an angle of 23.5° so that view of the ecliptic may be straight. Pole, Tropic of Cancer, Tropic of Capricorn, Equator on the Earth, orbit of the Moon and ecliptic may be seen in the picture. It can also be understood from the picture as to how Moon complete its rotation around the Earth with an inclined angle of 5.14° with reference to the ecliptic and how it intersect the ecliptic at two different points 'K' and 'B'. Rahu and Ketu are created when Moon transit towards north and south respectively after crossing the ecliptic. Position of creation of Rahu is shown by a rectangle. This rectangle is enlarged and shown in picture-35. Solar and lunar eclipse occur as and when angular difference between position of Sun and Moon is either 0° or 180° respectively, during their motion in their respective orbits and position of Moon also coincides with the ecliptic. Moon intersects the ecliptic after completing its rotation in about 27 days and it intersects ecliptic a little earlier in comparison to its 27 days earlier intersection position. Both these situations are shown in the picture by a small arrow. Earlier Rahu was created by the motion of Moon at point 'A' at the time of intersecting the ecliptic and after completing the rotation

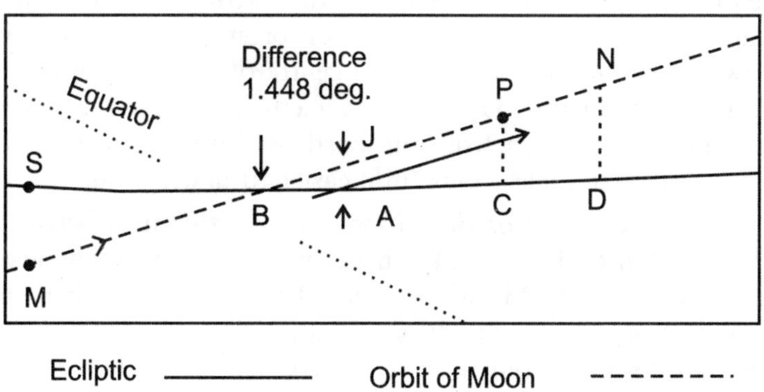

Picture – 35
Creation of Rahu

around the Earth by the Moon in about 27 days, next Rahu was created at point 'B' at the time of intersecting the ecliptic. At present angular difference between 'A' and 'B' is 1.4484°. Calculation and details of this degree will be described later on. If it is presumed that initially Sun and Moon were at point 'A' then after 27 days Sun will be at point 'C' on its orbit and Moon will be at point 'B'. Thus Sun will be about 28° away from point 'B'. Moon will take about two days in reaching to point 'P' from point 'B'. Sun will also move by 2° during these two days and will reach to point 'D'. Again Moon will take some extra time for reaching to point 'N', while moving on its orbit 'M, B, P, N'. Only after this, at the end of dark night, the Sun and Moon will again be at the same sign, degree after about 29.5 days from the earlier dark night. Degree-sign position of 'D' and 'N', 'C' and 'P' is same.

Moon rotates around the Earth in such a way so that its inclination with the ecliptic will always be 5.14°. This point is clearly shown in picture-36. For understanding this point more practically, take two bangles of different size and place small bangle inside another bangle with an angle of about 5°, presuming bigger and small bangle as ecliptic and orbit of the Moon respectively. After this, keep on rotating small bangle in different backward position as shown in picture-36 to easily understand the phenomenon of intersection of the ecliptic by the orbit of the Moon as seen from the Earth i.e. centre of the bangles. Three different position of orbit of the Moon is shown in picture-36. Sun is in the centre of orbit of the Earth as shown in picture-31, which is factually correct. But the same position as seen from the Earth is shown in picture-34 and 36, so that subject may little easier to understand.

Because distance of the Moon from Earth varies between 3.57 lakh km to 4.06 lakh km hence motion of the Moon also varies accordingly. Motion of the Moon increases when its distance from the Earth decreases and its motion decreases when its distance from the Earth increases. As nearest planet Mercury from the Sun, takes only 88 days in completing one rotation around the Sun whereas farthest planet Saturn from the Sun takes about 30 years in one rotation around the Sun.

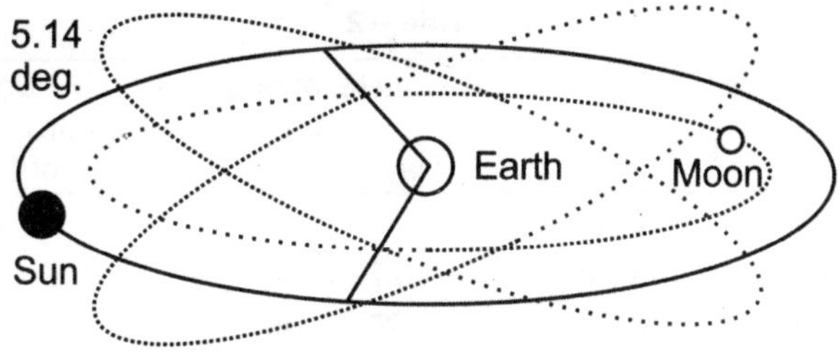

Ecliptic ————
Orbit of Moon above plane of Sun, Earth ....
Orbit of Moon below plane of Sun, Earth ....

Picture – 36
Orbit of the Moon

Distance of the Earth from the Sun, varies because orbit of the Earth around the Sun is elliptical hence Sun takes different time for covering one degree with reference to Earth. Likewise Moon takes different time in completing one rotation around the Earth due to change in its distance in accordance with the combined effect of gravitation of Sun and Earth, which can be calculated by law of motion. Various details have been incorporated in table-2 to clear this point of different time taken by the Moon in one constellational month for reappearing at 0° of Aries sign during its transit in twelve signs in one year. From these data it can easily be observed that Moon takes 27 days 5 hours 25 minutes to 27 days 10 hours 15 minutes in one rotation around the Earth due to effect of the Sun and Earth. At present there is a change of 1.4484° i.e. 1° 26' 54.24" in formation of Rahu after one rotation by the Moon. This fact may easily be understand from picture-35 that ecliptic is being crossed by the Moon by 1.4484° earlier, just before completing one rotation around the Earth in about 27.25 days and Moon takes 2 hours 38 minutes extra in covering the difference of 1.4484°. If it is presumed that Rahu is formed at 0° of Aries sign situated at point 'A' then next Rahu will be formed 2 hours 38 minutes earlier from the days shown under constellational month of table-2, which is calculated on the basis of time taken by the Moon in transit from point 'A' to point 'J' i.e. from 0° of Aries sign to next

Table – 2

Date	Time	Constellational month Day-Hour-Min.	Daily retro. motion of Rahu
17-01-2005	6-00	—	—
13-02-2005	14-30	27-08-30	3' 11.39"
13-03-2005	0-35	27-10-05	3' 10.92"
09-04-2005	10-25	27-09-50	3' 11.00"
06-05-2005	18-25	27-08-00	3' 11.53"
03-06-2005	0-30	27-06-05	3' 12.09"
30-06-2005	5-55	27-05-25	3' 12.29"
27-07-2005	12-15	27-06-20	3' 11.02"
23-08-2005	20-40	27-08-25	3' 11.41"
20-09-2005	6-45	27-10-05	3' 10.92"
17-10-2005	17-00	27-10-15	3' 10.88"
14-11-2005	1-55	27-08-55	3' 11.26"
11-12-2005	8-15	27-06-20	3' 12.02"
07-01-2006	13-55	27-05-40	3' 12.21"
03-02-2006	20-15	27-06-20	3' 12.02"
03-03-2006	5-30	27-09-15	3' 11.17"

arrival at 0° of Aries sign, as shown in picture-35. Interval between formation of two consecutive Rahu may be ascertained by deducting two hours 38 minutes from the period given under constellational month in table-2. For example after deducting two hours 38 minutes from 27-8-30 days, we get 27-5-52 days i.e. 27.244 days. When Rahu retrograde by 1.4484° in 27.244 days then daily retrograde motion of Rahu may be worked out by simple calculation i.e. 1.4484 / 27.244 = 0.05316° and daily retrograde motion in minutes may be worked out by multiplying 0.05316 with 60. As 0.05316 × 60 = 3.19' and except 3' remaining 0.19' may again be multiplied by 60 to get 11.39". Thus daily retrograde motion of Rahu works out to 3' 11.39". This daily retrograde motion is shown in last column of table-2. This whole process is again explained as follows to clear the concept and result incorporated in table-2.

Time between 6-00 on 17-1-2005 to 14-30 on 13-2-2005

= Time taken in transit from 0° or Aries sign to 0° of Aries sign by the Moon

= Time taken in transit of 360°

= 27 day 8 hour 30 minutes = 27.35416 days

Retrograde degree of crossing the ecliptic by the Moon in one constellational month

= Distance between point 'A' and point 'B' in picture-35

= 1.4484°

If time taken by the Moon in transit of 360° is 27.35416 days then time taken in transit of 1.4484°

= 27.35416 × 1.4484 / 360 = 0.11 day

= 2 hour 38 minutes

Interval between consecutive formation of Rahu

= 27.35416 – 0.11 = 27.2444 day

Daily retrograde motion of Rahu

= 1.4484 / 27.2444 = 0.053164°

= 0.053164 × 60 = 3.1898'

= Remaining 0.1898 × 60 = 11.39"

Daily retrograde motion of Rahu = 3' 11.39"

If we presume on every date shown in table-2 that Rahu is at 0° of Aries sign situated at point 'A' and work out the motion of Rahu then we will see that daily retrograde motion of Rahu varies, which is being shown in the last column of table-2. Though presently actual position of Rahu in the year 2005 may be in some other degree under Aries or Pisces sign yet retrograde motion will vary in the same manner, because reason behind change in retrograde motion of Rahu is elliptical orbit of the Earth and Moon. As described earlier Moon continuously crosses the ecliptic a little earlier during its rotation around the Earth and eclipses repeated after 6585 days or 223 lunar month (about 29.5 days) or 241 constellational month (about 27 days) as mentioned in earlier chapter. Now we will understand the scientific reasons behind repetition of eclipses.

As has already been described that full eclipse formed only when plane of Sun and Earth (refer first plane in picture-33) is crossed by the Moon, during its rotation around the Earth, in such a way so that Sun, Moon and Earth may be in one line. Now after full eclipse, Moon complete its one rotation in about 27 days i.e. the time taken by it in returning to the same constellation; and Moon intersect the ecliptic a little earlier by 1.4484°. In other words if Sun and Moon were at 0° of Aries sign at the time of full solar eclipse then after one rotation by the Moon, Rahu will be formed when Moon intersect the ecliptic from Pisces sign at 358.5516° i.e. 1.4484° back. In this way Rahu is retrogradely formed in zodiac. Sun will also reach at 27° of Aries sign during this period with a motion of about 1° per day. After completing twelve rotation of about 27.33 days each by the Moon in about 328 days, Rahu i.e. situation of intersecting the plane of Sun, Earth; will be formed at 12 × 1.4484 = 17.38° retrogradely i.e. at 342.62° (360 – 17.38 = 342.62) in Pisces sign; Moon will be as usual at its original position at 0° of Aries sign, whereas Sun will be at 328° ahead from 0° of Aries sign i.e. in Aquarius sign. There will be still a difference of 14.62° between Rahu and Sun. This difference will be covered by the Sun in 14-15 days, whereas Moon will be away from ecliptic after 15 days, because orbit of the Moon is inclined by an angle of 5.14°. Hence Moon crosses ecliptic only after 27 or 13.5 days for creating Ketu after creation of Rahu. In this way eclipse is not repeated either at the vicinity of 342° or of 356° and process of rotation by the Moon continue. Different eclipse occurred as and when Sun, Earth and Moon happens to be in a line during this rotation. But Sun and Moon reunited in the vicinity of original position after 18 years 10 days or 6585 days or 223 lunar months or 241 constellational months and it is repetition of the eclipse due to complete retrograde rotation of Rahu during this period. Because position of Rahu after 241 constellational month will be at 241 × 1.4484 = 349.06 retrograde or about 10° Aries sign. Whereas position of the

Sun after 18 years will not change but after next 10 days it will reach to 10° of Aries sign. Hence every eclipse repeat after this time.

Table-3 contains the details of one full lunar eclipse, which was repeated after every 223 lunar months, during 400 years. All other solar and lunar eclipses were also repeated in the same way. It may be seen from table-3 that there was a full lunar eclipse on 4-6-1621. At the time of lunar eclipse, Sun and Moon were at 55.08° and 235.08° respectively. This lunar eclipse was repeated on 15-6-1639, when Sun and Moon were

Table – 3

Retro. motion of Rahu at full lunar eclipse after 18 years

Date	Degree of Sun	Degree of Moon	Difference	Transit	Retrograde motion
04-06-1621	55.08	235.08	(10.22)	—	—
15-06-1639	65.28	245.28	10.20	349.80	1° 27' 5.22"
26-06-1657	75.46	255.46	10.18	349.82	1° 27' 5.52"
07-07-1675	85.64	265.64	10.18	349.82	1° 27' 5.52"
17-07-1693	95.84	275.84	10.20	349.80	1° 27' 5.22"
29-07-1711	106.05	286.05	10.21	349.79	1° 27' 5.08"
09-08-1729	116.30	296.30	10.25	349.75	1° 27' 4.48"
20-08-1747	126.59	306.59	10.29	349.71	1° 27' 3.88"
30-08-1765	136.93	316.93	10.34	349.66	1° 27' 3.13"
11-09-1783	147.33	327.33	10.40	349.60	1° 27' 2.24"
22-09-1801	157.80	337.80	10.47	349.53	1° 27' 1.19"
03-10-1819	168.34	348.34	10.54	349.46	1° 27' 0.14"
16-10-1837	178.94	358.94	10.60	349.40	1° 26' 59.25"
25-10-1855	189.62	9.62	10.68	349.32	1° 26' 58.05"
04-11-1873	200.36	20.36	10.74	349.26	1° 26' 57.16"
16-11-1891	211.16	31.16	10.80	349.20	1° 26' 56.26"
27-11-1909	222.02	42.02	10.86	349.14	1° 26' 55.36"
08-12-1927	232.93	52.93	10.91	349.09	1° 26' 54.62"
19-12-1945	243.86	63.86	10.93	349.07	1° 26' 54.32"
30-12-1963	254.81	74.81	10.95	349.05	1° 26' 54.02"
10-01-1982	265.76	85.76	10.95	349.05	1° 26' 54.02"
21-01-2000	276.71	96.71	10.95	349.05	1° 26' 54.02"
31-01-2018	287.64	107.64	10.93	349.07	1° 26' 54.32"

at 65.28° and 245.28° respectively. Though there were many full lunar eclipse during these two dates but every eclipse was repetition of earlier eclipse occurred before 18 years 10 days. Direct difference between the position of Sun or Moon in above two lunar eclipses was 10.2° (245.28° – 235.08° = 10.2°). Because Earth complete its rotation in one year hence relative position of the Sun from Earth would remain same even after 18 years but its position changes by about 10° only in remaining 10 days. It is, therefore, clear from this full eclipse that Rahu may be formed or meet at this point after 18 years 10 days. Accordingly Rahu must have retrogradely moved by 349.8° {235.08° + (360° – 245.28°) = 349.8°} during this period. This retrograde motion of Rahu has also been incorporated in table-3. This difference was covered by Rahu during 223 lunar months or 241 constellational months. After dividing this difference by 241 constellational months, we can easily workout or clearly see from table-3 that average retrograde motion of Rahu was 1° 27' 5.22" during every constellational month of about 27 days i.e. in every rotation, in between above two dates. It may also be seen from the last column of table-3 that maximum and minimum retrograde motion of Rahu was 1° 27' 5.52" and 1° 26' 54.02" respectively during 350 years. Average daily retrograde motion of Rahu during a constellational month may be worked out by dividing this average retrograde motion by about 27 days. At present average retrograde motion of Rahu during a constellational month i.e. difference between two subsequent formation of Rahu is 1° 26' 54.02", according to the details given in table-3. Average daily retrograde motion of Rahu may be worked out after dividing this retrograde motion by a constellational month of about 27 days. Daily retrograde motion of Rahu worked out after dividing the motion by constellational month is shown in table-2, which varies between 3' 10.88" to 3' 12.29". This whole process is again explained as follows on the basis of data incorporated in table-3.

Change in position of the Sun during 18 years 10 days i.e. from 4-6-1621 to 15-6-1639

= 65.28° – 55.08° = 10.2°

Position of Moon at full lunar eclipse

= 65.28° + 180° = 245.28°

Retrograde change in position of Rahu during 18 years 10 days or 241 constellational months

= 235.08° + (360° – 245.28°) = 349.8°

Retrograde change in position of Rahu during one constellational month

= 349.8 / 241 = 1.45145° or 1°

Balance 0.45145 × 60 = 27.087' or 27'

Balance 0.087 × 60 = 5.22"

Thus retrograde change in position of Rahu in one constellational month of about 27 days

= 1° 27' 5.22"

Last data of table-3 indicate present status. According to which presently there is a retrograde change of 349.07° / 241 = 1.4484° in the position of Rahu during a constellational month. Procedure of working out daily retrograde motion of Rahu as incorporated in table-2 is based on this change. Average retrograde motion of Rahu, in degree, minute, second in a constellational month during every 18 years 10 days i.e. 241 constellational month, is shown in the last column of table-3. If daily retrograde motion of Rahu in every constellational month is calculated individually then retrograde motion will again vary as shown in table-2.

It may be observed from table-3 that at the time of full lunar eclipse in the year 1657 and 1675 there was lowest difference of 10.18° in the position of Sun and Moon from their earlier position, which resulted in highest retrograde motion of Rahu. This difference was increased to 10.20° and 10.22° at the time of previous full lunar eclipse in the year 1639 and 1621 respectively. Likewise the maximum difference was 10.95° at the time of full lunar eclipse in the year 1963, 1982 and 2000, which resulted in lowest retrograde motion of Rahu. This difference was reduced to 10.93° at the time of full lunar eclipse in earlier and later year 1945 and 2018 respectively. This whole situation may easily be understood from a graph shown in

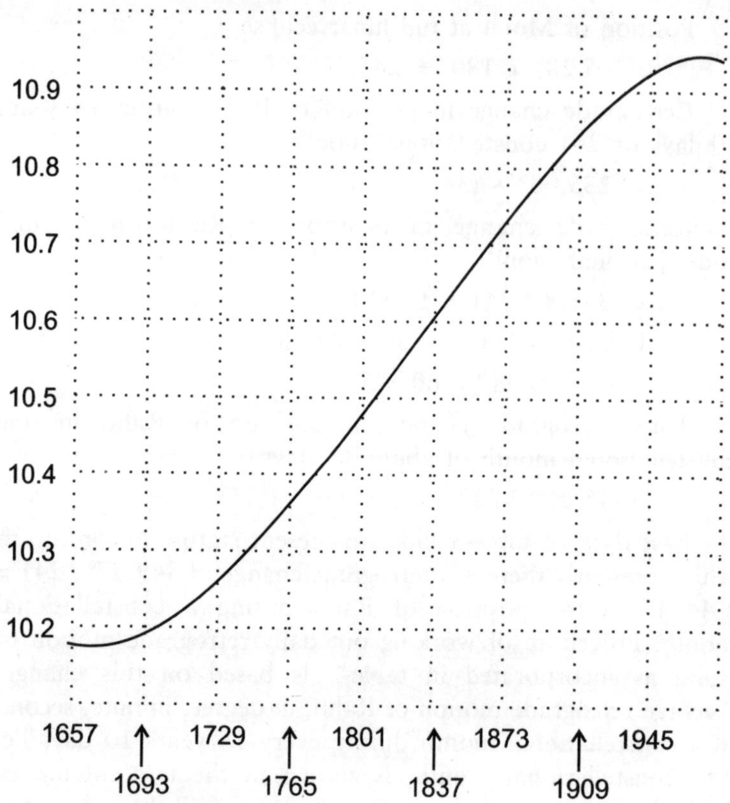

Picture – 37

Difference in the position of Sun or Moon at eclipse

picture-37 that how this difference was increasing since AD 1675 and likewise this difference will continuously reduce for next 306 years 6 months from the mid-position at AD 1982.

This situation may also be understood from the position of Sun as shown in table-3. Sun was at 85.64° in the year 1675 and it was at 265.76° after a change of 180° i.e. half zodiac, in the year 1982, after 306 years 6 months. Likewise Sun will be at 85.88° after next change of 180° in 306 years 6 months at the time of full lunar eclipse. This position of Sun will be nearer to its original position. In this way one cycle of change in retrograde motion of Rahu is completed in 613 years.

Main reason behind variation in difference from 10.18° to 10.95° as shown in table-3, is transit of Sun with reference to the Earth. At that time when this difference is minimum i.e. 10.18°, Sun happens to be completed its summer solstice and reached at the maximum north in Gemini sign and it is at maximum distance from the Earth with minimum motion i.e. on 23rd June. Contrary to this, when this difference is maximum i.e. 10.95°, Sun happens to be completed its winter solstice and reached at the maximum south in Sagittarius sign and it is at minimum distance from the Earth with maximum motion i.e. on 23rd December. This position may be understood from picture-33.

It is evident from the description given so far that retrograde motion of Rahu / Ketu never remains constant at 3' 11" as is being believed. Now you may have a question in your mind that if retrograde motion of Rahu / Ketu was not constant at 3' 11" then why there is an eclipse when Rahu / Ketu happens to be within 14° from the position of the Sun-Moon and if there is a variation in the motion of Rahu / Ketu then it will not be possible to perform correct calculation about the eclipse? Details of some lunar and solar eclipses are being shown in table-4 for giving an answer to this question. Dated degree minute position of Moon, Sun and Rahu or Ketu are shown in part (A) of the table, when distance of Rahu or Ketu was less than 14° from the Moon, on the basis of their daily retrograde motion of 3' 11", but even then there was no lunar eclipse. Contrary to this some position are shown in part (B) of the table, when distance of Rahu was more than 14° from the Sun, but even then there was solar eclipse. It may be seen from both type of details as contained in table-4 that on 3-3-1988, the difference between the Moon and Ketu was only 10.52°, which was sufficiently less than required 14° for an eclipse, but even then there was no lunar eclipse. Likewise on 21-7-1982, the difference between the Moon and Rahu was 15.20°, which was sufficiently more than so-called upper limit of 14° for an eclipse, but even then there was a solar eclipse. Thus it would have been quite clear that fixed retrograde motion of Rahu / Ketu is totally wrong. Quantum of error in

Table – 4

Erroneous position of Rahu / Ketu based on fixed retrograde motion of 3' 11"

Date	Degree of				
	Sun	Moon	Rahu-Ketu		Difference
(A)					
Lunar eclipses not occurred even when difference between Moon and Rahu / Ketu was less than 14°					
21-01-1981	276.71	96.71	108.00	Rahu	11.29
20-12-1983	244.12	64.12	51.63	Rahu	12.49
15-05-1984	31.02	211.02	223.84	Ketu	12.82
08-11-1984	203.01	23.01	34.43	Rahu	11.42
03-03-1988	319.74	139.74	150.26	Ketu	10.52
30-01-1991	286.23	106.23	93.95	Ketu	12.28
18-11-1994	212.05	32.05	20.40	Ketu	11.65
13-03-1998	328.70	148.70	136.23	Rahu	12.47
31-01-1999	287.62	107.62	119.03	Rahu	11.41
(B)					
Solar eclipses occurred even when difference between Moon and Rahu was more than 14°					
21-07-1982	94.24	94.24	79.04	Rahu	15.20
02-07-2000	76.49	76.49	91.93	Rahu	15.14

present calculation can very well imagine from the above clarification.

Now we will deeply understand about solar and lunar eclipse by calculating the visual diameter of the image of Sun and Moon and see that what was the relation between Rahu / Ketu and eclipse in sixteenth century when recognised book of astrology viz. '*Grahlaghav*' was written and some more fact contained in picture-32.

Visual angle of image of Sun / Moon

As has already been pointed out that from Primitive age to Pre-modern age it was believed that Earth is stationary, Rahu / Ketu are demons and other planets including Moon are deities. For pre-assessing an eclipse it is essential to calculate the size of

Sun, Moon and Rahu / Ketu. Such related calculations as given in '*Grahlaghav*' was certainly more precise in comparison to those as prevailed since Primitive age. But it was far behind in comparison to latest information about the solar system. Because, correct knowledge about the solar system and celestial position of the planets therein was not known till that time when Ganesh, who born in 1507, was writing '*Grahlaghav*', as in AD 1543 Copernicus of Poland was first to discover the concept of solar system as shown in picture-2 about the celestial position of the planets. Whereas, '*Grahlaghav*' was written prior to this discovery. Presently, concept of '*Grahlaghav*' is being used in astrological calculations performed in India. Thus it is clear that we have not yet incorporated latest astronomical information in astrological calculations and scientific information are only being referred in the books of astrology for ostentation.

As per principle of Bhaskaracharya formulated in twelfth century, diameter of the visual Moon in *angul* (the then measurement of length in fingers) was calculated after dividing lunar motion in minutes by 74. Likewise diameter of Rahu (*Bhubha*) in *angul* was also calculated after deducting 716' from the lunar motion in minutes, and dividing remainder by 22 and adding 32. Similarly, diameter of visual Sun in *angul* was also calculated after multiplying solar motion in minutes by 11/60. As per principle laid down in '*Grahlaghav*', after applying a minor correction, diameter of visual Sun in *angul* may be calculated after dividing double of solar motion in minutes by eleven.

It is clear from the description given in '*Grahlaghav*' that solar motion is essential for working out the diameter of visual Sun, and lunar motion was only essential for working out the diameter of visual Moon and Rahu. Description for understanding the shape of Rahu will be given later on. At present we confine our discussion to know the diameter of visual Sun and Moon. Following two data have taken for calculating and analysing the diameter of these planets. Diameter of visual Sun, Moon and Rahu will be calculated from these data, according to the principle as laid down in '*Grahlaghav*' and as per latest information of the solar system with the help of trigonometry.

	Motion of		Distance in lakh km	
Date	Sun	Moon	Sun	Moon
29-10-1985	60' 00"	11° 49'	1486.04	4.06
27-08-1988	59' 58"	15° 07'	1511.26	3.58

Calculation as per *Grahlaghav* :–

Diameter of visual Moon (*Chandravimb*)

on 29-10-1985 :–

Motion of Moon = 11 × 60 + 49 = 709'

Chandravimb = 709 / 74 = 9.58 *angul*

on 27-8-1988 :–

Motion of Moon = 15 × 60 + 7 = 907'

Chandravimb = 907 / 74 = 12.25 *angul*

Diameter of visual Sun (*Suryavimb*)

on 29-10-1985 :–

Suryavimb = 60 × 2 / 11 = 120 / 11 = 10.9 *angul*

on 27-8-1988 :–

Motion of Sun = 59' 58" = 59.966'

Suryavimb= 59.966 × 2/11 = 119.93/11 = 10.9 *angul*

Calculation on the basis of Trigonometry :–

On the basis of latest scientific information we know that :–

Diameter of Sun = 13.81 lakh km

Diameter of Moon = 3.45 thousand km

= 0.0345 lakh km

Diameter of Earth = 12.65 thousand km

= 0.1265 lakh km

For calculating the visual angle of these planets with the help of trigonometry, we have to draw a triangle by joining two end points of diameter of the Sun or Moon and centre of the Earth as a third point. In this triangle, line of diameter of the Sun or Moon will be perpendicular and line from one point of diameter to the centre of the Earth will be base. Distance from the centre of the Earth to the centre of the Sun or Moon may be taken as distance from centre of the Earth to one side of the diameter of the Sun or Moon respectively for simplification. Help of picture-39 may be taken after doing a little modification for understanding the concept of these two triangles. Further calculation is being done on the basis of two triangles PP'R and SS'R in the picture, where point R is centre of Earth, line PP' and SS' is diameter of the Moon and Sun respectively.

As per formula of trigonometry we know that

Tangent angle at point R = Perpendicular / Base

= Diameter / Distance

After converting angle to radian

Angle = Arctangent (Perpendicular / Base) radian

For converting radian angle to angle

Angle = Radian angle × 180 / Pi (Pi = 22 / 7)

Hence for calculating angle at the centre of the Earth

Angle at point R = Arctangent (Diameter / Distance) × 180 × 7 / 22

Visual angle P'RP of the Moon on :–

29-10-1985 = Arctangent (0.0345 / 4.06) × 1260 / 22

= 0.49°

27-8-1988 = Arctangent (0.0345 / 3.58) × 1260 / 22

= 0.55°

Visual angle S'RS of the Sun on :–

29-10-1985 = Arctangent (13.81 /1486.4) × 1260 / 22

= 0.53°

27-8-1988 = Arctangent (13.81 /1511.26) × 1260 / 22

= 0.52°

Above angle is formed at the centre of the Earth. We have to deduct radius of the Earth which is 0.0632 lakh km from distance of the Earth i.e. base of the triangle to workout very precise angle in seconds from the surface of the Earth from where we used to see Sun and Moon.

It is clear from the study of calculations based on the principles laid down in '*Grahlaghav*' that visual size of Sun and Moon would be more or less in proportion to their motion. Likewise it is also clear from the study of calculations based on trigonometry that visual angle of Sun and Moon will be more when their distance from the Earth is less and their visual angle will be less when their distance is more. According to Kepler's law of circular motion, transit of Moon and Sun (with reference to Earth) is inversely proportionate with reference to the distance. In other words velocity i.e. motion of the Sun or Moon will increase whenever they are nearer to the Earth. Contrary to this transit of Moon or Sun is reduced whenever they are away from the Earth. From this fact it can be realised that despite lack of knowledge about the correct distance of the Sun and Moon at the time of drafting of '*Grahlaghav*', their roughly correct size were calculated on the basis of their motion. Though, as per calculation based on the principle of '*Grahlaghav*' there is a difference of 28% in between the visual size of Moon on both dates, which were 9.58 and 12.25 *angul*. Whereas this difference is merely 12.5% (between 0.49° and 0.55°), when it is calculated with the help of trigonometry. Thus when we have up-to-date information about the distances of these planets at every time then there is no justification in doing rough and wrong calculation about their size on the basis of their motion as laid down in '*Grahlaghav*'. Because visual size of anything varies only on the basis of its distance and not on the basis of its motion. Hence it is absolutely correct to measure the visual size of these planets in angle instead of measuring them in length i.e. in *angul*. Thus at the time of full solar eclipse, there would be annular eclipse (only circumference of the Sun is visible) when visual angle of the Sun is more than the visual angle of Moon and in case of reverse position of visual angle of these planets there would be full solar eclipse. Beside this correct position and size of Rahu / Ketu may also be calculated with the help of trigonometrical formula.

There is variation in visual angle of the Sun and Moon from the centre of the Earth during one rotation. As such visual angle of Sun varies from 0.52° (distance and motion

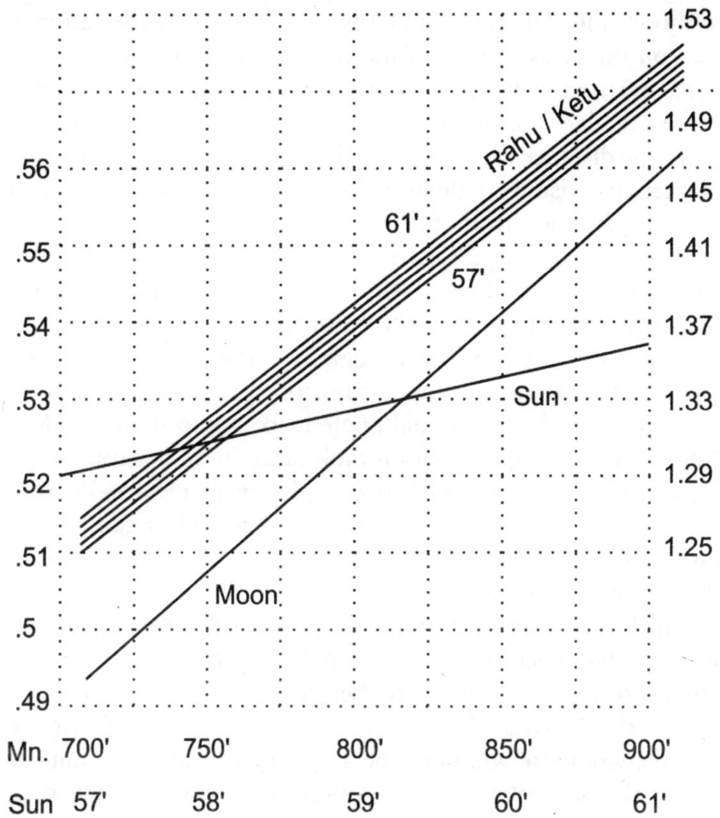

Picture – 38

Visual angle of Sun, Moon and Rahu

was 1521 lakh km and 57' respectively on 6-7-1982) to 0.5377° (distance and motion was 1471 lakh km and 61' respectively on 3-1-1983). Likewise visual angle of Moon also varies from 0.4942° (distance and motion was 4.06 lakh km and 708' respectively on 9-6-1982) to 0.5626° (distance and motion was 3.57 lakh km and 912' respectively on 22-6-1982). Variation in the visual angle of Sun and Moon is shown in the graph of picture-38. Different motion of Sun and Moon in minutes is shown in horizontal line and visual angle in degrees is shown in left vertical line. Visual size of Sun and Moon on the basis of different motion is shown in the graph by sun-line and moon-line. Though visual angle of Sun and Moon directly varies on the basis of their distance from the Earth. But due to inverse relation between distance and transit, their size may also be calculated on the basis of transition. As, when Sun is at maximum distance from the Earth and it's motion is 57' per day then its visual angle is 0.52°, whereas when Sun is at minimum distance from the Earth and its motion is 61' per day then its visual angle increases to 0.5377°. This change in visual angle of Sun took place in six months. Likewise when Moon is at maximum distance from the Earth and its motion is 708' per day then its visual angle is 0.4942°, whereas when Moon is at minimum distance from the Earth and its motion is 912' per day then its visual angle increases to 0.5626°. This change in visual angle of Moon took place in 13.6 days. Graph of visual angle of Sun and Moon is shown in picture-38 from where change in visual angle may be understood. It can also be clearly understand that visual angle of the Moon at a motion of 838' per day is almost equal to the maximum visual angle of the Sun. Hence, there will never be an annular solar eclipse but full (or partial) solar eclipse when motion of the Moon happens to be more than 838' per day, because in this situation visual angle of the Moon will be more than the visual angle of the Sun. Likewise there will never be a full solar eclipse but annular (or partial) solar eclipse when motion of the Moon is less than 787' per day, because visual angle of the Moon will be less than the visual angle of the Sun. In this way size and type of solar eclipse based on motion of the Sun and Moon may be understood with the help of the graph shown in picture-38.

Visual angle of Rahu / Ketu

Astrological principles were formulated on the basis of the qualities of Rahu / Ketu considering them as demons, which was based on religious perception as prevailed in the Primitive age. Their fixed retrograde motion of 3' 11" per day was recognised on the basis of eclipse and various calculations are still being done on this basis. You have already studied about the error in deciding this retrograde motion and their scientific reasons. Hence now we will have to understand about the size of Rahu before we go ahead to calculate the visual angle of Rahu.

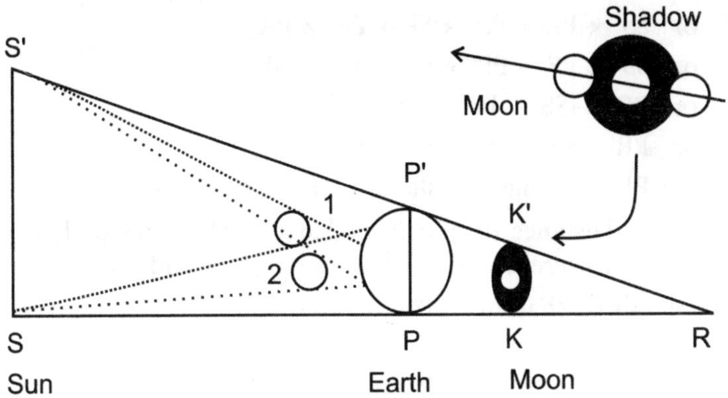

Picture – 39

Shadow of the Earth and size of Rahu

Size of Rahu at the time of lunar eclipse is actually the size of shadow of the Earth at a distance of the Moon and lunar eclipse occurs only when this shadow falls on the Moon. Shadow of the Earth is always in the opposite direction of the Sun and towards the ecliptic. This phenomenon has already been described along with the description of picture-32. Length of shadow of the Earth is always near about fourteen lakh km and length of shadow reduces whenever the Sun is nearer to the Earth and it increases whenever the Sun is far away from the Earth. Because there was no science based and well recognised information about various facts regarding solar system, shadow of the Earth etc. at the time of drafting of '*Grahlaghav*' hence there was gross misconception and confusion. But see picture-39 to understand this fact in view of scientific information. Distance between Earth and Sun is shown by line SP and shadow of the Earth is shown by triangle P'PR. Diameter of the Sun and Earth is shown by SS' and PP' respectively. According to general principle of geometry we know that angle at point R is same in two triangles S'RS and P'RP. Hence according to simple mathematics :–

$$SS' / SR = PP' / PR$$

or $SS' / (SP + PR) = PP' / PR$

or $SS' \times PR = PP' \times (SP + PR)$

or $SS' \times PR = PP' \times SP + PP' \times PR$

or $SS' \times PR - PP' \times PR = PP' \times SP$

or $PR \times (SS' - PP') = PP' \times SP$

or $PR = SP \times PP' / (SS' - PP')$

or PR i.e. length of shadow of the Earth

= Distance of Sun from Earth × Diameter of Earth / Difference in the diameter of Sun and Earth

Length of shadow $= SP \times 0.1265 / (13.81 - 0.1265)$

$= SP \times 0.1265 / 13.6835$

$= SP \times 0.0092447$

Hence length of shadow of the Earth on 29-10-1985

$= 1486.04 \times 0.0092447$

= 13.73 lakh km

Likewise length of shadow of the Earth on 27-8-1988

$= 1511.26 \times 0.0092447$

= 13.97 lakh km

Thus length of shadow of the Earth, having diameter of about 13,000 km, continuously varies between 13.61 lakh km to 14.07 lakh km and diameter of the shadow also reduce gradually as we move away from the Earth. This fact may easily be understood by observing picture-39, where shadow of the Earth P'P is extended up to point R. At the time of lunar eclipse, Moon actually passes through the shadow of the Earth shown between K'K. As has already been explained, according to general principle of geometry we know that angle P'RP is same in two triangles S'RS and P'RP. Hence according to simple mathematics :–

$KK' / KR = PP' / PR$

$KK' / (PR - PK) = PP' / PR$

$KK' = PP' \times (PR - PK) / PR$

KK' i.e. Diameter of shadow of the Earth at a point from where Moon passes through i.e. Diameter of Rahu

= Diameter of Earth × (Length of shadow of Earth – Distance of Moon from Earth) / Length of shadow of Earth

Hence diameter of Rahu at the position of Moon on 29-10-1985

= 0.1265 × (13.73 – 4.06) / 13.73

= 0.1265 × 9.67 / 13.73

= 0.08909 lakh km

= 8909 km

Visual (apparent) angle of Rahu (according to calculation of visual angle of Sun / Moon)

= Arctangent (Diameter / Distance) × 1260 / 22

= Arctangent (0.08909 / 4.06) × 1260 / 22

= 1.256°

Likewise diameter of Rahu at the position of Moon on 27-8-1988

= 0.1265 × (13.97 – 3.58) / 13.97

= 0.1265 × 10.39 / 13.97

= 0.09408 lakh km

= 9408 km

Visual (apparent) angle of Rahu

= Arctangent (Diameter / Distance) × 1260 / 22

= Arctangent (0.09408 / 3.58) × 1260 / 22

= 1.504°

In this way size and visual angle of Rahu or Ketu varies between 8900 to 9400 km and 1.2° to 1.5° respectively, while Moon passes through the shadow of the Earth. Entire above mathematical procedure may be cut short and visual angle of Rahu may easily be calculated with the help of following trigonometrical formula by placing distance of Sun and Moon from the Earth in place of Sun and Moon respectively.

Visual angle of Rahu

= Arctangent [13.6835 × {(Sun × 0.0092447) – Moon} / (Sun × Moon)] × 57.2727

It is clear from the study of the above formula that knowledge of distance of Sun from the Earth is also essential beside distance of Moon from the Earth for scientifically calculating the visual angle of Rahu while Moon passes through the shadow of the Earth. Because only then shadow of the Earth and size of Rahu may correctly be calculated. As has been explained during description of picture-38 that rough assessment of eclipse was possible due to inverse relation between the distance and transitional motion of the Moon. In those days *bhubha* (size of Rahu) was calculated only on the basis of motion of the Moon according to the principle formulated by Bhaskaracharya and procedure laid down in '*Grahlaghav*'. But size of Rahu cannot be calculated correctly by following the procedure contained in '*Grahlaghav*' because *bhubha* (size of Rahu) is calculated as follows leaving aside the impact of shadow of the Earth, which is directly related to distance of the Sun.

Calculation of *bhubha* (size of Rahu) as per procedure given in '*Grahlaghav*'

Bhubha on 29-10-1985 :-

Transitional motion of Moon = 11 × 60 + 49 = 709'

Bhubha = {(Motion of Moon – 716) / 22} + 32

= {(709 – 716) / 22} + 32 = 31.68 *angul*

Bhubha on 27-8-1988 :-

Transitional motion of Moon = 15 × 60 + 7 = 907'

Bhubha = {(907 – 716) / 22} + 32 = 40.68 *angul*

There is a difference of about 29% in *bhubha*, calculated as on above both dates. Whereas the difference is only 20% on these dates in case of visual angle of 1.256° and 1.504° calculated earlier with the help of trigonometrical formula. Hence it is clear that '*Grahlaghav*' based calculation relating to position, size of Rahu / Ketu referred for precise duration of eclipse as is being done now-a-days is not correct.

Distance of the Sun has an important role in calculating the size of Rahu at the time of lunar eclipse, because size of Rahu varies according to the change in distance of the Sun. As per Kepler's law of circular motion, distance and motion are inversely proportionate to each other. Effect of change in motion or distance of the Sun on the size of Rahu may be seen in the graph of picture-38. Various motion of Moon is shown in horizontal line and visual (apparent) angle of Rahu is shown in vertical line of right-hand side. Five lines in the graph show visual angle of Rahu i.e. angle of shadow from where Moon passes. These lines are drawn on the basis of five different motion of the Sun. Lowest line is drawn on the basis of motion of 57' per day of the Sun, subsequent three lines are also drawn for the Sun on the basis of motion of 58', 59' and 60' per day respectively, whereas top line is drawn for the Sun on the basis of motion of 61' per day. Variation in the size of the Rahu may be understood from this graph. For example, if motion of the Sun is 57' then visual angle of Rahu will be 1.25° and 1.49°, when motion of the Moon is 708' and 912' per day respectively. Likewise if motion of the Sun is 61' then visual angle of Rahu will be 1.27° and 1.52°, when motion of the Moon is 708' and 912' per day respectively. Effect of motion (distance) of the Sun may be understand with the help of different lines representing visual angle of Rahu. Because phenomenon of the effect of distance or motion of the Sun on the formation of Rahu / Ketu was not known at the time of drafting of '*Grahlaghav*', hence now, it is quite essential to have substantial change in astrological calculation in view of the latest information about the solar system.

Concept of Rahu and Ketu was devised in the Rising age due to solar and lunar eclipse on the basis of the then knowledge. After studying various eclipses and synchronising them with retrograde motion of Rahu / Ketu it was observed that if Rahu or Ketu happens to be up to 14° away from the Sun and Moon at the time of solar and lunar eclipse respectively then there may be an eclipse and if Rahu / Ketu is far away then there will be no eclipse. If size of Rahu / Ketu may be worked out on this basis their capacity of creating eclipse then their radius and diameter (visual angle of Rahu / Ketu) will be 14° and 28° respectively. Whereas you may have seen from earlier trigonometrical calculations that their (shadow of the Earth) visual (apparent) angle remains between 1.25° to 1.52° at the time of lunar eclipse; and between 0.49° to 0.56° (visual angle of Moon) at the time of solar eclipse. Enormous 28° size of shadow planet Rahu / Ketu and their capacity of grabbing Sun or Moon from 14° was main reason to classify them as distinct demons in astrological principles. Whereas their correct size, reason of creation can only be understand with latest scientific knowledge.

At the time of formulating the principles of astrology relating to calculation and prediction, in primitive age, Rahu / Ketu were considered as demons because they were responsible for creating eclipse on Sun and Moon. It was believed in those days that Earth is stationary and Sun is the nearest planet (see picture-1) hence neither it was known nor there was any concept that solar and lunar eclipse occurred due to Moon and shadow of the Earth respectively. Intersection points of orbit of the Moon and ecliptic are now being referred as Rahu / Ketu only after the knowledge and recognition of solar system, because eclipse formed on these points. Now everybody knows that shadow of the Earth falls on the Moon during lunar eclipse and Moon transits between Earth and Sun during solar eclipse. These both eclipses may occur either due to Rahu (transit of Moon towards north of ecliptic) or due to Ketu (transit of Moon towards south of ecliptic). Thus it is clear that the shadow of the Earth was considered as Rahu / Ketu at the time of lunar eclipse. You have studied about the size of shadow of the Earth or Rahu (it may be Ketu also) at the time of lunar eclipse. Contrary to this, size of the Moon became the size of Ketu (it may be Rahu also) at the time of solar eclipse. But size of Rahu / Ketu may reduce only to an intersection point when there is no eclipse. If correct position of Rahu / Ketu would have been known in the Primitive age then definitely shadow of the Moon and Earth would have been classified as Rahu and Ketu respectively and their motion was also alike Moon and Sun or they may not be classified as demons in case of their formation on intersection point of orbits. Thus in both these conditions principles of astrological calculation and prediction would have been quite different. Hence it is clear that principle of astrological calculation and prediction based on the concept of considering them as demons is totally wrong. Thus it is the need of this hour to do thorough revision in this matter instead of beating the bush.

By now you may be aware from the description given so far that how much astrological calculations relating to the formation of Rahu / Ketu, motion, position and size etc. are deviated from the reality. Now we will analyse their impact.

Impact of Rahu / Ketu

Moon is nearest from the Earth hence orbit of the Moon remains at an height of about 4 lakh km (distance of Moon), whereas distance of the Sun is more from the Earth hence ecliptic remains at a height of 15 crore km (distance of Sun). Hence actually these both orbits may not intersect each other; otherwise Sun and Moon would have been collided with each other. But as Sun appears (due to inclined rotation of the Earth) to swing in a year by 23.5° towards north till Tropic of Cancer and towards south till Tropic of Capricorn from equator or in other words with reference to the centre of the Earth. Likewise during rotation around the Earth, Moon also swing between 28.64° (23.5° + 5.14° = 28.64°) towards north i.e. by more than 5° 8' 24" or 5.14° from the Tropic of Cancer and towards south by more than 5.14° from Tropic of Capricorn from equator or in other words with reference to the centre of the Earth. Hence it appears from the Earth that both orbits are intersecting each other. When Moon swing towards north up to 28.64° then correspondingly it also swing towards south up to 28.64°. This position remains under continuous change due to retrograde motion of the orbit of the Moon as shown in picture-35. After rotating nine years around the Earth from the above status, Moon swing up to 18.36° (23.5° – 5.14° = 18.36°) towards north i.e. by less than 5.14° from the Tropic of Cancer and about 18.36° towards south i.e. by less then 5.14° from Tropic of Capricorn from equator. In this way Rahu created at a point of intersection of the ecliptic by the Moon, took 18 years to return its original position. Thus eclipses repeat themselves after this time and this point has already been explained.

This phenomenon may be understood from picture-40 and table-5. Picture incorporates ecliptic of one year and orbit of the Moon in the years of 1983, 1987, 1992, 1997 and 2001

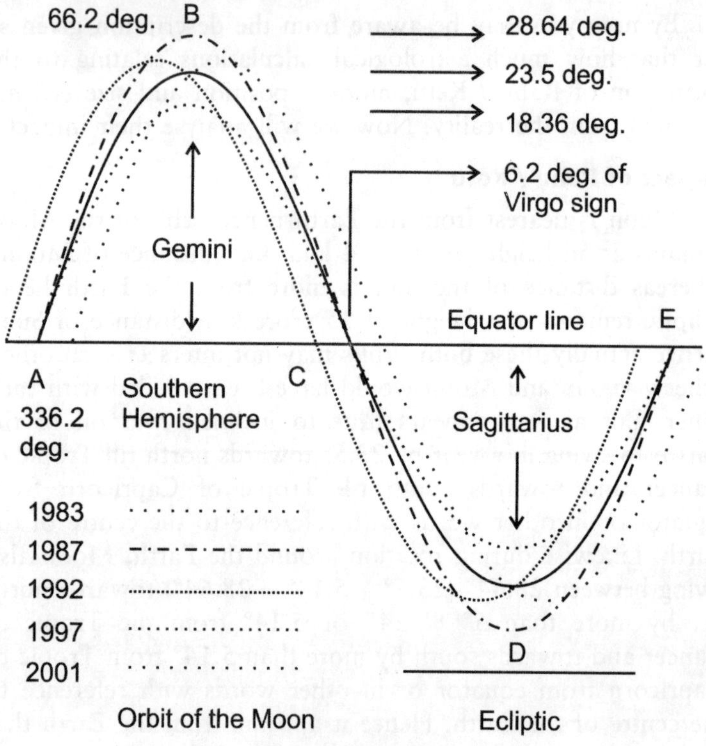

Picture – 40
Ecliptic and orbit of the Moon on Earth

Table – 5
Rahu / Ketu created on equator and ecliptic calculated on changing motion as explained earlier

Date	Formation	Sign	Moon	Rahu	Ketu
22-3-1983	Rahu	Gemini	66.2	66.2	—
17-11-1987	Ketu	Virgo	156.2	—	156.2
13-7-1992	Rahu	Sagitta.	246.2	246.2	—
10-3-1997	Ketu	Pisces	336.2	—	336.2
5-11-2001	Rahu	Gemini	66.2	66.2	—

by different type of line. Front as-well-as back face of the Earth is covered in the picture with a view to cover entire ecliptic and orbit. Sun enters in Southern Hemisphere after crossing equator at 6.2° of Virgo sign. Because summer solstice starts when Sun transit from 6.2° of Sagittarius sign, which is 90° away from 6.2° of Virgo sign. Moon also creates Rahu and Ketu while transiting towards north and south respectively after crossing the ecliptic. Now we will analyse the position to clear the concept according to the data given in table-5. On 22-3-1983, while Moon was moving in its orbit, it crossed the ecliptic 90° earlier from 6.2° of Virgo sign i.e. at 6.2° of Gemini sign (66.2°) and created actual Rahu at point B (corresponding Ketu was created 180° ahead i.e. at 6.2° of Sagittarius sign). In this way Moon was ahead in the Universe after crossing the plane of Sun and Earth (see picture-31 and 33). In this way ecliptic was repeatedly crossed a little earlier by the Moon with a retrograde creation of Rahu and subsequently after four year eight months i.e. about after 60 constellational months (constellational month = about 27.3 days) it created actual Ketu at point C on 17-11-1987 after crossing the ecliptic at 6.2° of Virgo sign (156.2°). Thus corresponding Rahu was created 180° from this point i.e. at 6.2° of Pisces sign (336.2°). After four year eight months i.e. on 13-7-1992 actual Rahu was created at 6.2° in Sagittarius sign (246.2°) at point D, after crossing the ecliptic by the Moon. After four year eight months i.e. on 10-3-1997 actual Ketu was created at 6.2° of Virgo sign at point E and corresponding Rahu was created, 180° ahead, at 6.2° of Pisces sign after crossing the ecliptic. Actual Rahu was again created at 6.2° of Gemini sign (66.2°) at point B after next four year eight months i.e. on 5-11-2001. As has been explained earlier that after 18 years 10 days Rahu, Moon and Sun again meets, but at a point, which is 10° away from earlier position, repeating same eclipse. But during this period Rahu does not complete its one rotation of 360° and it is short by about 10°. This shortfall of about 10° is covered in about seven months. Hence Moon creates repeated Rahu after about 18 years and 7.5 months as explained just now with the help of picture-40.

After about nine year four months, Ketu is created at the same degree-sign where Moon created Rahu after crossing the ecliptic. As may be seen from picture-40 that after nine year four months from 1983 i.e. in 1992 Ketu was created at 6.2° of Gemini sign (which was 180° ahead from 6.2° of Sagittarius sign), where Rahu was created in 1983. As has been described in picture-31 that celestial position of the Moon in Universe swing ahead and backward relative to the plane of the Sun and Earth after creating Rahu and Ketu respectively. Thus there is no question of same impact of the Moon on both hemisphere of the Earth with reference to the ecliptic instead of equator; due to reverse position of the Moon after nine year four months, relating to the plane of Sun and Earth.

From picture-34, 36 and earlier description about the motion of Rahu / Ketu you may clearly understand that (a) the location on the Earth from where the intersection point of ecliptic and the orbit of Moon may be imagined or seen perpendicularly, will be (b) on the line joining the centre of Earth and point of Rahu / Ketu i.e. (c) on the line joining centre of the Earth, centre of the Moon and ecliptic. Different three orbits of the Moon are shown in picture-36 to clear this phenomenon a little more. That part of the orbit of Moon, which is above than ecliptic, is shown by dark dots, whereas below part of the orbit is shown by light dots. There is always an angle of 5.14° and distance of more than 14 crores km between the orbit of Sun and Moon. Thus it is quite clear that any location on the Earth from where we see or imagine the position of Rahu / Ketu i.e. intersection points of orbits will always be on the joining line of the centre of Earth and Rahu / Ketu. Because Sun always remain within Tropic of Cancer in north and Tropic of Capricorn in south situated 23.5° on either side with reference to the equator, hence it is clear that Sun never moves beyond Tropic of Cancer in north and Tropic of Capricorn in south, with reference to perpendicular visual position from these lines on the surface of Earth. We can clearly understand this phenomenon from the circle drawn on the Earth by Tropic of Cancer and Tropic of Capricorn in picture-34. We can also say that line adjoining centre of the Sun and centre of the Earth will always touch the surface of the Earth in between Tropic of Cancer and Tropic of Capricorn. In other words line adjoining, orbit of the Moon (circle formed by different celestial position of centre of the Moon), centre of the Earth and ecliptic (circle formed by different celestial position of centre of the Sun) can be drawn only from any location situated in between Tropic of Cancer and Tropic of Capricorn on the Earth.

Latitude of Rahu / Ketu

It is essential to know the degree-sign position of creation of Rahu / Ketu for working out their latitude which in turn can correctly be used for assessing impact of Rahu / Ketu. Rahu and Ketu are actually created when Moon crosses the plane of Sun and Earth (see picture-31) and at that time degree-sign position of the Moon must match with the calculated position of Rahu and Ketu. In this way they are created alternatively after about 13.6 days. For calculating the position of Rahu / Ketu their retrograde motion may be taken as 3' 11" per day or may be changed according to explanation given earlier for precise calculation. When *ayanansh* was 0° in so-called AD 285, at that time summer solstice falls on 0° of Capricorn sign and Sun crossed the equator when it was at 0° of Aries sign. But now, while moving towards north, Sun crosses the equator line from 6° 12' or 6.2° of Pisces sign (360° – 23° 48' = 336° 12' = 336.2°), in the year 2004, when *ayanansh* was 23° 48'. In this way if position of creation of Rahu / Ketu was also at 6° 12' of Pisces sign then altitude of their creation would also be 0°, as they would have been created at equator, where latitude is 0° as shown by point E in picture-40. For example on 19-6-2006, Rahu will be created at 336° 12' on the basis of fixed retrograde motion of 3' 11", because at that time Moon will also be at 336° 12' while crossing the plane of centre of Sun and Earth. Degree-sign position of Sun at the time of crossing of equator will be changed in future due to change in *ayanansh*; hence position of 0° latitude of Rahu / Ketu will also be changed accordingly. In view of this following calculation may accordingly be corrected in future.

See in picture-40 that ecliptic is extended in north and south hemisphere up to 23.5° from equator. In this way, when

Rahu / Ketu will be created at 90° away from 336° 12' i.e. at 6.2° of Gemini sign (66.2°) then their latitude will be 23.5°, which is the latitude of Tropic of Cancer. From this description you can understand that there is a change of 23.5° latitude in the creation of Rahu / Ketu when position of their creation have a transit of 90°. In this way their latitude will change from 23.5° to 0° to –23.5° (southern latitude) and to 0° according to retrograde creation of Rahu / Ketu from 66.2° to 336.2° to 246.2° and to 156.2° respectively, with every change of 90°. On this basis, latitude of creation of Rahu / Ketu at any position may be calculated as follows :–

1. If Rahu / Ketu created between 336.2° to 66.2° (between point A and B in picture-40).

For example, Rahu or Ketu is created at 30° (30° of Aries sign) i.e. after transit of 53.8° (360° – 336° 12' + 30° = 53° 48' = 53.8°) in Northern Hemisphere after crossing of equator at 336° 12'. Remember that 360° – 336° 12' = 23° 48' = 23.8°, which is *ayanansh*.

Hence latitude of Rahu or Ketu = 23.5 × 53.8 / 90

= 14.4° northern latitude

2. If Rahu / Ketu created between 66.2° to 156.2° (between point B and C in picture-40).

For example, Rahu or Ketu is created at 120° (30° of Cancer sign) i.e. after transit of 143.8° (360° – 336.2° + 120° or *Ayanansh* + 120 = 143.8°) in Northern Hemisphere after crossing equator at 336.2°. Latitude starts to decrease from 66.2° i.e. after transit of 90° from 336.2°. Because Rahu or Ketu is created after transit of 53.8° (143.8° – 90°) from Tropic of Cancer.

Hence latitude of Rahu or Ketu

= 23.5 – (23.5 × 53.8 / 90)

= 23.5 – 14.04 = 9.46° northern latitude

3. If Rahu / Ketu created between 156.2° to 246.2° (between point C and D in picture-40).

For example Rahu or Ketu is created at 210° (30° of Libra sign) i.e. after transit of 233.8° (*Ayanansh* + 210° = 233.8°)

after crossing of equator at 336.2°. Southern latitude starts from 156.2° i.e. after transit of 180° from 336.2°. Because Rahu or Ketu is created after transit of 53.8° (233.8° – 180°) in Southern Hemisphere after crossing of equator.

Hence latitude of Rahu or Ketu

= – (23.5 × 53.8 / 90)

= – 14.04° latitude or 14.04 southern latitude

4. If Rahu / Ketu created between 246.2° to 336.2° (between point D and E in picture-40).

For example Rahu or Ketu is created at 300° (30° of Capricorn sign) i.e. after transit of 323.8° (*Ayanansh* + 300° = 323.8°) after crossing of equator at 336.2°. Southern latitude starts to decrease from 246.2° i.e. after transit of 270° from 336.2°. Because Rahu or Ketu is created after transit of 53.8° (323.8° – 270°) in Southern Hemisphere from Tropic of Capricorn.

Hence latitude of Rahu or Ketu

= (23.5 × 53.8 / 90) – 23.5

= 14.04 – 23.5 = – 9.46° latitude

= 9.46° southern latitude

Following two situations emerges after calculating the latitude of creation of Rahu / Ketu, regarding visual (apparent) creation and impact of Rahu / Ketu at different places on the Earth :–

1. Formation of Rahu / Ketu may be recognised from the surface of the Earth, which is on the line of intersection point of ecliptic and orbit of the Moon (i.e. point of formation of Rahu / Ketu) and the centre of Earth. In such case perpendicular position of Rahu / Ketu will always be in between Tropic of Capricorn and Tropic of Cancer.

2. Formation of Rahu / Ketu may be recognised from any place of the Earth from where intersection point of ecliptic and orbit of the Moon (i.e. point of formation of Rahu / Ketu) is visible then that place of the Earth will not be on the line adjoining Rahu Ketu and centre of the Earth. But that place will be at different latitude

and longitude irrespective of any boundaries of Tropic of Capricorn and Tropic of Cancer.

Now we will discuss in detail about the formation of Rahu / Ketu and their impact in above two situations.

First situation

If it is presumed that Rahu / Ketu is formed at a point of visual intersection of the orbit of Moon and ecliptic then their point of formation will always be perpendicular from a location on the surface of the Earth and that location which will be on the line of adjoining the centre of Moon, centre of the Earth and ecliptic. In this situation that location of the Earth will always be in between Tropic of Cancer and Tropic of Capricorn (23.5° on both sides from equator line). Because line adjoining any point of ecliptic with the centre of the Earth will always cross the surface of the Earth in between Tropic of Cancer and Tropic of Capricorn as shown in picture-34. Hence Rahu / Ketu formed after intersecting the ecliptic by the Moon will also form within Tropic of Cancer and Tropic of Capricorn. Perpendicular location of subsequent formation of Rahu / Ketu; calculated either on the basis of slight change in retrograde motion as explained earlier in 'Motion of Rahu / Ketu' or on the basis of their fixed retrograde motion; will always be at different longitude, latitude and Hemisphere of the Earth. In this way if Rahu is formed anywhere in frontal portion of the Northern Hemisphere of the Earth i.e. perpendicular from any northern latitude, then Ketu will be perpendicularly formed in Southern Hemisphere on the back of Earth nearly at the same southern latitude. This phenomenon may be understood from picture-40. For example, Rahu was formed in Gemini sign at 23.5° northern latitude after intersecting the ecliptic by the Moon in the year 1983. Thereafter, Ketu was formed after intersecting the ecliptic in Sagittarius sign at 23.5° southern latitude after about 13.66 days. In this way daily retrograde motion of Rahu / Ketu was near about 3' 11" per day, which has already been extensively explained in 'Motion of Rahu / Ketu'. But Ketu is not formed at a longitudinal distance of 180° from the longitude of formation of Rahu i.e. exactly at an opposite location of the

Earth. Because rotation of the Earth is completed by the Moon in about 27.33 days (27 days 8 hours) hence though position of the Moon is 180° away in zodiac from the degree-sign position of formation of the Rahu i.e. behind the Earth, after 13.66 days yet Moon is not at a geographical distance of 180° from the perpendicular formation of Rahu on the Earth.

This phenomena may be understand on the basis of details shown in picture-41 in which North Pole of the Earth is kept in the centre for easy going. Now suppose formation of Rahu was apparently observed or understood in India from Jabalpur situated just on Tropic of Cancer at the time of crossing of ecliptic by the Moon at 6.2° of Gemini sign (66.2°) and 80° geographical eastern longitude. This position of the India, Moon and Sun is shown in dark shadow in a line at right-hand side of the picture. After about 13.66 days, Sun will nearly reach at 20° of Gemini sign and Moon will form Ketu at 6.2° of Sagittarius sign (246.2°) after covering half rotation of the

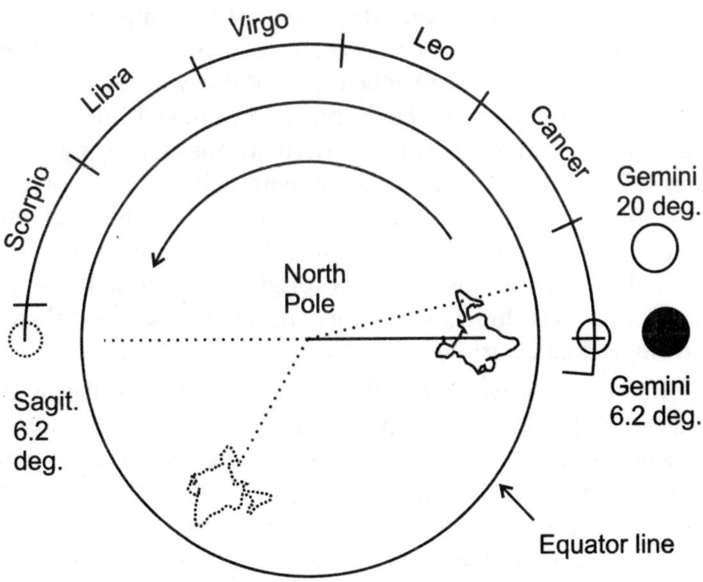

Picture – 41

Geographical formation of Rahu / Ketu

zodiac. These positions of the Sun and Moon is shown by light shade in the picture. Moon takes about 13 days, 16 hours in completing half rotation of the zodiac. Because Earth revolve once in a day on its axis hence position of Jabalpur on the Earth will match with the original position of the Gemini sign after 13 days, but geographical longitudinal location of Jabalpur cannot match with formation of Ketu (where Moon is present), due to more than half revolution of the Earth in remaining 16 hours. Because position of the Jabalpur revolves by 240° in 16 hours with a revolving speed of 15° per hour. This position of the India is shown by light shade in the picture. By observing the picture it may clearly be understand that perpendicular formation of Ketu will be at 60° west from the geographical longitude of Jabalpur or at 20° geographical eastern longitude and at 23.5° southern latitude i.e. over South Africa. Whereas, as per normal thinking formation of Ketu must be over South America, which is just opposite from the Jabalpur, where original Rahu was formed in Gemini sign. But Ketu will not form over South America, which will be just opposite to Leo sign. Indian subcontinent will again revolve by 240° and will be in front of Libra sign when next Rahu will be formed in Gemini sign in Northern Hemisphere after next 13.66 days. At the time of 2nd formation of Ketu in Sagittarius sign after next 13.66 days, Indian subcontinent will again revolve by 240° and it will be in front of Gemini sign. In this way after next 1.5 constellational month (41 days) or after three constellational months from the original position, Rahu will be formed over India. Only then its effect may be taken in astrological calculations.

Rahu / Ketu were considered as demons since Rising age and on the basis of eclipse it was believed that they are always present in the sky hence they were considered as moving shadow planets with retrograde motion of 3' 11" per day. But now when it is theoretically accepted that with reference to the centre of Earth, they are formed at intersection points of ecliptic and orbit of the Moon, then it is very funny to still move them with a fixed retrograde motion considering their continuous presence. Whereas they are formed for a while like visual total solar eclipse from any location on the Earth and this location also changes as has been explained above. Hence if Rahu is once formed over the India then though next Rahu will be formed over India after about three constellational month i.e. after about 82 days, but not over Jabalpur as per previous example. Likewise their position continuously changes and after about nine years Ketu will continue to form over the India. In this situation it is totally unscientific to include Rahu / Ketu in the horoscope of every individual.

Some astrologer may say that it is correct to move intersection points of orbit of the Moon and ecliptic because ecliptic is almost fixed (except slight change due to *ayanansh*) and orbit of the Moon as a whole is retrogradely changing its position as shown in picture-36, hence intersection point of orbits will also retrogradely move. To clear this doubt, see description of picture-24, where it was clearly explained that solar system as a whole is moving in three-dimensional Universe; and thus in strict sense there is no fixed path either for the Earth or Moon, which is known as ecliptic (orbit of the Sun with reference to the Earth) and orbit of the Moon. Because if we join various position of the Earth and Sun in picture-24 then actually it will not form a plane but a swirled form of lines will be formed; as Sun is moving in a direction around the Black-hole and angle between Sun and Earth is also changing due to summer solstice and winter solstice. Thus there is no fixed plane as such. Likewise there is no fixed plane between Earth and Moon. But for general understanding of a concept, a picture is drawn in which either Earth or Sun kept fixed as shown in picture-36 or 31 respectively. In this way there is no substantial change in primitive concept of Rahu / Ketu and latest astrological concept in which though intersecting point is being recognised as Rahu / Ketu, but they are still retrogradely moving in analogy of primitive concept without in-depth study of motion of solar system in the Universe. Because Rahu / Ketu is actually formed only when Moon crosses the "instant plane" created by expanding the line joining Sun and Earth, which is continuously changing due to movement of Earth and Sun. Thus it is totally wrong to move Rahu / Ketu with a retrograde motion. With this retrograde motion we can at the most calculate next formation of Rahu / Ketu.

From the above explanation it is quite evident that Rahu / Ketu are formed at about same northern and southern latitude but at different geographical longitude. As in the root of the astrology itself, importance was always given to visual position of the planets since Primitive age and presently as per instructions contained in '*Grahlaghav*'; hence *nirayan* system was recognised after discovering *ayanansh* on the basis of changing celestial position of the planets. Thus impact of eclipse and assessment of degree-sign position of the planets is based on celestial position and not only on mathematical calculation. Thus it is clear that there is no impact of Rahu / Ketu in various cities situated above the Tropic of Cancer passing through Ratlam, Bhopal, Jabalpur, Ranchi in Northern Hemisphere of the Earth, at a latitude of 23.5° and in various countries situated below the Tropic of Capricorn passing through Australia, South Africa, Argentina etc. Because Rahu / Ketu can never be observed or imagined perpendicularly i.e. in line of centre of the Earth, from these cities either by moving them with a fixed retrograde motion of 3' 11" or by moving them with a changing motion as explained earlier. It can be understand from picture-40 that formation of Rahu continuously and slowly shift towards Southern Hemisphere from Northern Hemisphere and accordingly Ketu shift towards Northern Hemisphere from Southern Hemisphere.

In the year 1987 Rahu and Ketu were formed on equator line at about 6.2° of Pisces and Virgo sign respectively and their perpendicular position could not be observed from entire India. Thus there was no justification in including their impact in prediction and astrological calculations. In continuation it is also mentioned that India is situated above 8° latitude in Northern Hemisphere of the Earth. Likewise it may also be understand from picture-40 that formation of Rahu / Ketu takes nine years in moving from Tropic of Capricorn to Tropic of Cancer, which is 47° (23.5° × 2) apart. Thus it may take about three years in moving from 8° southern latitude to 8° northern latitude or *vice versa*, during crossing of equator in complete cycle of 18 years. During these three years perpendicular formation of Rahu / Ketu can never be observed or imagined in India. Thus it is evident that there will be no impact of Rahu and Ketu at any place in India during these three years out of every nine years. This fact is again explained as follows :–

Time taken by Rahu in complete rotation = 18 years

Time taken by Rahu in reaching to 6.2° of Virgo sign from 6.2° of Sagittarius sign = 4.5 year

Change in latitude between 6.2° of Virgo sign and 6.2° of Sagittarius sign = 23.5°

Distance of southern tip of India from 8° of southern latitude = 16° latitude

Hence time taken in change of 16°
= 4.5 × 16 / 23.5 = 72 / 23.5 = 3 years

Above time relates to the movement of Rahu from 8° of northern latitude to 8° of southern latitude or *vice versa* movement of Ketu from southern latitude to northern latitude. We can easily calculate concerning calendar year of above three years as follows :–

Change in retrograde deg. in 6.2° of Virgo sign from 6.2° of Sagittarius sign = 90°

During change of 23.5° of latitude by Rahu, change in retrograde position = 90°

Hence during change of 8° of latitude by Rahu its change in retrograde position = 90 × 8 / 23.5 = 720 / 23.5 = 30.63°

In this way if Rahu is present within periphery of 30.63° from 6.2° of Virgo sign (156.2°) i.e. 6° 50' of Libra sign (156.2° + 30.63° = 186.83°) to 5° 34' of Leo sign (156.2° – 30.63° = 125.57°) or if Ketu is present in between these degree (186.83° to 125.57°) then there will be no impact of these shadow planets on entire India, because the location of view of their perpendicular formation will be outside from India. Rahu (Ketu was just opposite) was in this slot from 1-8-1995 to 30-9-1998 (as per fixed retrograde motion of 3' 11") and Ketu (Rahu is just opposite) remains in this slot from

19-11-2004 to 18-1-2008. Hence there will be no impact of Rahu / Ketu in the horoscope of any child born during this period in entire India.

Detail of actual perpendicular formation of Rahu / Ketu during the year 2007 along with date and time is given in table-6. You are now aware that Rahu / Ketu are created

Table – 6

Actual perpendicular formation of Rahu / Ketu during the year 2007

Date	Time	Deg. of Moon		Latitude of
		Rahu	Ketu	Rahu / Ketu
09-01-2007	2-45	—	145.80	4.23
22-01-2007	21-45	325.05	—	– 4.49
05-02-2007	7-50	—	144.30	4.82
19-02-2007	4-20	323.61	—	– 5.06
04-03-2007	12-15	—	142.92	5.38
18-03-2007	12-55	322.16	—	– 5.63
31-03-2007	15-30	—	141.41	5.97
14-04-2007	21-15	320.71	—	– 6.21
27-04-2007	18-30	—	139.98	6.54
12-05-2007	3-40	319.26	—	– 6.77
24-05-2007	22-20	—	138.54	7.10
08-06-2007	7-30	317.82	—	– 7.33
21-06-2007	3-20	—	137.07	7.67
05-07-2007	10-20	316.39	—	– 7.88
18-07-2007	9-15	—	135.66	8.22
01-08-2007	14-20	314.95	—	– 8.44
14-08-2007	14-45	—	134.19	8.77
28-08-2007	20-30	313.50	—	– 9.01
10-09-2007	19-20	—	132.82	9.30
25-09-2007	4-25	312.05	—	– 9.54
07-10-2007	22-35	—	131.38	9.84
22-10-2007	12-20	310.61	—	–10.06
04-11-2007	1-25	—	129.93	10.37
18-11-2007	18-10	309.16	—	–10.61
01-12-2007	5-30	—	128.47	10.90
15-12-2007	21-40	307.72	—	–11.13
28-12-2007	11-45	—	127.02	11.42

alternately, when plane of ecliptic and centre of the Earth is crossed by the Moon as shown in picture-31. Thus position and altitude of the Moon will match with the position of Rahu / Ketu. Plus or minus latitude indicates that Rahu or Ketu is created in Northern Hemisphere or Southern Hemisphere respectively with reference to the equator. From the table it may also be seen that Rahu is being created in Southern Hemisphere as indicated by minus sign in the last column of the table, and only after 18-7-2007, Ketu will start to form from 8.22° latitude and above in Northern Hemisphere; and due to this some time it may also form over southern India as explained in picture-41 and it will gradually move up to Tropic of Cancer.

In this way following position emerges from above explanation :–

1. Rahu / Ketu is not forming on any place of India or world wide situated above north of Tropic of Cancer. Hence there is no impact of Rahu / Ketu in the horoscope of any individual born in such place.
2. Though independent calculation may be done for particular place of birth, lying between Tropic of Cancer and Kanya Kumari in south, in respect of any individual born in India. Even then Rahu / Ketu has no impact during three years in every half cycle of nine years, as they are not formed over this area.
3. After formation of Rahu over the India, next formation of Rahu over Indian subcontinent may take place only after 82 days, whereas Ketu is formed at a distant place from India in Southern Hemisphere. In this way during remaining six years, as explained in s.no. 2 above, Rahu can only be formed at the most four or five times in a year.

Second situation

It has already been explained that there is an angle of 23.5° and 5.14° in between the equator and ecliptic, and in between ecliptic and orbit of the Moon respectively. See picture-42 and picture-31 for understanding it. Thus while rotating around the

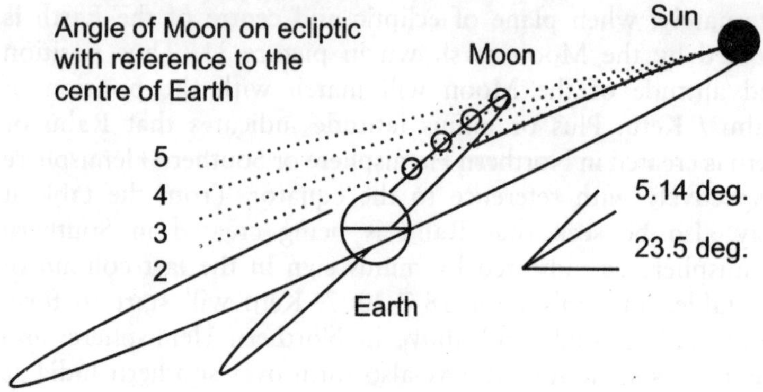

Picture – 42
5.14° inclined orbit of the Moon

Earth; Moon transit in its orbit, which maintains an angle of 5.14° with ecliptic. In this way Moon (not orbit of the Moon) has a 0° angle with ecliptic at the centre of the Earth, at the time of intersection of plane of ecliptic and Earth. After covering a distance of 90° in about 6-7 days, from the degree-sign of this intersection point, Moon has an angle of 5.14° with ecliptic at the centre of Earth. Likewise this angle reduced to 0° after next 90° rotation and thereafter during next 90° rotation in southern direction this angle again increased to 5.14° and at the time of next intersection of the plane of Earth and ecliptic, after complete rotation by the Moon in about 27 days, this angle again reduced to zero. When this angle is more than 1°, at that time line adjoining the centre of the Sun and centre of Moon will never touch the Earth. This fact is shown in picture-42 by the lines adjoining the centre of Sun and centre of Moon, when angle of the Moon is more than 1° with ecliptic. It may be observed from various orbits of the Moon shown in picture-40 that Moon never moves beyond 5.14°. In this way Moon never move beyond 28.64° (23.5° + 5.14°) northern latitude i.e. 5.14° north from the Tropic of Cancer passing through 23.5°. Hence whenever there is an angle up to 1° (actually 0.99°) between the Moon (not orbit of the Moon) and ecliptic at the centre of the Earth, only then line adjoining the centre of Moon and ecliptic (Sun at the time of solar eclipse) will touch the Earth at a place which is 90° altitude from the crossing point of the plane of ecliptic (Sun at the time of solar eclipse) on the Earth. In this way if Sun is actually on equator line and Moon is 1° towards northern latitude from equator line in its orbit, in other words if there is an angle of 1° between the Sun and Moon (not orbit) at the centre of Earth then line adjoining the centre of Sun and centre of Moon will touch the North Pole. Thus full solar eclipse may be seen from North Pole because shadow of the Moon will fall on North Pole despite presence of the Sun and Moon nearly over the equator line. Likewise solar eclipse may be seen at a distant place, based on the longitudinal, latitudinal angle of the Moon, from the perpendicular position of the Sun. Full solar eclipse may be seen whenever degree-sign and latitudinal difference between Moon and Sun will be less than 1°. This phenomenon may be understood from the study of picture-42. Though, position of difference of 1° latitude is not shown in the picture yet you can understand that whenever there will be an angle of 1° between the Sun and Moon then line adjoining the centre of Sun and centre of Moon will pass nearly from 90° altitude from the crossing point of the plane of ecliptic. Likewise it can also be understood that when Sun is at equator line and degree-sign position of the Sun and Moon is same then whenever there will be a difference of 1° southern latitude between the Sun and Moon then line adjoining the centre of Sun and centre of Moon will touch South Pole and full solar eclipse may be seen from South Pole.

Now we will understand this position with the help of picture-35. In which position of the Sun and Moon is at 'S' and 'M' respectively in their respective orbit and none of them is on equator. There is an angle of 1° southern latitude between these two points from the centre of Earth. As has been explained earlier, in this situation shadow of the Moon will fall on 90° southern altitude from crossing of the plane of ecliptic on the Earth (South Pole with reference to ecliptic and not with reference to equator). In other words line adjoining the centre of Sun and centre of Moon will pass from the South Pole with reference to ecliptic and full solar eclipse will be visible from there. Hence it is evident from this fact that crossing of ecliptic by the Moon will be visible from South Pole (of ecliptic) i.e. creation of Rahu may be seen and full solar eclipse will be visible due to presence of the Sun on ecliptic at that time whereas if we move towards north side on the Earth and see this situation from the equator line in place of centre of the Earth then we will find that there is an angle of more than 1° between the position of Sun or ecliptic and Moon, moreover due to absence of intersection of orbits neither solar eclipse nor creation of Rahu can be seen. If we further move towards north after crossing the India and see this position from North Pole then we will find that there is an angle of more than 2° between the position of Sun and Moon. Thus it is clear from this explanation that actual Rahu was already created when Moon was at point 'M', due to view of crossing of ecliptic by the Moon from South Pole (of ecliptic), instead of creating Rahu at point 'B' (see picture-35) after crossing the ecliptic by the Moon as is being presumed and recognised in the astrological calculation. In this way Rahu may be created at some place and may not be created at some other place of the Earth due to relative change in position of these planets in their respective orbit. Visibility of solar eclipse from different locations of the Earth also varies only due to this reason.

In Primitive age Rahu / Ketu were considered as demons and accordingly they were included in astrological calculations and principles. But to cover-up this wrong astrological notion of sages of primitive age, with the help of modern science, now-a-days it is proclaimed that intersection points of ecliptic and orbit of the Moon are Rahu / Ketu. If we examine this statement in view of the explanation contained in previous paragraph then it will be clear that Rahu was created as and when it was observed from South Pole, after intersecting the ecliptic by the Moon and thus not only it must be recognised in astrology but it may also be included in horoscope and so-called predictions accordingly. On the basis of this argument, it was explained in the chapter of "Rahu and Ketu" contained in first part, with the help of various data related to solar and lunar eclipse that if formation of Rahu / Ketu may be considered at intersection point of orbits than their retrograde motion of 3' 11" will not remain fixed, but it may vary between direct motion of 1' 53" to retrograde motion of 8' 53" and instead of their fixed mutual distance of 180°, it may also swing between 165° to 195° (see table-5 in the chapter of "Rahu and Ketu"). You have already studied this phenomenon.

Position of intersection of ecliptic with the orbit of the Moon is just now explained with the help of full solar eclipse. But it is not essential that the Sun may always be present in ecliptic, at the point of creation of Rahu or Ketu by the Moon. Because Rahu Ketu are created only when ecliptic is crossed by the Moon. We will understand this position with the help of picture-35. There is an angle of 1° latitude between ecliptic and Moon at point 'M' as seen from the centre of the Earth. There is a difference of about 17.5° geographical longitude between points 'M' and 'B' (position of Rahu created on the basis of so-called fixed retrograde motion of 3' 11"). Because a latitudinal angle of 5.14° is formed by the Moon with ecliptic, as seen from the centre of Earth, after transiting 90° or three signs by the Moon (see picture-40). Hence for forming a latitudinal angle of 1°, Moon has to transit by 90 / 5.14 = 17.5° longitude. Likewise there is a geographical longitudinal angle of 17.5° between point 'B' and 'P', and latitudinal angle of 1° between ecliptic and point 'P' as seen from the centre of the Earth. Because Moon transit towards north side from the ecliptic after crossing it from points 'B'. That's why full solar eclipse may be seen from North Pole if the Sun and Moon are at point 'C' and 'P' respectively. In this way it can be understood that if the Sun is neither present at point 'S' nor at point 'C' even then creation of Rahu may be seen from South Pole and North Pole (with reference to ecliptic, see picture-34), when Moon may be at point 'M' and 'P' respectively. Creation of Rahu may also be seen from in between location of South Pole and North Pole on the Earth during transit of Moon from point 'M' to 'P'. There is a difference of 35° between points 'M' and 'P'; and Moon may cover this distance in 2 days 13.5 hours with an average motion of 13° 40' per day. Hence process of creation of Rahu continuously transit from South Pole to North Pole during this

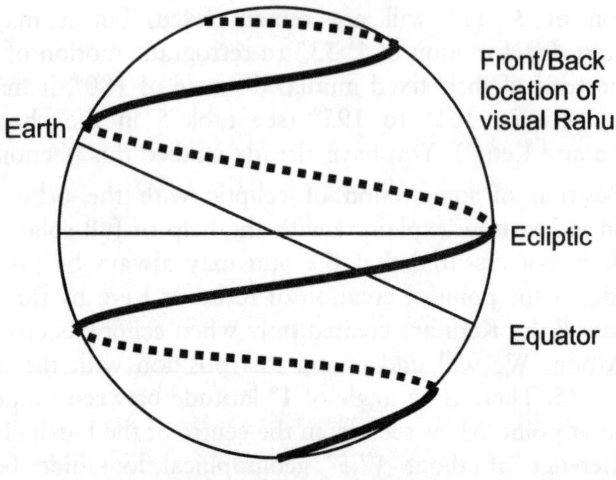

Picture – 43
Location of creation of Rahu

period and in this way Rahu complete 2.5 rounds (according to position of the Moon) of the Earth covering 180° latitude (South Pole to North Pole). Location of Rahu, according to its creation and its motion on the Earth may be understood from picture-43. This phenomena may also be understood from the fact that full solar eclipse may only be seen for a while (till creation of Rahu or Ketu) from any location on the Earth. But aeroplane is used for studying the solar eclipse for a longer period by flying it towards east, so that position of crossing of ecliptic (creation of Rahu or Ketu) may exist for a longer period and full solar eclipse may also be visible for a longer period. Those places on the Earth where creation of Rahu i.e. position of crossing of ecliptic by the Moon remains visible is shown by a thick line in the picture. Likewise continuity in creation of Ketu may also be understood. But visibility of creation of Ketu continuously transits from North Pole to South Pole. Because during creation of Ketu; Moon transits from Northern Hemisphere to Southern Hemisphere (with reference to 23.5° inclined ecliptic), as shown by point 'K' in picture-34.

From the above description, that it is possible to assume crossing of ecliptic by the Moon i.e. full solar eclipse when there is a difference of 1° latitude between the Sun and Moon, subject to condition that degree-sign position of the Sun and Moon may be same; a natural question arises that there will be a difference of 17.5° between the first situation of the Moon (at point 'M') at the time of solar eclipse (when line adjoining centre of the Sun and Moon does not pass from the centre of the Earth) and in second situation when there is a difference of 0° between ecliptic and the Moon (when line adjoining the centre of the Sun and Moon passes from the centre of the Earth) i.e. when Moon is at point 'B' (at the time of perpendicular creation of Rahu / Ketu from the Earth), as shown in picture-35. In this situation why solar eclipse is visible only when there is a difference of maximum 14° between the position of creation of Rahu / Ketu and same degree-sign position of the Sun and Moon as shown in picture-32 and prevailed in present astrological practice, instead of maximum difference of 17.5°?

For understanding the answer of this question we have to understand the calculation and description in view of the physical position of India on the Earth. As has been explained earlier that if there is a difference of 1° latitude between the Sun or ecliptic with the Moon then solar eclipse or creation of Rahu / Ketu respectively may be seen from a distance of 90° altitude with reference to the perpendicular position of the Sun or ecliptic on the Earth respectively, whereas calculated position of the Rahu / Ketu may be 17.5° away. During transit in Sagittarius sign (Capricorn sign in Primitive age) Sun remains at maximum 23.5° southern latitude in Southern Hemisphere. If Moon is also at the same degree-sign but with an angle of 1° towards northern latitude from the Sun then there may be a full solar eclipse and according to the given description, centre point of this eclipse on the Earth may be 90° towards northern latitude from 23.5° southern latitude (see detail of picture-43) i.e. at 66.5° (90° – 23.5° = 66.5°) northern latitude. Beside full solar eclipse, partial solar eclipse is also visible within a sphere of about 3200 km from the central location of full solar eclipse i.e. up to a location situated within about 30° latitude and longitude. In this way when centre of full solar eclipse is located at 66.5° northern latitude then partial solar eclipse is visible within a circular range of about 30° i.e. beyond 36.5 northern latitude (66.5° – 30° = 36.5°). Because this northern latitude was never in India hence correct position could not be analysed. But if calculated position of the Rahu / Ketu may be 14° away from the position of the Sun and Moon then solar eclipse may be seen from a distance of 72° altitude (90 × 14 / 17.5 = 72). Accordingly centre of solar eclipse will be 48.5° (72° – 23.5° = 48.5°) towards northern latitude and partial solar eclipse may be seen within a range of 30° i.e. beyond 18.5° northern latitude (48.5° – 30° = 18.5°) in India. All important places related to development of astrology in India were situated above 18° northern latitude hence when correct formation of solar system (picture-2), creation of Rahu / Ketu and shape of the Earth were not known in the Primitive age even then on the basis of eclipse it was calculated that eclipse occurred when Rahu / Ketu was up to 14° away from the Sun / Moon. But as per present astrological calculations there is factual mistake in the concept of 14° distance for any eclipse due to discrepancies regarding motion of Rahu / Ketu (see picture-37) and their position, as believed in Primitive age and as explained on the basis of latest scientific knowledge. This mistake has already been highlighted on the basis of table-4 that there may be eclipse even if difference is more than 14° and there may not be an eclipse even though difference is less than 14°. In this way it would have been quite clear on the basis of latest scientific information that how the concept of eclipse in case of distance of 14° of Rahu / Ketu was developed and what type of confusion is prevailing now-a-days in doing various astrological calculations.

Creation of Rahu will take transit from South Pole to equator as shown in picture-43 in accordance with the transit of the Moon from point 'M' to 'B' as shown in picture-35. Beside this creation of Rahu may also be seen up to a distance of 90° longitude from any location on the Earth, which is parallel with the ecliptic. Because after adjoining these locations with the centre of the Moon they will touch ecliptic on any point, which is either side of, point 'S' on ecliptic.

Above phenomena of creation of Rahu / Ketu may easily be understood by performing a simple experiment. Tie a thread at two places about a height of five foot to keep it straight. This straight thread will represent ecliptic. Now hold or place a small ball at a distance of about two feet in front of your eyes, so that it may be little below and about 5-6 feet from thread. This ball and your eyes will represent the position of the Moon and your location on the Earth respectively. In this way position of picture-35 will be created. Now if you slightly bend beneath the ball and see the ball i.e. from South Pole then only you will find that centre of the ball and thread are in line of your eyesight. Whereas ball is actually slightly lower than thread i.e. Moon is at an angle of 1° with reference to the ecliptic. Your eye is the location in the Southern Hemisphere of the Earth where Rahu is being created. You may easily move left or right and can also maintain matching of the centre of ball with the thread. Similarly, Rahu is also created at different locations on the Earth up to a distance of 90°. If you lift the ball above the thread and see the position i.e. after moving the Moon by 35° (from point 'M' to 'P' in picture-35) or with angle of 1° northern latitude. Then you have to move up a little i.e. up to North Pole, to match the centre of the ball with the thread. In this way you can understand the creation of Rahu on the North Pole. Likewise Ketu is created, when ball is lowered in this experiment. In this way you can easily understand the creation of Rahu / Ketu, other position shown in picture-35 and visual motion of Rahu as shown in picture-43, by performing this experiment.

Creation of Rahu on any location on the Earth can easily be ascertained from the following calculation.

Cities situated on the Tropic of Cancer

Sun remains between Tropic of Cancer and Tropic of Capricorn during its motion in ecliptic. At the initial time of summer solstice, when Sun is transiting over the Tropic of Capricorn then Sun is visible at an inclined angle of 47°

(23.5 × 2 = 47) towards southern latitude from the cities situated on the Tropic of Cancer. From the earlier description we know that crossing of ecliptic by the Moon may be seen in Southern or Northern Hemisphere from an altitude of 90°; when Moon is at an angle of 1° (north or south) with the ecliptic or at a longitudinal angle of 17.5° from the Rahu (created after transit of Rahu with a retrograde daily motion of 3' 11" on crossing of ecliptic by the Moon). Hence if Moon is 31' (60 × 47 / 90 = 31.33') north from the ecliptic or at a longitudinal angle of 9° 7' 48" (17.5 × 47 / 90 = 9.13°) from Rahu (9.13° ahead from point 'B' in picture-35) then creation of Rahu may be seen (assumed) towards south from zenith at an inclined angle of 47° from the cities situated on the Tropic of Cancer. For example according to almanac, on 16-6-1992, position of Rahu was at 247.3° i.e. 7° 18' of Sagittarius sign (daily position of Rahu is shown in almanac whereas Rahu is actually created after about 27 days. Hence it is presumed that Rahu was actually created on this date and leaving the difference in motion as shown in picture-37), then for the cities situated on the Tropic of Cancer, actual Rahu would be created when Moon will transit from 256.43° (247.3° + 9.13° = 256.43°) i.e. when Moon will be at about 17° of Sagittarius sign. In other words, crossing of the ecliptic by the Moon, which was passing through Sagittarius sign, may be seen (assumed) from the Tropic of Cancer when Moon will be nearly 17° in Sagittarius sign (see picture-35 and 40). After about nine years from the above date calculated Rahu (with a retrograde motion of 3' 11") will be created at 7° of Gemini sign when ecliptic is perpendicular from the Tropic of Cancer and actual Rahu will be created when Moon will cross the ecliptic from 7° of Gemini sign or when Moon will also be perpendicular from the Tropic of Cancer. At that time there will be no latitudinal change in the position of the Rahu. In this way according to almanac Rahu was at 67° on 9-10-2001 and actual Rahu was created when Moon was also at 7° of Gemini sign (67°), because centre of the Moon and corresponding point of ecliptic were perpendicular from the Tropic of Cancer. Hence position of Rahu will change from

256.43° to 67° instead of 247.3° to 67° during about nine years for the cities situated on Tropic of Cancer.

Likewise Ketu will be created when Moon will be longitudinally in opposite direction. For example actual Rahu was created 9.13° ahead from the calculated position of Rahu in Capricorn sign for the cities situated on the Tropic of Cancer, because creation of Rahu was inclined by an angle of 47° towards southern latitude from these cities. But creation of Ketu will be visually seen before 9.13° from calculated position of the Ketu, from the cities situated on the Tropic of Cancer. Thus Ketu will be created at an angular difference of 170.87° (180° – 9.13° = 170.87°) instead of fixed angular difference of 180° from Rahu. But again at the time of creation of Ketu at Tropic of Cancer after about nine years there will be no latitudinal change in actual and calculated position of Ketu.

From the above description it would be clear that there is a difference up to 9.13° in the position of Rahu / Ketu in the horoscope of the individuals born in the cities situated on the Tropic of Cancer.

Cities situated towards south of Tropic of Cancer

In accordance with the description given above, as we move towards south from Tropic of Cancer, the difference between the concerning city and Tropic of Capricorn will correspondingly decrease and the difference of 9.13° in assumed view of Rahu will also be reduced. This difference will be reduced to zero from southern altitude of 47° from Tropic of Cancer i.e. from Tropic of Capricorn. In this way there will be a reduction of 11' 39" (9.13 / 47 = 0.194°) in creation of Rahu from 9.13°, for change of every 1° altitude. (Actual orbit of the Moon is slightly spiral as shown in picture-40, whereas this calculation is based on straight line as shown in picture-45 in next chapter, hence due to fast motion of the Moon there may be a negligible variation in precise calculation.) Thus in the cities situated at 1° southern latitude from Tropic of Cancer, the difference in the actual position of Rahu, calculated as per retrograde motion of 3' 11", would be 9.13° – 0.194° = 8.936°. In other words actual Rahu for these cities will be created when Moon would be 8.9° ahead from the calculated position of Rahu with retrograde motion of 3' 11". Accordingly, the Moon will create Rahu for these cities 0.194° ahead for change of every 1° altitude, from the creation of Rahu after crossing of Tropic of Cancer.

Example

Line of 21.5° latitude, passes near about from Raipur, Sambalpur, which are nearly 2° south from the Tropic of Cancer, which is situated at 23.5° latitude. Hence for calculating degree-sign of actual formation of Rahu, we have to multiply the difference of both latitudes with 0.194°.

If position of Rahu calculated either on the basis of fixed retrograde motion of 3' 11" or changing retrograde motion explained earlier = 247°.

But Rahu will perpendicularly be created on Tropic of Capricorn (23.5 southern latitude) when Moon will also transit from 7° of Sagittarius sign (247°).

Hence latitude of actual formation of Rahu or Tropic of Capricorn = 23.5° southern latitude.

Hence difference of latitude of Raipur and latitude of actual formation of Rahu

= 21.5° northern latitude – 23.5° southern latitude

= 21.5 – (– 23.5)

= 45° altitude

Creation of Rahu from Raipur may only be seen when Moon will further transit by 45 × 0.194°

= 45 × 0.194° = 8.73°

= 8° 43' 48" after creating Rahu on Tropic of Capricorn.

Thus Rahu will be created for Raipur when Moon will transit from 247° + 8.73° = 255.73°, hence position of Rahu will also be at 255.73° for Raipur instead of 247°.

In this way creation of Rahu for Raipur may be considered after such time, which was taken by the Moon in moving 8.73°, after creating Rahu on the Tropic of Capricorn and after adding 8° 43' 48" in the position (247°) of Rahu, created on Tropic of Capricorn.

Position of creation of Ketu may also be calculated accordingly.

If Ketu is created at 67° (247° – 180°) on Tropic of Cancer (23.5 northern latitude) at a distance of 180° from Rahu.

Difference between Raipur and Tropic of Cancer

= 21.5 – 23.5 = – 2° latitude

Difference between calculated Ketu and actual creation of Ketu for Raipur

= – 2 × 0.194° = – 0.388°

= – 23' 18"

In this way creation of Ketu for Raipur may be understood before such time, which was taken by the Moon in moving 0.388°, from creating Ketu on the Tropic of Cancer and after deducting 23' 18" in the position (67°) of Ketu, created on Tropic of Cancer. Thus correct position of Ketu for Raipur at 66° 36' 42" (67 – 23' 18") may be ascertained.

From the above description it would be clear that there is a positive and negative difference of 9.13° in actual position of Rahu / Ketu in the horoscope of individuals born in the cities situated towards south of Tropic of Cancer.

Cities situated towards north of Tropic of Cancer

In accordance with the description given above, as we move towards north of Tropic of Cancer, the difference between the concerning city and Tropic of Capricorn will correspondingly increase and the difference in assumed view of Rahu will also be increase from longitudinal 9.13°. In this way after moving 1° north from Tropic of Cancer, position of creation of Rahu will also be changed by 9.13° + 0.194° for change of every degree of latitude. Thus if we calculate the position of Rahu for Delhi then due to difference of 5° (28.5 – 23.5) between Tropic of Cancer and 28.5° latitude of Delhi, there may be difference of 9.13 + 0.194 × 5 = 10.1° in the creation of Rahu. Thus creation of Rahu may be seen or imagined from Delhi when Moon will be 10.1° ahead from the calculated position of Rahu on the basis of fixed retrograde motion of 3' 11" or otherwise. Likewise if Rahu is created at 7° of Gemini sign i.e. on Tropic of Cancer even then there may always be minimum 0.194 × 5 = 0.97° difference. The difference between creation of Rahu and Ketu will not be 180° as in the case for the cities situated on the Tropic of Cancer. Thus actual difference between them may be calculated on the basis of distance of actual location from the Tropic of Cancer.

From the above description it would be quite clear that there is always a difference in the actual position and calculated position of creation of Rahu / Ketu in the horoscope of the individuals born in the cities situated towards the north of Tropic of Cancer.

Calculation of the position of Rahu / Ketu

According to different situations explained above, actual position of effective and visual creation of Rahu / Ketu at the point of crossing of ecliptic by the Moon for any city may easily be calculated as follows and time of actual creation of Rahu / Ketu may also be worked out on the basis of transit of Moon from the above position.

Position of actual creation of Rahu for any place or city = Calculated position of Rahu in degree + (Latitude of city – Calculated latitude of Rahu) × 0.194°.

Position of actual creation of Ketu for any place or city = Calculated position of Ketu in degree + (Calculated latitude of Ketu – Latitude of city) × 0.194°.

Notes

1. Calculated position of Rahu / Ketu means the position, which was calculated either on the basis of their fixed retrograde motion of 3' 11" or changing retrograde motion as explained earlier and Moon may also transit from that position.
2. Calculated latitude of Rahu / Ketu means the latitude of their perpendicular position on the Earth, which was calculated either on the basis of their fixed retrograde motion of 3' 11" or changing retrograde

motion as explained earlier and Moon may also transit from that position.

3. Take latitude in minus for geographical southern latitude.

In this way independent calculation of position of Rahu / Ketu for any city may be performed on the basis of above description.

Following position emerges from the above description of second situation regarding effect and motion of Rahu / Ketu.

1. Retrograde daily motion of Rahu / Ketu is not fixed at 3' 11" because they are created after in between 27 days 5 hours and 27 days 10 hours. Thus their daily retrograde motion continuously varies between 3' 10.88" to 3' 12.29".
2. Position of creation of Rahu on the basis of fixed retrograde motion will not match with the calculated Rahu; hence there is no eclipse despite less than 14° distance of Rahu from the Moon as shown in table-4.
3. Position of creation of Rahu continuously shift from South Pole to North Pole hence its span of impact may be narrowed down only for the cities situated between Tropic of Capricorn and Tropic of Cancer. Because line adjoining the centre of the Earth and Moon may pass from the intersection of both ecliptics, which may be seen or imagined only from these cities.
4. Rahu / Ketu are created at different places on the Earth, at different time. Because crossing of the ecliptic by the Moon may be seen from every place on the Earth at different time. In this way Moon, move ahead in the Universe after creating Rahu by crossing the ecliptic on a plane formed with a particular place of birth (not with the centre of Earth as shown in picture-31) on the Earth and centre of the Sun or lag behind in the Universe with reference to this plane after creating Ketu. Hence position of actual Rahu / Ketu must be shown in the horoscope like position of other planets, which is shown in the horoscope on the

basis of their actual position with reference to the place of birth.

5. Every city of India is situated at different latitude with reference to equator hence there may never be a fixed difference of 180° between the position of Rahu and Ketu. Because difference of 180° is fixed for the cities situated on equator and there is no such city in India.

From the above description you would have clearly understood that instead of doing some fruitful research at present how Almanac, Manual drafting of horoscope, Computerised horoscope, Yog, Prediction, Controlling evil effect of planet etc., type of all astrological work are being performed on the basis of fixed retrograde motion of Rahu / Ketu devised in the Primitive age, only on the basis of belief and faith without having any scientific reasoning and which has no connection whatsoever with the bare truth, just to exploit an individual having weak mentality.

Now we will discuss the calculation of solar and lunar eclipse on the basis of creation of Rahu and Ketu. On the basis of which minute calculation of eclipse may not only be performed but erroneous calculation being practised since long may also be corrected.

Eclipse

Trigonometrical formulas for calculating the size of Sun, Moon and Rahu / Ketu have already been mentioned. Minute calculation of the visual angle of the Sun, Moon and Rahu / Ketu may either be performed on the basis of those formulas or from the graph shown in picture-38 on the basis of their daily motion. Calculation of solar and lunar eclipse may easily be performed on the basis of their visual angle.

Happening of lunar eclipse may be worked out after calculating the visual angle of Rahu / Ketu / shadow of the Earth and Moon, referred as AR and AM respectively in the following formulas.

Partial lunar eclipse = {(AR + AM) / 2} × 90 / 5.14

Full lunar eclipse = {(AR – AM) / 2} × 90 / 5.14

Example

Motion of the Sun = 60' / day

Motion of the Moon = 800' / day

Visual (apparent) angle of Rahu = 1.38°

Visual angle of Moon = 0.525°

(On the basis of graph shown in picture-38)

Position of partial lunar eclipse

$= \{(AR + AM) / 2\} \times 90 / 5.14$

$= \{(1.38 + 0.525) / 2\} \times 90 / 5.14$

$= 0.952 \times 90 / 5.14$

$= 85.68 / 5.14$

$= 16.66 \;\; = 16° \; 40'$

Position of full lunar eclipse

$= \{(AR - AM) / 2\} \times 90 / 5.14$

$= \{(1.38 - 0.525) / 2\} \times 90 / 5.14$

$= 0.427 \times 90 / 5.14$

$= 38.43 / 5.14$

$= 7.47 \;\; = 7° \; 28'$

In this way, first calculate the visual angle of Rahu and Moon according to trigonometrical formulas given earlier, which are 1.38° and 0.525° respectively in the above example. Thereafter calculate maximum distance of Rahu / Ketu as shown above for partial and full lunar eclipse. After adding 180° in the position of the Sun, we may easily know the position of centre of the shadow of the Earth. If the position of Rahu or Ketu (after calculating on the basis of changing retrograde motion or fixed retrograde motion of 3' 11" with little mistake as may be seen from the almanac), whoever is near to 180° from the Sun and within 16° 40' on either side from the position of centre of the shadow of the Earth then there may be partial lunar eclipse. If the position of Rahu / Ketu is within 7° 28' on either side, from the Sun + 180° (centre of the shadow of the Earth) then there may be full lunar eclipse. Size and time of partial or full lunar eclipse will inversely increase in the ratio of angular distance or Rahu / Ketu from the centre of the shadow of the Earth.

Solar eclipse may be calculated as follows after calculating the visual angle of the Sun and Moon, referred as AS and AM respectively in the following formulas.

Partial solar eclipse = {(AS + AM) / 2} × 90 / 5.14

Full solar eclipse = {(AS – AM) / 2} × 90 / 5.14

Example

Motion of the Sun = 60' / day

Motion of the Moon = 800' / day

Visual angle of the Sun = 0.533°

Visual angle of the Moon = 0.525°

(On the basis of graph shown in picture-38)

Position of partial solar eclipse

= {(AS + AM) / 2} × 90 / 5.14

= {(0.533 + 0.525) / 2} × 90 / 5.14

= 0.529 × 90 / 5.14

= 47.61 / 5.14 = 9.26 = 9° 15'

Position of full solar eclipse

= {(AS – AM) / 2} × 90 / 5.14

= {(0.533 – 0.525) / 2} × 90 / 5.14

= 0.004 × 90 / 5.14 = 0.36 / 5.14 = 4'

In this way first calculate the visual angle of Sun and Moon according to trigonometrical formulas given earlier, which are 0.533° and 0.525° respectively in the above example. Thereafter maximum distance of Rahu / Ketu may be calculated as above for partial and full solar eclipse. If the position of Rahu or Ketu (after calculating on the basis of changing retrograde motion or fixed retrograde motion of 3' 11" with little mistake as may be seen from the almanac), is within 9° 15' on either side from the position of the Sun then there may be partial solar eclipse. If the position of Rahu / Ketu is within 4' on either side, from the position of Sun then there may be full solar eclipse. Size and time of partial or full lunar eclipse will inversely increase in the ratio of angular distance of Rahu or Ketu from the centre of the Sun. But in the above example visual angle of the Moon (0.525°) is less than visual angle of the Sun (0.533°), hence in case distance of Rahu / Ketu is less than 4' from the position of the Sun then there will be annular solar eclipse instead of full solar eclipse. Outer circumference of the Sun remains visible in annular solar eclipse, because visual size of the Moon is less than visual size of the Sun. Here you can observe that only size of the Moon represents Rahu or Ketu during solar eclipse, whereas they are represented by the shadow of the Earth during lunar eclipse. But this fact was not known to the sages of Primitive age.

Sun is always visible from half of the Earth and there is night in another half portion of the Earth, because shadow of the Earth is always extended towards the side of the night. Hence shadow of the Earth may be seen or imagined from half dark portion of the Earth. Because Moon transits from the shadow of the Earth during lunar eclipse hence visual shape and size of lunar eclipse is same from half dark portion of the Earth, whereas Moon (which was not visible hence presence of Ketu was believed during solar eclipse in the Primitive age) is in between the Sun and Earth during solar eclipse. Hence due to distance (9° 15' in above example) between the Sun and Moon; solar eclipse may only be seen from a place on the Earth, which is perpendicular from the Sun. But as explained in the description of picture-35, 39 and 42 that shadow of the Moon may fall on different places on the Earth hence different type of solar eclipse may be seen from different places. In this way partial solar eclipse of the example may be seen as a full or missing solar eclipse from different places on the Earth. Thus solar eclipse is visible from different places on the Earth even in case of 1° (latitude or longitude) difference between the Sun and Moon. On the basis of place of visual solar eclipse on the Earth, precise calculation of diameter of the Sun and Moon is calculated with the help of trigonometry for conducting precise scientific research.

If visual angle of diameter of the Sun and Moon may be taken as 1° instead of about half degree or in other words there may be a difference of 1° between their centres then calculation for partial solar eclipse may be done as follows :–

Position of partial solar eclipse

$$= \{(AS + AM) / 2\} \times 90 / 5.14$$
$$= \{(1 + 1) / 2\} \times 90 / 5.14$$
$$= 1 \times 90 / 5.14$$
$$= 17.5°$$

In this way solar eclipse may be seen if position of Rahu or Ketu as explained earlier is within 17° 30' either side from the degree-sign position of the Sun. But this solar eclipse may only be seen from an angular distance of 90° altitude from the perpendicular position of the Sun instead of perpendicular view of the eclipse from the Earth. This phenomenon has already been explained in detail. In this way size and zone of eclipse on the Earth from the perpendicular position of the Sun will increase according to the reduction in 17° 30' difference of Rahu / Ketu from the Sun.

From the detailed description given in this chapter it would be clear that retrograde motion of 3' 11" per day in the position of Rahu / Ketu is not correct. Beside this, it is also a fact that difference between actual position of Rahu, calculated on the basis of various eclipse and position shown in almanac is continuously reducing as described during explanation of picture-37 and table-3. In this way actual Rahu was at 356°, whereas in almanac it was shown at 355° 37' on 18-6-2005. Hence at present the difference in actual position of Rahu is reduced to about +23' (356 – 355° 37') and this difference relates only for the perpendicular location on the Earth situated between Tropic of Cancer and Tropic of Capricorn. Rahu / Ketu will be created at different degree for different locations on the Earth. In this situation it is quite essential to take care of this point along with other points during precise calculation of eclipse and correct incorporation of Rahu / Ketu in the horoscope.

20

AYANANSH

> **TIP** : If you are amateur reader or find any difficulty at any time in understanding this chapter then you may left it and continue your study from the chapter of 'Deep thought', remembering that *ayanansh* as used in astrology is scientifically not correctly applied. Try to understand this left out portion in next reading.

After a little understanding regarding the concept of Rahu / Ketu, it will be easy to understand about the *ayanansh*, which is also known as 'precession of the equinoxes'. For understanding the concept of Rahu / Ketu we have presumed that Sun is a stationary body (see picture-31). Whereas actually the Earth as well as Sun are moving in the Universe. You will be surprised to know that Earth is moving in a circular motion around the movable Sun with a speed of about 1,06,000 km per hour. In the same way Sun along with its entire solar system, is also moving in the galaxy around the Black-hole with an enormous speed of 7,69,000 km per hour as shown in picture-24. If Sun and centre of the galaxy i.e. Black-hole may be kept in a plane so that motion of the Sun may be perpendicular to this plane, then there would be an angle, between the first plane made up of the Sun and Earth as shown in picture-31, with reference to this new plane as shown in picture-33. During its rotation around the Sun, as and when the Earth crosses this plane of the Sun and Black-hole (vertical plane is shown by a line in picture-33) i.e. when it is on the verge of moving towards backward or lagging behind with reference to this plane; in other words during mid of summer solstice when Sun is just to cross the equator for entering in Northern Hemisphere; corresponding degree of the Sun at that time is *ayanansh* and the Sun is only visible in this situation once a year during summer solstice. We know that duration of the day and night is equal twice a year, when Black-hole, Sun and Earth are on the same plane. After crossing the plane, Earth lag behind the Sun in the Universe and complete its half rotation, whereas Sun appears to move towards northern side of the equator, if we look it from the equator. In this way in the Northern Hemisphere duration of the day increases in comparison to the duration of the night and on the other hand, in the Southern Hemisphere, duration of the day decreases in comparison to the duration of the night in the same ratio. After completing its half rotation around the Sun in about six months, Earth is again in a position to cross the plane of Sun and Black-hole during winter solstice when it will move ahead with reference to the Sun in the galaxy. As a result of this, duration of the day will reduce in comparison to the duration of the night in the Northern Hemisphere and on the other hand in the Southern Hemisphere duration of the day will start to increase in comparison to the duration of the night in the same ratio. After six months from this i.e. after one year from the earlier position, Earth will again came in a position to cross the plane of the Sun and Black-hole and move behind the sun. Again, at this time the position of the Sun in degree, as seen from the Earth, will be *ayanansh*. Actually Earth crosses this plane about 50" earlier in its every rotation. But relatively we say that Sun is retrogradely lagging with a motion of 50" per year. Thus difference of *ayanansh* in two successive years is about 50" and hence *ayanansh* increases continuously.

Concept of picture-33 can clearly be understood after observing it as picture-31; where Sun, Earth and Moon may be presumed and observed as Black-hole, Sun and Earth respectively. As Moon retrogradely crosses the plane of Sun and Earth by forming Rahu / Ketu; likewise after observing Moon as Earth as explained just now, we may understand that Earth will also retrogradely cross the plane of Black-hole and Sun. When Earth retrogradely cross this plane on 23rd March and move behind the plane of Black-hole and Sun (like moving of Moon after creating Ketu) then corresponding change in the position of the Sun in zodiac is known as *ayanansh*. The change in *ayanansh* of 50" per year due to rotation of the Earth can further be understood from picture-44. In this picture the position of crossing of the plane by the Earth is shown for four years. Earth lag behind by an angle of 50" per year but relatively as we see the situation from the Earth, it appears that Sun is lagging behind by an angle of 50" per year in the zodiac. On the basis of change in *ayanansh* by 50" per year, it is believed that *ayanansh* was 0° in the year AD 285; and position of the Sun was 0° of Aries sign, when it was on the equator line on 23rd March, when Earth was

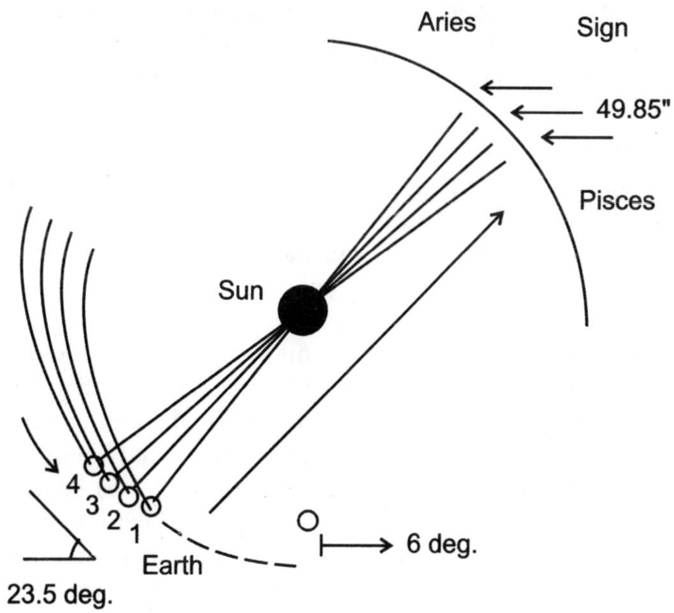

Picture – 44

Change in *ayanansh* by 49.85" per year

actually on the plane of Sun and Black-hole. But now the *ayanansh* is about 23.8°. In this way while crossing the equator, Sun is at 6.2° of Pisces sign and its northern latitude is actually about 6° by the time it transits from 0° of Aries sign. In this way the northern altitude of the Sun, with reference to the equator, by the time of transiting from 0° of Aries sign, also increases by 12.5" per year with the corresponding increase in the *ayanansh*. This position can also be understood from picture-44.

Like Rahu / Ketu of other planets, this position of ayanansh is also retrograde with reference to the Sun. In the Primitive age when it was believed that Sun is exalted at 10° of Aries sign; at that time *ayanansh* was –10°. Hence after deducting this *ayanansh* from the *sayan* position of the Sun of 0° of Aries sign; exalted position of the Sun at 10° of Aries sign in *nirayan* was concluded. Now-a-days the *ayanansh* is more than +23° or there is a change of 33° since Primitive age. In this way after deducting this much *ayanansh* from the 0° of Aries sign, we get 7° of Pisces sign. Hence Sun may be exalted at 7° of Pisces sign in accordance with the concept and calculation of the Primitive age. This fact has already been explained in the chapter of 'Exalted-debilitated Planets'.

As has been explained about the Rahu / Ketu of other planets, likewise if you consider the Rahu and Ketu of the Earth then *sampaat* position will be created as and when the Earth crosses its Ketu. Because only in this situation Sun was at 0° of Aries sign, known as *sayan* and after deducting *ayanansh* from this position we may work out the *nirayan* position of the Sun. In other words, we may say that when Earth crosses its Ketu (when duration of the day become more in comparison to the duration of night in Northern Hemisphere) then the visual position of the Sun in the zodiac will be actual longitude of the Sun in *nirayan* and difference between *sayan* (0° of Aries sign) and *nirayan* is *ayanansh*. The angle formed between the inclination of the orbit of the Earth and the plane formed by the Sun and Black-hole is actually well-known to us as an inclination of the Earth and we try to understand every position formed during its rotation around the Sun as an inclined Earth as shown in picture-30. The angle between these two planes is about 23.5°. That's why Earth swing with reference to the Sun by 23.5° while rotating around the Sun and also move to keep pace with the Sun in the galaxy. We visualise this inclination of the Earth in the form of winter solstice and summer solstice of the Sun. You can also understand this from picture-33. Orbit of all other planets is also inclined with reference to the plane of the Sun and Black-hole like the inclination of orbit of the Earth.

If we try to understand the ecliptic and orbit of other planets with reference to the Earth at a time then it can be understood from the picture-45. Line H L is projected line of equator in the sky with reference to the Earth. The position of the sky, which may be seen from the Northern Hemisphere, is shown above this line whereas the position as seen from the Southern Hemisphere is shown below the line. The position of ecliptic in earlier Primitive age is shown by dark line A, B, C, D, E; from which it may be observed that Sun crosses the equator from 10° of Aries sign shown as point X and thereafter it enters in the Northern Hemisphere, due to which the duration of the day start to increase in comparison to the duration of the night in the Indian subcontinent. Thus Sun was considered as exalted at 10° of Aries sign as has already been explained in the concerning chapter. Sun was at a maximum northern point B after summer solstice when it transit from 10° of Cancer sign i.e. at 23.5° latitude or at Tropic of Cancer which is shown by the P, I, B, W points. After touching this point, Sun enters in the phase of winter solstice during its motion and it remains in this phase till point D of 10° of Capricorn sign, after which it re-enters in the phase of summer solstice. That's why the union (*sankranti*) of Capricorn got importance over all other unions.

All other planets while rotating around the Sun remains in the close vicinity of this line (ecliptic). Point B of the orbit was in Cancer sign and in Pushya constellation as shown in the picture. Hence extremely illuminated Jupiter was visible in the sky from the northern India when it was very near to zenith i.e. at a maximum altitude during its rotation, which may be

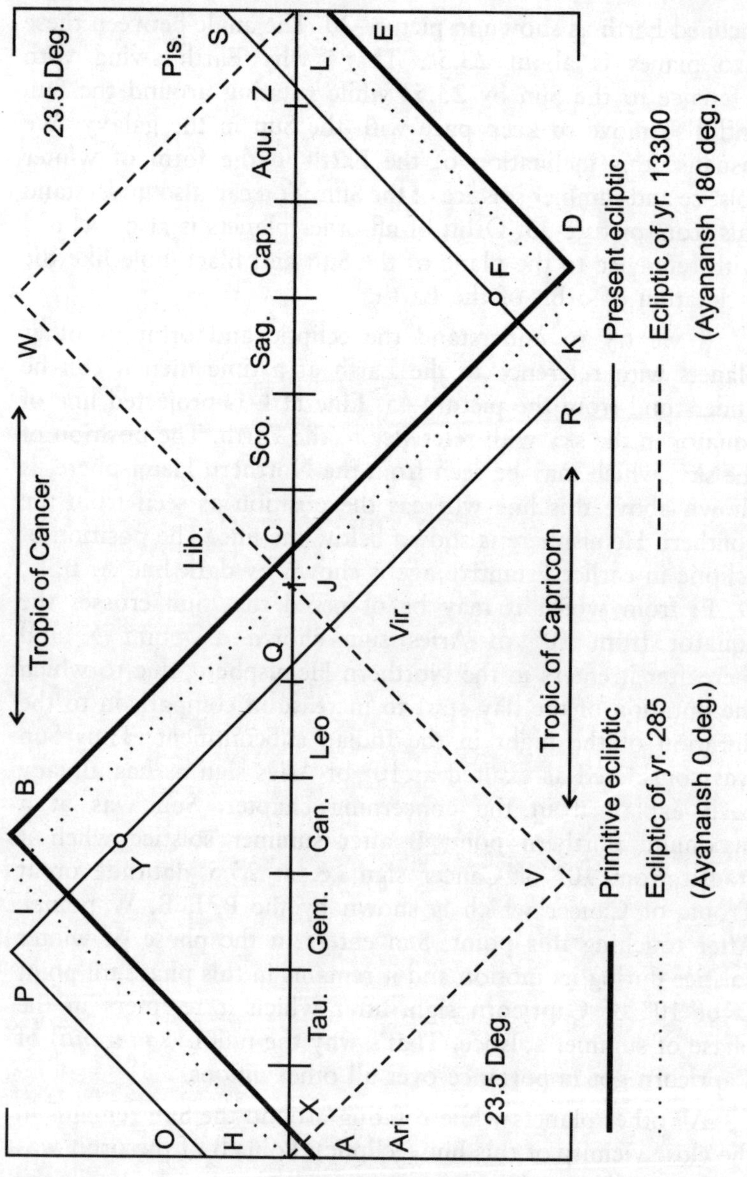

Picture – 45

Changing ecliptic of the Sun due to *ayanansh*

1.3° away from the ecliptic and due to which Jupiter was considered as exalted at the 5° of Cancer sign.

Due to continuous increase in the *ayanansh* it become (so-called) 0° in the year AD 285. The orbit of the Sun of that year is shown by the dotted line H, I, J, K, L in the picture-45. As *ayanansh* was 23° 48' in the year AD 2003 hence shifted ecliptic is shown by a thin line O, P, Q, R, S. You may observe from this line that Sun enters in summer solstice from 23rd December when it happens to be at 7° of Sagittarius sign, shown by point R. But we are still celebrating the union of Capricorn (*Makar Sankranti*) when Sun take transits from point F in Capricorn sign on 14th January during summer solstice, like practice as followed in the Primitive age. Whereas Sun actually covered a distance from point R to F in summer solstice. Point X of 10° of Aries sign on line A B is retrogradely moving due to change in *ayanansh* and has reached to point Z situated near 7° of Pisces sign. Similarly this point will continuously retrograde due to increasing *ayanansh* and will reach to point J situated at 0° of Libra sign in the year AD 13300. The ecliptic of that time is shown by broken line H, V, J, W, L in the picture. At that time Jupiter will not be visible at zenith, when it will transit from Cancer sign, but it will be visible nearly southern horizon and there will be no trace of its exaltation in Pushya constellation, because actually it will be 47° away towards south from the Pushya constellation. Beside this Sun will be at point W when it will be in the Capricorn sign and Sun will be on the verge of winter solstice. But surprisingly, if primitive practice prevailed till that time then we would have been celebrating the festival of summer solstice at the time of winter solstice.

In this way you can realise that Sun may be seen either in northern or in southern span of 23.5° from equator. Any planet which was visible in the Primitive age at an altitude in a sign either in northern or southern side with reference to the equator i.e. nearly a constellation, will be visible in the same sign but at a different altitude with reference to the equator, with passage of time. In astrological principles, the span of a constellation was considered up to 13.33°. Thus if a circle having a radius of 6.66° may be drawn as its orb and if a planet is situated within this circle then only it can be presumed that the planet is in that particular constellation. Because to locate the celestial position of any planet, sky was divided in the constellation and sign well before Primitive age and all 27 constellations are situated nearly to the line A, B, C, D, E. All planets remain very near to the ecliptic and appears to complete their rotation of zodiac while moving from close vicinity of these constellations. But due to change in *ayanansh* the orbit of the planets is now in the vicinity of the line O, P, Q, R, S (latest ecliptic), which is 33° (distance between point B and P representing corresponding shifting in ecliptic) away with reference to the primitive zodiac; and deviated by about 8° with reference to the equator. Because any planet, which was visible at point B in the Cancer sign in Primitive age, is now visible at a lower point Y, which is 8° away from the point B, though same planet is in the Cancer sign. Thus if the orb of a constellation was considered within the range of 6.66° and when at present all planets take transit from a distance of more than 8° from the actual location of the constellation then what is the logic in considering the planet in that constellation and that too when these constellations are not even in our galaxy (refer chapter of 'Modern Concept of Universe'). It is a serious question for deep thinking.

Thus there is a continuous change in the position of the planets in the sky. As it is essential to prepare new set of ferry in the event of change in the stream of a river and there is no use of old ferries. Likewise, we may have to decide new set of constellations in the orbit of the planets according to the change in their orbit, so that celestial position of the planets may be assessed correctly. Otherwise, with the passage of time, ecliptic along with orbit of the planets will further shift and it will be completely reversed by the year AD 13300 and become like H, V, J, W, L, which is just opposite to the ecliptic of the year AD 285 when *ayanansh* was 0° and even then all astrological calculations, prediction would have been based on the ecliptic (shown by A, B, C, D, E) of the Primitive age and constellations situated on that primitive ecliptic; and that situation will completely be foolish. In this way you can very well understand that how much variation may take place in the celestial position of the planets due to *ayanansh*. That's why it is pertinent to completely modify the astrological principles accordingly. But instead of correctly using this knowledge after doing necessary modifications in the astrological principles, now-a-days public at large is actually being misguided and exploited on the basis of wrong and outdated principles and concept.

Sun happens to be in winter solstice when it was in Cancer sign hence perpendicular transitory position of the Sun, as seen from the Earth, was regarded as Tropic of Cancer. Likewise in the summer solstice when Sun happens to be in the Capricorn sign then perpendicular transitory position of the Sun as seen from the Earth was regarded as Tropic of Capricorn. But since AD 285, winter solstice and summer solstice commenced when Sun transits in Gemini and Sagittarius sign respectively, due to increase in the *ayanansh*. Because in India we are following the *nirayan* system and Indian knowledge of astrology is only the oldest and recognised in the world, hence geographical Tropic of Cancer and Tropic of Capricorn must now be renamed as Tropic of Gemini and Tropic of Sagittarius respectively. Because Sun will be in the phase of winter solstice and summer solstice when it will transit in Gemini and Sagittarius sign respectively till AD 2453. Thereafter, Sun will be in the phase of winter solstice and summer solstice when it will transit in Taurus and Scorpio sign respectively till AD 4621. Hence there is now no justification in keeping the name of these geographical lines as Tropic of Cancer and Tropic of Capricorn.

When a planet crosses the ecliptic O, P, Q, R, S of the Sun and move towards the northern side of the Universe then it create its own Rahu. Likewise when a planet after crossing the ecliptic, move towards the southern side of the Universe / ecliptic, then it create its own Ketu. You have already studied about this in length in the previous chapter. But there is no research on the change in impact of the planet on the Earth, after or at the time of passing through such situation.

Variation in *ayanansh*

Till now we are not able to calculate correct *ayanansh*. Distinguished astrologer like Aryabhatt, Parashar, Varahmihir, Bhaskar etc. adopted different *ayanansh* based on different methods, and their *ayanansh* varied between 46.3" to 1' per year. If we expand their yearly *ayanansh* then year of 0° *ayanansh* may fall anywhere between the year 388 BC to AD 522. *Ayanansh* was estimated as 18° 18' in the year AD 1620, when '*Grahlaghav*' was available and at that time change in *ayanansh* was regarded as 1' per year. If we calculate on this basis then *ayanansh* may be 0° in the year AD 522. Whereas, now-a-days it is claimed that *ayanansh* was 0° in the year AD 285 and rate of change in *ayanansh* is 49.85" per year. In this way *ayanansh* will be 24° in the year 2018. Different estimated *ayanansh* is being adopted for preparing different almanac due to absence of correct and precise calculation of *ayanansh*. However, if we work out the *ayanansh* for the year AD 1620 and AD 522 with present rate of change (49' 85") then *ayanansh* may be about 18° 29' and 3° 17' instead of 18° 18' and 0° respectively. From this explanation it would be quite clear that there is sufficient variation in the estimation of *ayanansh* as adopted by the astrologers of the pre-Modern age and as adopted in the Modern age.

As you know that *ayanansh* has an important role in calculation of ascendant, and *ayanansh* is deducted from *sayan* position of the planet to work out vivid position of planets in *niryana*. Thus horoscope is totally based on these two building blocks. Due to this much variation (up to 3° 17') in the estimation of *ayanansh*, not only ascendant and birth horoscope would totally change but position of the planets will also change in *chalit, navansh* etc. horoscopes. Beside this, exalted-debilitated planets, *vinshottary dasha* etc. would also be drastically change. In this situation it is a matter of concern as to how so-called correct prediction would have been assessed by Varahmihir in sixth century or how prediction of all other astrologers of Pre-modern to Primitive age would have been regarded as correct?

Answer of this question may easily be traced in first section of this book. Wherein it was disclosed, as to how astrological principles were formulated on wrong concept of solar system (see picture-1) and how they differ from each other and lead to different direction. In this situation it was very easy to predict some thing according to one's sweet will from various possibilities; and due to psychological effect (which was not known in those days) some prediction may appears to be correct since Primitive age, despite substantial mistake in *ayanansh* and all astrological principles.

Transit of the Earth and Sun is responsible for creation and change in *ayanansh* (accumulated yearly change in the position of Sun with reference to 0° of Aries sign or Ashwini constellation which is not in our galaxy and situated in some other galaxy), like transit of Moon and Earth with reference to the Sun is responsible for creation and retrograde motion of Rahu / Ketu. As has been explained during description of picture-24 that Sun travels 674 crores km per year in our own Milkyway. In this way there is continuous change in the position of the plane formed with the Sun and Black-hole, which is crossed by the Earth with a different motion during its rotation around the Sun. This change is responsible for minute variation in rate of per year change in *ayanansh*. Thus it may easily be concluded that fix rate of change in *ayanansh* i.e. 49.85" per year cannot be regarded as correct.

Mangal Dosh

In *Vedic* period astrology was limited to study the movement of planets (now known as astronomy). After developing the skill of forecasting eclipse (trouble on deity) and weather, it was gradually modified to forecasting the future of an individual on the basis of the then concept, which your have already studied.

Our sages observed that Mars is not only masculine, fiery, chief of army of deities, arrogant and evil but only this planet also has self aspect (refer chapter of "Aspect of Planets"). Therefore its evil power gets multiplied. In this way a concept of unwarranted fear was developed and percolated in generation to come that only Mars is responsible for any negative incident in married life.

Status of body, relation of couple and inclination of mind, which were main function of married life were studied through Lord of ascendant, Venus and Moon respectively and position of Mars was studied in horoscopes drawn after placing the sign of (1) ascendant (known as birth horoscope), (2) Venus (3) Moon in 1st house and placing other planets in their respective signs. If Mars (refer picture-17) is in 1st, 4th, 7th, 8th and 12th house (also 2nd house in south India) in any of these three different horoscopes then that horoscope is classified as *Lagn* (ascendant) *mangali* (evil Mars), *Suka*-Venus *mangali* and *Chandra*-Moon *mangali*.

To dilute the evil effect or for so-called matching of horoscopes, our sages formulated a method that horoscopes of the couple must have same evil effect, or there may be some strong planet (some combinations are there) or any other evil planet like Sun, Saturn, Rahu or Ketu may be in same house or marriage may be performed after 28 years of age (when evil energy of an individual may automatically be cooled). To avoid complications in the arranged marriage, now-a-days prominence is only given to *Lagn mangali* and parents of *mangali* individuals remain in uncalled-for tension.

In Primitive age, when there was neither a scientific method to judge the correctness of any principle nor there was any communication with distant civilisation. Thus in those days this concept was accepted by the society due to unquestionable faith towards sages and fear of planet (deity). But now-a-days when we have fast system of communication, interaction, conveyance and scientific knowledge about the planets that there are not deities then following this unscientific concept is totally our ignorance.

21

DEEP THOUGHT

So far you may have well acquainted with the primitive misconcept about fundamental formation of the Universe. Thus there is no importance of these astrological principles based on such misconcept in view of the modern and scientific knowledge about the Universe as well as various impact of heavenly bodies like gravitation etc. Beside various astrological principles formulated on the basis of misconcept of the Universe, many supportive astrological principles have also completely lost their ground due to continuous change in the *ayanansh*. Because there is a change of 33° in the celestial position of the planets and change of more than 8° in their altitude due to *ayanansh* since Primitive age. In this situation present form of the astrology is completely baseless and these principles have no scientific approach. Although sages actually tried their best, by their continuous observation and deep thinking to understand the Universe and devised many sort of horoscopes and periodicities to assess the planetary impact due to their various celestial position. It was only their endeavour by which they could discovered various mysteries of the Universe that too without any modern equipment and could formulate various astrological principles; a part of which has now been developed as astronomy, geography etc., but predictive astrology is popular only due to psychological effect, which was not known in the Primitive age, and principle of predictive astrology is not supported scientifically. In the Primitive age, Rulers were also advised by the sages to act upon after assessing the celestial position of the planets. But even in those days sages not tried to mould the mindset of the Ruler or the society in the rigid frame of destiny on the basis of astrology. Lord Krishna himself conveyed the message of importance of work beside mortality of the body and immortal soul. If we want to know about immortality of the soul in modern scientific prospect then it can easily be understood as a form of energy. Eminent scientist Albert Einstein has not only founded the famous principle of relativity but also proved that energy can never be destroyed, but it can only be transformed. In the same way our soul or energy also hold in by physical matter i.e. body, while remaining immortal.

Deep study of the astrology has now been lost in time. Due to increase in materialistic mentality and unfulfilled superfluous desire, everybody is inclined or forced to believe in fixed destiny instead of performing some active, sincere honest hard work. To find a shortcut for fulfilling his desire to get much more than his own ability or requirement is pushing him in the trap of an attractive and manipulated prediction, due to which astrology has turned into a new type of roaring business with the help of computer and everybody is now trying to search one or other remedial dexterity to fulfil his every irrational and irrelevant desire, and wasting his money and valuable time of life by swinging in between hope and desperation.

When a magician perform some unimaginable feat then it appears to be quite real and trick behind that magic cannot be detected even by an intelligent person. Similarly, past events as narrated by an astrologer are actually not correct, but a best astrologer, who may be a good psychologist, explains past events in such a twisted and skilled manner so that every event appears to be correct. A magician actually admit that every magic is performed by some trick, whereas unscientific and unfounded (in view of latest knowledge of solar system) basis behind the astrology is not only continuously being concealed but public at large is also being misguided and exploited through modern methods referring astrology as science.

It is an ordinary fact that a person suffering from some disease will contact a doctor, likewise a person suffering from some trouble will contact an astrologer and remain confused due to his own weak mentality and full confidence on astrologer / predictive astrology. As one patient may feel relief in his illness after taking only some ordinary medicine or even coloured water in the form of medicine after sympathetic behaviour of a decoy doctor, due to change in his mental status because of full confidence on a doctor. Similarly, a person having weak mentality may feel that events and circumstances are turning in his favour after performing some spell, religious offering or after wearing a ring due to change in his mental status, whereas, circumstances which is result of the deed of someone else are not changing at all. Such exploitation of general public by astrologers can only be plugged in present scenario of confusion when astrologers may be dragged to consumer forum and may be asked to pay compensation for their wrong prediction.

We must not jump to the conclusion that any prediction, which is being inferred on the basis of the horoscope, is definite and cannot be mutilated and it will certainly happen, because any unfavourable prediction can be overturned by blending it with our good deed, correct implementation of judicious discretion and hard work. Because every presumption whether it is supported by experience of our own life or by astrology, which was again based on the lifetime experience of sages, has a role of our guideline. For example if we know by our experience that rash driving is hazardous and if we will not act according to our experience then we may be in hot water and thus it would be our guideline and we can advise accordingly. If some one will not follow this guideline than he has to face the music or even may not face the music. But anyhow our advice was not a forecast but our experience. We can see many example of such type, which is based on our lifelong experience and sometimes their result may not be according to our experience. Likewise primitive astrological presumption must also be viewed in the same analogy that during a particular transitory position of planets some favourable or unfavourable incident may take place. Because it is based on primitive experience and the basis of which has already been discussed in detail in the first section and it has nothing to do with fixed destiny, because all astrological principles are unscientific.

We would have been fortunist at one time or another on the basis of our horoscope. But in the next chapter you will understand that how horoscope was also designed with a view to perform some work at every stage of life and it is not a record of fixed destiny as has been manipulated and propagated by the astrologers since Primitive age. Hence never sit idle in the hope of fixed destiny and always have a faith on yourself and in the favourable result of your best deed. Always try to blend your hard and honest work with judicious discretion. Experience and knowledge learned from the surroundings can only be converted into judicious decision (*vivek*) by deep thinking (*chintan*). Hence always try to enhance your knowledge and experience. Because only these habits can convert the seed of circumstances to fulfilment of your desire and have a potential to override negative circumstances and any success can be achieved only by patience, devotion, self-confidence and implementation of judicious decision. In the next chapter you will know that how these three qualities repeat themselves in the horoscope. Contrary to this if you rely on fixed destiny and try to match any combination of planets in your horoscope with the same planetary combination in the horoscope of any eminent personality then you will simply be plundered by the astrologers and remain confused. *Yog*, periodicity, inter periodicity (*mahadasha, antardasha*) and inauspicious period of seven and half years due to Saturn (*saade-saati*) etc. have major role in fixing you in the utter confusion. As you have studied that various predictive astrological principle leads to different predictions hence you will find that result of some predictions may match with your present condition, circumstances and you will psychologically convinced that astrology is correct, but it is not so. If some sort of planetary combination of your horoscope is matching with the same sort of combination of some eminent person then it doesn't mean that same type of favourable or unfavourable result would come across to you. Because result of same action performed at different time is totally different; as time, period and circumstances continuously changes. Hence in this situation any prediction will be alike as if someone say that your nose is like our Prime Minister hence you would definitely be a Prime Minister. At one time or another you may like to believe in fixed destiny and turned away yourself from any sort of exertion after entangling in various forecasts being published in many magazines and books of astrology and act upon with a confused mind to modify the impact of a moving planet in the Universe according to your wishes with the help of a ring or something like this. Have you ever thought that when your body having the surface area of about two square meter is being continuously exposed for the impact of a planet then what difference it is going to make on the planetary impact by a gem of one square cm. When every planet has its definite impact in the Universe according to its size, distance and motion, which you have already studied then how you may defend yourself from that impact? We will later on discuss with a scientific angle, about the impact of planets.

A complete confused and illusive condition is persisting and it is further being complicated by the wordiness of so-called astrologers. On one hand we are forced to believe that every event, even every movement is pre-decided and pre-written; and only astrologer can decode it from the horoscope with the help of so-called primitive astrological principles. Just imagine, in this situation, we are like a puppet and when each and every event on every part of the Earth has to follow this so-called pre-written destiny then why we are as an ordinary actor is so much worried and anxious. On the other hand, by following the so-called sincere advice of learned astrologers, we also want to modify the whole script of so-called fixed destiny for our petty gains with the help of so-called ring, spell etc. being easily provided by the astrologers and consultants. Just have a sincere thinking over the fact that even if, it is possible to modify the written destiny then in this circumstance even a minor manipulation in the written destiny has a all-round cascading effect thus many related and inter-related incidents will also be changed.

Above fact may be clear from the example of an event. Suppose a renowned astrologer has predicted after consulting horoscope of an individual and after implementing all other related astrological principles that on a particular day, leg of individual will be amputate in an accident. Now that individual has only two options. Firstly, he may wait till that date when his leg will be amputate, believing that destiny is fixed and weaken his will power due to mental worries; and it may also be possible that in such a weak and worried mental status, he may be victim of any accident nearly that date. As an other option he may try to avert this accident by following the advise of the astrologer and wear some costly gem or do some spell etc. In both these above situations if there would be even a minor accident near about that date then quite naturally it will be concluded that forecast was correct and destiny is fixed and no body can change it. Now from the above explanation it can be concluded that every incident is pre-decided and nobody is in a position to change it. In this situation what is the propriety of virtuous or sinful work. Because virtuous or sinful action were itself pre-decided. In this situation what is the propriety in teaching someone to abstain from sinful action. Because he is neither performing any virtuous action nor any sinful action but he is simply following the track of pre-decided destiny and he is neither eligible nor supposed to use his intellect or knowledge for performing any action. Now, it is a very strange situation, as firstly someone may be forced to do some sinful act by following so-called fixed destiny and thereafter, he may be punished for that sinful act. Beside this, description of virtuous act of someone else may be praised in front of him in the hope that he will also follow the correct path and it is also expected from him to do some virtuous act. Whereas that poor fellow is not involve in any sinful act, because every incident is pre-decided, which may be decoded and forecasted by the astrologer from the horoscope and he is only performing his part according to the pre-decided script, like an actor of a film. In this situation he is neither supposed to use his skill, wisdom nor he is required to worry nor there is a need to know about the future because whatever is pre-decided would automatically happen.

In other situation, if that individual followed the advise of the astrologer and wear some costly gem or do some spell etc. to avoid the amputation of leg in an accident and subsequently there was no such accident. In this situation too that individual would not only have a complete and unquestionable faith on the forecast of the astrologer but he would also be mentally moulded to have a faith on the effect of the gem etc. and will have a firm opinion that any fixed incident of future may be changed or amended by following the advise of the astrologer like averting his own accident and he would be trapped in this swirl for rest of his life. Now-a-days almost everybody is suffering from this mentality and nobody has a vision for thinking logically or scientifically beyond this point. Whereas, when the astrologer forecasted from the fixed destiny about the amputation of leg in an accident of an individual on the basis of primitive astrological principles than this incident was not isolated but future of many persons was linked with this accident. Because any incident can never be isolated and it is always linked with a chain of incidents. Thus, when amputation of the leg was decided in the fixed destiny of the individual then in continuation of this incident it was also decided in the future of an auto-rickshaw driver that after this accident that poor auto-rickshaw driver who would have not earned a rupee would be awarded after taking him to hospital and subsequently, it was also decided in the future of the dying mother of that driver that she would be saved from the medicines purchased from this income. But that individual modified his fixed destiny on the advice of the astrologer by wearing a costly ring etc. Thus neither there was an accident, nor auto-rickshaw driver took him to the hospital, nor he was awarded, nor he could purchase the medicine for his dying mother and ultimately his mother died. In this way old mother of auto-rickshaw driver who was destined to survive after taking medicine purchased from the awarded money was actually died due to minor modification in the predicted fixed destiny of the individual by using gem, ring, spell etc. We may continue to add many more persons in the above incident, whose fixed destiny was also changed. In this way all linked incident and linked incident of linked incident would also be changed after averting or slightly changing any favourable or unfavourable fixed destiny and a person who was not even remotely connected would be effected as old mother of driver in the above example.

Just imagine if every Tom, Dick and Harry may be able to modify that so-called fixed destiny then the volume of destiny of entire world will be a mess and then what would happen to that so-called prediction, which was based on original destiny and assessed by a learned astrologer from the horoscope. In this way the concept of fixed destiny is only a psychological defensive tool for consolation for the persons having weak will-power or unsuccessful or who are facing opposite situations. But if we try to understand the reasoning of development of astrology and basic idea of the sages and then try to improve the astrological principles in view of latest knowledge of solar system and Universe by estimating the impact of the planet then we will definitely be able to calculate the impact, and can be able to take benefit of that impact in our favour. Most important factor required for this is that our mentality must be logical, modern instead of orthodox; and action oriented, intellect instead of believer of fixed destiny, only then we can carve out our future according to our desire and also create some destiny for next birth in accordance with our good deeds in this life.

What is my destiny, it is that inquisitiveness, which is enquired by every body through astrology. But it is a grave mistake to form an opinion that any prediction made after analysing the horoscope on the basis of illogical primitive astrological principles (as described in first part) is definite. Because present circumstances are being created on the basis of action performed by others and myself in the present life. These circumstances are destiny for the present and any event will take shape after executing any action by someone on the basis of judicious or injudicious decision. Any event will not take place only on the basis of destiny but result of present incident will be foundation for creating the circumstances in future. Thus despite so-called fixed scope of destiny, there is too much scope of uncertainty within this fixed scope. As someone is man then his scope of action and duty is somewhat fixed according to family, society, religion, city, country etc. in comparison to women but still there is too much scope for various action. Thus circumstances are being created regularly and final sequence of events will depend on intelligent, judicious or injudicious decision and action performed in the present transition of the planets.

You may have heard that though astrologer's narration of the event relating to the past was correct but for events relating to the future was not correct. Your present is actually the result of past deeds. If harvest has dried then anyone can say that it is due to draught, because the event of the past has already taken shape after union of your action with destiny i.e. circumstances which were created around you. But at present you only have so-called destiny i.e. circumstances which will be created around you and blending of your action in those circumstances is still pending according to which event of the future will be modified and take shape. As has been clarified earlier, generally it is believed that whatever is destine will be materialise in due course and horoscope is studied to know the destiny according to the transit of the planets i.e. "Destiny + Transit = Result". In this way your judicious or injudicious action has no contribution in deciding the event. This belief is absolutely wrong and illusive. Whereas actually desired result can only be carved out from any circumstances by doing the correct and appropriate action based on correct decision at correct time i.e. "(Destiny + Transit) × Action = Result". In this way if you will not perform your duty sincerely with devotion and correct wise judgement then whatever may be the potential of your destiny i.e. favourable circumstances and transitory position of the planet; the result will be zero, because multiplying zero action with destiny and transit is zero. A complete picture of destiny, transit and action (duty) can be understand by the example of cricket. Where you can presume the destiny in the form of pitch, circumstances created by the players like studying the horoscope. On this pitch you have to get success in the form of run during transit of the opposite team having nine players in the shape of nine planets and if we add Uranus and Neptune then this team will be of eleven players. At every time, one or another planet / player is impressing you in the form of impact / bowling and you have to perform your action / play in a day / over during a very little time of the day i.e. when you have to take some judicious decision or perform a duty which is going to effect the shape of event and in turn success in future. A best player always take decision about his action only after assessing the position of the pitch, calibre of the opposite team and own capacity i.e. after understanding destiny (circumstances) and transit, and finally get success. Whereas a person who believes in fixed destiny, try to get success after assessing the unfavourable condition of the pitch and opposite team by enticing the umpire i.e. by performing some illogical action for cooling down the impact of planets on the advice of astrologers or he become idle and remain unsuccessful in both conditions.

It is believed that we start our life in a particular planetary position according to our deeds in the previous birth. This particular opening celestial position of the planets is known as horoscope. Probably you may be surprised to know that planetary position in various houses as shown in the horoscope of a person, remains so only for near about two hours around the birth time i.e. till the ascendant is not changed. After that the same particular planetary position will neither be repeated in the future nor it was ever formed in the past. I have verified this fact on several horoscopes that same planetary position is never repeated even in a period of twenty-five thousand years of past and future. Even in two hours time span of an ascendant, there is also a continuous minor change in the position of every planet and ascendant as believed in the Primitive age and as per scientific calculations too. You may also be aware till now that there is a change of thousands km in the distance of a planet from the Earth in a moment. In this way effect of impact of planets on twins may also be varied due to continuous change in the impact of planets.

We can at the most assess the impact of planets at the time of birth by studying the horoscope, because it is so-called opening balance for present life. But favour of destiny i.e. circumstances can be materialised only when it is blended with our good deed. In this way we can also destroy the favour of destiny by blending it with misdeed. Likewise unfavourable destiny may only be materialised when it get support from our misdeed. Contrary to this, we may reduce the disfavour of destiny by our good deed. Good and misdeed may easily be ascertained. If your self-confidence improves with any action then it is good action and contrary to this if your self-confidence shattered with some action then it is a misdeed. Thus we can understand that chain of events of future is not pre-decided, which may be ascertained from the horoscope. It may also be understand by an example that though we may have seeds of best quality, yet the best harvest can be achieved only by putting a hard labour and neither by careless working nor by sitting idle by keeping a faith over destiny. Now what is the good deed for getting best harvest from the seed? Definitely it is the ability to pre-assess the information about the condition of the land, weather, rainfall, water etc. and ability to mould our action accordingly. We must also be careful about our every action at every stage of harvest and simultaneously, we may have to weed it. Likewise to get the maximum benefit from our destiny we may have to know the planetary transit and during their best transitory position we may have to exert devoted hard work in accordance with the various stages of our life. Simultaneously, we may have to reduce the unfavourable trend of our destiny like weeding out useless plantation by our good action, only then we may be able to get success in our life according to the potential of our destiny. At the end of life, as believed a net result of all deeds of this life, our soul may carry a new opening balance of destiny according to its net energy and may again proceed to incarnate in next life in appropriate planetary combination.

As we are not able to get the same harvest from each and every seed of the same quality. Because despite bearing the same weather during the journey of a seed to became a fruit, it has to bear substantial deviation in our action of weeding and effect of useless plantation. In the same way despite approximately same planetary position in the horoscope of twins i.e. same seed and despite same weather i.e. same family, atmosphere and care etc., the fate and result would be different because of their individual decision, which were taken during different stages of life and their action during different transitory position of the planets. In this way outcome may substantially differ, despite same action of two individuals with different intelligence. On this basis you can also realise that though there may be a slight difference in the correct time of your birth yet it makes no substantial difference in assessing the impact of the planets. We will again discuss this point later on.

Now you can realise that so-called commercial advice given by the astrologer was only based on those astrological principles, which were formulated on wrong, illogical and primitive information. You have already gone through these facts in the first section of this book. If we give a philosophical swing to the earlier example of cricket then the success achieved after performing your duty may be attached with the team or with your family. The success may instantaneously be linked with your life or body. But your record is made only on the basis of your good or bad action, which will be linked with your soul or energy and in turn it will alter the potential of your energy and on the basis of which you may get a best or weak team in the shape of a family in the next birth. In this way despite the defeat of your team i.e. materialistically unsuccessful in your life, you may get a best team i.e. best family in the next birth due to your best and good action or in other words due to strong potential of your energy. Contrary to this despite getting materialistically success by your team, you may take birth with weak destiny and become a part of weak team due to your misdeeds or weak potential of your energy. Hence you may only assess about the pitch and team with the help of astrology to decide about the correct time for performing hard work, best and good action according to your judicious decision and not for becoming a fast believer in fixed destiny. Even though, either you may get or may not get materialistic success in the life i.e. in the game yet atleast your personal record or potential of your soul i.e. energy level, self-confidence can be increased by performing good deeds. Because we must always remember that our action is based on our known or unknown decision and our decision in turn is based on experience and knowledge of our own or of our advisor. Whereas, any event may be net result of mixture of our action; time, circumstances and period over which we have no control. In this situation our ability is limited to our action, which is finally decided on the basis of our experience and knowledge. Thus we may succeed in life only after improving in these basic factors. If we consider three different forms of time i.e. past, present and future as three different forms of matter i.e. solid, liquid and gas then we may presume that future remains in the form of gas, which has no definite shape. At present time, future may be converted in the form of liquid for moulding in any shape by facing the circumstances with the help of our action. After which any event may be converted in the form of solid, as past and then it is not possible to change it. Hence it is essential to take judicious and firm decision with hard labour for converting every circumstances in your favour.

In the next chapter we will discuss with a scientific angle about the houses of the horoscope, how it indicates to work hard and creation of favourable conditions from the impact of the transitory planets.

Year

Measurement of year was an important and essential discovery since beginning of the civilisation. Various civilisations developed and adopted different type of calculation for measuring and commencement of a year, which were based on some important event, religious considerations, transit of the Sun, transit of the Moon, combined transit of the Sun and Moon etc., so that duration of a year may correctly be calculated and weather may also reoccur at correct time. Initial astrology played an important role in calculating the duration of a year because it has developed sufficient calculations for working out the correct position and transit of the planets.

Indian sages developed the calculation of *Tithi, Paksh, Maah* etc. on the basis of combined transit of the Sun and Moon for working out the duration of the year, since rising age. They have also devised a novel method of adding an *Adhimass* for matching the position with Sun, so that weather may reoccur at correct time.

At present about 35 different calendars are being used in the world. Thus New Year is being celebrated every month at some place of the world. Though, most developed and recognised, Gregorian calendar is being used since AD 1528, but still it is not modified as astronomical calendar in the present age of science.

Position of the Sun may be taken as main basis for devising an astronomical calendar and duration between recurrence of same position of the Sun may as usual be taken as a year. There are four important positions of the Sun with reference to the Earth. They are (1) When the Sun takes transit in summer solstice i.e. 23rd December (2) When the Sun crosses equator i.e. 23rd March (3) When the Sun takes transit in winter solstice i.e. on 23rd June (4) When the Sun crosses equator i.e. on 23rd September. Sun crosses the equator, two times in a year and at that time duration of day and night is equal. If we consider the time of commencement of summer solstice as a starting date of the year then it will not only be a justified astronomical calendar but this target may also be achieved very easily by backward shifting of the dates of Gregorian calendar by only eight days. Such correction of 15 days was also carried out previously in Gregorian calendar. There may not be any difficulty in calculation of duration of a year after correcting it astronomically and Gregorian calendar will also be recognised astronomically beside its scientific recognition and New Year falling on 1st January will automatically match astronomically with summer solstice.

Summer solstice was recognised in India since Rising age. Hence intellectual class and scientist of India may take initiative in this regard.

PART 3

PART 3

22

HOUSE OF HOROSCOPE

In the previous chapters you have studied about the factual position and the basis of formation of astrological principles as laid down by sages during Primitive age. Now-a-days prediction is being concluded on the basis of these scientifically illogical principles. But even if we omit these illogical principles, still there are some principles in which the view, study and meditation of the sage appear to be very ponderous and logical. These principles include House of the horoscope and their linking with the events of life, Activator planet of the house, Element beside signs. In the Primitive age sages tried to assess the impact of a planet after formulating many principles mainly on the basis of these facts and the then available knowledge about the Universe. Though these principles doesn't proved to be logical and correct after analysing them with a scientific angle and modern knowledge about the solar system and Universe hence this third part of the book is prepared on the basis of results obtained after blending remaining logical principles with modern scientific knowledge. I found that results are very convincing and logically correct. Though the subject matter of this section is also original. But because you may have elementary knowledge of the astrology hence it will not be difficult to understand the concept.

Extension of house

After calculating the ascendant, either on the basis of tables given in the almanac or *lankodaya* or with the help of computer, you may proceed further taking it as a correct ascendant. Requirement of correct and precise time of birth is always emphasised by the astrologers. But that much correct time is also not essential for taking the benefit of this section. If there is a difference in the time of birth even then there will not be a substantial change in assessing a time for taking a decision. Have you ever drawn your attention towards the fact that leave aside the availability of watch even sun-watch in the crude shape as may be seen in *Jantar-mantar* was also not available with the sages in the Primitive age and time, required for preparation of a horoscope, was assessed on the basis of shadow of a stick for further calculation. Use of watch for ascertaining the time is extensively started only in the modern age. Manufacture of wall-clock based on the principle of oscillation of long pendulum was started in Britain from the year 1670. Just after this, wall-clock also enters in India, when most part of the world came under direct rule of Britain. As you have already studied earlier that there was no significant development in the field of astrology during Pre-Modern age (from 1600 AD to 1900 AD); but astrologers have devised a new and easy way to save their skin for any wrong prediction based on primitive astrological principles (already explained in detail in first part about their wrong basis), mainly by taking shelter of mistake in the time of birth. Now-a-days this escape route is being used very easily. Similarly, latitude and longitude had no place in the primitive astrology, because it was not known in the Primitive age. Longitudes were only known from the Greek civilisation after well connection of our civilisation with them in the first century. Thereafter it was used in the astrology by the eminent mathematician of the Middle age.

You will observe from the *chalit* horoscope that ascendant is placed somewhere in the middle of the first house and the portion from conjunction of twelfth house till ascendant is also treated as a part of first house and placed before the ascendant. In this way the span of first house actually started from about 15° earlier from the ascendant and it is up to about 15° after the ascendant. In the same way span of other houses is being calculated. Thus you can realise that whatever be the planetary position in the eastern sky at the time of birth, a visible part of about 15° from the eastern horizon and the portion of sign and planet which rises from the eastern horizon within about an hour after the birth may found place in the first house and they have their impact on the matter relating to the body etc. which is considered from the first house. You may know about the matters related with the various houses of the horoscope from any book of the astrology or from the concerning box.

In the Krishnamurti system, which was developed in southern India, ascendant is treated as starting point of the first house. In this way the portion of a sign and planet which rises from the eastern horizon within about next two hours after the birth i.e. span of next 30° from ascendant, is considered as a span of first house. Thus, between both these systems there is a difference of about 15° in the span of every house of a horoscope.

If ascendant is 29° of Aries sign then according to Krishnamurti system, span of first house will be up to about 29° of Taurus sign. It is quite natural that there may be impact of the sign of first house on the matter related to first house i.e. body of an individual. But according to this system there may be impact of Aries sign and lord of constellation of ascendant, on the body of the individual. Whereas actually the entire span of the first house would have their impact on the individual. In this way, individual would have a combined effect of Aries and Taurus signs. If the impact may be worked out on the basis of respective portion of the signs in the first house then there is one part of Aries sign and 29 part of Taurus sign in this house. If impact may be worked out in percentage basis then it is 3% of Aries sign and 97% of Taurus sign. Thus it is clear that despite ascendant is in Aries sign yet Taurus sign has a major impact on the individual. Contrary to this, according to north Indian system, where commencing point of the first house start well before (about 15°) the position of ascendant and extended up to about next 15°. Hence according to this system, first house will commence 15°

earlier from the ascendant, thus it will actually commence from about 14° of Aries sign and will be extended up to 14° of Taurus sign, in the above example. If we work out the impact according to the respective span of the sign then first house has 16 part of Aries sign and 14 part of Taurus sign. Thus impact on the percentage basis will be 53% of Aries sign and 47% of Taurus sign. Thus it appears that there may be combined impact of both signs. Which is more logical. In this way if we continue to shift the time of birth i.e. for twins or for two individual births then it will be clear that impact of the signs will also be continuously and slightly deviate. Thus in the above example, impact of the Aries sign will continuously decrease and impact of the Taurus sign will increase accordingly in the same ratio. On this basis, it can be concluded that north Indian system in which span of house is extended on both sides from the ascendant is more appropriate and logical.

Mathematical complication is kept at lowest level in the description given ahead and there is also no need for minute calculation. Because assessment of the result is worked out in percentage basis. The object of this part of the book is not to ascertain the future, which is not fixed as has already been discussed, but the aim is to ascertain the favourable time for executing a work to enable us to get the maximum benefit from the transit of a planet, so that future may be carved out according to our wishes. For this you may simply add 15° in the position of ascendant to know the ending point of the first house and thereafter continue to add 30° for easy calculation of the ending point of every house. After twelfth house remaining 15° may be added in the first house to make it of 30°. For example, if the ascendant is 10° of Gemini sign i.e. 2-10°, then after adding 15° to it, we get 2-25° as ending point of first house. In this way second house will be up to 3-25°, third house up to 4-25°, fourth house up to 5-25°, fifth house up to 6-25°, sixth house up to 7-25°, seventh house up to 8-25°, eighth house up to 9-25°, ninth house up to 10-25°, tenth house up to 11-25°, eleventh house up to 0-25°, twelfth house up to 1-25° and thereafter first house which has already been decided up to 2-25°.

In this way every house may have a portion of two signs. Thus every house may have different impact according to the portion of the respective sign. The impact of the sign on a house can be worked out on the basis of the element of the sign falling in that portion of the house. Though it has been clarified that when astrological principles were formulated; it was believed that constellations / signs are situated just above the Moon (see picture-1), whereas actually they are not even in our galaxy. Hence their impact may not be taken as it is. But scientifically we know that every solid body exert some impact on other bodies. Accordingly, for an easy approach, we may consider consolidate impact of all other stars visible in the sky including 27 constellations in the form of impact of element of a sign. For example, if ascendant is 0-12° (12° of Aries sign) then span of first house will be from 11-27° to 0-27°. In this way first house will comprise of 27° of Aries sign and 3° of Pisces sign. Thus there would be 27 × 100 ÷ 30 = 90% impact of the element and nature according to Aries sign and remaining 10% impact would be according to the element and nature of Pisces sign on the first house. Element of Aries sign is fire, whereas element of Pisces sign is water. Hence nature of the individual and result of the first house will be effected accordingly i.e. result related to body will also be effected in the same ratio and nature, body makeup of the individual will be 90% fiery and 10% watery. In this way result of other houses may also be ascertained on the basis of the element of the sign falling in the span of that house.

You can observe that personality of every individual varies according to the ratio of two elements. If we take example of individuals having Aries sign as ascendant. Out of which, one individual having ascendant of 15° in Aries sign i.e. 0-15° then full span of 30° of Aries sign will fall in first house. Thus individual will have a full impact of fiery element of Aries sign. Another individual, whose ascendant is 1° of Aries sign i.e. 0-1°, then first house will have 16° of Aries sign and 14° of Pisces sign (± 15° from ascendant). In this way he will have 16 × 100 ÷ 30 = 53% effect of fiery element of Aries sign and remaining 47% effect of watery element of Pisces sign. Third individual whose ascendant is 29° of Aries sign i.e. 0-29°. Then first house will have 16° of Aries sign and 14° of Taurus sign. In this way he will have 53% effect of fiery element of Aries sign and remaining 47% effect of earthen element of Taurus sign. In this way body and nature of every individual having Aries sign as ascendant may have more than 50% impact of fiery element whereas remaining impact would either be watery or earthen element. In this way impact of different combination of elements can be worked out in per cent for every house.

Celestial position of the horoscope

If horoscope may be rotated in such a way so that tenth house may be in top position as shown in the picture-46 then you may be able to visualise actual celestial position of the sign and planets which prevailed at the time of birth.

As an example, black circle in the middle of the picture-46 is position of our Earth. We are at the top of this circle, from where we may see all planets and signs rising from the east and setting in the west. From this picture we may see that sign of tenth house and Sun which is in the Capricorn sign was visible at zenith. Moon in eighth house indicates that Moon was going to set in the west. Jupiter is in ascendant in Aries sign i.e. Jupiter was going to rise in the east. If degree of the Jupiter was more than the degree of the ascendant then Jupiter would rise after the birth, whereas if the degree of the Jupiter was less than the degree of the ascendant then Jupiter was visible in the eastern sky. Mars is in fourth house with Cancer sign i.e. it would rise in the east after about six hours from the time of birth and it is in the other part of the Earth. As 30° of a sign takes two hours for rising in the east or setting in the west. In this way all twelve signs i.e. 360° rises from the east, during one day and night. Aries sign relating to first house was visible in the east direction at the time of birth as shown in the horoscope of the picture and Capricorn sign relating to the house of duty, action was at zenith.

In this way six signs and planets situated in those signs which were visible in celestial span of 180° at the time of birth

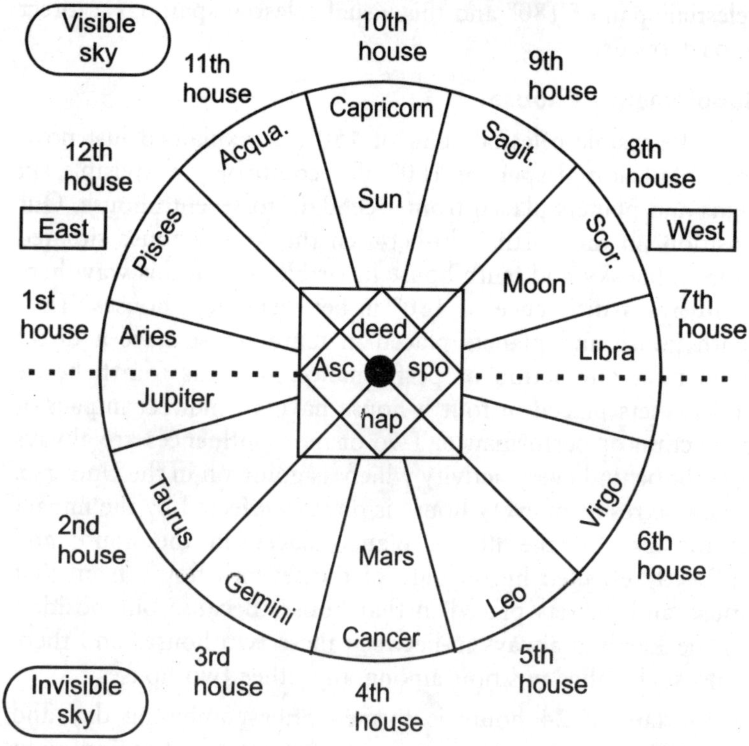

Picture – 46
Celestial position of the planets of horoscope

are shown in the horoscope under respective signs from seventh house to ascendant. All these visible signs, planets and houses have a direct impact on the tenth house related to action i.e. matter related to the tenth house. Because all these visual signs, planets and houses are within the ambit of 90° from the tenth house related to action. At the time of birth tenth house will always be at zenith. In this way span of tenth house is always perpendicular with reference to our then position. Thus middle angle of all visible seven houses with reference to our position are always at an inclination of 0°, 30°, 60°, 90°, 60°, 30°, 0° respectively. Beside this it is also clear that at a time we can see celestial span of 180° and this visual celestial span has a direct impact on us.

Supplementary house

Like visible celestial span of 180°, as explained just now, invisible celestial span of 180° also comprises of invisible six signs and planets placed from ascendant to seventh house. Our position on the Earth is in-between the fourth house situated in invisible sky and tenth house in visible sky. In this way there is always a difference of 180° in-between these houses. Thus tenth house and planets placed in tenth house have a direct impact on our action or performance, whereas fourth house and planets placed in fourth house have an indirect impact of our action or performance. Two or more influences are always present behind every activity which, is going on in the Universe. Likewise result of every house is directly effected by the impact of the sign of the house, planet placed in the house and indirectly effected by the sign of the seventh house from that house and planets placed in that house. Because our position on the Earth is always in-between these two houses and there is no such other position among any other two houses.

A date of 24 hours is formed after combining day and night. Thus in this date, day is supplement of night and night is supplement of day i.e. date has combination of both. Likewise every house of the horoscope is supplement of seventh house. Thus every house is incomplete without combining the supplement house. We may review in short the details of houses of the horoscope to make this point quite clear. First house is related to own body and supplement house of first house is seventh house, which is related to his companion, wife etc., without which accomplishment of having a body cannot be achieved. Similarly first house act as a supplement house for seventh house and provide completeness to that house i.e. with reference to reproduction of life and body etc. they are supplement of each other. Second house relate to primary knowledge and eighth house relate to profound, intricate and mysterious knowledge and such knowledge cannot be achieved without primary knowledge and on the other hand this knowledge provide completeness to primary knowledge. Thus they are supplement of each other. Third house relates to power and bravery whereas ninth house relates to luck or fortune. To get success in bravery support of luck is essential contrary to this to materialise the favourable luck it is essential to exert power or industrious. Fourth house relates to luxury and its counterpart tenth house relates to duty. Our desire to lead luxurious life forced us to perform our duties and accomplishment of duty lies in its result in the shape of comfort. Fifth house relates to knowledge, children and eleventh house relates to income. Here too, knowledge and experience is required for attaining income. Thus accomplishment of knowledge is income, fame etc., whereas accomplishment of income etc. lies in the children who may take the benefit of all this. Sixth house relates to disease and twelfth house relates to death. Here too, completeness of any disease is death and supplement of death is disease. In this way you can realise that how every house is main and seventh house become its supporter by supplementing it.

Date of birth and time from horoscope

Generally astrologer impress an individual by telling time and date or month of birth by observing a horoscope. If you clearly understand picture-46 then with little practice you may also be able to know the time and date of birth.

See from the picture that Sun remains in first house or ascendant, at the time of sunrise, in tenth house at noon, in seventh house at sunset and in fourth house at midnight. In this way due to change in ascendant after every two hours, position of the Sun rotates in all twelve houses during 24 hours. Thus rough time of birth may be known on the basis of the position of the Sun in a particular house after allowing two hours for every house.

Sun remains in Aries sign during mid April to mid May and changes its sign in a month. In this way approximate month may be ascertained on the basis of sign of the Sun. Sun and Moon remains in same sign at the commencement of a month from the first day of *Shukla paksh*. Moon changes its sign in every 2.5 days. On the day of full-moon i.e. after about 15 days, position and sign of the Moon will be seventh from the Sun in a horoscope. In the same way, after next 15 days, Sun and Moon will again meet in next sign on the day of dark-night (*Amavasya*). After a little practice you may be able to work out the date, month and time on the basis of relative position of the Sun and Moon in a horoscope.

Saturn, Rahu and Jupiter complete their rotation of zodiac, approximately in 30, 18 and 13 years respectively. If you remember relevant sign on any date then after multiplying the difference of sign of Saturn, Rahu and Jupiter in the horoscope with your standard sign by 2.5, 1.5 and 1 year respectively, you may easily work out the matching year i.e. year of birth.

23

CENTRAL HOUSE AND PERIODICITY

There are three types of central house among twelve houses of a horoscope. First central house comprises of 1, 4, 7, 10th house, second central house comprises of 2, 5, 8, 11th house and third central house comprises of 3, 6, 9, 12th house. These three central houses belongs to body, knowledge and power respectively. All four houses of these three types of central houses always have a particular ratio of respective two elements among fire, earth, air and water. These signs have also been classified in fixed, movable and dual nature as shown in the chapter of "Lord of Signs". Thus combination of nature among the sign of central house will always be same. If we divide all houses of a horoscope in four parts after taking one house from every central house then we may have first part comprises of 1st, 2nd and 3rd house. Next three houses 4th, 5th and 6th will form the second part and third part will comprise 7th, 8th and 9th house, likewise fourth part will have 10th, 11th and 12th house. If we re-examine these four parts then we can easily observe that every part now comprises of one house each from central house relating to three types of important activities i.e. body, knowledge and power, which leads the life. Likewise entire life of every man and woman is also actually distributed in four parts.

Total of number of three houses of the first part of the above mentioned horoscope will be 6 (1+2+3 = 6), total of three houses of second part will be 15 (4+5+6 = 15), total of three houses of third part will be 24 (7+8+9 = 24) and total of fourth part of three houses will be 33 (10+11+12 = 33). We can analyse the life of a man equal to the above total in solar years and equal to lunar years for a woman through a horoscope. Solar year i.e. time taken by the Sun for taking transit through twelve signs or one year. Likewise for supplement of a man i.e. for a woman, lunar year is 354 days or about 11.5 months which is time taken by the Moon i.e. supplement of the Sun, for taking transit through twelve signs with reference to the Sun. About 27 days are taken by the Moon for rotating in twelve signs but during this period Earth also transit in its circular motion around the Sun. Hence Moon takes about additional two days to cover this distance. Thus lunar year is equal to 354 days. We can say that lunar year is about 3% less in comparison to solar year. In this way total of all four parts of the horoscope will be 78 years for a man and about 76 years for a woman. Impact of all these twelve houses of horoscope are imparted respectively in the corresponding age group on all individuals.

Periodicity of houses

Duration of first part comprises of first three houses of the horoscope, is 6 years, which represents childhood. First house in this part relates to the body i.e. body is the main requirement and concern for a child till the age of one year. During this period of one year he get stability in his body i.e. he is able to manage the movement of his body. After this, periodicity of two years of second house started. This is the first house of the central house related to knowledge i.e. first house of 2, 5, 8 and 11th house. The primary knowledge required for a child i.e. identification by observation, attraction and holding of an article or toy etc., is learned by him during these two years. Only on the footing of this primary knowledge later on he may be capable to unde: ·and the bookish knowledge during the next periodicity of the knowledge. After this, three years periodicity of third house started. This is the first house of the central house related to power and possessions i.e. first house of 3, 6, 9 and 12th house. During this period child start to use his power. The meaning of power is his possessive and defensive capacity and he develop his capacity to take action for any possession. His tooth start to grow and he start to walk in this age to enable him to demonstrate his power by eating any thing, acquire an area by walking, by snatching any toy, by breaking his toy etc. All these actions are evidence of his capability to make use of power. Above explanation clearly shows an impact of periodicity of these houses. Beside this, during this period there is also an indirect or supplement impact of seventh, eighth and ninth house. Seventh house, which relates to his companion and as a result of this, his doctor or nurse etc. enter in his life as his companion to take care of his body and fulfil his requirement. After this, during periodicity of second house, supplement supportive impact of eighth house related to age is very essential otherwise he may also die. Maximum children die in this age due to absence of this support. During this period child also has permanent imprint of fear, darkness etc. in his subconscious mind due to supplement impact of 8th house. After this, during periodicity of third house, absence of supplement supportive impact of ninth house related to fortune may force him to lead his childhood in scarcity and lack of support of fortune in this age may turn the stream of his entire life.

Second part of life has duration of 15 years, which ends in the age of 21 years. In this part of life impact of 4th, 5th and 6th house reappears in the same earlier order of body, knowledge and power. Periodicity of four years of fourth house relating to comfort of body started after the age of six years. In this age every action of a child relates to his bodily comfort, happiness. Due to influence of this house and supplement impact of 10th house relating to action, his attention remains engaged in the demonstration of his active bodily capacity by his playful nature. Strong tooth starts to replace his earlier weak tooth for giving strong support to body. After this, periodicity of five years of fifth house relating to knowledge start. Direction, interest, inclination towards any particular subject can only be anticipated only in this period. This knowledge form a platform for subsequent development of capacity to take judicious decision during periodicity of third house of central house of knowledge or eighth house of horoscope. After this, periodicity of six years of sixth house came in the form of second house of central house of power. During this periodicity, capacity for struggling against any disease is developed and acquired by a youth. He takes an initiative and go ahead to show his capacity of power and bravery in every field of life. He increases this capacity by forming his group of friends. During this period, if at any time he felt that it is not possible to control the adverse situation even by applying his all power and courage then he may take a decision for committing suicide or to ran away from the house only due to reduction in struggling power and courage. Because twelfth house of death or destruction also has an indirect impact on sixth house. In this way two part of the life passes away. Only these two parts remain in the invisible sky at the time of birth, which can be seen in picture-46. Likewise this 21 years part of the life also remain completely invisible. Hence there is no direct or visible impact of a youth of this age on the family, society etc. and till this age he has no independent, individual and apparent identification.

Third part of actual apparent life of 24 years commenced from the age of 21 years and remains effective up to the age of 45 years. During this period impact of 7th, 8th and 9th house again reappears in the revised form and in the same order of body, knowledge and power. Periodicity of seven years of seventh house remains effective up to the age of 28 years. This house also related to life partner. During this young age he is quite able to show his bodily capacity. He extensively uses this capacity after marriage. A girl by the age of +20 years, after passing through various periodicities according to lunar year also become able to use extensively her bodily capacity for next seven lunar years. During this periodicity both are very careful about caring, appearance and get-up of their body. After this, periodicity of eighth house for a period of eight years commenced. The impact of this periodicity remains effective up to the age of 36 years in the form of third central house of knowledge. During this period he learn the knowledge relating to life by practical experience i.e. working knowledge related to his duties in office, profession or business, its complication and remedy, knowledge of sorting out odds during earning livelihood and for girl it is the time to learn to deal with day-to-day complications arising in the family, efficiently performing daily household work etc. along with social obligation. Thus they enrich their knowledge by exposing themselves in the light of practical realities. Remaining part of his life is only completed on the basis of sharpness of intelligence and practical knowledge acquired during this period. He also try to manage proper matching in between his bookish and practical knowledge and learn the main ingredients of the life by judicious application of his discretion which in turn will form the basis of spiritual knowledge according to his capacity. After this age, nine years periodicity of third central house of power or ninth house commenced. This periodicity remains effective up to the age of 45 years in the life of an adult. During this period he was able to demonstrate his competence in his working area, beside this luck also plays an important role to lift him in the life during this period and he undertake many task like professional competition, extension of working area, facing and control of odd situation etc., which is an indication of his power, courage and industrious nature due to indirect impact of third house.

Fourth part of life of 33 years commenced from the age of 45 years and remains effective up to the age of 78 years. During this period, impact of 10th, 11th and 12th house again reappears in the revised form and in the same earlier order of body, knowledge and power. Ten years periodicity of tenth house remains effective up to the age of 55 years. This is the house of duty and diligence. Indirect influence of fourth house in front of this house exaggerates the desire of bodily comfort i.e. to have a house, servant, conveyance etc. Hence one may involve in those activities which may provide bodily comfort to him. Though he may be conscious about the decreasing efficiency and strength of the body (due to increasing effect of 12th house, which will be explained in the forthcoming para of 'Expansion of impact of house') yet he will try his best to get mental and bodily comfort. By the end of the periodicity of tenth house capacity of bodily exertion also reduces.

Thereafter, time arrives for the periodicity of eleven years in respect of eleventh house related to income, which is last house of the centre of knowledge. During this later part of life one may have daughters-in-law, grandchildren etc. in the shape of income due to influence of house of income. Result of the performance of duty and various decisions taken according to his capacity during the entire life start to appears in the shape of income and source of financial income may stabilise. Feeling of ending phase of life emerges during this period, which remains up to the age of 66 years. In this changing scenario, he may be inclined towards the spiritual knowledge, religion, aversion etc. as a result of his learning from the experience, knowledge, intelligence and circumstances of his entire life due to the influence of fourth house of centre of house relating to knowledge. Desire to do something for his children and their proper settlement, also get fulfilled. Thus there is indirect influence of fifth house too. After this periodicity of twelve year of twelfth house commenced, which exist up to the age of 78 years. During this period one may start to demonstrate his physical power due to the influence of fourth house of centre of house relating to the power. For this he remain busy in overriding every sort of bodily deficiencies with his will and wealth. He develops a feeling that everybody must obey him, take advice. Thus feeling of power consciousness get satisfied. Sixth house relating to disease and twelfth house relating to death or destruction indirectly supplement each other and thus there is always a danger of some disease. Death in this age group is regarded as full life. After living all four parts of the life one may be classified to enjoy longevity. Because if one may be able to save his life energy by this age then only he may be able to enjoy next part of his life. After this age, fifth part of 42 years may came in the life. During this period, impact of first, second and third house again reappears for a period of 13, 14 and 15 years respectively in the revised form and in the same earlier order of body, knowledge and power. After commencing from the age of 78 years, this part may remain active till the age of 120 years.

Above periodicity of house is so much perfect that there is no need to give any example of a horoscope. Life of everyone mainly passes through the same passage and main events of the life are not only dependant on the fact that individual house of a horoscope has been occupied by which sign and planet, but it is also dependant on the action and decisions which have been taken during various periodicities of life, transit and celestial position of the planets and sign. Detailed description about this will be given later on.

Expansion of impact of house

Six signs are always present in the visible sky of 180° and due to direct exposure of these signs they effect our body according to their original qualities i.e. element, nature and occupied house of horoscope. This can be clearly understood by the example of the Sun. Sunrise in the morning activate stagnated life and activity of the life get momentum according to the rising altitude of the Sun. Likewise activity of the life diminished according to the descending altitude of the Sun after mid-day. As soon as Sun rises, all individuals get ready to perform their duties and they stop their activities after sunset.

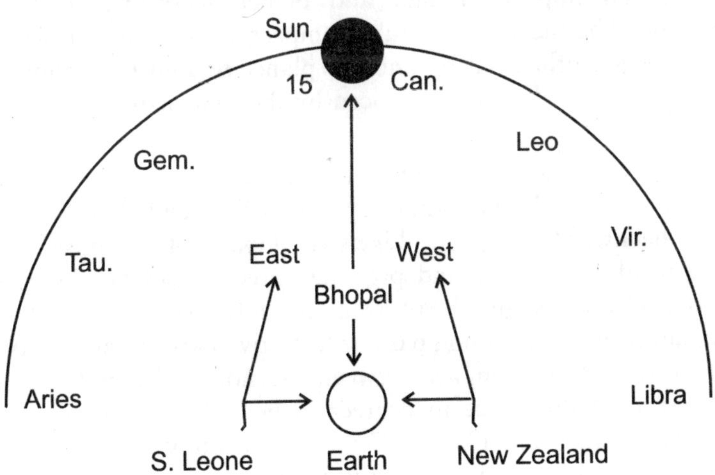

Picture – 47
Impact of the Sun

This may further be understood from another example based on picture-47. Suppose Sun is transiting at 15° of Cancer sign. When Sun will be at zenith (point in the sky above the head) in the noon in Bhopal i.e. when Sun will be at an altitude of 90° at 78° longitude (longitude of Bhopal). At that time Sun would have been rising in Sierra Leone, a country of Western Africa situated towards 90° western longitude from Bhopal and activity of the life would be just beginning there. Cancer sign would be rising in the East, whereas Aries sign of 15° would be at zenith in Sierra Leone. In the same way Sun would be setting in New Zealand, situated towards 90° eastern longitude from Bhopal and activity of life would be limping there. At this time Cancer sign would be setting, whereas Libra sign of 15° would be at zenith. Thus effect of the Sun, which is extreme at zenith in Bhopal is extended and gradually decreased up to New Zealand in east and Sierra Leone in west i.e. both side. In this way you can very well understood from picture-47 that span of impact of a sign or planet is expended up to 90° in forward as well as in backward direction. As impact of a planet may be different according to their celestial position, likewise there is difference in mutual impact of sign and planet according to their altitude. The meaning of mutual impact is that when a planet or sign get influenced by another planet or sign then another planet or sign also get influenced by the first planet or sign in the same ratio.

As you have seen that impact of a sign or planet continuously reduced within a span of 90° extended in forward and backward direction. Likewise impact of a house also expanded up to next and previous three houses i.e. forward and backward span of 90° from the effective point (will be explained in forthcoming para of 'Effective part of periodicity') of house. Mutual impact between the house also reduced in the ratio of difference in degrees in both directions, like the impact of sign and planet. We will now study the impact of houses on this basis. Following two examples as direct evidence will be quite sufficient to understand this impact :

1. Fourth house start from an angular difference of 90° from the starting point of first house. Fourth house represents mother. We can observe that the attachment of the mother towards her child increases day-by-day after the birth and similarly attachment of the child towards his mother also increases in the same ratio. Abortion is comparatively less grievous for mother if it is before natural birth. Because 1st house representing body of son is beyond 90° span of 4th house of mother. Whereas her attachment towards child gradually increases after taking birth, even though child may be disabled. Because fourth house of mother came within the span of 90° from the ascendant of the child after taking birth. In this way mutual attachment between them would be extreme during the periodicity of fourth house i.e. in the age of 6 years to 10 years. Because there is minimum angular difference between the effective periodicity and fourth house. Henceforth the impact of mother would gradually reduced with the passage of time. Because, son is now in the increasing influence of fifth and sixth house related to knowledge and power. You can observe that mother has no direct influence over the son when he completes the periodicity of seventh house by the age of 28 years, because point of his effective periodicity is beyond 90° from the 4th house related to mother. Likewise the mutual impact of 10th house related to father gradually increases after the age of 21 years. Which remains effective for rest of his life i.e. by the end of the periodicity of 12th house. There is difference of opinion among the scholars about the house, which may be treated as related to father. Very few scholars gave importance to ninth house whereas larger group gave importance to tenth house for the matter related to father. But if we examine this point logically and practically then tenth house must be taken into consideration for the matters related to father. Because only then it is seventh and

can correctly act as a supplement for the fourth house related to mother. The impact of fourth house as well as tenth house is lowest during the periodicity of seventh house, which is effective in-between the age of 21 years to 28 years. Because seventh house is placed after` 90° from the starting point of fourth house and it is 60° away from the ending point of fourth house. Hence the impact of the mother is going to dilute. Similarly, starting point of seventh house is behind 90° from the starting point of 10th house. Hence the impact of father is in the initial stage. Thus there is minimum impact of the parents on the children of this age group. Whereas the impact of the seventh house i.e. supplement of body in the form of life partner is maximum hence naturally there is maximum mutual attraction. It is quite natural that effect of periodicity of seventh house generates attachment towards the counterpart of body, and a young boy between the age of 21 years to 28 years or a young girl between the age of 20 years to 26 years (according to 21 and 28 lunar years) may revolt against the family. Incidents like inter-caste marriage, separation from the family, eloping with the counterpart happens due to effect of the periodicity of seventh house.

2. Another example may be seen for clearing the concept of impact of house. There is seven years periodicity of seventh house during the age from 21 years to 28 years. For simplifying the situation, if we take the middle age and analyse than it can be realised that required development of body in this age was actually commenced in the age of 8 years i.e. in the age group of 6 years to 10 years or during the periodicity of 4th house which is 90° earlier from the 7th house. Likewise strength and ability of the body acquired during the age between 21 years to 28 years may be effectively active till the periodicity of house which is 90° ahead from the 7th house i.e. by the age of about 55 years or in other words till the end of periodicity of 10th

house. Contrary to this, 33% mutual impact of 10th house commenced by the age of 28 years to meet the requirement in the periodicity of the 10th house. This fact may be clearly observed in the women. Essential development of her body which is required between the age of 20 years to 26 years for conception, may actually commenced between the age of 8 years to 10 years and the development of the body may be at peak during the age of 20 years to 26 years (21 to 28 lunar years). Similarly, ability of conception may gradually be reduced from the age of 26 years i.e. 28 lunar years and it may remain effective till the periodicity of 10th house which is 90° ahead from the seventh house i.e. by the age of 53 years or 55 lunar years. After this age the influence of 7th house in the form of ability of reproduction of a baby may be finished.

Thus impact of a house gradually increases when it is 90° ahead from the actual point of periodicity and likewise impact of a house gradually reduced and remains effective till it is within 90° from the actual point of periodicity. If we look it with a spiritual angle then we can realise that the impact of periodicity of 10, 11 and 12th house may have its forward influence up to 90°, which may fall beyond the age of 78 years i.e. these houses may have gradually increased impact for the age which is beyond 78 years. This impact is also a mutual impact. If we consider the period, which is after the age of 78 years, in the form of next birth or regeneration then the result of our good deed or misdeed, executed after the age of 45 years may gradually increase in the ratio of impact of periodicity and perhaps may be linked with our soul in the form of destiny for next birth. Because soul, which is a form of energy, cannot be destroyed according to our religious belief, as well as scientifically proved by Einstein that energy can never be destroyed and it can only transform in any other shape. In this way if our soul may absorb the result of our action according to their merit in the form of destiny and proceed to next birth then our body which is also a combination of five elements or matter, may also be continuously effected by the impact of planets (every matter which exist in the Universe). In this way, perhaps we may face favourable and unfavourable condition in the shape of happiness and sorrow during our present life, and continuously perform our journey towards the next birth by effecting our soul and body according to the destiny and planetary position in the horoscope, transit and by our judicious action.

Effective part of periodicity

There is always a continuous main impact of a house, reduced impact of adjoining houses and indirect impact of respective seventh house exist during every moment of entire life. We can also work out the effective part or inter-periodicity of a house by dividing the 30° of a house with the periodicity of that house and can ascertain that which part of a sign or planet is appearing in this effective part. For example periodicity of first house is one year and by dividing this house by 30 we may easily work out that one part of the house is equal to about 12 days. In this way after 12 days from the birth inter-periodicity of second part or 2nd degree of the house would be effective. During the periodicity of 3rd house, every 10° of this house would represent one year. During the periodicity of 10th house, every 3° of this house would represent one year. In this way, you may easily work out the inter-periodicity of an effective part of a house, sign and planet appearing in that part of house, according to your age. We may consider the impact of a house as a main periodicity and effective part of a house as inter-periodicity like *vinshottary* system.

You can very well understand the procedure to work out the percentage power of periodicity of a house, from the picture-48. In this picture all twelve houses are arranged in a line. Number of house is given below the house, which also indicates the periodicity of that house. Age, at the time of commencement of a periodicity, is also mentioned in the lower part. A bold line is marked below the seventh house.

At the time of commencement of periodicity of 7th house in the age of 21 years, we may observe after extending the

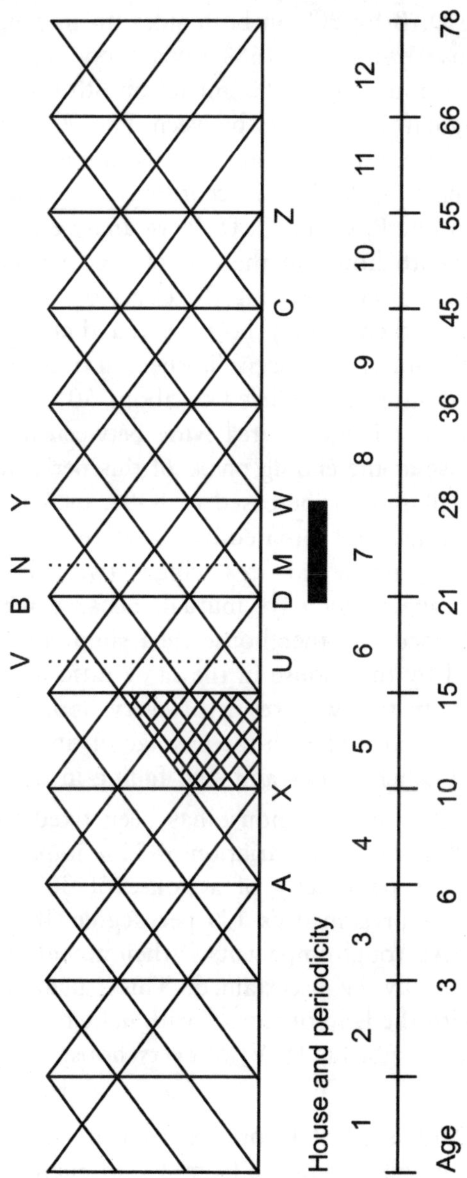

Picture – 48
Impact of house periodicity

effect of line D, B by 90° on both sides up to point A and C that 7th house has about 16% impact on 4th house, 50% impact on 5th house and 83% impact on 6th house according to the triangular area lying between line A, B and A, D. Likewise 7th house also has about 50% impact on 8th house and 16% impact on 9th house according to the triangular area lying between line B, C and C, D. If we analyse the position of impact of seventh house at the end of this periodicity in the age of 28 years after extending the effect of line W, Y up to point X and Z then it may be observed that impact of 7th house on 4th house has been finished, it reduced to about 16% on 5th house and reduced to about 50% on 6th house according to the triangular area lying between line X, Y and X, W. Likewise at the ending phase of this periodicity, impact on 8th house has been increased to 83%, increased to about 50% on 9th house and initiated by about 16% on 10th house according to the triangular area lying between line Y, Z and W, Z. This impact is always mutual. Because when a house exert its influence on other house then simultaneously it also get influenced by that house in the same ratio and it is also a scientific fact. In this way result of every house continuously increased and decreased with the passage of time, according to the impact of other houses and sign falling in that house.

Because span of every house has been fixed to 30° hence you can see that there is a variation of 33% impact on a house during complete periodicity of a house of 30°. This impact may roughly be presumed as 1% per degree. If we add 10% impact in above rough impact itself then actual percentage of impact may easily be ascertained. This calculation may be performed with the help of simple arithmetic or geometry after presuming the height (as U, V) of every house as 100 units.

Example

If ascendant is 5° of Capricorn sign at the time of birth then 1st house will commence from 20° of Sagittarius sign (as has been explained earlier that first house commence from 15° earlier from ascendant) and remains up to 20° of Capricorn sign. Accordingly, starting and ending point of Gemini sign in sixth and seventh house is shown by lines U, V and M, N respectively. Because seventh house started from 20° of Gemini sign. Thus it is clear that a part of 10° of Gemini sign will remain in seventh house. In this way at the time of commencement of periodicity of seventh house, its effect would be extended up to fourth house. The quantum of effect can be worked out in the following manner.

Effect on fourth house

Length of vertical line from point X to the line A, B will be 33 units and length of line from point A to the line A, B will be 0.

Area of house

= Length of house × Height of house ÷ 2

= 30 × (33 + 0) ÷ 2 = 495

Complete area of house = 30 × 100 = 3000

Impact of effective degree on fourth house

= 495 × 100 ÷ 3000 = 16.5%

Effect on fifth house

Effect in percentage can be worked out by comparing the area of shaded portion with the area of full house. Vertical distance between point X to the line A, B will be 33 units and the length at the other side of the house will be 66 units.

Area of house

= Length of house × Height of house ÷ 2

= 30 × (33 + 66) ÷ 2 = 1470

Complete area of house = 30 × 100 = 3000

Impact of effective degree on fifth house

= 1470 × 100 ÷ 3000 = 49%

The impact of Gemini sign and this house on fourth house will be nil at the time of effect of 30th degree of Gemini sign and 10th degree of the house. Whereas effect of seventh house and Gemini sign on fifth house can be worked out by reducing 10 + 1 = 11% (1% per degree + 10% of it as explained earlier) from 49% and thus actual effect will be 38%.

In this way you can understand that there is always an impact of the periodicity of a house on adjoining houses as well as there is impact of the adjoining houses on the active house. Thus it is a mutual impact. In this way the impact of effective part of a house may be effective up to 90° on both sides, in the ratio of their distance in degree, and this periodicity may also get effected in the same ratio from the houses of both sides. The impact of periodicity continuously reduced in those houses, whose periodicity has been passed, whereas it is continuously and gradually increased for those houses whose periodicity is still pending. Likewise planets also exert their influence like gravitation etc. on every other planet and get influenced from other planets of the solar system. As we can see after mixing cold water with hot water that cold water always try to cool down the hot water and at the same time correspondingly it looses its coldness in the same ratio due to mutual effect.

Span of a house and effective degree of the house is again being explained by an another example. If ascendant of an individual is 10° of Taurus sign. We have to simply add 15° and deduct 15° from this ascendant to ascertain the span of first house. In this way span of the first house will be from 25° of Aries sign to 25° of Taurus sign. Likewise after calculating span of other houses, span of seventh house will be from 25° of Libra to 25° of Scorpio. This house may have effect of airy element till effective periodicity up to 5° of Libra sign and thereafter it may have effect of watery element of Scorpio sign till effective periodicity up to next 25°. Periodicity of seventh house is effective for seven years i.e. 84 months. In this way every degree may have an effect for 2 months 24 days (84 ÷ 30). Thus effect of airy element of last 5° of Libra sign will be finished within one year and two months. After this, effect of watery element of Scorpio sign will commence. In this way effect of 10th degree of this sign or effect of 15th degree of the house will be finished after a period of 2 years 4 months i.e. totally after 3 years and 6 months i.e. in the age of 24 years 6 months.

24

RISE AND SETTING OF SIGNS

Throughout the life we always have increasing and decreasing influence of six adjoining houses, as per description given in the previous chapter and accordingly their favour or disfavour also remains under continuous change. All signs including those signs who have occupied the house, whose periodicity is effective, remain continuously rising and setting in the sky. It is a scientific fact that we always get influenced by each and every celestial body, with reference to their position from us. Thus if a body is in perpendicular position with reference to our position then we will get maximum influence and the influence will be minimum when that body is inclined towards horizon. Suppose there is Sagittarius sign in the ninth house related to fortune then this Sagittarius sign will exert its maximum impact whenever it may be near to meridian line (line adjoining Pole star and zenith) passing through zenith in the sky with reference to your city i.e. its influence will be maximum whenever it may be at an altitude of 90° from the eastern horizon i.e. at that time it will be more favourable and you may get support from your fortune. The per cent of favouritism would be according to its altitude in the sky. As you know that these signs continuously rises from the east. In this way every constellation, planet and signs continuously rises in the east at a motion of 1° per four minutes and likewise they set in west with the same motion. Thus favourable influence of a sign will also increase according to its altitude i.e. at the rate of 1% for every change of 1°

altitude per four minutes. Thus after ascertaining the effective periodicity of a house and sign according to your age, if that part of Sagittarius sign related to house of fortune which has been worked out according to your age, is rising in the east and nearer to horizon at an altitude of 1° then fortune will also be favourable with 1% power. The power of sign will continuously increase at the rate of 1% due to increasing altitude after every four minutes. When this sign will cross the meridian line passing through zenith i.e. at 90° altitude then favourable effect of the Sign will be 90 + (10% of 90) = 99%. After this the favourable effect will start to reduce at a rate of one per cent after every four minutes, because altitude of sign will continuously decrease and it will move to set in the west. In this way you can understand that favourable effect of every house and sign continuously changes according to its celestial position.

The favourable effect of various subject matters related to an active house and its sign, according to your age group, will increase correspondingly to its celestial altitude. Beside this effect of adjoining six houses, three on each side of the active house will also vary according to their celestial position after rising in the east. Every sign crosses the meridian line passing through zenith in about six hours after rising and it will set in about next six hours. The same process remains continuously operative for every sign as well as planet. Hence maximum favourable effect of sign and planet may be obtained by planning the work after ascertaining the favourable time on the basis of maximum altitude of the sign and planets. Detailed description about the strength of a planet will be discussed in next chapter.

There is no need to do complicated calculations to ascertain the celestial position of the signs for maintaining their impact in your favour. But you may have a little idea that which sign is moving from the meridian line at a particular time and to which house of your horoscope it is related. All houses of the horoscope are generally good except 6th and 12th who are believed to be related with disease and death respectively. These two houses are supplement to each other and combined 30° span of these two houses is always present in the sky. In this way, it can also be realised that we are always in the ambit of disease or death and it can also be understood from the earlier discussion related to 'Periodicity of house' that these houses have their impact during entire life irrespective of any periodicity. As can be seen that third house is within the range of 90° from the 12th house related to death and it may have 33% impact during the age group of 3 years to 6 years, when periodicity of third house is effective. Thereafter, the impact of 6th house commenced after this age. The impact of 6th house may continuously increase from 0% to 100% and thereafter it may continuously decrease to 0% by the age of 45 years. After this age, impact of 12th house related to death may start to increase from 0% onward. Likewise, we are always in the clutch of impact of a house and corresponding 7th house. Thus while performing any important work we may only be aware and may take care that the signs of 6th and 12th houses may not be at meridian line and if we have sufficient cushion of time then we may further take care that any sign related to these houses may not be risen from the east. Because after this, the impact of this sign will continuously increase during next four five hours. If we have sufficient time then it may be favourable to perform important work while the concerning sign is going to set in next two hours. Because during this time the impact of the sign of this house will be diluting and corresponding 7th sign will be rising in the east. But the impact will be lowest because both signs will be nearer to horizon. Similarly, impact of any particular house or supplement house may be increased or decreased by little presumption about the celestial position of relevant sign.

You may feel a little hardship in ascertaining the actual position of sign in the sky. The easiest way to know about the sign and its celestial location is that a particular sign, in which Sun or Moon are taking transit, is moving in the sky, where Sun or Moon are moving in the sky. Next sign is towards east from the location of the Sun or Moon and previous sign is toward west from the location of the Sun or Moon. In this way at the time of sunrise, previous six signs from the sign of Sun; in noon three next signs and three previous signs from the sign of Sun; and at the time of sunset, next six signs from the sign of Sun are present in the fixed order in the sky. Likewise, the celestial position of the signs can also be ascertained with reference to the position of the Moon. You can also understand this position from picture-46. It is not at all a difficult task, when generally you have to take care that signs related to 6th and 12th houses may not be near to meridian line. Once you have worked out the timing of these signs as to when they are at meridian line then reduce 4 minutes from this time for next day and so on. Suppose 15th degree of a sign is at meridian line at 2 PM in noon, then on next day the same position of the sign will appear at 1-56 PM in noon and on further next day the same position will appear at 1-52 PM. In this way the same position will continue to repeat 4 minutes earlier.

The celestial position of these signs according to their altitude from southern horizon also varies with reference to your geographical position on the Earth. All signs are spread within 47° (difference between Tropic of Capricorn and Tropic of Cancer) latitude. In this way the celestial position of these signs are located within the latitude from 23.5° north to 23.5° south from equator line. If you want to see Scorpio and Sagittarius sign i.e. the signs in which, presently planets remain in southern most situation, from the cities which are situated either north or south from the cities like Bhopal which is situated on Tropic of Cancer then you have to simply deduct the latitude of the city from 23.5° and add 43° or deduct the latitude of the city from 66.5° to work out the altitude of these signs from southern horizon. The entire shape of a sign was visible up to 8° towards north in the Primitive age, as has already been explained during the description of point Y in picture-45. The position will be more clear from the following two examples.

1. Latitude of Amritsar = 31.5°

   Altitude of Scorpio and Sagittarius sign in Amritsar from the southern horizon

   = 23.5 – 31.5 = – 8 + 43 = 35°

   or 66.5 – 31.5 = 35° (A)

Expansion of these two signs is from 35° to 43°.

2. Latitude of Chennai = 13°

   Altitude of Scorpio and Sagittarius sign in Chennai from the southern horizon

   = 23.5 – 13 = 10.5 + 43 = 53.5°

   or 66.5 – 13 = 53.5° (A)

Expansion of these signs is from 53.5° to 61.5°.

The celestial position of other signs would be changed according to these two signs. The position of Libra and Capricorn signs would be at 8° above the position shown at (A) i.e. in the above example these signs would be visible at an altitude of 43° to 51° and 61.5° to 69.5° respectively. The position of Virgo and Aquarius signs would be at 16° above the position shown at (A). The position of Leo and Pisces signs would be at 24° above the position shown at (A). The position of Cancer and Aries signs would be at 32° above the position shown at (A). The position of Gemini and Taurus signs would be at 40° above the position shown at (A). The planets transiting in these signs would also be visible at the same altitude, whereas these signs were visible in the Primitive age at a difference of 8°. Specific position may be seen from picture-45.

The fact that zodiac has shifted by 33° due to *ayanansh* since Primitive age is very important in the above example. Though position has already been explained through picture-45, yet you may have a fresh look on the position. In the Rising and Primitive age all constellations, which were present in the zodiac were actually in the close vicinity of ecliptic. In this way all constellations and signs formed by these constellations were visible nearby line A, B, C, D, E of picture-45. All planets take transit according to inclination of their orbit and also remains very close to ecliptic. At that time maximum southern-most point of ecliptic was at point D situated at 10° of Capricorn sign. Due to which Sun crosses the celestial equator at vernal equinox when it was at 10° of Aries sign. Actual shapes of Scorpio and Sagittarius signs were in between the line C, D of this picture. But now all planets take transit beside line O, P, Q, R, S and now southern-most point of ecliptic is at 7° of

Sagittarius sign shown as R, which is 33° towards west from point D and 8° south from an actual point of 7° of Sagittarius sign on line C, D due to 33° *ayanansh* since then.

The astrological principles formulated by sages in the Primitive age after experiencing impact of a planet when it was transiting in Capricorn sign; the same planetary impact may now be experienced when it takes transit from Sagittarius sign because altitude of the planet from the southern horizon would be same due to *ayanansh*. Likewise impact of a planet during its transit may be understood from picture-45. Planetary altitude from horizon is most important factor in view of latest scientific information instead of its position in a constellation or sign formed by constellations, because constellation have no independent individual impact at all, as they are situated in other galaxies and consolidated impact of all stars visible in the sky at a time has been discussed in this chapter through impact of a sign.

During continuous monitoring of the sky our sages observed in Rising age that planets are moving among some specified group of stars. Thereafter they nominated these specified groups of stars as constellation and name of month was also decided on the basis of nearest star from the Moon on the night of full-moon. These names are still prevailing. In those days it was believed that constellation are situated below the Mercury planet or very near from the Earth as you have already studied from picture-1. In this situation it was quite natural that impact of constellation got prominence. Thus impact of constellation and sign was incorporated in the astrological principles. But if we analyse the situation in the light of scientific information then we can understand that though actual size of constellations are more than million times in comparison to our Sun yet all these constellations are not in our Milkyway having a enormous size of one lakh light-year i.e. 946,000,000,000,000,000 km. Beside this it is also correct that every solid body has impact on us according to its altitude from our location on the Earth. Thus scientifically every visual star or group of stars viz. Polestar, Seven stars, *Lubdhak, Hans, Prajapati, Garud, Yam, Aritra, Jatayu, Buck,*

Yamuna etc. have an impact on us, though it may be very little. Because our sages were not aware about the impact of every individual star due to availability of limited information about them in Rising age hence they formulated various astrological principles considering the impact of constellations believed to be situated very near from the Earth and in the orbit of the planets. In this way actually that impact of a planet, which was being experienced in the primitive age, while transiting between Mula to Purvabhadrapad constellations situated in Sagittarius, Capricorn and Aquarius sign, may be experienced now-a-days when that planet transit between Swati to Uttarashada constellations situated in Libra to Capricorn sign due to change of 33° *ayanansh*. Impact of planetary position will now be discussed in next chapter.

Constellation based month

There is a reference as follows about 12 lunar months and 360 days in *slok* 1,164, 48 of *Rigveda*.

.....द्वादश प्रवयश्चक्रमेकं त्रीणि नभ्यानि क उ तश्चिकेत
तस्मिन्त्साकं त्रिशता न शंकवोऽर्पिता: षष्टिर्न चलाचलास:

360 days of a year was derived from the fact that it has 12 months comprising of 30 *tithi* each and sky was divided in 360 parts on the basis of these 360 days (12 × 30 = 360) of a year taken by the Sun for one rotation which was subsequently converted into 360°. Geometry adopted this concept for further development and in this way 360° is still being used in all calculation related to circle.

Name of 12 months is mentioned in *slok* 1.4.14 and 4.4.14 of *Tettariya Sanhita*. It clarifies from the description contained in *Prashnavyakarnang* that name of respective month was known as traditional name on the basis of position of the Sun in a particular constellation during a month. Name of these months, season and English names are as follows:

Traditional Month	Season	English Month	Constellation of Rising age	Traditional name
Madhu	Spring	March	*U. falguni*	*Falgun* .
Madhav	Spring	April	*Chitra*	*Chaitra*
Sukra	Summer	May	*Vishakha*	*Vaishakh*
Suchi	Summer	June	*Jyestha*	*Jyesth*
Nabhas	Rainy	July	*Uttarashada*	*Ashad*
Nabhasya	Rainy	August	*Shravan*	*Shravan*
Ish	Autumn	September	*U.B. pad*	*Bhadon*
Urza	Autumn	October	*Ashwini*	*Ashwin*
Sahas	Cold	November	*Kratica*	*Kartik*
Sahasya	Cold	December	*Mragshira*	*Agrahan*
Tapas	Winter	January	*Pushya*	*Paush*
Tapasya	Winter	February	*Magha*	*Magh*

25

PLANETARY SHADBAL

In the previous chapter we have studied about ascent / setting and impact of signs on the Houses of horoscope. We may take it as a fixed impact over the Houses. Periodicity of Houses has a gradual impact in one's lifetime. But the planet placed in a particular House has its definite impact irrespective of the impact of sign and constellation of that House. Thus by observing the planetary placement in a horoscope, we may ascertain about the planets, which will be active during the periodicity of a particular House.

As you have studied in the previous chapter that according to my discovery, impact of a House change according to the age. Thus, during the periodicity of a particular House, as seven years effective period of seventh House after the age of 21 years then any planet placed in seventh House will have its impact according to its element and for which it is an activator. For example if Jupiter is placed in seventh House and we also know that Jupiter is an activator planet for 2, 5, 9, 10 and 11th House. Thus it is clear that during the periodicity of seventh House, Jupiter would have a leading role for providing the result of seventh House as well as for those Houses, for which it is an activator. Thus, planet and House has mutual instigating affect on each other. In this way you may easily understand the impact of any planet situated in any

House and its active period in one's life. Scientifically every planet has following six powers:

1 – Positional power of planets
2 – Transitional power of planets
3 – Rising power of planets
4 – Exalted power of planets
5 – Distant power of planets
6 – Motional power of planets

Now we will discuss about these powers of a planet from which potential of a planet can be ascertained.

Positional power of planets

As we have studied in detail about the expansion of impact of a sign and House up to 90°. Similarly, during the periodicity of a House, not only the planets situated in the House have full impact but the planets situated in the vicinity up to 2-3 Houses also have impact during this period in the ratio of their angular difference in degree from the effective part of the House. For example, if Venus of 15° is placed in eighth House and we know that nearly in the age of 25 a native is effected by that part of seventh House, which is at 15°. Thus in that age the effect of Venus will be about 66%, because it is situated at an angular difference of 30° from this operative part of seventh House. If the Venus of 15° would have been in ninth House, then it would have exerted about 33% effect due to its angular difference of 60° and if this Venus of 15° would have been in tenth House, then its effect would have been just started due to its angular difference of about 90°, which is the threshold limit. Thus, it would be clear that the impact of planets, situated in the Houses which are ahead from the effective House, would continuously increase day-by-day, whereas according to same analogy the impact of the planets situated in those Houses which are behind the effective House, would continuously decrease day-by-day.

To calculate the impact of a planet, we simply calculate the angular difference in degrees between the planet and effective part of the House. Deduct this difference from 90 and add 10% to it, to arrive at the power of impact of the planet on the House at that point of time. For example, if Venus of 20° of Sagittarius sign i.e. 260° is situated in a House and effective part of the House is situated at 10° of Scorpio sign i.e. 220°. Then to arrive at the impact of Venus at that point of time, we have to calculate the angular difference in between these two points, which is 40°. Now, deduct it from 90 to get 50 and add 10% to it i.e. 5, and we may easily get 55%. Thus, we can easily conclude that at that point of time Venus would have about 55% impact on the subject related to Venus as well as to the subject of seventh House. Suppose, we have Jupiter in place of Venus then we may conclude that being the activator of 2, 5, 9, 10, 11th House, Jupiter will exert an impact of 55% relating to the subject of these Houses along with impact of 7th House.

Transitional power of planets

As we have calculated the positional power of planets on every House of a horoscope. In the same way, we can also calculate the day-to-day Transitional power of planets on various Houses. For this we simply draw a horoscope with the same ascendant, which was in the birth horoscope and place all planets according to their present transitional position in a sign. Remember that the expansion of every House will be in accordance with the birth horoscope thus every House will generally have two signs. For example if Sagittarius is the Ascendant in birth horoscope then we will have to draw a horoscope and mark 9 in Ascendant and accordingly fill in all other subsequent Houses with a sign. Thereafter, we will place the planets in the House according to their transitional sign. Thus we can easily prepare our day-to-day horoscope. From this we can calculate the power of impact which a planet is exerting on a House which will definitely be according to birth horoscope. For example, if Venus of 15° of Cancer sign is placed in eighth House of birth horoscope and during transition Venus is moving at 15° in Taurus sign, thus it would be placed in sixth House of daily horoscope because ascendant is as usual Sagittarius. Thus it would be very clear that Venus of birth horoscope is having 66% impact on seventh House at a particular time and transitional Venus is also exerting an impact of 66% at the same point of seventh House from the sixth House of daily horoscope. Thus the native may feel an increase in the result of seventh House in coming days due to transition of Venus towards Gemini sign. Accordingly, power of planet that is being exerted on a House during transition may very easily be calculated.

Rising power of planets

Impact of power as calculated above may be most effective when the concerning planet is crossing the meridian line, which may be drawn from Pole-star to zenith and extended further towards south horizon. Every planet rise in the east and after remaining in the sky for about 12 hours it set in the west. Thus keeping in mind the description given in the previous chapter about the movement of sign from east to west, you may easily understand the movement of a planet, which also moves from east to west. The impact of a planet, which is just rising i.e. which is at 0° altitude in the eastern horizon, will have 0% impact because of its horizontal location in the sky and we will not be in a position to get the impact of the planet. But the planet will continue to rise at a speed of 1° per four minute and on the same analogy power of the planet will also be increased at a speed of about 1% per four minute. After about six hours it will cross the meridian line and it will be at 90° with reference to our position and at that time it will have maximum potential. After this, planet will move towards western horizon and the power will also decrease at a speed of 1% per four minute and subsequently the influence of the planet will completely be diluted after setting in the west. Next day the same cycle will again be repeated.

Full cycle of rotation followed by every planet may easily be understood from the rotation of Sun. We can observe that effect of the light, heat, various rays, flux etc. which is being continuously emitted by the Sun, remains at lowest ebb during every night and the impact is actually 0%. Whereas, the effect of Sun on us, started as soon as it appears in the east. The impact of Sun is maximum i.e. 100% at noon, when its position is at 90° altitude with reference to our physical location on Earth. Thereafter, the impact of Sun started to diminish during its journey towards west. In the same way, impact of every other planet on us changes according to their altitude in the sky with reference to our location on the Earth.

Because, Sun is the activator of life and our existence on Earth is only possible due to Sun and none else. Therefore, we start our activity as soon as Sun rises in east and activity of our body is at maximum level at noon and we can feel stagnation in our activity after sunset. Thus, during our entire life, we always try to synchronise our activity with the Sun. Thus it would be clear that to maintain our body in a proper and perfect shape and for taking maximum out of it, it is essential that we must synchronise and decide our activity according to the position of Sun from east to west, who is the activator of first House i.e. body. In the same way, for fulfilling the desire related to a particular House, we must synchronise and decide our activity according to the position and movement of that planet from east to west, who is activator of the House and the planet which is situated in that House. So that, the way in which Sun is influencing our body as an activator of first House, in the same way, we may extract the maximum favourable result of a House after anticipating the time of rising, setting and crossing of meridian line i.e. noon of that planet, who is the activator or who is placed in the House. Because we can realise that after rising of the Sun, it can at the most inform us to get ready for performing our duties, but it can never pickup from our bed and drop at our duty point. For that we have to understand the system of information being adopted by the Sun and must use our intelligence for extracting maximum benefit of the day. Likewise we have to understand the system of information being adopted by various planets, only then we may be able to get the maximum benefit during favourable conditions being created by the planet. We learn since our childhood and mentally prepared to get ready by the time of sun-rising. In other words, we know the system of information being adopted by the Sun, but we are not able to understand the system of information of other planets and whenever unknowingly our performance synchronises with the condition created by the planets then we may also get favourable support, otherwise not. Hence maximum benefit of the favourable condition being created by the planets can only be obtained if we scientifically understand the system of information of the planets.

It is really not very difficult to ascertain the time of rising of a planet in east. As I have already explained that it takes about 4 minutes for rising 1° of a sign and it take about two hours for rising a sign of 30° in east. Because planets are also visible in a sign hence they also move in the sky like our Sun while remaining in that sign. If the transitory degree (Sign × 30 + degree) of a planet is more than the degree of the Sun then deduct the degree of the Sun from the degree of that planet and multiply the remainder by 4 to get the time in minutes. Thus planet will appear in the eastern sky after passing of this much time followed by sunrise. Thus a very nearby timing of rising of a planet may easily be calculated. After six hours from this time, this planet will be at the meridian line and will set in west after next six hours from this time. Although, we may not be able to see the planet in the light of Sun during day time but the planet is very much in the sky and also exerting its effect on the subject for which it is activator and subject of the House in which it is placed in the horoscope. We may see these planets after sun-set. If the transitory degree of a planet is less than the degree of Sun, then deduct the degree of planet from the degree of Sun and multiply the remainder by 4 to get the time in minutes. Thus planet will appear in the eastern sky before this much time of sunrise. The planet will in turn crosses the meridian line after six hours and will set in after six hours, but before sun-set. The planet will be in a position of exerting its effect, on the subject of the House for whom it is an activator and subject of the House in which it is placed in the horoscope, well before sunrise. Such planet may actually be seen before sunrise.

In this way, after calculating the actual timing of crossing of meridian line by a planet, which is activator of a House, we may calculate daily critical timing of crossing of meridian line by simply deducting 4 minutes per day. We may periodically correct this time, because the timing of crossing of meridian line is actually the noon of the concerning planet, when it is most effective. For convenience of the readers, difference of time in hours, between rising of Sun and planet is enlisted in column 5 of appendix-2. If any planet is rising in east before actual sunrise then negative sign is placed before the time.

If you want to see a planet in the sky, or for getting maximum direct impact of a planet by observing it, after calculating the favourable time, we must also know true east direction. Generally, we decide the east direction with reference to the position of sunrise and correlate it to identify all four directions with reference to four walls of our House. Due to shifting of Sun from winter solstice to summer solstice, it actually takes a swing of about 47°. Thus it is not possible to realign all four direction with reference to new direction of east due to daily shifting of sunrise. But Pole-star always remains at true North direction. Thus true east direction is 90° towards east from this true north. Sun always rises within the span of 23.5° north and south from this true east direction. On 23rd of March and September, Sun rises from the true east direction in the cities situated on equator line. In the same way all planets neither rises from the true east nor they rises from the point of sunrise. Because all planets including Earth take rotation of the Sun hence the point of rising of planets also changes continuously according to their sign.

Planet transiting in Taurus, Gemini sign may rise from about 90° to 98° towards east from pole star; planets in Aries, Cancer sign may rise from about 98° to 106° towards east; planets in Pisces, Leo sign may rise from about 106° to 114° towards east; planets in Aquarius, Virgo sign may rise from about 114° to 122° towards east; planets in Capricorn, Libra sign may rise from about 122° to 130° towards east; planets in Sagittarius, Scorpio sign may rise from about 130° to 137° towards east from Pole-star in the cities like Bhopal who are situated on Tropic of Cancer. Direction of rising of a planet with reference to the Pole-star in other cities may easily be ascertained by deducting 23.5° from the latitude of that city and by adding this to the above mentioned degrees. For example, if latitude of a city is 25.5° then Taurus and Gemini sign will appear to rise from 90 + (25.5 – 23.5) = 92° to 100° and so on. Try to understood this point from picture-45. In this way those Planets who are transiting in Taurus or Gemini sign nearly point P on line O, P, Q, R, S, which is present ecliptic of the Sun may rise from extreme northern position and planets transiting in Scorpio or Sagittarius sign nearly point R may rise from extreme southern position.

Exalted power of planets

Well before Primitive age, Jupiter moves so closely to Pushya constellation that it was difficult to differentiate them from each other. At that time Pushya constellation was visible in Cancer sign nearly at zenith on meridian line. It was recorded in the Tettariya Brahmin at step 3-1-1 that "बृहस्पति: प्रथमं जायमाना:। तिष्यं नक्षत्रमपि संबभूव।।". Thus due to immense closeness of the Jupiter with Pushya constellation, it was presumed that the Jupiter has taken birth from Pushya constellation. It was also observed that the impact of Jupiter also increases as it comes closer to the Pushya constellation, hence the Jupiter was considered as exalted in Pushya constellation. This has already been explained in the chapter of "Exalted-debilitated Planets". As per explanation already given in support of picture-1, you have already studied that all constellations were considered to be situated in between Moon and Mercury planets. Because all 27 constellations of zodiac were considered to be nearer than Mercury and all planets moves among these constellations. Thus our sages always took help of these constellations for locating a planet in the sky. Hence in the process of formulation of astrological principles, constellational position of a planet had important contribution. From all this explanation, it would be clear that our sages were also aware of the fact that the impact of a planet at zenith situated at meridian line increases. But due to some misconception about the formation of Universe, position of planets and lack of other scientific information they could not properly formulate more befitting principles of astrology.

From the description given in support of picture-45, you may have understood that in Primitive age, it was observed that all planets were passing through 27 constellations. But zodiac is also continuously shifting its position and till today the position of this zodiac from Cancer to Scorpio sign has been shifted by more than 8° towards south and from Capricorn to Taurus sign, it has been shifted by more than 8° towards north, due to continuous change in *ayanansh*. This position can be seen in picture-45, where part of ecliptic as seen in Primitive age and as on today, have been marked by B C D and Y Q R; D E / A B and R S / O P respectively. Above variation is only due to change in *ayanansh* by 33° since Primitive age. This has resulted in fall of winter solstice and summer solstice when Sun transits from point P and R instead of point B and D respectively. There is a difference of 33° in between point B and P. Thus, it would be clear that planetary path (adjoining area of ecliptic) of today does not embrace 27 constellations in it, which were once situated in zodiac and planets also do not transits besides these constellations. Thus, it is pertinent and a matter of research to decide the impact of 27 constellations in this shifted situation of the ecliptic. Actually we have to decide the impact of new set of 27 constellations which may be marked in present zodiac (O, P, Q, R, S in picture-45) after marking the daily position of the Moon in consonance with the concept of Primitive age. Because now it is also a well-known fact that these constellations are neither situated in our solar system nor even they are in our Milkyway. It is still not known that in which galaxies they are actually situated. But it is in accordance with the scientific theory and logical that planetary inclination does have a varied impact hence we will now discuss in detail about the exalted power of planets.

You may have understood from the Rising power of the planets that they exert their maximum impact when they are at zenith like the Sun. It is known that zenith is the topmost point in the sky and is 90° above from all directions. Whereas extended line joining Pole-star and zenith is called meridian line. It is not essential that every planet may pass through zenith after six hours from its rising in east, but every planet including Sun crosses the meridian line after about six hours from its rising in east. Hence, the angle of elevation from the southern horizon (for Northern Hemisphere) to that point of meridian line at which a planet crosses this line is actually responsible for Exalted power of that planet. This angle is the basis of calculation of Exalted power of that planet and it is most powerful among all sort of powers.

In India, Tropic of Cancer passes nearly from Ahmedabad, Banswara, Ratlam, Bhopal, Ranchi etc. Hence at the time of winter solstice i.e. on 23rd June, Sun remains at zenith in noon in these cities. Thus nearly after six hours from rising, when Sun crosses the meridian line, it remains at zenith i.e. 90° above from southern horizon. Whereas, in the cities which are situated towards north side of this Tropic of Cancer, Sun remains at southern side from the zenith while crossing meridian line at noon. In this way on 23rd June at the time of winter solstice, in the cities like Gwalior, though Sun attains the highest slanted elevation at noon from the eastern horizon i.e. 90°, but it is not at an elevation of 90° from southern horizon, instead of this Sun crosses the meridian line at a low elevation. Table of appendix-2 contains the position of 26° latitude i.e. the latitude, which is in the vicinity of the latitude of Gwalior. From the column 8 of the above table you can observe that on 23rd June, Sun crosses the meridian line at a maximum elevation of 86-87°. Contrary to this, though at the time of crossing the meridian line by the Sun at noon of 23rd June on those cities which are situated towards the southern side of the Tropic of Cancer, Sun was at an elevation of 90° from the eastern horizon but the elevation is more than 90° from the southern horizon. Thus it crosses the meridian line from northern side of it. In this way it would be clear that Sun remains at zenith two times in a year in those cities which are situated in the southern side of the Tropic of Cancer. In these cities Sun passes from zenith at the time of moving towards winter solstice and again at the time of moving towards summer solstice. Thus it would be clear that in the cities of south India, Sun passes from the zenith twice in a year i.e. at the elevation of 90° from east direction as well as from south direction. You can also clearly understand it with the help of picture-49 given below.

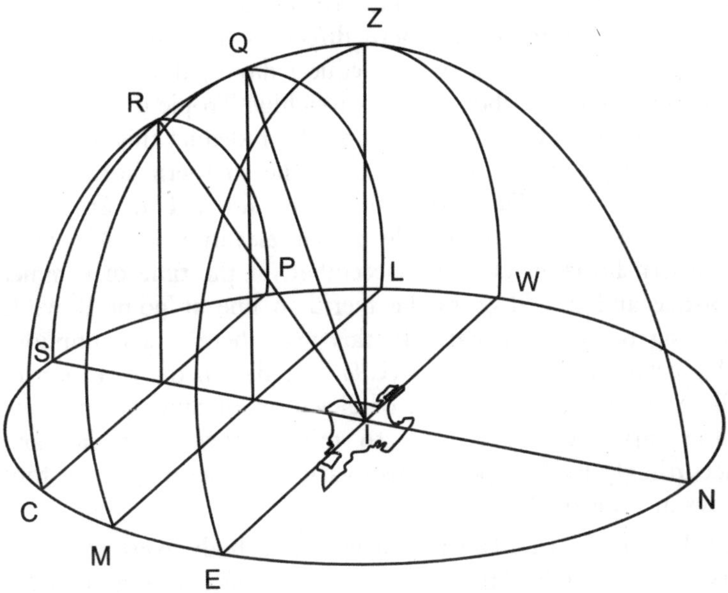

E, W = Tropic of Cancer

C, P = Tropic of Capricorn

Q, I, Z = R, I, Q = 23.5°

R, I, S = 43°

I = India

Picture – 49

Transitory movement of the planet in the sky

Straight line N, S running from north to south is longitudinal line on the Earth. Whereas, circular line N, Z, S, which is touching the point of north direction, zenith and south direction is a meridian line (projected longitudinal line) in the sky. Straight line M, L in the picture is Equator line on the Earth. In the same way circular line M, Q, L, which is starting from the east direction and ending in west direction, depict the projected equator i.e. path of movement as followed by Sun on 23rd March and September. You can see from the picture that on 23rd June when Sun follows the path of E, Z,

W, which is projected Tropic of Cancer and passes over the city like Bhopal etc., which are situated on this line, then at the time of crossing of meridian line N, Z, S, it is visible at point Z which is actual zenith. Whereas, after this date due to winter solstice, day-by-day Sun crosses this meridian line at a point which is in the southern direction from zenith. In this way the Exalted power of Sun reduces day-by-day. Sun takes a southern swing of about 47° for touching Tropic of Capricorn from Tropic of Cancer. Therefore, if we deduct this 47° from the elevation of 90° of zenith from the southern horizon, we simply get 43°. Thus from the cities situated at Tropic of Cancer, Sun may be visible at an elevation of 43° from southern horizon, on 23rd December, at the time of summer solstice and it will cross the meridian line at point R while moving on C, R, P path. In this way there is a continuous change of about 16 minute (*kala*) per day in the elevation of the Sun. In this way angle of elevation of Sun at any fixed time varies at a speed of 16 minute (*kala*) per day and accordingly Exalted power also varies by one per cent in four days at a particular time.

It is a scientific fact that whenever a body exert any force from a perpendicular position of 90°, then at that time its impact would be maximum due to absence of any factor of reflection etc. As we go on deviating the perpendicular position of an impacting body and reduce its elevation, the impact of the body will also be reduced accordingly due to increase in the factor of reflection etc. This principle always has its effect on energy, light, magnetic flux, magnetic storm, radiation, different type of rays like Alpha, Beta etc., which are being continuously emitted by a planet. In India we may verify the effect of this principle from the position of Sun and Moon. We may feel maximum heat and cold respectively, when Sun and Moon happens to be at an elevation of 90° in the summer and in the night of full Moon respectively. Contrary to this, we may feel less heat and cold respectively, when Sun crosses the meridian line at noon in winter at a lower elevation from southern direction and when Moon remains nearer to horizon at the time of rising in the east and setting in the west. This change in the impact of these planets is only due to inclination in the line of effect. Whereas, actual distance of the Sun from the Earth is minimum during winter in comparison to its distance during summer, even then impact of Sun reduces during winter only due to inclination in the path of its movement with reference to our position on the Earth. Thus it would be quite clear that perpendicular position of a planet exert maximum impact and in turn Exalted power will also be highest.

To work out the Exalted power of a planet in per cent, we must know the angle of elevation from the southern horizon, at the time of crossing of the meridian line during its daily movement in the sky. We may simply add 10% of the angle of elevation in it to know the percentage of Exalted power, which is being exerted by the planet at that time. In the previous example it was explained that Sun will cross the meridian line in the cities like Bhopal, which is situated on the Tropic of Cancer, at noon of 23rd June at an elevation of 90° from southern horizon. Thus the Exalted power of the Sun at that time can be worked out by adding 10% of 90 in 90 itself to get 99% or say cent-per cent. Whereas, the Exalted power of the Sun on 23rd December, when it will cross the meridian line at an elevation of about 43° (90 – 23.5 × 2) would be 43 + 4.3 (10% of 43) = about 47%. In the same way every planet crosses the meridian line at a different elevation, resulting in continuous variation in the Exalted power of that planet. As has already been explained that the position of signs with reference to the southern horizon for every city of the Earth is fixed, hence planet also remains at about the same elevation of the sign, in which they are situated during transition.

If we consider about those cities, which are situated towards the northern side of the Tropic of Cancer, which is at an altitude of 23.5°, like Amritsar, which is situated at 31.5° latitude. Then it would be clear from the picture-49 that this city is situated at 8° north from Tropic of Cancer. Thus when Sun will be at zenith and in a position to cross the meridian line at noon of 23rd June at Bhopal, then at that time it will not be at zenith of Amritsar like its position at Z as seen from Bhopal. Instead of this it will be 8° southern from zenith i.e. it will be at an elevation of 82° from southern horizon of Amritsar. Thus the Exalted power of the Sun will be 90% in Amritsar. In the same way on 23rd December elevation of the Sun will be 43° (90 – 23.5 × 2) as seen from the Tropic of Cancer and it will also be reduced by 8° in Amritsar. Thus the angle of elevation will be 35° (43 – 8) and the Exalted power will also be about 39% (35 + 3.5) in Amritsar.

Thus Exalted power of planet gradually increases and after reaching to a maximum point according to the latitude of the city, it starts to reduce gradually in the cities situated towards north of Tropic of Cancer. This power increases after reaching to the point of minimum Exalted power. In this way the maximum Exalted power is dependable and varies according to the latitude of a city. Yet, according to present *ayanansh*, every planet has maximum exalted power due to its maximum altitude, in the cities situated towards north of the Tropic of Cancer when it is at about 7° of Gemini sign. Accordingly, every planet has lowest exalted power due to its minimum altitude, with reference to entire India, when it is at about 7° of Sagittarius sign.

For the cities situated on Tropic of Cancer and above, it took same time in completing one cycle from maximum Exalted power to the next maximum Exalted power, which is the time cycle of a planet to cover the entire zodiac of 12 signs i.e. roughly one year by Sun, one month by Moon, three months by Mercury, nine months by Venus, two years by Mars, thirteen years by Jupiter and thirty years by Saturn.

Every planet like Sun appears to be in northern direction while it is crossing the meridian line, during its transit in Taurus and Gemini sign, and angle of elevation from southern horizon will be more than 90° from the cities situated in the belt between Tropic of Cancer and Equator. Thus angle of elevation of the planet from northern horizon will be less than 90°. To calculate the actual angle of elevation, we have to reduce to angle of elevation from southern horizon, by the angle, by which it is more than 90° or in other words calculate the angle of elevation from northern horizon. Thereafter, as usual we may add 10% of it to get correct Exalted power of the planet. In this way you can understand that for the cities situated in-between these two geographical lines, the Exalted power will be slightly reduced after reaching to 100% point and thereafter it will again touch the point of 100% power. Only after this repetition it will continuously reduce till its threshold limit of minimum Exalted power. From where it will again increase gradually. In this way these cities actually enjoyed two occasions of 100% Exalted power. For further clarification we may take the example of Mysore, which is situated at 12° latitude. At noon of 8th May, Sun appears to cross the meridian line of this city at an elevation of 90° from southern direction i.e. from zenith. At that time Sun will exert 100% Exalted power. The point of zenith will be somewhere in between Z and Q of picture-49. After this date too Sun will continue its movement towards north till it reaches at Tropic of Cancer. At that time the elevation of the Sun at noon will be 101.5° with reference to southern horizon of Mysore or 11.5° slanted towards northern side from zenith of Mysore and its elevation will be 78.5° from the northern horizon. Thus its actual elevation will be 90 – 11.5 = 78.5° and Exalted power will be reduced to 78 + 8 (10% of 78) = 86%. During winter solstice nearly on 8th August, Sun will again cross the meridian line of Mysore and transit from an elevation of 90°. Thus its Exalted power will again be 100%. After this date Sun will continue its movement towards south and on 23rd December it will cross the meridian line at an elevation of about 54.5° (90 – 23.5 – 12) and its Exalted power will be 60% (54.5 + 5.4). Thus cities situated in south of Tropic of Cancer will be in a position to enjoy Exalted power of a planet twice in every cycle.

Those cities which are situated in between the Equator line and Tropic of Capricorn may enjoy maximum Exalted power in opposite situation i.e. when the Exalted power may be reducing in the cities situated towards the north of Tropic of Cancer, during winter solstice then the cities situated towards southern side of Equator line will get higher Exalted power. Thus as we have taken the angle of elevation from south horizon at the time of crossing the meridian line, for calculating the Exalted power for the cities in India, contrary to this, for the habitat of Southern Hemisphere of the Earth, Exalted power may be calculated by the angle of elevation from north horizon. Because India is situated in Northern Hemisphere of the Earth hence detailed analysis for the position of Southern Hemisphere is not covered in the book. But if we simply try to access the position of Exalted power in both hemisphere then it would be clear that whenever the Exalted power is decreasing in India then at the same time countries like Australia will be in the increasing phase of Exalted power. Thus you can very well understand that for any two places of the Earth, Exalted power will be different due to difference in elevation of sign and planet from the south as well as east horizon.

To ascertain the different power of the planets according to the description given in this chapter, necessary details have been incorporated in the tables contained in appendix-2. In column 8 of the table, angle of elevation of a planet from the southern horizon has been exhibited. This angle of elevation is based on 26° latitude, which is near to Gwalior. On the basis of this information you can very easily calculate the angle of elevation from southern horizon for any city. For this you have to simply deduct the latitude of the concerning city from 26 and add this figure to the figure exhibited in column 8 of the table. Thus you can ascertain the angle of elevation of the planet with reference to southern horizon at the time of crossing of meridian line of that city. Add as usual, 10% of this angle to the angle itself and you will get the Exalted power of that planet in per cent. We can also understand the above example on the basis of the table in the following manner. There is no need for any minute calculation, because power is ascertained in per cent.

Latitude of Mysore = 12°

Latitude of table (appendix-2) = 26°

Difference in both latitude = 26° – 12° = 14°

Exalted power of the Sun on the basis of angle of elevation of the Sun as shown in column 8 of appendix-2

= Angle of elevation at 26° + Difference in latitude

On 8-5-2007 = 76 + 14 = 90 + 9 = 99%
or say cent-per cent Exalted power

On 23-6-2007 = 87 + 14 = 101
It is more than 90 by 11 hence
90 – 11 = 79° + 7 = 86% Exalted power

On 8-8-2007 = 76 + 14 = 90 + 9 = 99%
or say cent-per cent Exalted power

As explained in the chapter of 'Actual Rahu-Ketu' that all planets remains in their respective orbit while rotating around the Sun and thus make an angle with reference to the plane of Sun and Earth (refer picture-31). The angle of inclination of the orbit of Moon is 5.14°, Mars is 1.85°, Mercury is 7°, Jupiter is 1.3°, Venus is 3.39° and Saturn is 2.49°. In this way all these planets may swing up and down by this much angle during their movement with reference to ecliptic i.e. path followed by the Sun. Thus whole band of movement covered by these planets around ecliptic is called zodiac. If it is further explained then at noon of 23rd December, Sun will be visible at an elevation of 43° while transiting from 7° of Sagittarius sign from the cities situated on Tropic of Cancer. Thus whenever a planet moves in Sagittarius sign, their angle of elevation may be more or less up to the angle of inclination of their orbit. For example, angle of elevation of Mercury, while transiting from 7° of Sagittarius sign will be within 36° (43° – 7°) and 50° (43° + 7°). However, actual calculation may be performed on the basis of data contained in appendix-2.

Now, I will like to further explain some points, though these points have already been explained but they need last punch in the light of above explanation regarding movement of planets.

1. Position of setting of a planet due to another planet has already been described in detail. From that description you may have understood that it is essential for a planet to transit behind another planet for classifying it as a set planet. After the description of inclination in the orbit of every planet with reference to the plane of Sun and Earth, it is essential to clarify

a little more regarding the setting of a planet. You may have grasped the explanation that during their daily movement, all planets cross the meridian line at different elevation with reference to southern horizon. In this way Sun and any other planet, for example, say Mercury and Sun are moving in same sign and at same degree, and say Mercury is far away in comparison to Sun, thus it is also transiting behind the Sun. It is quite possible that Mercury may be treated at set due to same position of the Sun and Mercury. But, you are also aware that the angle of inclination of orbit of Mercury is 7°. Thus if Mercury and Sun are crossing the meridian line with an angular difference of more than 1° then Mercury will not actually move behind the Sun and thus it cannot be termed as set due to Sun. Because in this situation transitory path of both planets will be at different elevation from the southern horizon. In this way, any planet can only be termed as set due to Sun or Moon, if the degree-sign of both the planets are within half degree and the angle of elevation of both the planets with reference to southern horizon must also be within half degree. Because the radius of the Sun and Moon is about half degree. If any of the above two conditions is not fulfilled than there is no setting of a planet at all. Thus it is prime requirement that two planets (one of them may either be Sun or Moon) must be within half degree. As at the time of solar eclipse, the degree-sign difference between the Sun and Moon is less than 1° (because total of radius of both these planets is 1°) and difference in elevation of Sun and Moon from southern horizon is also less than 1°. You may also understand it with the help of data enlisted in the table.

According to the table, nirayan degree of Sun and Mercury were 170° and 171° respectively i.e. they are in Virgo sign on 7-10-2004 and angle of elevation on meridian line with reference to southern horizon were 60.4° and 64.1° respectively. As per present practice, Mercury was treated as set due to difference of 1°

Table – 1
Data of Sun and other planets

Planet	Date	Degree	Elevation
Sun	7-10-2004	170	60.4
Mercury	7-10-2004	171	64.1
Mercury	7-05-2003	22.7	76.5
Sun	7-05-2003	22.2	76
Sun	9-07-2004	83	83
Saturn	9-07-2004	83	82.8

between the nirayan degree of Sun and Mercury but you can see that the difference in angle of elevation on meridian line is more than 3° (64.1° – 60.4° = 3.7°). Thus actually Mercury was not moving behind the Sun hence in turn it could not be termed as set due to Sun. Contrary to this situation, nirayan degree of Mercury and Sun were 22.7° and 22.2° respectively on 7-5-2003 and the angle of elevation from southern horizon at the time of crossing of meridian line were 76.5° and 76° respectively as seen from 26° latitude. Thus it would be clear that transitory degree as well as elevation of both planets were within half degree. Because Sun is behind the retrograde Mercury, hence technically Sun must be treated as set instead of Mercury. Supportive explanation in this regard has already been given in earlier chapters. Above position was actually seen in the sky, which itself prove that Mercury may come nearer to the Earth in comparison to Sun against the concept of Primitive time, which was followed by our sages at the time of formulation of astrological principles, when Mercury was considered as far away from Sun and Moon as shown in picture-1. *Nirayan* degree of Sun and Saturn was 83° on 9-7-2004 and the angle of elevation from southern horizon at the time of crossing of meridian line was 83° and 82.8° respectively. Thus there was no difference in nirayan degree and the difference in elevation was also less than half degree, hence Saturn was correctly termed as set.

2. I have already explained about the Rahu and Ketu of every planet. For example, which was also quoted earlier in table-1 of chapter "Actual Rahu-Ketu" that on 27-1-2004 Mercury crossed its own Ketu and moved in a backward position with reference to the plane of Sun and Earth. You can also observe this position from the table that on this date the angle of elevation of Mercury was 44.2° and nirayan position was 260°. Angle of elevation of Mercury was continuously reducing between 1-1-2004 to 31-1-2004. The angle of elevation of Sun was 44.2° and nirayan position was 260° on 5-1-2004, while moving towards the southern side of ecliptic.

Table – 2

Data of Sun and Mercury

Planet	Date	Degree	Elevation
Sun	05-01-2004	260	44.2
Mercury	06-01-2004	243	51.5
Mercury	16-01-2004	248	45.4
Mercury	27-01-2004	260	44.2

Thus it can be observed that Mercury crossed ecliptic i.e. it created its own Ketu and remained in trailing position in the Universe. You can also understand from this explanation that Mercury was in southern position with reference to the plane of Earth and Sun i.e. orbit of the Earth.

In the same way Mercury crossed this plane nearly on 17-3-2004 after creating its own Rahu at the elevation of about 63° and remained in a leading position in northern direction in the Universe with reference to the plane of Earth and Sun. You can very well understand these positions for other planets too. Thus any planet which is moving in the northern direction after creating its own Rahu would exert more impact on India because it is situated in the Northern Hemisphere of the Earth.

3. Now, if we consider a totally different view for understanding the impact of the Exalted power in view of the fact that all 27 constellations and signs comprised of these constellations are not even in our galaxy i.e. Milkyway. Then impact of these signs would definitely be nearer to zero. We have already studied from the picture-45 that till now the position of zodiac has been shifted by 33° since Primitive age, when all sort of predictive principles of astrology were being formulated. At that time our sages observed the movement of planets in the background of various shapes of different sign and considered that impact was due to movement in particular sign, which was considered between Moon and Mercury (refer picture-1). Whereas, actually the impact of a planet was only based on the power exerted due to its angle of elevation, which is also scientific. If we reconsider all these situational position of various planets having a particular angle of elevation, which they have in Primitive age then we can realise that sign will always remain changing due to change in *ayanansh*. For example, if it was formulated at that time that Jupiter placed in Cancer sign in a horoscope, will give some particular result. Now, we can see from the picture-45 that in Primitive age when Jupiter used to transit from Cancer sign then angle of elevation was 90° at the time of crossing of meridian line of the cities situated on Tropic of Cancer. If we consider the angle of elevation then we may see that now-a-days Jupiter remains at 90° elevation, at the time of crossing of meridian line of the cities situated on Tropic of Cancer, in Gemini sign instead of Cancer sign. In this way the entire swing of 94° (23.5 × 4) taken by the Sun during winter solstice and summer solstice may be

converted into twelve zones, each of about 8°. Thus one zone each of winter solstice and summer solstice will fall in a belt of 8° and entire new revised set of predictive aspect of astrology may be developed on the basis of change in elevation by every degree in place of division of a sign on the basis of *Navansh, Saptmansh* etc., in view of the modern concept of solar system and *ayanansh*. These new principles will remain effective even after change in *ayanansh* and these principles may be everlasting because there will be no change in inclination of orbit of the Sun.

Thus we have to reallocate the prediction to Gemini sign, which was once related with Cancer sign. In this way we have to reformulate entire predictive astrology accordingly. But it is a matter of continuous research, analysis and processing of various data before modifying any principle outrightly and we have consider as to whether future is definite and fixed, only then we have to verify as to whether a particular prediction itself has sufficient validity or not. Otherwise instead of psychologically believing any prediction regarding indefinite future on the basis of above principles as correct, it would have been quite correct to scientifically assess the impact of planet in per cent and then act according to our best judicious decision.

Distant power of planets

It is a well-known scientific fact that any body or mass which has a capacity to exert an effect over another body, then the quantum of effect will be inversely proportionate to distance between these two bodies or in other words the effect would be more if the distance between two bodies is less and the effect would be less if the distance is more.

We know that the distance between Earth and every planet is continuously changing. If the difference of maximum and minimum distance of a planet from the Earth, may be divided by 100 then the percentage of Distant power of that planet can be ascertained for any given distance of a day. For example the minimum and maximum distances between the Moon and the Earth is 3.57 lakh km and 4.07 lakh km respectively. Hence, if the difference between these distances, which is 50,000 km, may be divided by 100 then we will get 500 km. Now if Moon is farthest from the Earth then the Distant power will naturally be 0%. If the distance of the Moon is 4 lakh km then after deducting it from the maximum distance of the Moon, we will get 7000 km (4.07 lakh – 4 lakh), which may be divided by 500 and we can easily get 14% (7000 / 500) Distant power of Moon at that point of time. Minimum and maximum distance of a planet from the Earth is provided in the chapter of 'Universe'. However, the difference between the maximum and minimum distances of a planet from the Earth is given in the column 3 of the table and the distance which is responsible for increasing the Distant power by 1% is given in the column 4. To calculate the percentage of the Distant power, we have to deduct the present distance from the maximum distance of that planet and divide it by the figure given in column 4. For the convenience of the readers, distance of every planet is provided in column 2 and percentage of the Distant power in column 3 of the tables contained in appendix-2, after a fixed interval of five days.

Table – 3

Planet 1	Maximum dist. 2	Difference 3	1% distance (in km) 4
Saturn	169.70 crore	5816 lakh	58.16 lakh
Jupiter	96.43 crore	3734 lakh	37.34 lakh
Mars	39.97 crore	3439 lakh	34.39 lakh
Venus	26.23 crore	2250 lakh	22.50 lakh
Mercury	22.16 crore	1426 lakh	14.26 lakh
Sun	15.27 crore	62 lakh	62 thou.
Moon	4.07 lakh	50 thou.	500

We have studied from the details provided in support of picture-27 that on the basis of relative position of Mars, Jupiter and Saturn with reference to the Sun, we can ascertain the direction of movement of these planets as to whether they are moving towards the Earth or moving away from the Earth.

Now, if we have a horoscope and we want to ascertain the Distant power of the planets then the approximate Distant power of these three planets may be calculated on the basis of the absolute difference in *nirayan* degree between concerning planet and the Sun, which may always be less than 180°. By dividing this difference by 1.8 we may immediately ascertain the percentage Distant power of that planet. For example if the absolute difference between Sun and a planet is 90° then the Distant power would be 90 / 1.8 = 50%. If the absolute difference between Sun and planet is 162° then the Distant power would be 162 / 1.8 = 90%. However, there may be a slight difference in the percentage of Distant power calculated on the basis of actual distance of the planet from the Earth.

Motional power of planets

It is also a scientific fact that the motion of a moving body has a direct relation with the quantum of impact and it is directly proportionate to the motion. Hence if a body is moving towards another body with a greater speed than the impact will also be more and this impact will be reduced with the reduction in the speed of the body. For example, we may have experienced on the railway station that the pitch of the whistle of a train is much more while it is coming towards the station, in comparison to the pitch of the whistle when the same train is moving away from the station. This effect due to motion of a body is known as Doppler's effect.

There are two different motions of every planet. According to first motion, every planet moves in his own orbit (refer picture-2) and its position from the Earth is ascertained on the basis of degree-sign. Whereas second motion is ascertained on the basis of change in direct distance of that planet from the Earth. For example, on any day the distance of the Sun from the Earth is 15 crore km and after 5 days the distance between them increased to 15.02 crore km. Then there is a change of 2 lakh km in 5 days. In this way daily motion of the Sun is 40,000 km per day, by which it is moving away from the Earth. This motion is the basis of calculating Motional power of planets.

The motion of the planets with reference to the Earth also continuously varies in the same way as the distance of the planets. If we divide the maximum motion of these planets, which they have with reference to the earth, by 100 then with the help of this number we can easily calculate the Motional power in per cent on that date. Detail of maximum motion per day of every planet is provided in the table. A planet may move towards the Earth or move away from the Earth up to this maximum motion. Because every heavenly body including the Earth and planets are moving in the Universe hence motion of every planet has been calculated on the basis of difference in their daily distance from the Earth. The value of 1% motion has been worked out after dividing the maximum motion by 100 and rounded for easy calculation of the Motional power. There may be a difference of 1% to 2% by adopting this rough method of rounding.

Table – 4

Planet 1	Maximum daily motion 2	1% motion (in km) 3
Sun	43 thousand	430
Mars	13.79 lakh	14000
Mercury	42.08 lakh	42000
Jupiter	24.39 lakh	25000
Venus	11.81 lakh	12000
Saturn	24.96 lakh	25000
Moon	7 thousand	70

The movement of all planets may be in both direction i.e. planet may move towards the Earth or it may also move away from the Earth. Thus the motion may be + or – respectively. We may calculate the + or – Motional power of any planet by dividing the motion on that day by the figure of 1% motion. Distance of every planet from the Earth at an interval of five days is provided in column 2 of the tables contained in appendix-2. We may calculate the daily motion of a planet by dividing the difference of these distances by five. For the convenience of the readers, column 6 of the table contains the motion of the planet at an interval of five days. This motion may be divided by the number of 1% motion provided in column 3 of the above table to ascertain + or – Motional power of that planet. Calculation of the Motional power of Jupiter is given in the following examples :–

Example 1

Distance of the Jupiter from the Earth as on
11-1-2004 = 7224 lakh km

Distance of the Jupiter from the Earth as on
16-1-2004 = 7125 lakh km

Difference of both distances
= 7224 – 7125 = + 99 lakh km

Daily motion = 99 / 5 = + 19.8 lakh km
= 1980 thousand km

(It is rough estimate as distance is calculated at an interval of 5 days.)

Actual motion of Jupiter on 16-1-2004 was 1931 thousand km.

Motional power
= + 1980 / 25 = + 79% (rough estimate)

Actual Motional power of Jupiter would be 77%.

Example 2

Distance of the Jupiter from the Earth as on
5-5-2004 = 7383 lakh km

Distance of the Jupiter from the Earth as on
10-5-2004 = 7493 lakh km

Difference of both distances
= 7383 – 7493 = – 110 lakh km

Daily motion = – 110 / 5 = – 22 lakh km
= – 2200 thousand km

(It is rough estimate as distance is calculated at an interval of 5 days.)

Actual motion of Jupiter on 10-5-2004 was – 2220 thousand km.

The difference is only due to different mode of calculation, which is based on daily position and the position at an interval of five days. But the difference was not substantial as we are calculating the per cent of Motional power.

Motional power = – 2200 / 25 = – 88%.

By following the procedure adopted in the above example, you may easily calculate the Motional power of any planet. You may observe after calculating the Motional power with both systems that there is no substantial difference in the percentage of the Motional power. Scientist Doppler proved that whenever any heavenly body move towards another body then there is a shift of light towards the band of violet colour in the spectrum which resulted in increase in the power of the band which is on the violet side. Contrary to this, whenever any heavenly body moves away with reference to another body then there is a shift of light towards the band of red colour in the spectrum which resulted in increase in the power of the band which is on the red side. The shift in the colour spectrum is directly proportionate to the motion of the planet. If we reconsider this situation in accordance with the concept of sages in Primitive age and classify the shift of light towards the band of red colour as a malefic impact and shift towards the band of violet colour as a benefic impact, then it may be clear that whenever any planet is moving towards the Earth then according to Doppler's theory there is a shift towards violet band and according to concept of sages there will be a benefic impact of the planet. In contrary to this whenever any planet is moving away from the Earth then according to Doppler's theory there is a shift towards red band and according to concept of sages there will be malefic impact of the planet.

In this way it may be quite clear that whenever any planet is moving towards the Earth then its Motional power would be + and its impact would be positive and favourable. Contrary to this whenever any planet is moving away from the Earth then its Motional power would be – and its impact would be negative and unfavourable. On the same analogy when two planets move nearer to each other then they exaggerate their mutual power and at the time of moving away from each other they dilute their mutual power. But neither sages nor astrologers have ever studied this aspect of mutual planetary behaviour in predictive astrology.

In the manner explained above we may calculate the planetary *Shadbal* in the form of Positional power, Transitional power, Rising power, Exalted power, Distant power and Motional power. Exalted power is most important among all and thereafter we may arrange other powers in the order of Positional power, Transitional power, Rising power and Distant power. The impact of above powers may then be classified as favourable on the basis of per cent of + Motional power and unfavourable on the basis of per cent of – Motional power. For calculating the power of all planets, necessary details may be seen in appendix-2.

Formula of *Shadbal*

You can easily and correctly assess the comprehensive favourable or unfavourable potential of all type of impacts of a planet from this formula of *Shadbal*. All powers in percentage have been shown by their first letter in the formula. Like Positional power by P, Transitional power by T, Rising power by R, Exalted power by E, Distant power by D and Motional power by M. If Rising power or Motional power is zero then this may be taken as one.

$$H = \{ (P + T) \div 2 \}$$

$$C = \{ (E + D) \div 2 \} \times R \div 100$$

$$\text{Shadbal} = (H \times C \times M) \div 10000$$

Average of, Positional power as worked out on the basis of effect of a planet at the point of effective periodicity of a House of the horoscope and Transitional power as worked out on the basis of transit of a planet is termed as H in this formula. Likewise celestial power C of the planet is worked out on the basis of average of Exalted power based on the altitude and Distant power multiplied by Rising power. Rising power of a planet would be 100%, when planet is at zenith and after dividing it by 100, we will get one. In that situation average of Exalted and Distant power would be effective. After multiplying

H, C and + or – of Motional power and dividing it by 10000, we may get comprehensive potential of planetary *Shadbal* in per cent. This would be favourable or unfavourable according to + or – Motional power respectively. Favourable and unfavourable timings may be worked out more appropriately if we also consider the + or – Motional power of a planet at the time of birth. In this way we must take appropriate judicious decision after assessing the impact of planets, so that maximum celestial benefit may be obtained from their impact.

Calculation of *Shadbal*

Four powers are calculated from the birth horoscope, whereas Positional power and Transitional power may be taken as 100%, hence there is no need to calculate them for working out the *Shadbal* of planets at the time of birth. Essential data for calculating four powers of the horoscope shown in appendix-1 is provided in table-5. It is not essential to get precise data for working out the powers, because it is being calculated in percentage, hence data and calculation have been rounded.

Table – 5

Planet	Deg.	Southern altitude	Distance in lakh km Birthday	Distance in lakh km Next day	Eleva. East
Ascen.	265	—	—	—	—
Sun	205	51.3	1480.86	1480.52	60
Mars	135	72.2	2527.78	2514.94	130
Mercury	199	55.6	2090.69	2102.70	66
Jupiter	273	46.8	8044.95	8066.33	–8
Venus	252	37.2	1106.96	1095.70	13
Saturn	144	69.5	14654.54	14632.78	121
Moon	86	89.4	3.89	3.85	179

Rising power

We have to ascertain the elevation of a planet for calculating Rising power. If a planet is elevated by 90°, it means that Rising power is maximum and it is placed in 10th house. If a planet is elevated between 90° and 180°, it means that Rising power is decreasing after attaining its maximum power and planet is placed between 7th and 10th house in birth horoscope. If a planet is elevated by more than 180° than it means that planet is set. The position may be clarified from picture-46. Degree-sign of ascendant is rising from the east at the time of birth hence after deducting the degree-sign of the planet from the ascendant we get degree of elevation for calculating Rising power. Thereafter there are following three situations.

First situation: If degree of elevation is up to 90° than simply add 10% of this degree to get Rising power.

After deducting 205° (25° of Libra sign) of Sun from 265° (25° of Sagittarius sign) of ascendant, we get 60. After adding 10% of this 60 i.e. 6, we get 66% Rising power of the Sun. In the same way Rising power of Mercury is 73% (265 – 199 = 66 + 6.6 = 73) and Rising power of Venus may be 14% (265 – 252 = 13 + 1.3 = 14).

Explanation: If Aries sign is in between tenth house and ascendant then above procedure may be followed after adding 360° in ascendant. For example, if ascendant is 45° (15° of Taurus sign) and Sun is placed in eleventh house with 340° (10° of Pisces sign) then deduct 340 after adding 360 in ascendant. Thus Rising power of the Sun will be 72% (45 + 360 – 340 = 65 + 6.5 = 72).

Second situation: If degree of elevation is in between 90° and 180° then deduct more than 90° from 90° and add 10% to get Rising power.

After deducting 135° of Mars from 265° of ascendant, we get 130, which is in between 90° and 180°. After deducting more than 90° i.e. 40° from 90° we get 50°, because planet is moving towards west after attaining its maximum power.

265 – 135 = 130

i.e. 40° more than 90° (130 – 90 = 40)

Deduct this 40 from 90 and we get 50.

90 – 40 = 50

After adding 10% of this 50 i.e. 5, we get 55% Rising power of the Mars. In the same way Rising power of the Saturn and Moon will be 65% and 1% respectively.

Ascendant – Saturn = Elevation from east
265 – 144 = 121
121 – 90 = 31
90 – 31 = 59
59 + 5.9 = 65% Rising power

Ascendant – Moon = Elevation from east
265 – 86 = 179
179 – 90 = 89
90 – 89 = 1
1 + .1 = 1% Rising power

Explanation: If Aries sign is in between 7th house and ascendant then above procedure may be followed after adding 360° in ascendant. For example, if ascendant is 45° (15° of Taurus sign) and Sun is placed in 9th house with 280° (10° of Capricorn sign) then deduct 280 after adding 360 in ascendant. Thus Rising power of the Sun will be 50% (45 + 360 – 280 = 125 – 90 = 45 and 90 – 45 = 45 + 4.5 = 50).

Third situation: If degree of elevation is more than 180° then planet is set, because difference between planet and ascendant is more than 180°, hence Rising power will be zero.

After deducting 273° of Jupiter from 265° of ascendant we get –8. Minus figure indicates that planet is set and it is not in the sky. Thus Rising power of the Jupiter will be zero.

Exalted power

Every planet daily rises in the east like Sun and set in the west. But when Rising power is maximum i.e. when planet is at meridian at that time angle of elevation from the southern horizon may not be 90° i.e. perpendicular. It is also not essential that every planet may be visible in the sky at the time of birth. But angle of elevation of a planet from southern direction at the time of crossing of meridian line of same latitude as of birth place (26° latitude in the example) i.e. with same latitude and which may be any other place on Earth, is exalted angle of that planet. Hence Exalted power may be worked out after adding 10% of exalted angle in it. Exalted power is shown in table-6, after adding 10% of the angle as shown in table-5.

Distant power

Deduct distance of the planet at the time of birth from maximum distance of the planet and thereafter divide it by 1% (detail given in Distant power of planets) to get Distant power of the planet.

Formula of Distant power of planet =

(Maxi. distance of planet – distance on birthday)/1%

Planet	Maximum	–	Birthday	=	Balance /1%	=	Power
Sun	1527	–	1481	=	46 / 0.62	=	74
Mars	3997	–	2528	=	1469 / 34.39	=	42
Mercury	2216	–	2091	=	125 / 14.26	=	9
Jupiter	9643	–	8045	=	1598 / 37.34	=	43
Venus	2623	–	1107	=	1516 / 22.5	=	67
Saturn	16970	–	14655	=	2315 / 58.16	=	40
Moon	4.07	–	3.89	=	18000 / 500	=	36

Motional power

Motion of a planet may be calculated on the basis of the distance of the planet at the time of birth and at next day.

Deduct motion of the planet from maximum motion of the planet and thereafter divide it by 1% (detail given in Motional power of planets) to get motional power of the planet.

Formula of Motional power of the planet =

(Distance on birth day – Distance on next day at the same time) / 1%

Planet	(Birth day	–	Next day)	/	1%	=	Mo. power
Sun	(1480.86	–	1480.52)	/	0.0043	=	80
Mars	(2527.78	–	2514.94)	/	0.14	=	92
Mercury	(2090.69	–	2102.70)	/	0.42	=	–29
Jupiter	(8044.95	–	8066.33)	/	0.25	=	–86
Venus	(1106.96	–	1095.70)	/	0.12	=	94
Saturn	(14654.54	–	14632.78)	/	0.25	=	87
Moon	(3.89	–	3.85)	/	0.0007	=	67

Four powers of horoscope are consolidated in table-6, for calculating *Shadbal* of a planet as per following formula :–

$$H = \{(P + T) \div 2\}$$

$$C = \{(E + D) \div 2\} \times R \div 100$$

$$Shadbal = (H \times C \times M) \div 10000$$

Present power of a horoscope is calculated after including Positional power and Transitional power. These two powers may be taken as 100 at the time of birth. Thus value of H in the above formula will be 100. Result of other calculation is shown in table-6.

Table – 6

Power of planet

Planet	Rising	Exalted	Distant	Motional	C	Shadbal
Sun	66	56	74	80	43	34
Mars	55	79	42	92	33	30
Mercury	73	61	9	–29	26	–8
Jupiter	0	51	43	–86	0.5	–0.4
Venus	14	41	67	94	8	8
Saturn	65	76	40	87	37	32
Moon	1	98	36	67	0.7	0.4

Consolidated effect of a planet at the time of birth may be assessed from table-6. Above four powers may be seen graphically in picture-50 for clearly understanding the concept of *Shadbal.* Twelve houses of 30° each are arranged in a row. Vertical big line at left-hand side indicates the position of ascendant (265° i.e. 15° of Sagittarius sign). Position of planets applicable for all graphs is shown in top line. Jupiter was not in the visible in the sky at the time of birth, resulting in 0% Rising power hence its effect is not visible in the graph of Rising power. Motional power of the Mercury and Jupiter were negative hence their effect in the graph of Motional power is shown by dotted line. Position of house and sign is given at bottom of the picture. Power of planets during their transit may also be scientifically worked out as explained and effect of both powers may be assessed.

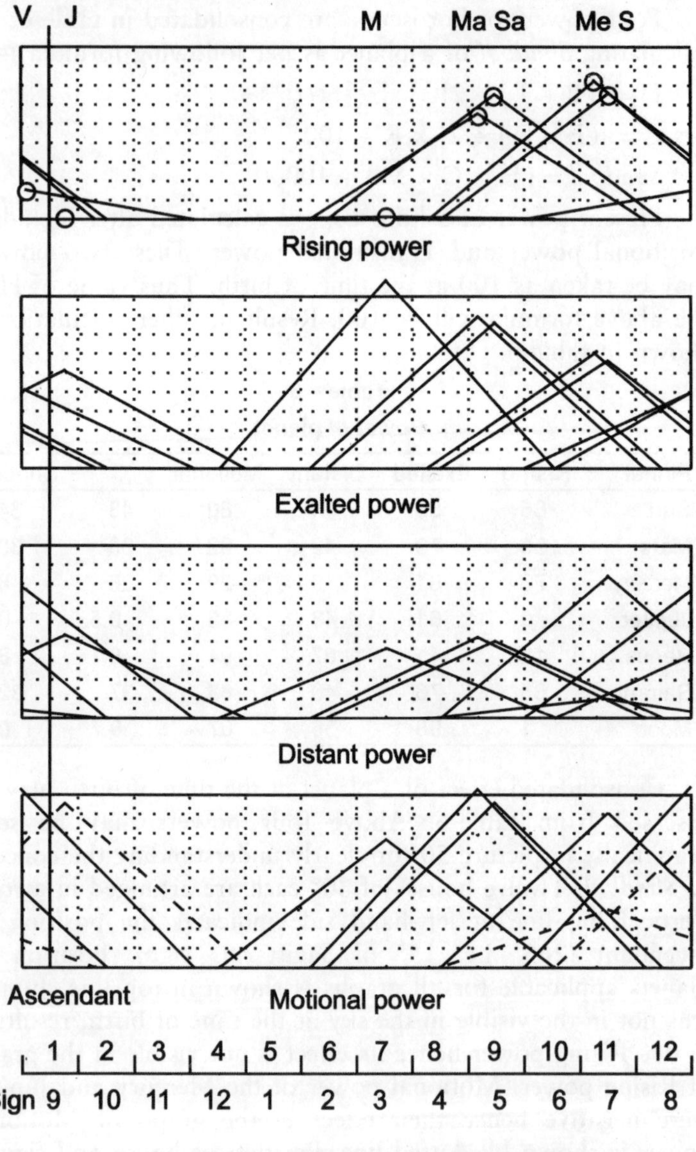

S = Sun, M = Moon, Ma = Mars, Me = Mercury,
J = Jupiter, V = Venus, Sa = Saturn

Picture – 50
Shadbal of planets

26

SUMMARY

From the description given so far, you may easily calculate the periodicity of effective House and impact of a planet. Because the impact of a House and planet is calculated in per cent hence there is no need for any cumbersome and minute calculations. I am again highlighting the important points.

1. Decide periodicity of a House according to your age.
2. Impact of that House would be more significant, when sign of this House is nearabout to meridian line.
3. When the elevation of the planet placed in a House and activator planets of the effective House, is maximum from southern horizon then they may exert their maximum effect due to Exalted power.
4. Any planet that is transiting nearby a House may be effective.
5. Exalted position of the planet will also be effective according to Rising power and will be more effective at the time of crossing meridian line.
6. During retrograde motion of a planet, when it is actually nearer to the Earth, it may be more effective due to higher per cent of Distant power.
7. If the planet is moving towards the Earth with an increased motion then it may be more effective due to higher per cent of Motional power.

8. Whenever you desire to take benefit of a House or planet then keep in mind about the timing when the House, planet placed in the House and the activator of the House may be nearest to the meridian line and plan your work accordingly to get maximum heavenly support from the planet and House.

Some readers may have problem as to how maximum favourable benefit of the power of planets may be obtained, if date of birth and time is not known. In this situation procedure mentioned at s.no. 1, 5, 6, 7 may be followed for sorting out this problem and day-to-day activity may be managed according to the transitory position of the planets. Thus favourable benefit of transitory planets may at least be obtained in the absence of basic information relating to planetary position in the horoscope. Those readers who have their horoscope may also follow this procedure for taking maximum favourable benefit of transitory planets.

We are generally taking help of many symbolic articles like Gem etc. for moulding the impact of planets or pleasing them for fulfilling our desire. Publicity of all type of symbolic articles are being carried out only for promoting the business, whereas, the concerning planet itself is moving daily in front of us. But due to our ignorance, neither we are paying any interest towards the planet nor we are being guided in this regard by the astrologers in view of their business interest and instead of this we are expending hefty amount in acquiring the symbolic representative of that planet. We have completely forgotten sky watching as described in the history, hence unable to locate and identify any planet. In this way, we have not only forgotten most effective planet itself but indulging ourselves in moulding their effect with the help of some useless symbolic articles due to blind faith, which has been unknowingly infused in our sub-conscious mind in childhood and this blind faith always block our judicious and logical decision.

As we keep our body fit, healthy and in good shape by exposing our body to the rays emerging from the Sun in sunlight or by doing *Surya Namaskar*. In the same way, if we bow before the planet and daily stare the concerning planet for some time, then we may immediately and effectively pass on the cosmic impact due to + Motional power, Distant power, Exalted power and Rising power in our body through our retina, where blood vessels are almost exposed and can increase the favourable impact of the planet. As it would not be prudential to perform *Surya Namaskar* in the night. Similarly, if we have a faith and want to mould the impact of the planet in our favour by some sort of donation or worship etc. (as for Saturn) then this performance will only be effective when the concerning planet is in exalted position i.e. nearabout to meridian line. If we expand this aspect then we must resolve our decision of marriage etc. at the time, when the activator of the matrimonial life i.e. Venus is moving nearabout to meridian line or in noon, because Venus always remain in the vicinity of the Sun and if the marriage ceremony is also performed in noon, under the direct impact of Venus, as was the tradition in Primitive age then it will definitely be best in comparison to perform marriage ceremony in the night when Venus, activator of matrimonial life is actually set.

As we always try to sail in the direction of the flow of the river to get the maximum mileage and not the other way round. In the same way we must also plan our action and try to synchronise it according to the movement of the planets to get the maximum heavenly support from them and not other way round by foolishly trying to bend the immense force of planets with the help of some symbolic articles according to your sweet will. Because neither they are deities nor demons nor they have any sort of man made feelings at all, as believed in the Primitive age and as has been fed in our mind. So try to come out from this suffocative and outdated behaviour and breath in fresh air with scientific approach towards these planets. Because Planets do have some qualities, but this is only due to the matter they contain and their location in the solar system.

Instead of ascertaining the destiny with the help of astrology try to get the benefit from this knowledge, because if the destiny is fixed only then it can be ascertained. But we will not be able to get any thing even after knowing some forecast about our destiny, if we are not performing our sincere and hard action according to our desire. Thus we cannot get anything from our destiny without adding our action to it. Because action is in our hand and we can also change our action according to our decision, thus there is a variation in our act, which blend with the then action of others and in turn the resultant outcome of destiny in the shape of an event is also varied. In this way, it is pertinent to do judiciously right action at right time for carving out our future accordingly, because prudent action is only and most important in our entire life.

Above fact may easily be understood with the help of a simple example. Suppose we have a tumbler containing cold water and we place it on a burner. After some time it will boil. This time will vary according to the effect of some other factors, as to whether water is dripping in/leaking from the tumbler, room temperature, circulation of air, external pressure on the water, initial temperature and quantity of water etc. Despite presence of these factors, we can calculate time required for raising the temperature to a fixed point. In the same way, we human beings, initially made up of matter, gets effected by all external factors i.e. cosmic rays, impact of planets, stars etc., which may be calculated as six powers (*Shadbal*) and synchronised with the periodicities of the Houses (as contained in Part 3). Can we calculate the time required for raising the temperature of water contained in the tumbler, if tumbler has some 'mind' and may jump from the burner according to his 'decision'? Definitely, in this situation it is not possible to calculate the time required for any pre-decided target of temperature. In the same way, though effect of planets etc. may be calculated yet we human beings have mind, thought, experience etc. and able to take judicious or foolish decision for doing some act in a particular situation, which after blending with surrounding situations and happenings, ultimately turns into an incident and course of our life may be decided accordingly.

There was a practice in the Primitive age to teach any complicated matter with the help of some symbolic incident.

Sages also tried to infuse the philosophy of life and the importance of prudent and judicious action with the help of a symbolic incident of *samudra-manthan* that when, we try to solve a problem like *Sumeru parvat* by clutching it with the help of rope of our experience and knowledge like *Shesh-nag*, which has a mouth of negative thought and tail of tolerance, over the fixed mental status like turtle and churn or deeply think over the unknown possibilities and conditions like the ocean then first of all sound represented by conch-shell comes out and we may be able to communicate our particular views among many possible answers in a particular situation. After further churning the possibilities, impressive and defeating thought represented by *Gada* and *Chakra* etc. respectively in the form of power comes out and thought of controlling the situation in our favour may emerge and we may act accordingly. After further churning with the help of our thought, we may be able to get the know-how to earn wealth, which was represented by *Lakshmi*. From this thinking (churning of thoughts) we may also get the destructive thoughts, which was represented by poison and which can only be contained by gentle and brave persons like Shiva, who has grown up wisdom represented by symbolic third eye. Because execution of such destructive thoughts may not only destroy others but may also destroy themselves. After extreme deep thinking we may be able to get in last the ultimate prudence and judicious conclusion represented by nectar, which is not only desired by gentleman but equally desired by crooked persons also, represented by deities and demons respectively. Because one, who performs his action with prudence may only achieve his target and may be immortal. With the narration that some drops of this nectar or ultimate wisdom fallen at Nasik, Ujjain, Haridwar and Allahabad, our sages only wants to convey that monasteries situated at these places were actually the origin of prudence and they could direct the society and could get immortality.

If we review the four parts of the horoscope then it can easily be understood that second part of life up to the age of 21 years is actually dependent on the knowledge acquired till the age of 6 years in the first part of life. Likewise third part of the life up to the age of 45 years is actually dependent on the knowledge and wisdom, which was acquired till second part of the life. Thus immortality may only be achieved with the deeds performed with prudence and judicious wisdom in the third and fourth part of the effective visual life.

The practice of formulating the astrological principles after continuous monitoring of the sky was discontinued by the end of Primitive age. But the astrological principles framed in that age are still alive only on the shoulders of faith. Though we may come forward to abolish these outdated principles in the light of modern knowledge yet the inquisitiveness behind the main idea to identify the impact of the planet on human being, which was once generated by our sages, cannot be extinguished and the procedure to ascertain the impact of heavenly bodies is also improving day-by-day in last 2500 years and very rapidly in recent years. Present form of astrology was only based on some wrong idea about the Universe and a concept that planets are living-being with some element and on the basis of some imaginary relationship between the planets. There was no any scientific support for these principles. After passing of sufficient time we have not only lost the track of basic idea behind the astrology and despite having sufficient astronomical information about our Solar system (refer picture-2) and Universe (refer picture-23), which is completely against our primitive concept (refer picture-1), we are determined and forcefully trying our best to support these principles based on outdated knowledge and concept, by this way or that way by exploiting the soft feeling and faith of the society on astrology due to ignorance, either with an idea to get cheap popularity or with an idea that the knowledge of our sages was complete and best.

But the time has come, when we must have to face the ground realities and must understand that the knowledge of astrology which was once based on some primitive concept can only and only be improved logically in the right direction for the constructive and practical help of the human being by following the scientific principles and by absorbing modern knowledge about these planets, Solar system and Universe and not merely by publishing the latest scientific photographs in the astrological books and deceiving propaganda through media and by internally following the same primitive concept to misguide the innocent lot either on the name of mismatching of horoscopes due to *Mangal dosh*, less *Gun* matching, *Saade-saati*, *Kaal-sarp yog*, periodicity of *markesh* etc. It is only a main and fundamental difference between faith and science that we tie up ourselves with faith and always try to avoid any logical or new scientific concept, which is against our belief and faith or try to anyhow link any modern knowledge with our primitive faith. Thus we are always very late in accepting the bare and hard truth thereby actually loose our confidence and falls in the trap of blind-faith. Whereas, scientific research always opens new horizon of knowledge.

It was disclosed by the Bhaskaracharya in his *Sidhant-shiromani* written in 12th century that if we drop heavy and light body simultaneously then both bodies will touch the Earth at the same time and on this basis he founded that Earth has some attraction force in it. But we have not given any cognisance to this research due to our the then baseless faith and belief and due to this apathetic attitude, later on when Newton discovered that the Earth has gravitational attraction and his discovery was recognised by the western countries then his name become immortal. Now we are trying to save our skin by mentioning that our Bhaskaracharya had already discovered this gravitational attraction long before Newton. But it is not a matter of pride, instead of this we must feel ashamed that how brutally we have sacrificed so many discoveries on the altar of our primitive faith and belief. Hence where on the one hand we must feel pride that despite paucity of correct information and technology in Primitive age our sages were able to enrich our knowledge by the concept of planetary impact and on the other hand we must realise that knowledge is always incomplete and unknown facts of the Universe is limitless. Thus we must always try to enrich our knowledge on the basis of latest information and we must not bind ourselves with the primitive astrological knowledge by classifying it as a matter of faith or covering up its hollowness with latest scientific photographs. Instead of this we must try to understand the basic idea behind it and not only try to improve it from the grass-root level by giving new dimension to this knowledge with the help of modern science but also try to use it for the constructive benefit of the society.

When we are not able to know the correct traces of our destiny with the help of present astrological principles due to gross mistake at the time of initial formulation in the Primitive age due to wrong concept of the Universe, principles based on myths, mistake about the planetary position and *ayanansh* then it will be more prudent, logical and scientific to ascertain the favourable time to enable us to realign our planning on the basis of explanation contained in third part of the book by taking benefit of modern science. Accordingly, instead of knowing the future with the help of primitive erroneous astrological principles, we must take the benefit of the impact of the planets for carving out our future by the proper use of this knowledge and we must understand that future is not a bunch of fixed incident which can be disclosed but it has immense possibilities which can be moulded according to our wishes by proper, sincere and judicious actions.

It is not the end but it is starting point of endless journey from unscientific and baseless primitive astrological principles towards developing it with logical and latest scientific discoveries. If you will come forward to save others from this blind faith and infuse correct, scientific and logical concept only then our society may get rid off from primitive bridle.

In last, I will like to quote the Buddha who said over 2500 years ago "... believe nothing, merely because you have been told it or because it is traditional or because you yourself imagined it. Do not believe what your teacher tells you, merely out of respect for the teachers. But whatever, after due examination and analysis you find to be conducive to the good, the benefit, the welfare of all beings, believe that doctrine and cling to and take it as your guide...".

APPENDIX – 1

Software covering various calculations related to horoscope and prediction was developed due to self-interest in astrology and computer. But as usual it was inconvenient to take care of all relevant output of a horoscope relating to Ascendant, *Chalit*, *Navansh*, *Saptmansh*, Status and degree of planet, Full half etc. Aspect, Periodicity (*Dasha*), Number of *Ashtak-varg*, Transit of planet, Exalted, debilitated planet, *Kaarak, Maarak*, Friend-enemy, *Tazik*, various information relating to Krishnamurti system etc., while concluding a precise prediction. Because all these informations are scattered on various pages hence it was not possible to simultaneously evaluate the impact of every chart. Astrologers generally conclude any prediction on the basis of some known and practised principles irrespective of the fact as to whether it may be correct or not. But for conveniently evaluating a horoscope from all angles and also considering various charts, irrespective of the fact as to whether those principles are well versed or not; I developed three charts of Eskain horoscope with the help of computer, to enable me to conclude a prediction after evaluating various output. Every chart is prepared only on a page, hence it is extraordinarily convenient to assess appropriately placed various points based on the traditional astrological system.

Chart of power (*Shakti chakra*)

Following informations are incorporated in one page of *Shakti chakra* :–

Ascendant horoscope, *Chalit* horoscope - North Indian, *Chalit* horoscope - Krishnamurti, *Saptmansh* horoscope,

Navansh horoscope, *Tazik* horoscope, House with *sandhi* - North Indian, Span of house - Krishnamurti system (KP), Lord of house, Degree of planets, Exalted-debilitated, *Aarohi*, *Avrohi*, *Kaarak*, *Kaarak* of house, Own house, Friend's house, Even house, Enemy's house, *Mool-trikon*, Full, 3/4th, half, quarter aspect, Set, Retrograde, Status of planet, *Ashtak varg*, Current Major and Minor periodicity (*Maha dasha*, *Antar dasha*), Next Major and Minor periodicity, Order of *dasha* since birth, Constellation of the Sun and Moon with their steps, Friend, enemy, own house of *Saptmansh* and *Navansh* horoscopes, *Tri-bal* (*Sthan-bal*, *Dig-bal*, *Nesargik-bal*) of planet in per cent, Significator of house, Favourable and unfavourable aspect on the Cusp of house - KP, Favourable and unfavourable aspect on a planet - KP, Conjunction of planet - KP, Lord, Sublord, Subsublord of a house - KP, Lord, Sublord, Subsublord of a planet - KP, Interchange of planet, per cent of distance of a planet from the Earth, Motion of a planet and its direction as to whether it is moving towards the Earth or away from the Earth.

It is very easy to read and understand all above information of *Shakti chakra*. If you go through the following description along with consulting the *Shakti chakra*. Thereafter it will be quite easy to assimilate various informations.

This *chakra* also has twelve house like general horoscope and they are enclosed by a border of double lines and central house 1, 4, 7, 10 has again been enclosed by a double border. Whereas house numbers 2, 3 and 5, 6 and 8, 9 and 11, 12 are separated by single line. Every house has two extra lines at the top to clarify status of the house, followed by ten lines as ten parts.

One sign has 30° hence every sign has been subdivided in ten lines, so that every line represents 3° of that sign. Because planet move from one sign to another after moving through these 30° hence position of the planet is shown on these lines according to their degree and line will change after movement of every 3°. Movement of planet is shown from top line to bottom line in respect of 1st house to 7th house and from bottom to top line for 8th house to 12th house. Planet is shown by first letter or first three letters as { S / SUR (ya), C / CHA (ndra), M / MAN (gal), B / BUD (h), G / GUR (u), U / SUK (ra), N / SAN (i), R / RAH (u), K / KET (u) }. {U} is used for first letter of *Sukra*-Venus and {N} is used for first letter of *Sani*-Saturn. Other related information of planet or commencement of an information is shown by a specific symbol.

First line of top two lines of every house has sign of house, Lord of house in {[ ]}, eight numbers of *sarvastak varg* and name of sign respectively. Eight numbers of *sarvastak varg* indicates the number of lines drawn in the *ashtak varg* by Sun, Moon, Mars, Mercury, Jupiter, Venus, Saturn and Ascendant respectively. As first line of first house has {9[GUR]16444542DHANU}. It means that individual has 9th sign as ascendant i.e. *Dhanu*-Sagittarius, lord of ascendant is *Guru*-Jupiter and in the ascendant house of *ashtak varg* of Sun has obtained one line, Moon has obtained 6 lines in ascendant house and likewise lines obtained by other planets in ascendant in the *ashtak varg* are shown.

Second top line of a house comprises the information based on KP and significator planet for a house is shown by the first letter. Planets having favourable aspect followed after a symbol {«} of double arrow, unfavourable aspect of the planets followed after a symbol {¥} and Lord, Sublord, Subsublord are followed after a symbol of small square { ■ }. Like second line of ascendant house has {SGC«SMBN¥RC■UBK}. It means Sun, *Guru*-Jupiter, *Chandra*-Moon are significators for the first house and Sun, Mars, *Budh*-Mercury, Saturn are favourable due to favourable angle on the cusp of the ascendant whereas Rahu and *Chandra* are unfavourable due to unfavourable angle on the cusp of the ascendant. At last, lord of the cusp of ascendant *Sukra*-Venus, sublord *Budh*-Mercury and subsublord Ketu are indicated. Likewise north Indian and KP status of every house may be ascertained from the top two lines.

Sign is divided in ten lines and every line covers 3° of that house. Every line has a number in the beginning as well as at the end. Starting and ending number of the line indicates the number of house according to KP and number of *chalit* house according to north Indian system. You may see that these numbers are increasing slowly in all twelve houses and there is symbol of line {– = ≡} in between, which indicates one, two and three degree respectively. As at left-hand side of the ascendant house 12 is indicated up to eight lines, thereafter there is a symbol of {–} on 9th line. It indicates that span of 12 house is up to 8 line × 3° = 24 + 1 line of symbol = 25° i.e. span of 12th house is up to 25° of Sagittarius sign according to KP. Thereafter 1st house of ascendant is commenced i.e. ascendant is in between 25° and 26° of Sagittarius sign. Likewise span of other houses according to KP may be seen. Similarly span of a house along with joints according to north Indian system may be seen at the end of every line. Like at the end of 5th line of 2nd house a symbol of {–} is shown. It indicates that span of first house is up to 4 line × 3° = 12 + 1 line of symbol = 13° i.e. span of first house is up to 13° of Capricorn sign according to north Indian system and thereafter joint of 2nd house will commence. On the 10th line of this house there is a symbol of three lines {≡}. It indicates that span of second house is commencing from 9 line × 3° = 27 + 3 line of symbol = 30° i.e. span of second house commencing from 30° of Capricorn sign. From the 6th line of third house of Aquarius sign, it can be seen that span of second house is up to 5 × 3 = 15 + 3 = 18° i.e. span of 2nd house is up to 18° of Aquarius sign. Likewise span of other houses according to both systems may be seen.

Planets in the horoscope are indicated by three letters after symbol of lines {–, =, ≡} indicating one, two or three degree. Degree of a planet may also be ascertained by multiplying the line number by 3 and adding line of symbol. For example see the position of *SUKra*-Venus, which is at the fifth line in ascendant house. Before the name of the planet their is a symbol {–} representing 1°. Venus has crossed 4 lines and placed at 5th line. Hence degree of *Sukra*-Venus is 4 × 3 = 12 + 1 = 13° i.e. Venus is at 13° of Sagittarius sign. Similarly position of other planets may also be ascertained.

There is a number between 0 to 100 after the name of the planet, which indicates per cent of *Tri-bal* i.e. *Sthan-bal*, *Dig-bal* and *Nesargik-bal*. Number zero indicates lowest power of *Tri-bal* and 100 indicate highest power of *Tri-bal*. From this number the potential of a planet can immediately be known. Like there is number 46 after *Guru*-Jupiter in second house. It means that *Tri-bal* of *Guru*-Jupiter is 46%. After this there is a symbol {+} or {/}, which indicate that planet is moving towards the Earth or moving away from the Earth respectively. After this there is again a number from 0 to 100, which indicates percentage distance of the planet from the Earth. Here zero indicates that planet is farthest from the Earth and 100 indicates that planet is nearest from the Earth. Like there is a symbol {/} after *Guru*-Jupiter, which indicate that *Guru* is moving away from the Earth and it is 43% near to the Earth.

After this there may be symbol {<}, {£}, {Ñ}, {^}, {¿} on this line. Which indicates that planet is in Retrograde, Exalted, Debilitated, *Aarohi* or *Avrohi* position respectively. Like there is a symbol {Ñ} after *Surya*-Sun on 9th line of 11th house indicates debilitated Sun and symbol {¿} after *Chandrama*-Moon on 9th line of 7th house indicates *Avrohi* Moon.

After this there may be symbol { | }, {#}, {*} on this line. Which indicates that planet is in own house, friend's house or enemy's house respectively. Position of the planets is indicated on *Panchadha* friendship system. Like *Guru* of second house is in enemy's house and *Mangal* in ninth house is in friend's house.

Symbol of {■} on the line of planet indicates that planet is *Kaarak*. Like this sign in sixth line from bottom in ninth house indicates that *Mangal*-Mars is *Kaarak*. Symbol of { | } indicates that planet is *Swa-bhav Kaarak*. Like this sign in second line of second house indicates that *Guru*-Jupiter is *Swa-bhav Kaarak*. Symbol of {Γ} and {Σ} indicates *Mool-trikon* and *Maarak* character of a planet respectively. Like symbol of {Σ} after *Sani* at ninth line in ninth house indicates that *Sani*-Saturn is *Maarak*.

After these symbols, planet is shown by one letter in the line. This letter indicates that planet indicated by first letter has a supportive and favourable aspect on the planet placed on the line and indicated by first three letters. Like {SC} indicated on the line of planet *Budh*-Mercury, in seventh line from the bottom of the eleventh house, indicates that Sun and Moon has supportive aspect on *Budh*-Mercury. First letter of planet is again indicated after a symbol {¥} on this line. This indicates that planet indicated by first letter has an unfavourable aspect on the planet placed on the line and indicated by first three letters. Like {¥R} indicated on the line of *Budh*-Mercury in eleventh house indicates that Rahu has an unfavourable aspect on Mercury.

After this last symbol as small square is { ▪ } on this line. After which first letter of three planets is indicated.. This indicates that planets represented by first letter are Lord, Sublord and Subsublord of the main planet according to KP. Like {KBC} indicated on the line of *Sukra*-Venus means that Lord of Venus is Ketu, Sublord of Venus is Mercury and Subsublord of Venus is Moon.

There is a symbol {∞} like eye, on some other lines out of ten lines of a sign, after which a number 1, 2, 3 or 4 is shown followed by first letter of a planet. It means that there is 1/4, 1/2, 3/4 or full aspect respectively of concerning planet on that part of the sign. After first letter of the concerning planet their is a symbol of {/} or {+}, which indicates as per earlier description that planet is moving away from the Earth or moving towards the Earth. After this *Tri-bal* of that planet has been reduced in the ratio of his aspect. Like after symbol of {∞} in ninth line of ascendant house {1S12+78,2N22+43,4C59+41} is inscribed. It is evident from this that on the last part of the Sagittarius sign of ascendant Sun has quarter, Saturn has half and Moon has full aspect. Accordingly the *Tri-bal* of Sun and Saturn have also been reduced to quarter and half respectively. From this it is also evident that all these planet are not aspecting *Sukra*-Venus. Which is though in the same sign but away by four lines i.e. 12°. Planet situated in friend's house is shown by capital letter and planet situated in enemy's house is shown by small letter.

Sign and planet in *Navansh* and *Saptmansh* horoscope in the same house is indicated on the vacant lines out of ten lines of a house. Symbol {7} and {9} in between the sign and planet indicates *Saptmansh* and *Navansh* horoscope respectively. Like {KUM 9 GUR*} and {SIN 7 KET#} as indicated in the fourth house indicates that fourth house of *Navansh* horoscope has *Guru*-Jupiter in enemy's house KUMbh-Aquarius sign and *Saptmansh* horoscope has Ketu in friend's house SINgh-Leo sign. After the planet there is symbol of {£, Ñ, ❙, #, *} which means Exalted, Debilitated, Own house, Friend's house and Enemy's house respectively as described earlier. Likewise other related information of *Navansh* and *Saptmansh* horoscope may be ascertained.

If relevant information of a planet is not covered within a line then it is shifted to other forward or backward line after a symbol of {½} or {¼} respectively. Like remaining information of ninth line of ascendant house has been shifted to tenth line after a symbol of {½}.

If two planets are on the same line or on nearby lines then there would be conjunction due to minimum difference between their degree. Likewise if a planet is situated within two lines from the line of the Sun then it may be treated as set. Because a sign has been divided in ten lines hence every two lines cover 6°. Thus status of a planet may be ascertained by treating consecutive two lines as *Bal*, *Kumar*, *Yuva*, *Bradh* and *Mrat* respectively. Likewise *Jagrat* and *Supt* position of planet may be ascertained.

Current and following *maha dasha* and *antar dasha* of a planet by three letters along with ending month and year is incorporated in the upper and lower space respectively between fourth and tenth house. Like {1 2005} and {SUKSUK} is indicated in the upper space and it indicates that *antar dasha* of *Sukra* would be effective under *maha dasha* of *Sukra* till January-2005.

Name, date of birth, time is shown in the upper part of the ascendant house. Likewise constellation and step of Sun and Moon is shown in the bottom part of 7th house. Thereafter, first letter of six planets, whose *maha dasha* would be serially effective after birth is shown. Those planets, who have interchanges their position are shown by their first letter on the outer side of the top and bottom corner of the outer border. Like on the outer corner {SNGU} is indicated, it means that Sun, Saturn, Jupiter and Venus have interchanges their position.

Effective date of commencement of *varsh kundali* is shown on the top line of the right-hand side. Like date {11/11/2002} is shown on top line. Whereas planetary position with sign in *varsh kundali* (*Tazik* horoscope), which is effective on the date of preparation of this *Shakti chakra* is also inscribed on the outer side of the border of the horoscope. Every line of this horoscope also represents 3° of a sign and planet is also placed on the corresponding line according to their degree. Planet is shown by first letter. Planet placed in 2nd house to 6th house is shown from top to bottom on left-hand side and planet placed in 8th house to 12th house is shown from bottom to top on right-hand side. Planet placed in ascendant and 7th house is shown from right-hand side to left-hand side and from left-hand side to right-hand side in the blocks created on top and bottom of the *chakra* respectively. Sign of the house is also indicated on the outer part of the main horoscope. Like {6} inscribed on the outer part of 2nd house denotes that 2nd house has *Kanya*-Virgo sign and thus ascendant of *tazik* horoscope is *Singh*-Leo sign. *Muntha* of the horoscope is shown by symbol {*} and it is also placed on the corresponding line according to its degree like other planets.

Description of all sort of symbol is also shown at top and bottom of the *chakra* in three lines for convenience.

Chart of transit (*Chal chakra*)

After preparing *Shakti chakra* of the horoscope, it is also essential to ascertain the position of the planet in transit for concluding any prediction. For this it is essential to correlate the transitory position of the planet with the *Ashtak varg*,

Dasha of the birth horoscope, *Mudda dasha* of *tazik* horoscope etc. It is very convenient from one page of the *Chal chakra* to ascertain various positions after a fixed interval.

Chal chakra comprises of birth horoscope, day-to-day changing position of the planets in various signs, number of lines of *Sarvastak varg* and their impact, *Tazik* horoscope, day-to-day *Vinshottary maha dasha, antar dasha, pratyantar dasha, sukshm dasha* beside *maha dasha* and *antar dasha* of *Mudda dasha*, day-to-day exalted, debilitated, own house, friend's house, enemy's house, retrograde, direct, *maarak* position of the planets, daily, monthly and yearly horoscope with *muntha*, 7½ and 2½ years of Saturn, per cent of distance of planet from the Earth, Significator planets of various houses as per KP etc.

Chal chakra is divided in 14 columns. Except first and last column, other twelve columns are created according to twelve signs of the horoscope. First column, out of these twelve columns relates to ascendant of birth horoscope, 2nd column to 2nd house and likewise 12th column relates to 12th house. Planets are indicated by the first letter of the planet as has been described in *Shakti chakra*.

Significator planets according to KP are shown on the first line of the *Chal chakra* at the top of the corresponding house. Like {SGC} shown in the first line of the first house indicates that *Surya*-Sun, *Guru*-Jupiter, *Chandrama*-Moon are significators for the first house. Likewise significators of other houses may be ascertained. Third line from the top indicates name of all signs. Every house is again subdivided in eight columns and each column can hold one letter. Thus every column represent the position of 3° 45' of that sign. In this way it matches with *ashtak varg*. Top second line indicates planetary position according to their degree in the birth horoscope. Thus first letter of the planet is shown on the correct position out of eight columns according to its degree. Fourth line indicates the correct planetary position according to their degree in *tazik* horoscope and its date. Position of ascendant and *muntha* is also shown according to their degree at the correct position by a symbol {@} and {*} respectively. Like symbol of ascendant and *muntha* is indicated in ninth and sixth column related to Leo and Taurus sign respectively. Number of lines given by a planet in various houses in the *ashtak varg* is shown in fifth line and order of planets for these lines is also given in the last column as {NGMSUBCL}, which indicates that the order of planets for number of *ashtak varg* is *Sani*, *Guru*, *Mangal*, *Surya*, *Sukra*, *Budh*, *Chandra* and *Lagn* (ascendant) respectively. Order of the planet in this way is kept due to the fact that result of the planet is given in the same order during transit. For example, {44415462} is mentioned in the fifth line of the column of the ascendant. It indicates that ascendant has four line from the *ashtak varg* of the Saturn, four lines from Jupiter and one line from Sun etc. In this way lines of other planets may be ascertained. Underlining the number of the *ashtak varg* in the concerning sign indicates the position of the constellation of the *Maarak* planet. Like such position of the constellation is indicated in the fourth house.

Order of *maha dasha* of all planets since birth is given in the first column of sixth line. Like {GNBKUSCMR} mentioned in the sixth line indicates that *maha dasha* of *Guru* was effective at the time of birth. After this *maha dasha* of *Sani*, *Budh*, Ketu etc. would be effective. Likewise order of *Mudda dasha* of *Tazik* horoscope is also mentioned in the last column of this line. Date and first letter of four planets followed by first letter of two planets is mentioned on the seventh line of the first column. It indicates that *maha dasha* of the planet of first letter, *antar dasha* of the planet of second letter, *pratyantar dasha* of the planet of third letter and *sukshmdasha* of the planet of fourth letter, thereafter *mudda maha dasha* of the planet of first letter and *mudda antar dasha* of the planet of second letter was effective on the date mentioned before this. Like {03/08 uUgb uB} mentioned on the seventh line indicates that *mahadasha* of *Sukra*, *antar dasha* of *Sukra*, *pratyantar dasha* of *Guru* and *sukshm dasha* of *Budh* along with *mudda maha dasha* of *Sukra* and *mudda antar dasha* of *Budh* was effective on 3/8/2003. *Dasha* is effective according to the degree of the planet in a sign. If planet is in the beginning of a sign then *dasha* would be effective in the initial part, if planet is in the middle of the sign then *dasha* would be effective in the middle part and if the planet is in the last portion of a sign then *dasha* would be effective in the last part. On the basis of this principle, first letter of the planet is mentioned in capital, if *dasha* is actually effective and first letter of the planet is mentioned in small letter, if *dasha* of that planet is ineffective. Like *maha dasha* of *Sukra* shown by small {u} is not effective but the *antar dasha* of *Sukra* shown by capital {U} is effective. Likewise if *dasha* of second planet is actually effective during periodicity (*dasha*) of first planet then this first planet is bolded and underlined. First letter of those planet, whose *dasha* is effective even before commencement or after the end of actual *dasha*, is respectively mentioned in the last column of second and third line, before or after the symbol of {<>}. Like {G<>SC} mentioned in the 2nd line indicates that periodicity of *Guru*-Jupiter would be effective well before commencement of its actual *dasha* and *dasha* of *Surya*-Sun and *Chandra*-Moon would remain effective even after end of actual *dasha*.

Dated position of the planets in various signs is shown under twelve columns according to their transit in a sign as mentioned in the third line. Position of the planet is shown by the first letter of the planet and it is placed in eight minor columns according to their degree. Planet is considered to be favourable whenever it move over a line drawn in *ashtak-varg*, hence this position is shown by capital letter of the planet and whenever it is not in a favourable condition then it is shown by small letter of the planet. Thus favourable and unfavourable position of the planet may easily be ascertained. The first letter of the planet is underlined, whenever it is moving towards the Earth and bolded letter shows retrograde planet. If two or more planet is moving within 3° 45' of a sign then first letter of second planet is shifted on vacant position under the same sign.

For preparing daily, monthly and yearly *tazik* horoscopes, daily position of the ascendant and *muntha* is shown by symbols {@} and {*} respectively in relevant columns of the sign. Hence these horoscopes may be prepared by placing the planets in the concerning signs, on the basis of sign mentioned at the top of the concerning columns. Dates for monthly and yearly horoscope are shown by a symbol of {▌} and {¥} respectively in the demarcation line of the first column. Like it is shown against the date of {12/8}.

The transitory positions of those planets, whose *maha dasha, antar dasha, pratyantar dasha* and *sukshm dasha* are effective, are also important. Hence position of these four planets is assessed by four different methods as mentioned below :–

Transitory position of these planets from the sign of :–

1. Moon of birth horoscope.
2. Ascendant of birth horoscope.
3. Respective planet of birth horoscope.
4. Transitory Moon.

The above order of four ways of analysis is also shown at sixth line from the top as {RASHI LAGN GRAH CHANDRA}. Like four numbers {2,2,3,3} as mentioned under Sagittarius sign at seventh line. It has nothing to do with this sign but vacant space is only being used. These numbers indicate that on the date, as mentioned in the first column, the transitory position of four planets whose *maha dasha, antar dasha, pratyantar dasha* and *sukshm dasha* are active i.e. sUkra, sUkra, Guru, Budh; is 2nd, 2nd, 3rd and 3rd from the sign of Moon (*rashi*) in birth horoscope. Likewise four numbers are again mentioned in the next column. It indicates that the transitory positions of four planets are 8th, 8th, 9th and 9th from the sign of ascendant (*lagn*) in birth horoscope. Again four numbers are shown in the vacant space. It indicates that the transitory positions of four planets are 8th, 8th, 8th and 11th from the sign of these respective planets in birth horoscope. Again four numbers are shown in the vacant space. It indicates that the transitory positions of four planets are 11th, 11th, 12th and 12th from the sign of transitory Moon on date. If a transitory position is not favourable with reference to the sign of Moon or ascendant of the birth horoscope then it is indicated by underlining that number.

Position of daily *muntha* from daily ascendant and effective *pratyantar dasha* or *sukshm dasha* of *Maarak* planet, is shown at the end of first line, in the last column of the chart by a number and symbol {▤} respectively. It is followed by friendly/enemy position of the planet during daily transit and is indicated by the first letter of the planet in capital/small letter. After this number of favourable transitory planets according to *ashtak varg* is mentioned. If Moon is moving through harmful constellation or if there is a harmful combination (*Ghaatak yog*) then it is indicated by a symbol {$}. If there is no change in the position of all these indications of the last column on next date then distance of planets is indicated by 0 to 9 number as 1/10th per cent. In this way number 9 will indicate that a planet is more than 90% nearer to the Earth. Order of the planet for this purpose is Sun, Mars, Mercury, Jupiter, Venus, Saturn and Moon. If unfavourable period of 7½ years or 2½ years of Saturn is running then it is also indicated after this.

First letter of the planet mentioned before a symbol {/} at the bottom of every column indicates that the planet transit through that sign and if this transit is through his own house then a symbol {|} is given after the planet, first letter is capitalised or normal in case of exalted or debilitated transit of the planet respectively. Capital or small letter after a symbol of {/} indicates transit of the planet through friend's or enemy's house respectively. Side of exalted/debilitated or friend/enemy from symbol {/} is shown at the bottom line of the first and last column.

If you want to see the planet in the sky on any date then a planet which is 24 letters towards the right-hand side from the Sun i.e. {S}, would be visible near meridian line passing through zenith just after sunset. Likewise a planet which is 24 letters towards the left-hand side from the Sun then it would be visible near meridian line passing through zenith just before sunrise. In this way position of every letter continuously transit through the zenith within 15 minutes.

Chart of aspect (*Drasti chakra*)

Consolidated effect of transitory and periodicity (*dasha*) of planet was assessed from the *Chal chakra*. Planet also has four types of aspect on other houses during transit. This *Drasti chakra* is prepared to assess the impact of these aspects of all planets. We can assess the position of aspect of planets after a given interval from the information contained on one page. When there is no aspect than that date is excluded. Like 27-8-2003 is not incorporated in the *chakra* of third type.

Drasti chakra is divided in thirteen columns. First column contains date whereas other twelve columns are allotted to twelve signs. Every column is again subdivided in ten columns. Hence every position indicate the status of 3° of a sign. Thus it is synchronised with the *Shakti chakra*.

In *Drasti chakra*, Potential of a planet is shown by 1/10th of the per cent, by a number from 0 to 9. Thus number 9 indicates the power of a planet between 90% to 100%. Number 0 indicates less than 10% power.

Power of planets in birth horoscope is shown in first and third line whereas related planet is shown in second and fourth line of *Drasti chakra*. Signs are given in fifth line. Span of a house according to *chalit* horoscope drafted as per north Indian system is shown at sixth line. Likewise span of a house according to KP is shown at the bottom of the *chakra*.

Dated transitory position of planet is shown by first letter of the planet in capital letter and aspect of that planet is shown by small letter. *Drasti chakra* is designed in following three versions.

1. It comprises of all transitory position of all planets along with 1/10th of power. Their power of aspect is also covered according to their aspect. If there are two planets at the same location i.e. within 3° then position of one planet is shown.

2. It comprises of all transitory position of all planets along with 1/10th of power as above. But only those aspects have been covered in this version, where either the aspect of the planet in the birth horoscope or position of the planet itself is matching with the transitory aspect.
3. Aspect of above version is included in this version but only those transitory position of the planets have been covered in this version, where either there is any aspect of the planet in the birth horoscope or position of the planet itself is matching with the transitory position.

In this way any repetition of an aspect or the position of a planet in birth horoscope during transit can be ascertained from this *chakra*, due to which effect of a planet may be increased and prediction may also be effected.

If readers desire to have above Eskain horoscope then information relating to their name, date of birth, time, place of birth (if place of birth is a village than nearby city) along with the name of desired *chakra* may be forwarded to the writer along with the cost as they may deem fit, in the form of postage stamp, money order or draft.

APPENDIX – 2

At present such almanac are not being prepared, which may contain the daily distance and motion etc. of the planets. But we may hope that such almanac will easily be available in future, after increasing trend of scientific approach towards astrology.

Appropriate information related to the planets at an interval of five days for the year 2007 is incorporated in the tables. These tables have planetary position at 26° latitude at 5-30 AM Indian standard time. Contents of the tables are as follows :–

	Column	Description
1	Date	Date.
2	Dist.	Distance of the planet from Earth in lakh km.
3	Dp	Distant power of the planet in per cent on the basis of their distance from the Earth.
4	deg.	Nirayan degree of the planet.
5	Rp	Difference of time in between sun-rise and rise of concerning planet in hours. – indicate that planet will rise before sun-rise.
6	M	Daily motion of the planet towards the Earth in thousand km. – indicate that planet is moving away from the Earth.
7	Mp	Motional power of the planet in per cent.
8	Elev.	Altitude of the planet at the time of crossing of meridian line with reference to the southern horizon at 26° latitude.

Power of planets may be worked out as follows :–

Per cent of Transitory power – Power on a house in per cent according to the birth horoscope may be worked out after placing the planet in the horoscope according to the degree shown in column 4.

Per cent of Rising power – Time of rising, crossing of meridian line and setting of a planet with reference to the Sun, may be ascertained from the information given under column 5.

Per cent of Exalted power – After deducting the latitude of a city from 26 and adding the number shown in column 8 and by further adding 10% to it, we may get per cent of exalted power.

Per cent of Distant power – Given in column 3.

Per cent of Motional power – Given in column 7.

(Please write with self-addressed envelope to writer for getting planetary position of desired year or for edited Hindi version of this book "ज्योतिष - कितना सही कितना गलत".)

Sun

Date 1	Dist. 2	Dp 3	deg. 4	Rp 5	M 6	Mp 7	Elev. 8
01/01/2007	1471	90	256	0	2	5	43.2
06/01/2007	1471	90	261	0	–1	–2	44.5
11/01/2007	1471	90	267	0	–5	–11	45.9
16/01/2007	1472	89	272	0	–8	–20	47.2
21/01/2007	1472	88	277	0	–12	–29	48.5
26/01/2007	1473	87	282	0	–16	–37	49.8
31/01/2007	1474	85	287	0	–19	–45	51.2
05/02/2007	1475	84	292	0	–22	–53	52.5
10/02/2007	1476	82	297	0	–26	–60	53.8
15/02/2007	1477	79	302	0	–28	–67	55.1
20/02/2007	1479	77	307	0	–31	–73	56.4
25/02/2007	1481	74	312	0	–34	–79	57.8
02/03/2007	1482	71	317	0	–36	–84	59.1
07/03/2007	1484	68	322	0	–38	–88	60.4
12/03/2007	1486	65	327	0	–39	–92	61.7
17/03/2007	1488	62	332	0	–40	–95	63.0
22/03/2007	1490	59	337	0	–41	–97	64.3
27/03/2007	1492	55	342	0	–42	–99	65.6

Sun (Contd.)

Date 1	Dist. 2	Dp 3	deg. 4	Rp 5	M 6	Mp 7	Elev. 8
01/04/2007	1495	52	347	0	–42	–99	66.9
06/04/2007	1497	48	352	0	–42	–99	68.1
11/04/2007	1499	45	357	0	–42	–99	69.4
16/04/2007	1501	41	2	0	–42	–97	70.7
21/04/2007	1503	38	7	0	–41	–95	72.0
26/04/2007	1505	35	12	0	–39	–92	73.3
01/05/2007	1507	32	16	0	–38	–89	74.5
06/05/2007	1509	29	21	0	–36	–85	75.8
11/05/2007	1511	26	26	0	–34	–80	77.1
16/05/2007	1512	23	31	0	–32	–75	78.3
21/05/2007	1514	21	36	0	–29	–69	79.6
26/05/2007	1515	18	41	0	–27	–63	80.8
31/05/2007	1517	16	45	0	–24	–56	82.1
05/06/2007	1518	15	50	0	–21	–49	83.3
10/06/2007	1519	13	55	0	–18	–41	84.6
15/06/2007	1520	12	60	0	–14	–34	85.8
20/06/2007	1520	11	64	0	–11	–26	87.1
25/06/2007	1521	10	69	0	–7	–18	86.7
30/06/2007	1521	10	74	0	–4	–9	85.4
05/07/2007	1521	9	79	0	0	–1	84.2
10/07/2007	1521	9	84	0	2	6	83.0
15/07/2007	1521	10	88	0	6	14	81.7
20/07/2007	1520	11	93	0	9	23	80.5
25/07/2007	1520	12	98	0	13	31	79.2
30/07/2007	1519	13	103	0	16	38	78.0
04/08/2007	1518	14	107	0	20	46	76.7
09/08/2007	1517	16	112	0	23	53	75.5
14/08/2007	1516	18	117	0	26	60	74.2
19/08/2007	1514	20	122	0	28	67	73.0
24/08/2007	1513	23	127	0	31	73	71.7
29/08/2007	1511	25	131	0	33	78	70.5
03/09/2007	1509	28	136	0	35	83	69.2
08/09/2007	1507	31	141	0	37	87	67.9
13/09/2007	1506	34	146	0	39	91	66.7
18/09/2007	1503	38	151	0	40	94	65.4
23/09/2007	1501	41	156	0	41	97	64.1
28/09/2007	1499	44	161	0	42	98	62.8

Sun (Contd.)

Date 1	Dist. 2	Dp 3	deg. 4	Rp 5	M 6	Mp 7	Elev. 8
03/10/2007	1497	48	166	0	42	99	61.6
08/10/2007	1495	51	170	0	42	99	60.3
13/10/2007	1493	55	175	0	42	99	59.0
18/10/2007	1491	58	180	0	42	98	57.7
23/10/2007	1489	61	185	0	41	96	56.4
28/10/2007	1487	65	190	0	40	93	55.1
02/11/2007	1485	68	195	0	38	90	53.8
07/11/2007	1483	71	200	0	37	86	52.5
12/11/2007	1481	74	205	0	34	81	51.2
17/11/2007	1479	76	210	0	32	75	49.9
22/11/2007	1478	79	215	0	30	69	48.6
27/11/2007	1476	81	221	0	27	63	47.2
02/12/2007	1475	83	226	0	24	56	45.9
07/12/2007	1474	85	231	0	20	48	44.6
12/12/2007	1473	87	236	0	17	40	43.3
17/12/2007	1472	88	241	0	13	32	41.9
22/12/2007	1472	89	246	0	10	23	40.6
27/12/2007	1471	89	251	0	6	15	41.8
01/01/2008	1471	90	256	0	2	6	43.1

Mars

Date 1	Dist. 2	Dp 3	deg. 4	Rp 5	M 6	Mp 7	Elev. 8
01/01/2007	3566	12	235	–1.4	656	46	43.0
06/01/2007	3532	13	238	–1.5	677	48	42.0
11/01/2007	3498	14	242	–1.6	697	49	41.0
16/01/2007	3463	15	246	–1.7	714	51	39.9
21/01/2007	3426	16	249	–1.8	730	52	40.5
26/01/2007	3389	17	253	–1.9	743	53	41.3
31/01/2007	3352	18	257	–2.0	755	53	42.2
05/02/2007	3314	20	260	–2.1	765	54	43.1
10/02/2007	3275	21	264	–2.2	773	55	44.0
15/02/2007	3236	22	268	–2.3	780	55	44.8
20/02/2007	3197	23	272	–2.4	784	56	45.7
25/02/2007	3158	24	275	–2.5	788	56	46.6

Mars (Contd.)

Date 1	Dist. 2	Dp 3	deg. 4	Rp 5	M 6	Mp 7	Elev. 8
02/03/2007	3118	25	279	–2.5	789	56	47.5
07/03/2007	3079	26	283	--2.6	790	56	48.4
12/03/2007	3039	28	287	–2.7	789	56	49.3
17/03/2007	3000	29	291	–2.8	787	56	50.2
22/03/2007	2961	30	294	–2.8	784	56	51.1
27/03/2007	2922	31	298	–2.9	780	55	52.0
01/04/2007	2883	32	302	–3.0	776	55	52.9
06/04/2007	2844	33	306	–3.1	771	55	53.8
11/04/2007	2806	34	310	–3.1	765	54	54.7
16/04/2007	2767	35	314	20.8	760	54	55.5
21/04/2007	2730	37	317	20.7	754	53	56.4
26/04/2007	2692	38	321	20.6	748	53	57.3
01/05/2007	2655	39	325	20.6	742	53	58.2
06/05/2007	2618	40	329	20.5	736	52	59.1
11/05/2007	2581	41	333	20.4	731	52	60.1
16/05/2007	2545	42	336	20.4	727	51	61.2
21/05/2007	2509	43	340	20.3	723	51	62.3
26/05/2007	2472	44	344	20.2	720	51	63.4
31/05/2007	2436	45	348	20.2	718	51	64.5
05/06/2007	2401	46	352	20.1	716	51	65.5
10/06/2007	2365	47	355	20.0	716	51	66.6
15/06/2007	2329	48	359	20.0	717	51	67.7
20/06/2007	2293	49	3	–4.1	720	51	68.8
25/06/2007	2257	50	6	–4.2	723	51	69.8
30/06/2007	2221	51	10	–4.3	728	52	70.9
05/07/2007	2184	52	13	–4.4	733	52	71.9
10/07/2007	2147	53	17	–4.4	741	52	72.9
15/07/2007	2110	54	20	–4.5	749	53	74.0
20/07/2007	2072	56	24	–4.6	758	54	75.0
25/07/2007	2034	57	27	–4.7	769	54	76.0
30/07/2007	1995	58	31	–4.8	781	55	76.9
04/08/2007	1955	59	34	–4.9	794	56	77.9
09/08/2007	1915	60	37	–5.0	807	57	78.9
14/08/2007	1875	61	41	–5.1	821	58	79.8
19/08/2007	1833	63	44	–5.2	836	59	80.7
24/08/2007	1791	64	47	–5.3	852	60	81.6
29/08/2007	1748	65	50	–5.4	867	61	82.5

Mars (Contd.)

Date 1	Dist. 2	Dp 3	deg. 4	Rp 5	M 6	Mp 7	Elev. 8
03/09/2007	1704	66	53	–5.6	882	63	83.4
08/09/2007	1659	68	55	–5.7	897	64	84.2
13/09/2007	1614	69	58	–5.9	912	65	85.0
18/09/2007	1568	70	61	–6.0	925	66	85.8
23/09/2007	1521	72	63	–6.2	937	66	86.6
28/09/2007	1474	73	66	–6.3	946	67	87.3
03/10/2007	1427	74	68	–6.5	954	68	87.0
08/10/2007	1379	76	70	–6.7	958	68	86.6
13/10/2007	1331	77	72	–6.9	958	68	86.2
18/10/2007	1283	78	74	–7.1	953	68	85.8
23/10/2007	1236	80	75	–7.3	942	67	85.5
28/10/2007	1189	81	76	–7.6	925	66	85.3
02/11/2007	1143	83	77	–7.9	899	64	85.1
07/11/2007	1099	84	78	–8.1	863	61	85.0
12/11/2007	1058	85	79	–8.5	817	58	85.0
17/11/2007	1018	86	79	–8.8	757	54	85.1
22/11/2007	983	87	78	–9.1	683	48	85.2
27/11/2007	951	88	78	–9.5	593	42	85.5
02/12/2007	925	89	77	–9.9	487	34	85.8
07/12/2007	904	89	75	–10	365	26	86.3
12/12/2007	890	90	74	–11	229	16	86.8
17/12/2007	883	90	72	–11	80	5	87.3
22/12/2007	883	90	70	–12	–75	–5	87.9
27/12/2007	892	90	68	–12	–235	–16	88.5
01/01/2008	908	89	66	–13	–394	–28	89.1

Mercury

Date 1	Dist. 2	Dp 3	deg. 4	Rp 5	M 6	Mp 7	Elev. 8
01/01/2007	2155	4	253	–0.2	–141	–3	37.0
06/01/2007	2149	4	261	0.0	281	6	37.3
11/01/2007	2122	6	269	0.2	737	17	37.4
16/01/2007	2070	10	277	0.4	1252	29	37.5
21/01/2007	1989	16	286	0.6	1854	44	41.0
26/01/2007	1876	23	294	0.8	2559	60	46.0
31/01/2007	1725	34	302	1.0	3329	79	51.4

Mercury (Contd.)

Date 1	Dist. 2	Dp 3	deg. 4	Rp 5	M 6	Mp 7	Elev. 8
05/02/2007	1537	47	310	1.2	3991	95	57.0
10/02/2007	1329	62	315	1.2	4178	99	62.3
15/02/2007	1136	75	316	1.0	3532	84	66.8
20/02/2007	1000	85	314	0.4	2094	49	69.7
25/02/2007	947	89	308	–0.3	394	9	65.3
02/03/2007	970	87	304	–0.9	–955	–22	61.4
07/03/2007	1044	82	302	–1.4	–1743	–41	58.5
12/03/2007	1143	75	302	–1.7	–2099	–49	56.5
17/03/2007	1252	67	305	–1.8	–2210	–52	55.4
22/03/2007	1362	59	309	–1.8	–2200	–52	54.7
27/03/2007	1470	52	315	–1.8	–2133	–50	54.3
01/04/2007	1574	45	321	–1.7	–2040	–48	54.2
06/04/2007	1673	38	328	–1.6	–1928	–45	54.2
11/04/2007	1765	31	336	–1.4	–1785	–42	54.2
16/04/2007	1849	25	345	22.9	–1585	–37	55.0
21/04/2007	1920	20	354	23.1	–1278	–30	59.9
26/04/2007	1970	17	4	–0.5	–789	–18	65.4
01/05/2007	1988	16	14	–0.2	–45	–1	71.5
06/05/2007	1961	18	25	0.2	943	22	78.1
11/05/2007	1883	23	35	0.6	1974	47	85.0
16/05/2007	1760	32	45	1.0	2739	65	88.4
21/05/2007	1610	42	54	1.2	3101	73	85.2
26/05/2007	1453	53	62	1.4	3133	74	86.2
31/05/2007	1301	64	68	1.5	2958	70	88.3
05/06/2007	1162	73	73	1.5	2656	63	88.2
10/06/2007	1040	82	76	1.4	2259	53	85.4
15/06/2007	942	89	78	1.2	1759	41	83.2
20/06/2007	872	94	77	0.8	1136	27	81.5
25/06/2007	837	96	75	0.4	385	9	80.3
30/06/2007	843	96	72	–0.1	–460	–10	79.2
05/07/2007	892	92	70	–0.6	–1324	–31	77.9
10/07/2007	983	86	69	–1.0	–2127	–50	76.1
15/07/2007	1111	77	70	–1.2	–2820	–67	76.3
20/07/2007	1269	66	73	–1.3	–3362	–80	78.1
25/07/2007	1447	53	78	–1.3	–3675	–87	79.8
30/07/2007	1631	41	86	–1.1	–3624	–86	81.5

Mercury (Contd.)

Date 1	Dist. 2	Dp 3	deg. 4	Rp 5	M 6	Mp 7	Elev. 8
04/08/2007	1799	29	95	–0.8	–3095	–73	83.1
09/08/2007	1927	20	105	–0.5	–2180	–51	84.6
14/08/2007	2006	14	115	–0.1	–1179	–28	85.7
19/08/2007	2039	12	125	0.2	–336	–8	81.2
24/08/2007	2036	12	135	0.5	289	6	75.9
29/08/2007	2007	14	144	0.8	744	17	71.1
03/09/2007	1959	18	152	1.1	1091	25	66.8
08/09/2007	1896	22	160	1.3	1376	32	62.8
13/09/2007	1819	27	168	1.4	1631	38	59.0
18/09/2007	1730	34	174	1.6	1876	44	55.4
23/09/2007	1629	41	181	1.7	2117	50	52.0
28/09/2007	1516	49	186	1.7	2347	55	48.6
03/10/2007	1393	57	191	1.7	2538	60	45.4
08/10/2007	1263	66	194	1.6	2615	62	42.4
13/10/2007	1137	75	195	1.3	2415	57	44.6
18/10/2007	1036	82	193	0.8	1649	39	48.0
23/10/2007	998	85	188	0.1	47	1	52.7
28/10/2007	1059	81	182	–0.6	–2047	–48	58.0
02/11/2007	1212	70	180	–1.1	–3594	–85	62.7
07/11/2007	1409	56	182	–1.2	–4051	–96	66.1
12/11/2007	1604	43	187	–1.2	–3726	–88	67.0
17/11/2007	1772	31	194	–1.1	–3096	–73	62.1
22/11/2007	1907	21	201	–0.9	–2432	–57	57.5
27/11/2007	2010	14	209	–0.8	–1826	–43	53.2
02/12/2007	2085	9	217	–0.6	–1291	–30	49.1
07/12/2007	2135	5	225	–0.4	–813	–19	45.2
12/12/2007	2162	3	233	–0.2	–372	–8	41.3
17/12/2007	2168	3	240	0.0	53	1	37.5
22/12/2007	2153	4	248	0.2	482	11	34.8
27/12/2007	2115	7	256	0.4	938	22	34.9
01/01/2008	2053	11	264	0.6	1442	34	35.0

Jupiter

Date 1	Dist. 2	Dp 3	deg. 4	Rp 5	M 6	Mp 7	Elev. 8
01/01/2007	9238	11	224	–2.1	1305	52	47.1
06/01/2007	9169	12	225	–2.4	1445	57	46.9
11/01/2007	9093	15	226	–2.7	1579	63	46.6
16/01/2007	9010	17	227	–2.9	1706	68	46.3
21/01/2007	8921	19	228	–3.2	1826	73	46.1
26/01/2007	8826	22	229	–3.5	1937	77	45.8
31/01/2007	8726	24	230	–3.8	2038	81	45.6
05/02/2007	8621	27	231	–4.1	2130	85	45.4
10/02/2007	8512	30	232	–4.4	2210	88	45.2
15/02/2007	8400	33	232	–4.6	2280	91	45.0
20/02/2007	8284	36	233	–4.9	2337	93	44.8
25/02/2007	8166	39	234	–5.2	2381	95	44.6
02/03/2007	8046	42	234	–5.5	2411	96	44.5
07/03/2007	7925	46	235	–5.8	2427	97	44.3
12/03/2007	7803	49	235	–6.1	2429	97	44.2
17/03/2007	7682	52	235	–6.5	2415	96	44.1
22/03/2007	7562	55	236	–6.8	2386	95	44.0
27/03/2007	7444	59	236	–7.1	2340	93	44.0
01/04/2007	7329	62	236	–7.4	2277	91	43.9
06/04/2007	7217	65	236	–7.7	2198	87	43.9
11/04/2007	7110	67	236	–8.1	2102	84	43.9
16/04/2007	7008	70	236	15.6	1990	79	43.9
21/04/2007	6913	73	236	15.3	1861	74	44.0
26/04/2007	6824	75	235	14.9	1716	68	44.0
01/05/2007	6743	77	235	14.6	1556	62	44.1
06/05/2007	6670	79	235	14.2	1383	55	44.2
11/05/2007	6606	81	234	13.9	1196	47	44.3
16/05/2007	6552	82	234	13.5	999	39	44.5
21/05/2007	6509	83	233	13.2	792	31	44.6
26/05/2007	6475	84	233	12.8	577	23	44.7
31/05/2007	6453	85	232	12.4	358	14	44.9

Jupiter (Contd.)

Date 1	Dist. 2	Dp 3	deg. 4	Rp 5	M 6	Mp 7	Elev. 8
05/06/2007	6442	85	231	12.1	135	5	45.0
10/06/2007	6442	85	231	11.7	–87	–3	45.2
15/06/2007	6453	85	230	11.4	–308	–12	45.4
20/06/2007	6475	84	229	11.0	–524	–20	45.5
25/06/2007	6507	84	229	10.6	–734	–29	45.7
30/06/2007	6550	82	228	10.3	–936	–37	45.8
05/07/2007	6603	81	228	9.9	–1128	–45	45.9
10/07/2007	6665	79	227	9.6	–1307	–52	46.0
15/07/2007	6735	77	227	9.2	–1473	–58	46.1
20/07/2007	6813	75	227	8.9	–1625	–65	46.2
25/07/2007	6899	73	226	8.6	–1762	–70	46.2
30/07/2007	6991	71	226	8.2	–1883	–75	46.2
04/08/2007	7088	68	226	7.9	–1989	–79	46.3
09/08/2007	7190	65	226	7.6	–2078	–83	46.3
14/08/2007	7296	62	226	7.3	–2151	–86	46.2
19/08/2007	7406	60	226	7.0	–2208	–88	46.2
24/08/2007	7517	57	227	6.7	–2250	–90	46.1
29/08/2007	7631	54	227	6.4	–2277	–91	46.0
03/09/2007	7745	50	227	6.1	–2289	–91	45.9
08/09/2007	7860	47	228	5.8	–2286	–91	45.8
13/09/2007	7973	44	228	5.5	–2270	–90	45.7
18/09/2007	8086	41	229	5.2	–2241	–89	45.5
23/09/2007	8197	38	229	4.9	–2199	–87	45.3
28/09/2007	8305	36	230	4.6	–2145	–85	45.2
03/10/2007	8411	33	231	4.3	–2080	–83	45.0
08/10/2007	8513	30	232	4.1	–2004	–80	44.7
13/10/2007	8610	27	232	3.8	–1918	–76	44.5
18/10/2007	8703	25	233	3.5	–1822	–72	44.3
23/10/2007	8791	23	234	3.2	–1718	–68	44.0
28/10/2007	8874	20	235	3.0	–1605	–64	43.8
02/11/2007	8951	18	236	2.7	–1484	–59	43.5
07/11/2007	9021	16	237	2.4	–1356	–54	43.2
12/11/2007	9085	15	238	2.2	–1222	–48	43.0
17/11/2007	9142	13	239	1.9	–1082	–43	42.7
22/11/2007	9192	12	240	1.6	–937	–37	42.4
27/11/2007	9234	11	241	1.4	–787	–31	42.1

Jupiter (Contd.)

Date 1	Dist. 2	Dp 3	deg. 4	Rp 5	M 6	Mp 7	Elev. 8
02/12/2007	9269	10	242	1.1	–634	–25	41.8
07/12/2007	9296	9	244	0.9	–477	–19	41.5
12/12/2007	9315	9	245	0.6	–318	–12	41.2
17/12/2007	9326	8	246	0.3	–158	–6	40.9
22/12/2007	9329	8	247	0.1	3	0	41.0
27/12/2007	9324	8	248	–0.2	165	6	41.3
01/01/2008	9311	9	249	–0.5	327	13	41.6

Venus

Date 1	Dist. 2	Dp 3	deg. 4	Rp 5	M 6	Mp 7	Elev. 8
01/01/2007	2426	8	272	1.1	399	33	43.5
06/01/2007	2405	9	278	1.1	426	35	44.6
11/01/2007	2383	10	285	1.2	454	37	45.8
16/01/2007	2360	11	291	1.3	481	40	46.9
21/01/2007	2335	12	297	1.4	509	42	48.4
26/01/2007	2308	14	303	1.4	538	44	50.5
31/01/2007	2281	15	310	1.5	566	47	52.6
05/02/2007	2251	16	316	1.6	595	49	54.8
10/02/2007	2221	17	322	1.7	625	52	56.9
15/02/2007	2189	19	328	1.8	655	54	59.0
20/02/2007	2155	20	335	1.8	685	57	61.1
25/02/2007	2120	22	341	1.9	716	59	63.2
02/03/2007	2083	24	347	2.0	747	62	65.3
07/03/2007	2045	25	353	2.0	779	64	67.4
12/03/2007	2005	27	359	2.1	810	67	69.5
17/03/2007	1963	29	5	–22	842	70	71.6
22/03/2007	1920	31	11	–22	874	72	73.7
27/03/2007	1875	33	17	–22	905	75	75.8
01/04/2007	1829	35	23	–22	937	78	77.8
06/04/2007	1781	37	29	–22	967	80	79.9
11/04/2007	1732	39	35	–21	997	83	81.9
16/04/2007	1681	41	41	2.6	1026	85	84.0
21/04/2007	1629	44	47	2.7	1054	87	86.0
26/04/2007	1576	46	52	2.7	1081	90	88.0

Venus (Contd.)

Date 1	Dist. 2	Dp 3	deg. 4	Rp 5	M 6	Mp 7	Elev. 8
01/05/2007	1521	49	58	2.8	1105	92	90.0
06/05/2007	1465	51	64	2.8	1128	94	88.0
11/05/2007	1408	54	69	2.9	1149	95	87.6
16/05/2007	1350	56	75	2.9	1168	97	89.5
21/05/2007	1291	59	80	2.9	1183	98	88.5
26/05/2007	1231	61	85	3.0	1196	99	86.7
31/05/2007	1171	64	90	3.0	1206	100	84.8
05/06/2007	1111	67	95	3.0	1212	101	83.0
10/06/2007	1050	69	100	3.0	1214	101	81.2
15/06/2007	989	72	105	3.0	1211	100	79.5
20/06/2007	929	75	109	3.0	1203	100	77.8
25/06/2007	869	77	114	3.0	1189	99	76.3
30/06/2007	810	80	117	2.9	1168	97	74.7
05/07/2007	753	83	121	2.8	1137	94	73.3
10/07/2007	697	85	124	2.7	1095	91	72.1
15/07/2007	644	87	126	2.5	1040	86	70.9
20/07/2007	594	90	128	2.3	967	80	70.0
25/07/2007	548	92	129	2.1	872	72	69.2
30/07/2007	508	93	129	1.8	751	62	68.7
04/08/2007	475	95	128	1.4	601	50	68.5
09/08/2007	450	96	126	0.9	420	35	68.5
14/08/2007	435	97	124	0.4	215	17	68.7
19/08/2007	431	97	120	–0.1	–4	0	69.0
24/08/2007	438	97	117	–0.6	–221	–18	69.2
29/08/2007	455	96	115	–1.1	–419	–34	69.4
03/09/2007	481	95	113	–1.5	–589	–49	69.7
08/09/2007	515	93	113	–1.9	–728	–60	70.4
13/09/2007	555	91	113	–2.2	–837	–69	70.8
18/09/2007	599	89	114	–2.4	–921	–76	71.0
23/09/2007	647	87	116	–2.6	–984	–82	71.0
28/09/2007	698	85	119	–2.8	–1031	–85	70.8
03/10/2007	751	83	122	–2.9	–1066	–88	70.4
08/10/2007	805	80	126	–3.0	–1091	–90	70.0
13/10/2007	860	78	130	–3.0	–1108	–92	69.4
18/10/2007	916	75	134	–3.1	–1119	–93	68.8
23/10/2007	972	73	139	–3.1	–1125	–93	68.1
28/10/2007	1028	70	144	–3.1	–1128	–94	67.3

Venus (Contd.)

Date 1	Dist. 2	Dp 3	deg. 4	Rp 5	M 6	Mp 7	Elev. 8
02/11/2007	1085	68	149	–3.1	–1126	–93	66.5
07/11/2007	1141	65	154	–3.1	–1122	–93	65.6
12/11/2007	1197	63	160	–3.1	–1116	–93	64.7
17/11/2007	1252	60	165	–3.0	–1107	–92	63.8
22/11/2007	1307	58	171	–3.0	–1096	–91	62.9
27/11/2007	1362	56	176	–2.9	–1084	–90	61.9
02/12/2007	1416	53	182	–2.9	–1070	–89	60.9
07/12/2007	1469	51	188	–2.9	–1055	–87	59.9
12/12/2007	1521	49	194	–2.8	–1038	–86	58.9
17/12/2007	1572	46	200	–2.7	–1021	–85	57.8
22/12/2007	1623	44	206	–2.7	–1002	–83	56.8
27/12/2007	1673	42	212	–2.6	–983	–81	54.7
01/01/2008	1721	40	218	–2.6	–963	–80	52.6

Saturn

Date 1	Dist. 2	Dp 3	deg. 4	Rp 5	M 6	Mp 7	Elev. 8
01/01/2007	12638	80	121	–9.0	1743	69	74.5
06/01/2007	12555	81	120	–9.4	1572	62	74.6
11/01/2007	12482	82	120	–9.8	1386	55	74.6
16/01/2007	12419	84	120	–10	1186	47	74.7
21/01/2007	12366	85	120	–10	974	38	74.8
26/01/2007	12324	85	119	–11	753	30	74.9
31/01/2007	12293	86	119	–11	525	21	75.0
05/02/2007	12274	86	118	–12	291	11	75.2
10/02/2007	12266	86	118	–12	54	2	75.3
15/02/2007	12271	86	118	–12	–181	–7	75.4
20/02/2007	12287	86	117	–13	–416	–16	75.5
25/02/2007	12315	86	117	–13	–646	–25	75.6
02/03/2007	12354	85	116	–13	–869	–34	75.7
07/03/2007	12403	84	116	–14	–1083	–43	75.8
12/03/2007	12464	83	116	–14	–1286	–51	75.9
17/03/2007	12534	81	115	–14	–1477	–59	76.0
22/03/2007	12613	80	115	–15	–1654	–66	76.1
27/03/2007	12701	78	115	–15	–1815	–72	76.1

Saturn (Contd.)

Date 1	Dist. 2	Dp 3	deg. 4	Rp 5	M 6	Mp 7	Elev. 8
01/04/2007	12796	77	115	–15	–1960	–78	76.2
06/04/2007	12898	75	115	–16	–2089	–83	76.2
11/04/2007	13006	73	114	–16	–2199	–87	76.3
16/04/2007	13119	71	114	7.5	–2292	–91	76.3
21/04/2007	13236	69	114	7.2	–2367	–94	76.3
26/04/2007	13356	66	114	6.9	–2424	–96	76.3
01/05/2007	13478	64	115	6.5	–2464	–98	76.3
06/05/2007	13602	62	115	6.2	–2486	–99	76.3
11/05/2007	13727	60	115	5.9	–2491	–99	76.2
16/05/2007	13851	57	115	5.6	–2480	–99	76.2
21/05/2007	13974	55	115	5.3	–2453	–98	76.1
26/05/2007	14096	53	116	5.0	–2412	–96	76.1
31/05/2007	14215	51	116	4.7	–2356	–94	76.0
05/06/2007	14331	48	116	4.4	–2286	–91	75.9
10/06/2007	14442	46	117	4.1	–2204	–88	75.8
15/06/2007	14550	44	117	3.8	–2109	–84	75.7
20/06/2007	14652	42	118	3.5	–2003	–80	75.6
25/06/2007	14749	41	118	3.2	–1887	–75	75.5
30/06/2007	14840	39	118	3.0	–1761	–70	75.4
05/07/2007	14924	37	119	2.7	–1626	–65	75.2
10/07/2007	15001	36	120	2.4	–1483	–59	75.1
15/07/2007	15070	35	120	2.1	–1333	–53	75.0
20/07/2007	15132	34	121	1.8	–1176	–47	74.8
25/07/2007	15186	33	121	1.6	–1013	–40	74.7
30/07/2007	15232	32	122	1.3	–846	–33	74.5
04/08/2007	15269	31	123	1.0	–674	–26	74.4
09/08/2007	15298	31	123	0.7	–499	–19	74.2
14/08/2007	15317	30	124	0.5	–321	–12	74.1
19/08/2007	15328	30	124	0.2	–141	–5	73.9
24/08/2007	15330	30	125	–0.1	39	1	73.7
29/08/2007	15322	30	126	–0.4	220	8	73.6
03/09/2007	15306	30	126	–0.7	400	16	73.4
08/09/2007	15280	31	127	–0.9	579	23	73.3
13/09/2007	15246	32	128	–1.2	756	30	73.1
18/09/2007	15203	32	128	–1.5	929	37	73.0
23/09/2007	15152	33	129	–1.8	1098	43	72.8
28/09/2007	15092	34	129	–2.1	1262	50	72.7

Saturn

Date 1	Dist. 2	Dp 3	deg. 4	Rp 5	M 6	Mp 7	Elev. 8
03/10/2007	15024	36	130	–2.4	1420	56	72.5
08/10/2007	14948	37	130	–2.7	1571	62	72.4
13/10/2007	14865	39	131	–3.0	1713	68	72.3
18/10/2007	14776	40	132	–3.3	1847	73	72.2
23/10/2007	14679	42	132	–3.6	1970	78	72.0
28/10/2007	14577	44	132	–3.9	2083	83	71.9
02/11/2007	14470	46	133	–4.2	2183	87	71.8
07/11/2007	14358	48	133	–4.5	2269	90	71.7
12/11/2007	14243	50	134	–4.8	2342	93	71.7
17/11/2007	14124	52	134	–5.1	2400	96	71.6
22/11/2007	14002	54	134	–5.4	2441	97	71.5
27/11/2007	13880	57	134	–5.7	2466	98	71.5
02/12/2007	13756	59	135	–6.1	2473	98	71.4
07/12/2007	13633	61	135	–6.4	2462	98	71.4
12/12/2007	13510	64	135	–6.7	2433	97	71.4
17/12/2007	13390	66	135	–7.1	2384	95	71.4
22/12/2007	13273	68	135	–7.4	2316	92	71.4
27/12/2007	13159	70	135	–7.7	2229	89	71.4
01/01/2008	13051	72	135	–8.1	2122	84	71.4

Moon

Date 1	Dist. 2	Dp 3	deg. 4	Rp 5	M 6	Mp 7	Elev. 8
01/01/2007	3.75	64	44	–14	–2	–30	89.0
06/01/2007	3.93	29	110	–10	–4	–59	79.3
11/01/2007	4.05	5	171	–6.4	0	–3	57.8
16/01/2007	3.88	38	232	–2.6	4	70	36.0
21/01/2007	3.68	77	301	1.6	2	32	52.5
26/01/2007	3.71	71	12	–18	–2	–30	78.0
31/01/2007	3.86	41	80	–14	–3	–46	89.9
05/02/2007	4.02	10	143	–9.9	–2	–37	67.5
10/02/2007	4.01	11	202	–6.3	2	36	46.4
15/02/2007	3.75	63	266	–2.4	5	81	40.4
20/02/2007	3.62	89	339	2.1	0	0	66.3
25/02/2007	3.78	57	51	–17	–4	–64	88.2

Moon (Contd.)

Date 1	Dist. 2	Dp 3	deg. 4	Rp 5	M 6	Mp 7	Elev. 8
02/03/2007	3.97	19	115	–13	–2	–41	77.3
07/03/2007	4.06	2	175	–9.8	0	–9	55.9
12/03/2007	3.94	27	235	–6.1	4	69	35.1
17/03/2007	3.64	85	303	–2.0	4	70	53.5
22/03/2007	3.62	89	18	–21	–2	–40	80.3
27/03/2007	3.89	36	87	–17	–5	–78	87.2
01/04/2007	4.04	5	148	–13	–1	–22	65.4
06/04/2007	4.04	6	208	–9.6	1	18	44.2
11/04/2007	3.83	48	270	–5.8	5	84	41.9
16/04/2007	3.59	96	341	22.6	2	39	67.2
21/04/2007	3.69	75	56	3.3	–5	–73	87.2
26/04/2007	3.98	17	121	7.3	–4	–66	74.8
01/05/2007	4.06	2	181	11.0	0	3	53.6
06/05/2007	3.97	20	241	14.7	2	41	34.4
11/05/2007	3.73	67	306	18.7	5	76	55.1
16/05/2007	3.60	94	20	–0.8	0	0	81.1
21/05/2007	3.80	53	92	3.7	–6	–87	85.3
26/05/2007	4.04	6	154	7.6	–2	–37	63.1
31/05/2007	4.01	12	214	11.2	2	28	41.9
05/06/2007	3.86	41	277	15.1	3	50	44.6
10/06/2007	3.68	78	345	19.3	3	45	68.9
15/06/2007	3.67	79	58	–0.1	–2	–34	87.1
20/06/2007	3.92	30	126	4.1	–5	–77	73.0
25/06/2007	4.05	5	186	7.8	0	0	51.6
30/06/2007	3.91	31	247	11.5	3	50	34.2
05/07/2007	3.76	62	314	15.7	2	38	57.9
10/07/2007	3.69	76	24	–4.0	0	3	83.0
15/07/2007	3.79	55	95	0.4	–3	–53	84.0
20/07/2007	4.01	13	158	4.3	–3	–50	61.3
25/07/2007	4.00	14	218	8.0	2	39	40.0
30/07/2007	3.79	56	282	12.0	4	58	46.8
04/08/2007	3.69	76	352	16.3	0	5	71.9
09/08/2007	3.76	62	63	–3.3	–2	–33	86.6
14/08/2007	3.92	30	129	0.8	–3	–51	71.5
19/08/2007	4.05	4	190	4.5	–1	–14	49.8
24/08/2007	3.91	32	251	8.3	5	71	35.8
29/08/2007	3.67	79	319	12.5	3	47	60.1

Moon (Contd.)

Date 1	Dist. 2	Dp 3	deg. 4	Rp 5	M 6	Mp 7	Elev. 8
03/09/2007	3.69	76	32	–7.0	–2	–35	86.0
08/09/2007	3.87	40	100	–2.7	–3	–52	81.8
13/09/2007	4.01	11	162	1.1	–2	–34	59.5
18/09/2007	4.04	7	222	4.7	1	22	38.3
23/09/2007	3.79	56	285	8.6	6	88	48.1
28/09/2007	3.60	94	357	13.1	1	17	73.8
03/10/2007	3.75	64	70	–6.4	–4	–71	87.8
08/10/2007	3.97	19	135	–2.4	–3	–49	69.2
13/10/2007	4.06	2	195	1.3	0	–9	47.8
18/10/2007	3.97	19	255	5.0	3	55	37.5
23/10/2007	3.68	77	321	9.0	5	83	61.0
28/10/2007	3.59	95	36	–10	–1	–22	87.8
02/11/2007	3.85	45	107	–5.9	–6	–87	79.1
07/11/2007	4.04	5	168	–2.1	–1	–28	57.2
12/11/2007	4.04	5	228	1.5	1	15	37.6
17/11/2007	3.87	39	289	5.2	5	72	49.9
22/11/2007	3.61	91	358	9.5	3	55	74.6
27/11/2007	3.65	83	74	–9.8	–4	–57	89.4
02/12/2007	3.95	24	141	–5.6	–5	–79	66.8
07/12/2007	4.06	2	201	–2.0	0	0	45.5
12/12/2007	3.97	20	261	1.7	2	36	40.0
17/12/2007	3.77	59	325	5.6	4	66	62.9
22/12/2007	3.62	90	37	–14	1	16	88.5
27/12/2007	3.77	61	110	–9.4	–5	–76	77.6
01/01/2008	4.02	10	173	–5.5	–3	–50	55.0

Torch
of Knowledge
is with you
and only
YOU
can destroy
ignorance

SPACE MAY BE USED FOR NOTING IMPORTANT POINTS

SPACE MAY BE USED FOR NOTING IMPORTANT POINTS